W9-AQN-975

School
Law for
Counselors,
Psychologists,
and
Social Workers

Second Edition

School Law for Counselors, Psychologists, and Social Workers

Louis Fischer
University of Massachusetts, Amherst

Gail Paulus Sorenson
State University of New York, Albany

Longman
New York & London

Tennessee Tech University
Cookeville, Tenn.
WITHDRAWN

**School Law for Counselors,
Psychologists, and Social Workers
Second Edition**

Copyright © 1991, 1985 by Longman Publishing Group.
All rights reserved.
No part of this publication may be reproduced,
stored in a retrieval system, or transmitted
in any form or by any means, electronic, mechanical,
photocopying, recording, or otherwise,
without the prior permission of the publisher.

Longman, 95 Church Street, White Plains, N.Y. 10601

Associated companies:
Longman Group Ltd., London
Longman Cheshire Pty., Melbourne
Longman Paul Pty., Auckland
Copp Clark Pitman, Toronto

Executive editor: Naomi Silverman
Production editor: Marie-Josée A. Schorp
Cover design: Anne M. Pompeo

Library of Congress Cataloging-in-Publication Data

Fischer, Louis, 1924–
    School law for counselors, psychologists, and social workers/
Louis Fischer, Gail Paulus Sorenson.
        p.   cm.
    Includes bibliographical references.
    ISBN 0-8013-0483-0
    1. Student counselors—Legal status, laws, etc.—United States.
2. Counseling—Law and legislation—United States. I. Sorenson, Gail Paulus. II. Title.
KF4192.5.G8F57   1991
344.73′079—dc20
[347.30479]   90-33733
                                                      CIP

ABCDEFGHIJ—DO—99 98 97 96 95 94 93 92 91 90

Contents

Topic Overview

4. Education Records and the Student's Right to Privacy

5. Legal Issues Related to the Testing and Grouping of Students

6. Students with Special Educational Needs

7. Behavior Control and Student Discipline   **139**

8. Child Abuse and Neglect   164

9. Rights Related to Schooling: Part I   181

10. Rights Related to Schooling: Part II

Preface

Counselors, psychologists, and social workers function in a complex legal environment. In their professional work, whether they are aware of it or not, a variety of laws and regulations apply to them. Some of these laws emanate from our national Constitution and federal laws, many from state laws and constitutions, and some from local ordinances and school board regulations.

Counselors and others who work with students cannot hope to keep abreast of all relevant laws and regulations. If they did, they could not possibly carry out their professional duties or keep up with developments in their field. Nor do they need such complete and up-to-date knowledge. They must, however, be sensitive to the legal issues inherent in their work; they must understand guiding legal principles controlling these issues and the processes whereby our legal institutions address and resolve conflicts, and know when to seek the advice of lawyers.

In recent decades, educators increasingly have found themselves in court, as defendants, in a wide variety of lawsuits. Some decry this litigation as an abuse of our legal system and a sign that "we have too many lawyers," whereas others claim that it signals a "democratization of the law" (i.e., an access to the courts by all people, not merely the wealthy few). Whatever the merit of these arguments, the fact remains that practitioners must become "legally literate" in order to avoid legal problems when possible and to deal with them intelligently when prevention does not work.

Counseling functions both inside and outside of schools are carried on at times by trained counselors, at times by psychologists and therapists, and at still other times by social workers, nurses, and so on. All of these categories are included whenever we refer to counselors or educators in this book. Only economy of expression and writing style prevent us from constantly mentioning each specialty. Our intention in this book is to focus on the legal aspects of counseling and to stay away from the substantive work a counselor does, as much as possible. Our book assumes that counselors are competent in their work and that they have had little or no exposure to legal materials. Our contacts with counselors and counselor-educators lead us to conclude that in their professional training, both pre- and in-service, almost no legal issues or principles were included. Our recent search of published materials also points to the need for an up-to-date work on legal issues of particular interest to counselors, psychologists, and social workers.

It is also our intention to present these materials in a manner understandable by an intelligent lay person who has no prior knowledge of the law. The legal principles and explanations are sound and accurate, but stripped of jargon and needless technicalities. Where technical explanations or materials are warranted, they are presented in appendixes.

Because this book is for laypersons rather than lawyers, we present principles and explain them, and refer to leading cases, but there is no effort to present an exhaustive analysis of all cases relevant to the principle under consideration. Practicing attorneys might have a need for all such cases, but counselors do not, for it is not our aim to turn counselors into lawyers. We aim to sensitize our readers to the legal dimension of their work, to make them aware of the "legal environment" in which they function, so that they can avoid pitfalls and carry on their work in confidence. At the end of each chapter we also include an edited case, relevant to the substance of the particular chapter. These edited cases, along with the additional Supreme Court cases in Appendix D, give readers some sampling of the language and reasoning used by judges as they work their way from facts through issues to their decisions. We have removed all technical citations, references, footnotes, and discussions of procedural issues. However, the case citation is always included, so interested counselors can easily find the entire case in any law library.

The materials we present should be of interest to counselors, psychologists, and social workers, whether they work in schools or in clinical practice, whether in the public or private sector. It should be understood, however, that not all the legal principles discussed here apply to all situations and, therefore, to the work of all of these professionals. For example, although the legal principles controlling confidentiality apply to all counselors, whether in private or public practice, the legal principles controlling student records, derived primarily from the Family Educational Rights and Privacy Act, apply only to schools that receive federal support. Similarly, civil and criminal liability may be incurred by professionals working in either the public or the private sector, but many of the legal issues related to testing and grouping of students relate primarily to public schools. However, counselors in private schools or private practice could certainly incur liability for negligence in the use of tests and possibly for violating certain provisions of federal law.

Thus, all of our work applies to counselors in public schools and much of it applies to counselors in other settings as well. Because counselors in private practice often work with clients who attend public schools, they need to know the legal principles applicable to the public schools. For example, counselors in such situations may need access to school records as they work cooperatively with school personnel.

No single volume can discuss thoroughly all the issues of law related to counselors, psychologists, and social workers; we selected those we consider most central in their daily work. Many of the issues we present are complex and the laws related to them are changing. New laws are passed, regulations change, courts are persuaded by novel legal arguments, and the Supreme Court may declare a law or policy unconstitutional. Therefore, no book in any area of law is the final, definitive word at the time of its publication or a substitute for competent legal advice when specific problems arise. A counselor who contemplates legal action should consult a lawyer or seek the help of a professional association. Anyone who has been associated with a lawsuit also knows that it can be an expensive, time-consuming, and unhappy affair, and one that should be avoided whenever possible. We have confidence that professionals who know the law applicable to their work will be in a better position to avoid legal problems, and, should such problems arise, to resolve them through negotiation rather than litigation.

Louis Fischer
Gail Paulus Sorenson
Amherst, Massachusetts

School Law
for
Counselors,
Psychologists,
and
Social Workers

CHAPTER 1

Anatomy of the Law

OVERVIEW

For school counselors, psychologists, and social workers, as for all of us, the law is a pervasive, sometimes overwhelming and frustrating, aspect of both personal and professional life. Although it is necessary on many occasions to consult those with specialized legal training, we believe that increasing one's knowledge of the law can go a long way toward demystifying perceived complexities and can give one a greater sense of control over law-related issues encountered in daily life; knowledge also can prevent legal problems from arising. As a first step, we briefly define some common legal terms, outline some concepts, and discuss the nature of law in general. We pay particular attention to the constitutional concepts most relevant to those who work with students, and stress the importance of state and local education law. We also outline the structure and function of the court system, in order to place judge-made law into appropriate legal perspective; and we discuss the evolution of legal precedent and how to read case law. The final section of this chapter (which can be read now or saved for a time when its relevance may be more apparent) provides some suggested resources that may prove useful in initial investigations of legal questions or problems of particular interest. Because few, if any, legal questions can ever be definitively resolved, the emphasis throughout this book is on the application of legal principles in a variety of problematic situations. A basic legal framework, a knowledge of fundamental principles of law, and a catalog of resources for further legal investigation provide a good beginning for practicing the kind of law that doesn't require a law degree—preventive law. As more educators* become familiar with basic legal principles and tools, they will be

---

*We use the term "educators" throughout the book in its broadest sense to include all who work with school-age children.

able to do their jobs more effectively and with greater assurance that their actions will harmonize with fundamental legal requirements.

What is law?

In the common-law tradition that we in the United States have inherited from England, law is much more than a prescriptive set of rules and regulations to guide human behavior. Unlike those countries where the civil law tradition is followed and behavior is thus governed by a master code—and despite the recent trend toward convergence of common law and civil law traditions—the common law countries have evolved legal systems that undergo a continual process of development. In addition to the U.S. Constitution, which establishes our tripartite system of government and sets out certain procedures, rules, and broad principles that guide the polity, an important aspect of law in the United States is judge-made law (i.e., legal rules and principles derived from cases). Judge-made law is often called *case law* or *common law*, indicating that it has evolved from the common thought and experience of a people.

In order to gain even a rudimentary idea of the law that applies to a particular educational issue, it often will be necessary to review cases that have considered the issue, to review school policies, state law, federal law and regulations, and perhaps even state and federal constitutional provisions. There are many sources of law in our society; it is only by creating some sort of logical amalgamation of the relevant principles, rules, policies, and practices and applying them to the facts of a particular situation that one can derive a general understanding of the larger issues.

An enumeration of the various sources of law, however, does not really tell us what the law is. Some people have viewed law as the command of a sovereign, or as the manifestation of a transcendental will, or as a closed system of rules and regulations backed up by sanctions, or simply as what lawyers and judges actually do. We believe it is important that educators *not* view law as something that can be known once and for all and applied without adaptation to new situations. Following John Dewey, America's great educator, psychologist, and philosopher, we take the view that law derives from a process of social interaction.[1] In Dewey's words, "The standpoint taken is that law is through and through a social phenomenon; social in origin, in purpose or end, and in application."[2] According to Dewey, law is an interactive, human process—"not something that can be said to be done or to happen at a certain date."[3]

Legal principles and rules, then, arise out of social interaction, as people form beliefs and habits that are shared and eventually become customary. Some of these customary beliefs and habits are later formulated into legal principles or rules that further reinforce the relative stability of the antecedent customary beliefs and habits. Dewey rejected, however, any suggestion that either customs or the rules and principles derived from them were necessary unchangeable. Although he understood the importance of the order and stability provided by the relatively slow evolutionary process of legal development, he also appreciated the flexibility inherent in relying on historical precedent as a tool to help us develop more effective, harmonious, and just human interactions. For Dewey, law was not a straitjacket for maintaining the status quo:

> Many . . . are now aware of the harm done in legal matters by assuming the antecedent existence of fixed principles under which every new case may be brought. They recognize that this assumption merely puts an artificial premium on ideas developed under bygone conditions, and that their perpetuation in the present works inequity. Yet the choice is not between throwing away rules previously developed and sticking obstinately by them. The intelligent alternative is to revise, adapt, expand and alter them. The problem is one of continuous, vital readaptation.[4]

John Dewey's philosophy of law had a considerable impact on judicial thought in the United States. Judge Jerome Frank, who wrote one of the most widely read books on American law, was greatly influenced by Dewey's theory of adjudication. Judge Frank noted that "the best available description of the logical method employed by judges is from the pen, not of a lawyer, but of a psychologist."[5] Dewey had said that people generally resolve problems by beginning "with some vague anticipation of a conclusion (or at least of alternate conclusions) and then . . . look around for principles and data which will substantiate it or which will enable us to choose intelligently between rival conclusions."[6]

We believe that John Dewey had some important insights about the process of adjudication and about the nature of law itself. We are particularly persuaded by his description of law as a flexible and adaptable process, neither rigidly adhering to historically derived rules and principles nor ignoring their possible relevance and importance to current problems. It is possible that adopting such a view will allow us to reconcile freedom with authority, and change with stability; a healthy respect for both the past and the present may provide us with a good measure of each of these alternatives. Although problems may be posed by the vital readaptation Dewey spoke of, these very problems provide grist for the mill of social development. If law is "through and through a social phenomenon," these problems are not only inevitable but welcome.

Why is the Constitution so important to education?

The Constitution nowhere mentions education, which is an enterprise left to state control under the reserved powers of the tenth amendment.[7] However, article VI, section 2 clearly states that the Constitution "shall be the supreme Law of the Land." This means that state and federal court decisions, state and federal legislation, rules and regulations of state and federal administrations, and local school policies that are inconsistent with the provisions of the Constitution are invalid. When controversy exists over the constitutionality of a particular rule or policy, it becomes the responsibility of the courts and, ultimately, of the Supreme Court to say what the law is. This power of "judicial review" was explicated by Chief Justice John Marshall over

180 years ago; although controversial at times, it is an important function of the Court today.[8]

What constitutional provisions are most relevant to educators?

Despite the fact that power over education is largely left to state governmental discretion,[9] in the last quarter-century the federal government has greatly increased its regulation of educational matters. From a constitutional point of view, this increased presence has been made possible by article I, which empowers Congress to collect taxes and spend money in order to provide for the general welfare,[10] and by provisions of the thirteenth and fourteenth amendments, which have allowed Congress to pass civil rights legislation. Familiar examples of legislation created pursuant to those provisions are the Education for the Handicapped Act,[11] which provides monies to states and local school districts in order to ensure that students with handicapping conditions receive a free and appropriate education, and Section 504 of the Rehabilitation Act,[12] which assures that the benefits of federally aided programs will be extended to handicapped individuals by prohibiting discrimination against them. (See Chapter 6, on students with special educational needs, for a fuller discussion of these federal provisions.)

Apart from constitutional provisions that affect the way in which educational authority is allocated between the federal government and each state, good arguments can be made that the fourteenth amendment is the most important constitutional provision of relevance to education. The fourteenth amendment contains two vital clauses that provide protections for individuals—the due process clause and the equal protection clause.

The due process clause, which says "nor shall any State deprive any person of life, liberty, or property, without due process of law," protects against state actions that are fundamentally unfair or that are accomplished without fair procedures. This prohibits states and local school districts (including counselors and teachers) from administering unreasonably harsh corporal punishment (a denial of substantive due process), and from expelling a student without providing for a hearing (a denial of procedural due process).

The distinction between substantive due process and procedural due process is sometimes difficult to comprehend. Educators are most familiar with procedural due process, which essentially provides that notice and a hearing must be given before an important right, such as the right to an education, can be taken away—even temporarily. The right to substantive due process, on the other hand, does not relate to procedures such as notice and a hearing but, rather, requires that state officials not impose punishments that are arbitrary, capricious, or unfair. An example of a denial of substantive due process would be punishing a child because her parents had not paid a required school fee. It is simply not fair to punish a child for something over which she has no control.

It is important to notice that the due process provision protects individuals only from penalties administered under state, not private, authority. Although other legal provisions or local school policy might provide protections for students in private schools, constitutional provisions generally do not apply in private situations. This prerequisite is often referred to as the "state action doctrine." Counselors working in private schools and institutions generally will not be bound by the Constitution as a matter of law; counselors in public schools will be bound by due process and other constitutional principles.

The equal protection clause, which says that a state may not "deny to any person within its jurisdiction the equal protection of the laws," assures persons of equal and, in many cases, fair and equitable treatment by the state. If a wave of foreign refugees entered the public schools and intentionally were not taught English, for example, it could be said that they were denied equal protection. This would be true even though the students were provided with all the same courses that other students were provided; it is not fair to teach those who are unequal, due to their limited English-language experience, in the same way that native-born, English-speaking students are taught.

The due process and equal protection clauses are the two most important substantive provisions of the fourteenth amendment, but the importance of this amendment to education goes far beyond its explicit substance; the fourteenth amendment has served a vital instrumental function as well. Although the important individual rights protections of the Bill of Rights were originally thought to limit only the power of the federal government, a long process of judicial interpretation has now made clear that all of the most important constitutional rights are also guaranteed secure from state encroachment. It is said, for example, that our right to freedom of speech is protected from state encroachment under the first *and* fourteenth amendments. The first amendment contains the substantive protection for freedom of speech, but its language says only that "*Congress* shall make no law . . . abridging the freedom of speech."[13] In order to prohibit *state* officials from interfering with this freedom, it is said that this fundamental liberty right is "incorporated" into the due process clause of the fourteenth amendment. This process of "selective incorporation" (selective because not all of the Bill of Rights has been incorporated) has the effect of prohibiting state officials from depriving persons of any important liberty right, without due process of law. Thus, through a process of judicial interpretation, the fourteenth amendment has become an extremely important source of individual rights and liberties.

The other constitutional provisions of greatest relevance and importance for public education are as follows: the first amendment's prohibition against an "establishment of religion" by public authorities and the corollary guarantee of "free exercise" of religion; the additional first amendment protections of speech, press, assembly, and petition (which the Supreme Court has said includes freedom of association as well); the fourth amendment's protection against "unreasonable searches and seizures;" and the due process clause of the fifth amendment. Because it limits the power of the federal government rather than the state government, this "second" due process clause provides due process protections for persons *not* covered by the fourteenth amendment's due process provision—students, counselors, and teachers in the Washington, D.C., public schools, for example. In addition, courts have said that the concept of due process in the fifth amendment is broad enough to encompass the principle of fairness that is inherent in the notion of equal protection. Thus, public school officials in the District of Columbia must respect both due process and equal protection principles established under the fifth amendment.

As important as these and other constitutional provisions have been to education, and particularly to public education, we would like to emphasize that the Constitution rarely provides optimal protections. For example, just because the Supreme Court has said that corporal punishment of schoolchildren is not "cruel and unusual" in the constitutional sense does not mean that we cannot go beyond what the Constitution requires. In fact, several states have decided that corporal punishment is an educational policy they do not wish to embrace. The important point here is that individual states and localities have a great deal of discretion when exercising their considerable authority over education and have often chosen to go beyond minimal constitutional guarantees. The importance of state and local education law and policy cannot be overstated and must always be considered by counselors and educators.

What is the structure of the court system in the United States?

In the United States there are really 51 court systems: the federal court system, and a court system in each of the 50 states. Each system has the power to decide both criminal cases and civil cases, but the jurisdiction of the federal courts is limited by the Constitution. Article III, which defines the judicial power of the federal courts, says that this power extends only to cases "arising under this Constitution [and] the Laws of the United States."[14] This limitation on the types of cases that can be decided by courts of the United States is the most important limitation for those who deal with legal issues in education. Often referred to as "federal question jurisdiction," it means that cases concerning the fourteenth amendment's equal protection provision or cases involving sex discrimination in education (which is prohibited by federal law) can be decided by federal courts. On the other hand, a case involving alleged defamation cannot be decided by a federal court, but generally would have to be tried in a state court. State courts, in addition to dealing with a variety of criminal and civil matters, also have the power to decide cases concerning issues of federal statutory and constitutional law. Because many legal problems in education involve federal questions (either constitutional or statutory), litigants in these types of cases have a choice as to which court system (federal or state) they initially will choose. A case filed in a state court can reach the U.S. Supreme Court if a controversy still exists after it has been heard and decided by the highest court of a state. Figure 1.1 shows the alternative paths of a judicial controversy.

The federal judicial system and most state judicial systems are three tiered. They have a relatively large number of trial courts, where the facts are determined and where the law is applied to the particular facts; a smaller number of intermediate appellate courts, which review the way the law has been applied to the facts; and one final court of appeals, which is the highest court of the particular jurisdiction. The names of these courts vary from state to state; they often are called superior

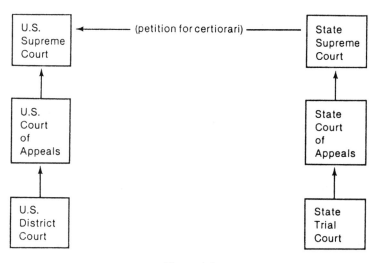

Figure 1.1

court, court of appeals, and supreme court, respectively, but this is not always true, so care should be taken in determining whether one is reading a case from a trial court or from the highest court of a state. In New York State, for example, the lowest trial court of general jurisdiction is called the "Supreme Court," while the state's highest court is called the "Court of Appeals." In the federal system, the nearly 100 trial courts are called United States District Courts, the 13 courts of appeals are called the United States Courts of Appeals, and the highest court is officially called the United States Supreme Court.

Judicial controversies generally move from the trial court level to the intermediate appellate court level and, finally, to the highest court of the jurisdiction. Additionally, a case can move from the highest court of a state to the U.S. Supreme Court, if the losing party submits a request to the Supreme Court to consider the case. This request usually comes in the form of a "petition for certiorari," which the Supreme Court can either accept or reject. After careful consideration, a vote is taken by the nine justices; if four vote in favor of considering the case, the Court will issue a "writ of certiorari" asking that the case be sent to the Court. This often occurs when the various federal courts of appeals are in conflict over a particular issue.

The workload of the Supreme Court is heavy, consisting of more than 5,000 cases per year. Of the approximately 300 cases actually accepted and decided by the Court in a given year, approximately half receive a hearing and are followed by full written opinions. The other half are decided without argument and are reported in memorandum opinions or in short "per curiam opinions" (opinions of the Court). The federal courts of appeals deal with over 25,000 cases a year, and the federal district courts with over 200,000 cases.[15]

When reading one of the many cases decided by the various state and federal courts, an important point to consider is whether or not the particular decision of the court (often called the court's "holding") is binding in your state or region. Decisions of the Supreme Court are binding everywhere, but the decisions of the lower federal courts are binding only in their respective territories. All federal courts of appeals (except for the one in Washington, D.C., and one dealing with special patent and copyright issues) cover more than one state, and there is more than one federal district court in most states. A map of the territories covered by the federal courts of appeals is contained in Appendix A. The opinions of state courts are binding only in the state where they are decided. However, decisions from courts other than the one deciding the case may be used as precedent; although not binding, these decisions are often considered persuasive in other jurisdictions. In fact there is a trend in education law to give great weight to the decisions of the lower federal courts and state supreme courts regarding issues that have not been addressed by the U.S. Supreme Court.

How can reports of court cases be found?

Because of the increased importance of education law to counselors and other professionals, one might find it interesting and perhaps necessary to read the complete opinion of a particular court from time to time. Although professional organizations keep their members advised of important legal developments in their fields of interest, there often is no fully adequate substitute for the unedited version of an opinion of special importance.

Supreme Court opinions of wide relevance to educators are now published (in lengthy excerpts) in *Education Week,* a comprehensive and widely circulated newspaper focusing on education at the elementary and secondary school levels. All Supreme Court opinions are made available within approximately two weeks in *U.S. Law Week,* a publication that can be found in any law library, including local or countywide law libraries. Within a few months, Supreme Court opinions are published in three different sets of reporters, called the *U.S. Reports,* the *Supreme Court Reporter,* and the *Supreme Court Reports, Lawyers Edition.* These also can be found in law libraries, and they are sometimes available in the libraries of colleges and universities. Access to cases in these reporters is facilitated if one has a complete citation, which includes the case name, the volume number, the name of the reporter, the page, and the date. A complete citation looks like this: *Brown v. Board of Education,* 347 U.S. 483 (1954). In addition, all cases of relevance to education are published in *West's Education Law Reporter.*

Although more information on how to locate particular court opinions will be found in Appendix A, we would like to stress the fact that not all court controversies are reported. This means there is always the possibility that a few interesting and relevant cases will not appear in the extensive series of reporters and thus will be generally unavailable. For example, when we say we have found no reported cases imposing liability on a school counselor for failure to report child abuse, this does not necessarily mean that it has never happened. However, many thousands of cases are reported every year, allowing us to learn a great deal about how the law is applied in a variety of contexts and, more importantly, how to reason by analogy in new situations.

What should one look for when reading a court case?

It is important to look for the following things when reading a judicial decision: the facts, the issue or issues, the holding (decision) of the court, and the reasons for the holding. Many students of the law write "briefs" or short summaries of cases in which they carefully sort out and enumerate the important and relevant facts and the major legal issues involved (the latter are often phrased in the form of questions). The holding is most important and must be distinguished from "dicta," which consist of often interesting but nonbinding statements of opinion found in a case. Just as the issues derive from the facts and the holding derives from the issues, so must the court's reasons be related to the holding. Briefs help the reader to identify particularly relevant information; to be most useful, they should be short—usually a page or less in length—and should be headed by the case name and a complete citation. Notes regarding particularly important dicta or other interesting information may be added at the end of the brief.

Where can books and articles about legal problems in education be found?

The most readily available resource for locating books on education law is *Books in Print.* This index is frequently updated and contains a special section called "law and legislation" where many books of interest are listed. A more specialized and more comprehensive index for locating books, listing books on law-related issues exclusively, is *Law Books 1876–1981: Books and Serials on Law and Law-Related Subjects.*

Because the law on a particular topic is continually evolving, it is often a good idea to look for current articles in addition to books. Law-related issues in education are dealt with occasionally in a wide variety of education journals; another place to look is in the law reviews that are published by the nation's law schools. Access to topics of special interest is provided by three major indexes: *Index to Legal Periodicals, Current Law Index,* and *Legal Resource Index* (a microform publication). At the present time, there are two journals that focus on legal issues in elementary and secondary education, the *Journal of Law and Education* and *West's Education Law Reporter;* the latter contains articles of interest to educators in addition to education-related cases.

How can one keep informed about legal issues in education in general?

In addition to daily general circulation newspapers, which are reporting more and more law-related news every year, *Education Week* contains several articles each week on current legal issues. A weekly newsletter, *School Law News,* and one national organization, the National Organization on Legal Problems of Education (NOLPE),[16] also focus exclusively on education-related legal issues. NOLPE publishes a newsletter, a "reporter" that briefly summarizes all cases of current interest to educators, and books, monographs, and minimonographs on topics of special

importance to education. In addition, the NOLPE newsletter briefly summarizes all
new books of interest to those dealing with legal problems in education.

NOTES

1. For a brief statement of John Dewey's views on law see J. DEWEY, *My Philosophy of Law,* in THE GREAT LEGAL PHILOSOPHERS 506 (C. Morris ed. 1959).
2. *Id.* at 507.
3. *Id.*
4. J. DEWEY, HUMAN NATURE AND CONDUCT 221 (Modern Library edition 1930), (1st edition 1922).
5. J. FRANK, LAW AND THE MODERN MIND 369 (1936).
6. Dewey, *Logical Method and Law,* 10 CORNELL LAW Q. 17, 23 (1924).
7. The tenth amendment states, "The powers not delegated to the United States by the Constitution, nor prohibited by it to the States, are reserved to the States respectively, or to the people."
8. *See* Marbury v. Madison, 5 U.S. (1 Cranch) 137 (1803).
9. *See* U.S. CONST. amend. X.
10. *See* U.S. CONST. art. I, § 8, cl. 1.
11. 20 U.S.C. § 1400 et seq. (1982).
12. 29 U.S.C. § 794 (1982).
13. U.S. CONST. amend. I (emphasis added).
14. U.S. CONST. art. III, § 2, cl. 1.
15. REPORT OF THE PROCEEDINGS OF THE JUDICIAL CONFERENCE OF THE UNITED STATES. Held in Washington, D.C., March 12 and 13, 1981, and September 24 and 25, 1981.
16. NOLPE's address is Southwest Plaza Building, 3601 S.W. 29th Street, Suite 223, Topeka, Kansas 66614.

CHAPTER 2

Confidentiality and the Duty to Warn

OVERVIEW

Counselors of every stripe, whether school counselors, psychologists, psychiatrists, or others, insist that confidentiality in relations with their clients is of utmost importance in their work. Central to the success of the counseling relationship is a feeling of trust, which cannot be established and maintained without assurance that the confidential relationship between client and counselor will not be breached. This is true whether the client is an adult, a child, a student, or anyone else. "The essence of much psychotherapy is the contribution of trust in the external world and ultimately in the self, modelled upon the trusting relationship established during therapy."[1]

Confidentiality is also essential to guarantee full disclosure during counseling or treatment. Clients tend to approach counseling with caution and different degrees of resistance. The possibility of disclosure would make this resistance more impenetrable. In fact, without the assurance of confidentiality, many in need of help would shy away from it. Even today we can't overlook the fact that there is a stigma attached to the seeking of psychological help and this stigma deters those in need from seeking such help. Confidentiality helps overcome such reluctance. In sum, it is clear that there are sound reasons to protect from public disclosure the communications that take place between clients and counselors.

All mental health professionals assert the need for confidentiality in their codes of ethics. Unless the situation is an exceptional one, such as a case involving child abuse, or court-ordered disclosure, it is unethical conduct to violate confidentiality. In fact, the counselor-therapist may be sued by the client for money damages for violating confidentiality.

On the other hand, there are situations where social policy might be best served by disclosure. What if a counselor-therapist learns during the course of the counseling relationship that the particular client has dangerous propensities? That he is likely to do serious harm to self or others? What if the client makes serious threats specifically focused on an individual? Should that be viewed the same or differently from threats of a more general nature? Does the counselor have a duty to warn an identified probable victim, or the public in general? Do parents have the right to know what transpires between the counselor and an unemancipated minor? These are some of the issues explored in this chapter.

What is the legal meaning of confidentiality?

We have all been told things in confidence, and we, in turn, have told things to others with the request or admonition that they hold them in confidence. There are "confidential employees" in the executive offices of most organizations. People "share confidences" of various kinds. Thus "confidentiality" is a term in common use. However, in law there is a special meaning to the term, namely, that no one can compel the disclosure of the information that was exchanged between two people.

While counselors usually speak of "confidentiality," the more generally accepted legal expression for the same concept is "privileged communication." As stated by Jagim et al., "Whereas confidentiality concerns matters of communication outside the courtroom, privilege protects clients from disclosure in judicial proceedings."[2] Such privilege refers to the right of a person in a "special relationship" to prevent the disclosure in legal proceedings of information given in confidence in the special relationship. Depending on the laws of the various states that govern the granting of such privilege, the "special relationship" *generally* includes husband–wife, attorney–client, clergy–penitent, and physician–patient relationships; in some states," special relationships" include those between counselors and clients, teachers and students, and even parents and children.

Does the law respect privileged communications in all professions?

No, it does not. In fact, courts and judges have always been reluctant to extend the right of privileged communications beyond its narrowest applications, and for good reasons. The administration of justice requires the fullest possible access to accurate information, which means that courts must be able to require everyone who has information relevant to a case to testify and thus furnish evidence.

Wigmore, the leading authority on the Anglo-American law of evidence, expressed this principle in the following way:

> For more than three centuries it has now been recognized as a fundamental maxim that the public . . . has a right to every man's evidence. When we come to examine the various claims of exemption, we start with the primary assumption that there is a general duty to give what testimony one is capable of giving and that any exemptions which may exist are distinctly exceptional, being so many derogations from a positive general rule.

Furthermore,

> The investigation of truth and the enforcement of testimonial duty demand the restriction, not the expansion, of those privileges. They should be recognized only within the narrowest limits required by principle. Every step beyond these limits helps to provide, without any real necessity, an obstacle to the administration of justice.[3]

This privilege originally existed only as an idea of "honor among gentlemen," and evolved into the attorney–client privilege, which is the oldest recognized privilege. English courts were impressed by the argument that clients would not speak freely with their lawyers for fear that the lawyers would be called to testify against them. This made it impossible for lawyers and clients to communicate completely and thus for the lawyer to defend a client effectively. An exception was created to the general rule that a court could require everyone to testify in a criminal case. This exception, the granting of "privileged communication," encouraged more thorough, detailed discussion between lawyers and their clients. The protection was for the client only, who could, if he or she so chose, disclose the communication with the lawyer, that is, waive the privilege.

The only other privileged communication originally recognized by common law (judge-made law) was the relationship between a married couple. The husband–wife privilege developed as a matter of sound public policy concerned with the preservation of marriage and family life. Early in English history it was recognized that marriages would suffer and deteriorate if spouses could be compelled to testify against each other. (Novelists have made use of this privilege by silencing a witness to a crime through a deceitful marriage.)

Whatever other professional or personal relationships might be protected by the doctrine of privileged communication is a matter of state statute. For example, many states have enacted legislation extending such protection to communications between physicians and patients, clergy and penitents; some to reporters and informants, psychologists and clients; and a few to counselors and counselees.

What are the criteria for privileged communications?

Professor Wigmore articulated the basis on which courts have supported the existence of privileged communication. According to his summary, four requirements must be met in order to justify the proposed privilege:

1. The communications must originate in confidence that they will not be disclosed.
2. The confidentiality must be essential to full and satisfactory maintenance of the relationship between the parties.
3. The relationship must be one which, in the opinion of the community, should be sedulously fostered.
4. The injury to that relation, caused by disclosure, would be greater than the benefit gained to the process of litigation.[4]

These criteria are generally accepted by modern scholars of the law of evidence as the appropriate test for what qualifies as privileged communication.[5]

Judges have been very reluctant to grant or acknowledge such a privilege and more reluctant still to extend it to new relationships. Even with long-recognized exemptions, such as the lawyer–client relationship, courts have demanded that certain conditions be met.

Three conditions must be fulfilled before a professional relationship arises: (1) One party in the relationship must be legally certified as a lawyer, doctor, or minister; (2) at the time of the communication in question he or she must have been acting in a professional capacity; (3) the person making the communication, if in possession of his or her faculties, must have regarded the professional person as his or her lawyer, doctor, or minister.[6]

As further evidence of judicial reluctance to extend the privilege, even the well-established medical profession was not able to secure it in this country until 1828. Even today, not all states recognize doctor–patient communications as privileged. Courts in many states have indicated that they are reluctant to extend the list of relationships accorded such privilege. Courts in California, Virginia, Washington, Florida, Wisconsin, Michigan, Minnesota, Indiana, and other states have ruled that only specific state legislative action can grant confidentiality to heretofore unrecognized privileged relationships. Furthermore, they tend to agree with the opinion of the Iowa Supreme Court that a state law enumerating professions accorded the privilege was "essentially artificial" in that no such privilege existed in common law.[7] In addition, the court indicated that such a statute would be strictly and narrowly interpreted and that courts had no power to extend the privilege. The Ohio Supreme Court ruled similarly, and called for a strict interpretation of the state statute, because it was in derogation of the common law of privileged communication.[8]

Although most cases involving counselor–client relationships are likely to be filed in state courts, some may involve issues implicating federal law or the Constitution and thus may be filed in federal court. Federal rules of evidence are less rigid; good arguments could be made under them to extend the privilege of confidentiality to counselor–client relationships. The applicable federal rules of evidence are the following:

Rule 26 of the Federal Rules of Criminal Procedure
In all trials the testimony of witnesses shall be taken orally in open court, unless otherwise provided by an act of Congress or by these rules. The admissibility of evidence and the competency and privileges of witnesses shall be governed, except when an act of Congress or these rules otherwise provide, by the principles of the common law as they may be interpreted by the courts of the United States in the light of reason and experience.[9]

Rule 43(a) of the Federal Rules of Civil Procedure
Form and Admissibility. In all trials the testimony of witnesses shall be taken orally in open court, unless otherwise provided by these rules. All evidence shall be admitted which is admissible under the statutes of the United States, or under the rules of evidence heretofore applied in the courts of general jurisdiction of the

state in which the United States court is held. In any case, the statute or rule which favors the reception of the evidence governs and the evidence shall be presented according to the most convenient method prescribed in any of the statutes or rules to which reference is herein made. The competency of a witness to testify shall be determined in like manner.[10]

These federal rules appear to be quite flexible and provide substantial discretion to the judge conducting the trial. Furthermore, various decisions of federal courts have warned against being controlled "by the dead hand of the common law,"[11] and the U.S. Supreme Court has reminded us "that the common law is not immutable but flexible, and by its own principles adapts itself to varying conditions."[12] Despite the apparent flexibility of the Federal Rules of Procedure and the admonition of the Supreme Court, federal courts have not extended the principle of privileged communications to new professional relationships, but they have reiterated that they will follow the law of evidence of the state where the conflict arose.[13]

In sum, it is clear that neither the common law, the U.S. Constitution, nor the Federal Rules of Procedure extend the protection of privileged communication to the counselor–client relationship. Therefore we must look elsewhere, namely to the statutes of the 50 states.

Do state laws protect the confidentiality of counselor–client relationships?

In several states they do, but in most they do not. Perhaps the following provisions of a Michigan statute provide the most complete protection:

> No teacher, guidance officer, school executive or other professional person engaged in character building in the public schools or in any other educational institution, including any clerical worker of such schools and institutions, who maintains records of students' behavior or who has such records in his custody, or who receives in confidence communications from students or other juveniles, shall be allowed in any proceedings, civil or criminal, in any court of this state, to disclose any information obtained by him from such records, or such communications; nor to produce such records or transcript thereof, except that any such testimony may be given, with the consent of the person so confiding or to whom such records relate, if such person is 18 years of age or over, or, if such person is a minor, with the consent of his or her parent or legal guardian (P.A. 1972. No. 87, Para. 1, eff. March 20, 1963).[14]

Similarly, the state of Nevada extends the privilege to both teachers and counselors in civil and criminal proceedings, except for proceedings in criminal offenses where the punishment might be life imprisonment or death.[15] South Dakota provides immunity from testifying to counselors only, not to teachers,[16] while Montana exempts anyone who teaches psychology or is "engaged in the observation of child mentality."[17] The latter provision is sufficiently vague and broad to include counselors and teachers. Delaware, Idaho, Indiana, Maine, Maryland, North Carolina, Oklahoma, Oregon, Pennsylvania, South Carolina, South Dakota, and Washington are the only other states that grant the privilege *directly* to counselors or teachers,[18] but some favorable arguments can be made by analogy in states where psychologists have received the privilege by statute.

It has been reported that "47 states and the District of Columbia have privileged communication statutes for psychologists, and 28 states have privileged communication statutes for social workers" as of 1985.[19] An argument can be made that certified counselors have the same need for confidentiality in their professional relationships with students as do psychologists; often, in fact, counselors are certified psychologists. Such an argument makes good sense, but in light of judicial reluctance to extend the privilege, and in light of the courts' tendency to interpret such statutes very narrowly, we should not expect the argument by analogy to succeed.

A further complication arises in relation to school counselors due to the very nature of their work. Counselors in private practice do their work in their offices, whereas school counselors interact with students not only in their offices but also in less formal settings such as the playground, the cafeteria, the hallways, and other places. For purposes of the law, do these interactions constitute counseling sessions? Although no cases give us authoritative guidance on this matter, it can be argued that it is not the formality of the setting but the intention of the parties that determines whether or not an exchange should be considered counseling. By way of analogy, the attorney–client privilege would apply whether the interaction took place in the attorney's office, on a tennis court, or in a supermarket, as long as the other criteria listed by Wigmore were satisfied.

In the absence of the confidentiality privilege, what should counselors do?

Situations where counselors have a need to claim confidentiality in a legal proceeding do not arise very often, because information that passes between counselor and student is rarely relevant to court proceedings. When it is relevant, the privilege may be claimed in the few states we mentioned, unless it is specifically waived by the client. It is important for the counselor to remember that the privilege is for the protection of the client, who has the choice to assert it or waive it if he or she is of legal age, or whose parent or guardian may do so if the client is a minor.

In states where no privilege has been enacted into law, the counselor must testify, when ordered to do so by a court, or face the consequences, which may be a fine or even a prison term. Much publicity has been given to reporters who went to prison in recent years for defying judicial orders to testify in states where reporters were not granted privilege by state legislatures. There are no reported cases of counselors who chose such penalty in defiance of a court order to testify.

An alternative course of action is organizational or political effort to change existing laws in states that do not provide for the privilege. In the meantime it is reasonable for counselors either to avoid discussions of criminal matters with counselees, or to advise them that the counselor will probably have to testify in court, if subpoenaed, about the content of the counseling sessions.

In the absence of a court order, counselors generally need not disclose such information, or their records, to businesses, the military, government officials, or others who might request it. (See Chapter 4 on laws related to confidentiality of school records.) Situations where counselors or school psychologists are commonly called to testify are in judicial proceedings related to divorce, child custody, and adoption. In such proceedings counselors might be considered important witnesses to establish the fitness of one of the parents in a custody case or in a contested adoption. A potential witness who wishes to avoid having to testify and thus reveal what he or she considers confidential information might inform the attorneys on both sides that there are serious questions about the fitness of each of the contesting parties. Attorneys are not likely to put such an unfavorable witness on the stand to testify.

In any event, it would be advisable for the counselor to consult a local attorney, perhaps the attorney for the school district or a local teachers' association, concerning the probable consequences of a proposed course of action.

May therapists withhold information from parents?

The law is not clear in this area. Traditionally, since parents make decisions concerning therapeutic services for their children, they had access to information and could even release it to others. Courts would so rule even today in the case of young children, but therapists can use professional judgment regarding when, how, and what information to share with parents.

The law is more complicated regarding teenagers. In states that allow them to seek the services independently, good arguments can be made that they should be able to control who has access to confidential information. This is also the case for emancipated minors, as well as those whom courts have recognized as "mature minors" with a legal capacity to seek treatment on their own. Such cases are rare, but it is important for therapists to find out what the law is in their own states concerning the treatment of teenagers.

May the counselor withhold information from parents?

Yes he or she may, except for the provisions of Family Educational Rights and Privacy Act (FERPA), discussed in Chapter 4. The foregoing discussion applies to the assertion of privilege in a court proceeding only. Many situations arise outside the court proceedings, in discussions with parents, teachers, and school administrators, where counselors must decide whether or not to disclose information gained in private counseling sessions.

Apart from special provisions related to educational records, discussed in Chapter 4, state laws typically do not address questions related to counselors keeping information from parents, and leave to local school boards' discretion the creation of policy in such matters. Unless required by local board policy, counselors do not have to make disclosures of the substance of their counseling sessions. However, in many situations it makes good educational sense to communicate with teachers and/

or parents, with care and sensitivity, about the substance of such sessions, so as not to violate expected confidence. Counselors must rely on their professional expertise to guide their behavior in such communications. We'll have more to say on this matter in Chapter 3, where we consider the possible civil and criminal liability of counselors. Aside from court proceedings or school situations controlled by school board policy, the ethical principles of the profession guide counselors' behavior regarding confidentiality.

Does the principle of privileged communication apply to group therapy?

In general, no. This is one of many situations where the technical and professional developments in a field have progressed at a rate faster than related legal principles. Group counseling and group therapy are widely accepted and practiced. There is evidence that the sharing of similar problems, feelings, and attitudes is more useful for the successful resolution of certain problems than is one-to-one counseling/therapy. Despite the professional soundness of such group work, courts have not accorded it the status of privileged communication.

The main reason for this is rooted in the historic reluctance of courts to grant the privilege and to extend it to new types of relationships. Furthermore, with courts' tendencies to interpret new legislation in this area strictly and narrowly, no group sessions will be privileged unless the legislation clearly and specifically provides for it. At this writing, only the state of Colorado recognizes such privilege for all participants in group therapy.[20]

Even in states that grant confidentiality to counselor–client communication, it is safe to assume that courts would not extend the privilege to group sessions. In analogous situations, with third parties present in an otherwise privileged relationship, the claim of privilege has been denied. An example of this occurred in Iowa,[21] where both a psychologist and a psychiatrist worked with the same individual, but the state law granted immunity from testifying only to the psychiatrist. Though they worked as a small group, the psychologist was ordered by the court to give testimony.

The historical view of courts has been that if more than two people are involved in the conversation, the privilege is lost to all, since there is no confidentiality intended. Although this view makes little sense in group counseling or therapy, counselors should realize that there is a significant lag between developments in their professional techniques and law. Thus they should avoid discussing in groups information they or their counselees are not willing to disclose in court.

Once granted, is confidentiality absolute?

No, it is not. There are circumstances where public interest in disclosure may override confidentiality normally accorded a relationship. Probably the best-known case to illustrate this point is *Tarasoff v. The Regents of the University of California,* which involved the confidential relationship between a University of California psychologist and his patient.

The **Tarasoff** *Case*[22]: *The Duty to Warn.* Tatiana Tarasoff was killed on October 27, 1969, by Posenjit Poddar. Two months earlier, Poddar confided his intention to kill her to his psychologist during therapy sessions. The psychologist, Dr. Moore, was employed by the University of California hospital at Berkeley. Tarasoff's parents filed suit, and among other issues, claimed that Dr. Moore had a duty to warn their daughter and them of the impending danger. Because there was no such warning (although Moore did notify the campus police), the plaintiffs alleged that the psychologist and his employer were negligent and that their negligence was the cause of Tatiana's death. They sought money damages against the psychologist and the university, among others.*

Do psychologists have a duty to warn of impending danger from their clients? Historically, under the common law, as a general rule one is not duty bound to control the conduct of another or to warn those endangered by such conduct. This laissez-faire attitude is consistent with other principles and practices in the individualistic social philosophy of Anglo-American tradition. For example, Mark Spitz, winner of seven Olympic gold medals in swimming, is under no legal obligation to make any attempt to save the life of a drowning child. His moral obligation is clear, but it is not a legal obligation or duty. However, courts have developed an exception to this general rule in cases where people stand in a special relationship to each other. If Spitz were a lifeguard or the child's parent or teacher, a "special relationship" would exist that would place a legal obligation upon him to make reasonable attempts to save the child.†

Similarly, the California Supreme Court ruled in the *Tarasoff* case that the psychologist–patient relationship is a special relationship out of which arises the duty to warn. When the defendants argued that the psychologist's relationship was with Poddar and not with Tarasoff, the court rejected the argument. It will suffice, the court ruled, to "stand in some special relationship to either the person whose conduct needs to be controlled or in a relationship to the foreseeable victim of that conduct."[23] The court cited various cases and scholarly analyses to conclude that "there now seems to be sufficient authority to support the conclusion that by entering into a doctor–patient relationship the therapist becomes sufficiently involved to assume some responsibility for the safety, not only of the patient himself, but also of any third person whom the doctor knows to be threatened by the patient."[24]

But what if the therapist has difficulty in predicting whether or not a patient presents a serious threat of violence? The court explained that therapists are required to exercise only "that reasonable degree of skill, knowledge, and care ordinarily possessed and exercised by members of [that professional specialty] under similar circumstances."[25] In the *Tarasoff* case, however, there was no doubt whatever about the seriousness of the threat or the identity of the intended victim.

Although the psychologist has a professional responsibility to his or her patient,

---

*The suit also named a supervising psychologist and the police department as defendants, but for our purposes we need not explore all aspects of the suit. Interested readers may find the entire case by looking up the citation provided at the end of the chapter.

†In 1983, Minnesota became the first state to require observers to go to the aid of one in danger or under attack. Failure to do so will incur a $100 fine. Reported in *The New York Times*, August 2, 1983.

the ultimate question to resolving the tension between the conflicting interests of patient and potential victim is one of social policy, and not professional expertise. . . . In sum, the therapist owes a legal duty not only to his patient, but also to his patients' would-be victim and is subject in both respects to scrutiny by judge and jury.[26]

But what about the need for full and open communication between the patient and the psychologist in a privileged, confidential setting? Isn't the giving of a warning a breach of confidential communication? Yes, it is, recognized the California court; however, the need to protect against the clearly identified danger outweighs the therapist's obligation to the client. The court even quoted from §9 of the Principles of Medical Ethics of the American Medical Association [1957]: "A physician may not reveal the confidence entrusted to him in the course of medical attendance . . . unless he is required to do so by law or unless it becomes necessary in order to protect the welfare of the individual or of the community."[27]

The majority of the California Supreme Court ruled that the psychologist had a duty to warn a known intended victim, although some justices dissented. They agreed with those who fear that this obligation will be counterproductive because some violence-prone patients will be less willing to communicate with therapists who, in turn, will have fewer opportunities to help them. It is also feared that psychologists will recommend many more patients for protective custody, as a cautious reaction to possible liability.

The aftermath of Tarasoff.   The *Tarasoff* case raised much furor among psychiatrists and other therapists. Since the case was decided, a number of state legislatures have enacted laws granting a psychiatrist–patient privilege, a psychologist–patient privilege, or both. These statutes tend to limit the effect of *Tarasoff* and similar cases. For example, a Maryland case decided there was no duty to warn, citing a post-*Tarasoff* Maryland statute as its authority.[28]

The *Tarasoff* court indicated that, in some situations, the therapist's duty may even go beyond the duty to warn and may include a duty to attempt to detain. A 1980 case in Nebraska agreed, and ruled that "this duty requires that the therapist initiate whatever precautions are necessary to protect the potential victims of his patient."[29] A Pennsylvania case limited the duty to warn only to those *readily identifiable* as a likely target of the patients' violence, in order to keep the rule of liability in *Tarasoff* within workable limits.[30]

No one can state with confidence the exact limits of the duty to warn derived from *Tarasoff*. Therapists need not interrogate their clients concerning the identity of an unknown potential victim. Nor are they under an obligation to conduct an independent investigation. The duty to warn or to protect arises, said the court in *Tarasoff,* and in a 1980 case, only when the probable victim is identified or could be identified upon a "moment's reflection."[31] However, the California Supreme Court extended the doctrine in 1983 to warn "persons in close relationship to the object of a patient's threat."[32] In this case the psychologists had been told their client intended to seriously harm an identified woman. The court ruled that the therapist should have warned the victim and that the duty to protect also applied to her infant son, who was with his mother and was traumatized by the shooting. Such an extension introduces more uncertainty into the work of therapists. For example, if the potential victim coaches a Little League team, should members of the team and their families be warned in addition to the coach?

It will take several more years of litigation to clarify the contours of the law regarding the duty to warn or to protect. Most courts that have followed *Tarasoff* applied the principle to identifiable probable victims, to those easily identifiable, or at most to those in "close relationship" to them. Furthermore, they applied it only when injury to persons was probable. There was at least one case in Vermont, however, that held a therapist liable for not warning the parents whose son disclosed during therapy sessions that he would burn down their barn, which he did.[33] With such unpredictable extension of the duty to warn, therapists must keep abreast of the changing law in their state and perhaps take political action and influence the legislature to enact laws specifying the limits of such duty or eliminating it completely. In the meantime, it is prudent to have a paid-up malpractice insurance policy.

Does a counselor have a duty to warn a known intended victim of his or her patient?

In all probability, yes. We can speak only in probabilities, for there are no reported appeals court cases to which we can go for authoritative answers. Not all cases that go to court are printed in the published reporters that catalog cases from state courts. However, all cases that are appealed do appear in these reports. Thus, because many if not most cases that go to trial are never appealed, there probably are cases involving counselors that have not been reported. All federal appellate court decisions appear in reporters, but not all cases tried at the federal district court level (see Appendix A). However, we can reason by analogy from *Tarasoff* and other cases.

Legally, there are significant differences between psychiatrists and psychologists as well as between either of these groups and school counselors. Even when they do similar work with clients, we have seen that the law accords greater privilege to psychiatrists and is most likely to extend confidentiality to them. Because they are trained as physicians, they benefit from the historic privilege extended to the doctor–patient relationship. Relationships between counselors and their clients and psychologists and their clients, however, would undoubtedly fall within the category of "special relationship" discussed in *Tarasoff*. This "special relationship" imposes a duty that does not exist among ordinary citizens. Every reason advanced to impose on psychiatrists an obligation to warn potential victims known to be in danger applies with equal force to psychologists and counselors. In fact, because these professionals have a weaker claim to privilege, courts are more likely to impose upon them the duty to warn intended probable victims of violence.

Whether social policy imposes the greatest obligation in this respect on school counselors is debatable. Typically their clients are minors; the counselors, together with other school personnel, are employees hired to enhance the social-emotional, as well as the intellectual, development of students, and they are responsible for the health and well-being of all students. Perhaps the very dearth of appeals court decisions is evidence of the generally held belief that counselors have such obligations and that they've been performing them. If any counselor were to find himself or herself in an ambiguous situation related to the duty to warn, it would be advisable to check with the appropriate administrator and school attorney.

It is also generally understood in our legal system that there are three situations in which a counselee automatically waives (loses) his or her privilege: (1) child custody cases in which either parent challenges the mental fitness of the other or where the therapist-counselor has reasonable suspicion of child abuse, (2) any case in which client-counselee introduces his or her mental condition as a relevant factor in the case, and (3) cases in which the client-counselee makes statements to a therapist-counselor in a course of psychiatric examination ordered by the court, after being told that the communication would not be privileged.

SUMMARY AND CONCLUSIONS

The need for confidentiality between psychiatrists, psychologists, social workers, counselors, and their clients is generally recognized. It is a necessity for effective counseling and even for encouraging those in need to seek the help of counselors. The ultimate legal test of such confidentiality is embodied in the principle of "privileged communication," that is, the exemption from having to testify in court proceedings.

Anglo-American law has always been reluctant to grant such privilege, for the legal process used to arrive at an accurate determination of facts needs all relevant testimony. Historically, exceptions to the obligation to testify were granted only to attorney–client and husband–wife relationships. Such statutes later exempted some other relationships, such as clergy–penitent, and doctor (including psychiatrist)–patient; a few states extended the privilege to psychologists and counselors. State laws that grant these exemptions are strictly and narrowly interpreted and most states still do not grant confidential, privileged status to counselor–counselee communications. While most states grant the privilege against testifying to psychiatrists and certified psychologists, and many to social workers, in most states counselors have a legal duty to testify if ordered to do so by a court, and refusal is likely to lead to a contempt citation with a resulting fine or jail term. Political action aimed at legislative change is probably the best way to secure the confidentiality privilege in states that currently do not grant it.

Even psychiatrists, psychologists, or counselors who have the privilege may have the duty to testify and even to give warning in certain circumstances. The claim of privilege is outweighed by considerations of public safety where the counselor learns of a counselee's intention to harm someone. The courts impose the duty to warn individuals who are specifically identified or readily identifiable as targets of threats or violence.

Aside from court proceedings, counselors may and probably should keep their communications with counselees confidential. School records kept by counselors are governed by provisions of the federal law, but counselors' relationships with parents are generally governed by local school board policy. In the absence of policy requiring disclosure to parents, a counselor has no obligation to breach the confidentiality of communications with counselees even if parents request it. Counselors usually can develop effective working relationships with parents, teachers, and administrators without revealing information received in confidence.

TARASOFF v. REGENTS OF THE UNIVERSITY OF CALIFORNIA
551 P.2d 334 (Cal. 1976)

TOBRINER, Justice.

On October 27, 1969, Prosenjit Poddar killed Tatiana Tarasoff. Plaintiffs, Tatiana's parents, allege that two months earlier Poddar confided his intention to kill Tatiana to Dr. Lawrence Moore, a psychologist employed by the Cowell Memorial Hospital at the University of California at Berkeley. They allege that on Moore's request, the campus police briefly detained Poddar, but released him when he appeared rational. They further claim that Dr. Harvey Powelson, Moore's superior, then directed that no further action be taken to detain Poddar. No one warned plaintiffs of Tatiana's peril.

. . .

We shall explain that defendant therapists cannot escape liability merely because Tatiana herself was not their patient. When a therapist determines, or pursuant to the standards of his profession should determine, that his patient presents a serious danger of violence to another, he incurs an obligation to use reasonable care to protect the intended victim against such danger. The discharge of this duty may require the therapist to take one or more of various steps, depending upon the nature of the case. Thus it may call for him to warn the intended victim or others likely to apprise the victim of the danger, to notify the police, or to take whatever other steps are reasonably necessary under the circumstances.

. . .

Plaintiffs' Complaints. Plaintiffs, Tatiana's mother and father, filed separate but virtually identical second amended complaints. The issue before us on this appeal is whether those complaints now state, or can be amended to state, causes of action against defendants. We therefore begin by setting forth the pertinent allegations of the complaints.

Plaintiffs' first cause of action, entitled "Failure to Detain a Dangerous Patient," alleges that on August 20, 1969, Poddar was a voluntary outpatient receiving therapy at Cowell Memorial Hospital. Poddar informed Moore, his therapist, that he was going to kill an unnamed girl, readily identifiable as Tatiana, when she returned home from spending the summer in Brazil. Moore, with the concurrence of Dr. Gold, who had initially examined Poddar, and Dr. Yandell, assistant to the director of the department of psychiatry, decided that Poddar should be committed for observation in a mental hospital. Moore orally notified Officers Atkinson and Teel of the campus police that he would request commitment. He then sent a letter to Police Chief William Beall requesting the assistance of the police department in securing Poddar's confinement.

Officers Atkinson, Brownrigg, and Halleran took Poddar into custody, but, satisfied that Poddar was rational, released him on his promise to stay away from Tatiana. Powelson, director of the department of psychiatry at Cowell Memorial Hospital, then asked the police to return Moore's letter, directed that all copies of the letter and notes that Moore had taken as therapist be destroyed, and "ordered no action to place Prosenjit Poddar in 72-hour treatment and evaluation facility."

Plaintiffs' second cause of action, entitled "Failure to Warn On a Dangerous Patient," incorporates the allegations of the first cause of action, but adds the assertion that defendants negligently permitted Poddar to be released from police custody without "notifying the parents of Tatiana Tarasoff that their daughter was in grave danger from Posenjit Poddar." Poddar persuaded Tatiana's brother to share an apartment with him near Tatiana's residence, shortly after her return from Brazil, Poddar went to her residence and killed her.

Plaintiff's third cause of action, entitled "Abandonment of a Dangerous Patient," seeks $10,000 punitive damages against defendant Powelson. Incorporating the crucial allegations of the first cause of action, plaintiffs charge that Powelson "did the things herein alleged with intent to abandon a dangerous patient, and said acts were done maliciously and oppressively."

Plaintiffs' fourth cause of action, for "Breach of Primary Duty to Patient and the Public," states essentially the same allegations as the first cause of action, but seeks to characterize defendants' conduct as a breach of duty to safeguard their patient and the public. Since such conclusory labels add nothing to the factual allegations of the complaint, the first and fourth causes of action are legally indistinguishable.

. . .

> Plaintiffs can state a cause of action against defendant therapists for negligent
> failure to protect Tatiana.

The second cause of action can be amended to allege that Tatiana's death proximately resulted from defendants' negligent failure to warn Tatiana or others likely to apprise her of her danger. Plaintiffs contend that as amended, such allegations of negligence and proximate causation, with resulting damages, establish a cause of action. Defendants, however, contend that in the circumstances of the present case they owed no duty of care to Tatiana or her parents and that, in the absence of such duty, they were free to act in careless disregard of Tatiana's life and safety.

In analyzing this issue, we bear in mind that legal duties are not discoverable facts of nature, but merely conclusory expressions that, in cases of a particular type, liability should be imposed for damage done. "The assertion that liability must . . . be denied because defendant bears no 'duty' to plaintiff 'begs the essential question—whether the plaintiff's interests are entitled to legal protection against the defendant's conduct. . . . [Duty] is not sacrosanct in itself, but only an expression of the sum total of those considerations of policy which lead the law to say that the particular plaintiff is entitled to protection."

Justice Peters recognized that liability should be imposed "for an injury occasioned to another by his want of ordinary care or skill" quoting "'whenever one person is by circumstances placed in such a position with regard to another . . . that if he did not use ordinary care and skill in his own conduct . . . he would cause danger of injury to the person or property of the other, a duty arises to use ordinary care and skill to avoid such danger.' "

We depart from "this fundamental principle" only upon the "balancing of a number of considerations"; major ones "are the foreseeability of harm to the plaintiff, the degree of certainty that the plaintiff suffered injury, the closeness of the connection between the defendant's conduct and the injury suffered, the moral blame attached to the defendant's conduct, the policy of preventing future harm, the extent of the burden to the defendant and consequences to the community of imposing a duty to exercise care with resulting liability for breach, and the availability, cost and prevalence of insurance for the risk involved."

The most important of these considerations in establishing duty is foreseeability. As a general principle, a "defendant owes a duty of care to all persons who are foreseeably endangered by his conduct, with respect to all risks which make the conduct unreasonably dangerous." As we shall explain, however, when the avoidance of foreseeable harm requires a defendant to control the conduct of another person, or to warn of such conduct, the common law has traditionally imposed liability only if the defendant bears some special relationship to the dangerous person or to the potential victim. Since the relationship between a therapist and his patient satisfies this requirement, we need not here decide whether foreseeability alone is sufficient to create a duty to exercise reasonable care to protect a potential victim of another's conduct.

Although, as we have stated above, under the common law, as a general rule, one person owed no duty to control the conduct of another . . . nor to warn those endangered by such conduct . . . the courts have carved out an exception to this rule in cases in which the defendant stands in some special relationship to either the person whose conduct needs to be controlled or in a relationship to the foreseeable victim of that conduct. Applying this exception to the present case, we note that a relationship of defendant therapists to either Tatiana or Poddar will suffice to establish a duty of care; as explained in section 315 of the Restatement Second of Torts, a duty of care may arise from either "(a) a special relation . . . between the actor and the third person which imposes a duty upon the actor to control the third person's conduct, or (b) a special relation . . . between the actor and the other which gives to the other a right of protection."

Although plaintiffs' pleadings assert no special relation between Tatiana and defendant therapists, they establish as between Poddar and defendant therapists the special relation that arises between a patient and his doctor or psychotherapist. Such a relationship may support affirmative duties for the benefit of third persons. Thus, for example, a hospital must exercise reasonable care to control the behavior of a patient which may endanger other persons. A doctor must also warn a patient if the patient's condition or medication renders certain conduct, such as driving a car, dangerous to others.

. . .

"[C]ase law should dispel any notion that to impose on the therapists a duty to take precautions for the safety of persons threatened by a patient, where due care so requires, is in any way opposed to contemporary ground rules on the duty relationship. On the contrary, there now seems to be sufficient authority to support the conclusion that by entering into a doctor-patient relationship the therapist becomes sufficiently involved to assume some responsibility for the safety, not only of the patient himself, but also of any third person whom the doctor knows to be threatened by the patient."

Defendants contend, however, that imposition of a duty to exercise reasonable care to protect third persons is unworkable because therapists cannot accurately predict whether or not a patient will resort to violence. In support of this argument amicus representing the American Psychiatric Association and other professional societies cites numerous articles which indicate that therapists, in the present state of the art, are unable reliably to predict violent acts; their forecasts, amicus claims, tend consistently to overpredict violence, and indeed are more often wrong than right. Since predictions of violence are often erroneous, amicus concludes, the courts should not render rulings that predicate the liability of therapists upon the validity of such predictions.

The role of the psychiatrist, who is indeed a practitioner of medicine, and that of the psychologist who performs an allied function, are like that of the physician who must conform to the standards of the profession and who must often make diagnoses and predictions based upon such evaluations. Thus the judgment of the therapist in diagnosing emotional disorders and in predicting whether a patient presents a serious danger of violence is comparable to the judgment which doctors and professionals must regularly render under accepted rules of responsibility.

We recognize the difficulty that a therapist encounters in attempting to forecast whether a patient presents a serious danger of violence. Obviously we do not require that the therapist, in making that determination, render a perfect performance; the therapist need only exercise "that reasonable degree of skill, knowledge, and care ordinarily possessed and exercised by members of [that professional specialty] under similar circumstances." Within the broad range of reasonable practice and treatment in which professional opinion and judgment may differ, the therapist is free to exercise his or her own best judgment without liability; proof, aided by hindsight, that he or she judged wrongly is insufficient to establish negligence.

In the instant case, however, the pleadings do not raise any question as to failure of defendant therapists to predict that Poddar presented a serious danger of violence. On the contrary, the present complaints allege that defendant therapists did in fact predict that Poddar would kill, but were negligent in failing to warn.

Amicus contends, however, that even when a therapist does in fact predict that a patient poses a serious danger of violence to others, the therapist should be absolved of any responsibility for failing to act to protect the potential victim. In our view, however, once a therapist does in fact determine, or under applicable professional standards reasonably should have determined, that a patient poses a serious danger of violence to others, he bears a duty to exercise reasonable care to protect the foreseeable victim of that danger. While the discharge of this duty of due care will necessarily vary with the facts of each case, in each instance the adequacy of the therapist's conduct must be measured against the traditional negligence standard of the rendition of reasonable care under the circumstances. ". . . The ultimate question of resolving the tension between the conflicting interests of patient and potential victim is one of social policy, not professional expertise. . . . In sum, the therapist owes a legal duty not only to this patient, but also to his patient's would-be victim and is subject in both respects to scrutiny by judge and jury."

. . .

The issue in the present context, however, is not whether the patient should be incarcerated, but whether the therapist should take any steps at all to protect the threatened victim; some of the alternatives open to the therapist, such as warning the victim, will not result in the drastic consequences of depriving the patient of his liberty. Weighing the uncertain and conjectural character of the alleged damage done the patient by such a warning against the peril to the victim's life, we conclude that professional inaccuracy in predicting violence cannot negate the therapist's duty to protect the threatened victim.

The risk that unnecessary warnings may be given is a reasonable price to pay for the lives of possible victims that may be saved. We would hesitate to hold that the therapist who is aware that his patient expects to attempt to assassinate the President of the United States would not be obligated to warn the authorities because the therapist cannot predict with accuracy that his patient will commit the crime.

Defendants further argue that free and open communication is essential to psychotherapy; that "Unless a patient . . . is assured that . . . information [revealed by him] can and will be held in utmost confidence, he will be reluctant to make the full disclosure upon which diagnosis and treatment . . . depends." The giving of a warning, defendants contend, constitutes a breach of trust which entails the revelation of confidential communications.

We recognize the public interest in supporting effective treatment of mental illness and in protecting the rights of patients to privacy and the consequent public importance of safeguarding the confidential character of psychotherapeutic communication. Against this interest, however, we must weigh the public interest in safety from violent assault. The Legislature has undertaken the difficult task of balancing the countervailing concerns. In Evidence Code section 1014, it established a broad rule of privilege to protect confidential communications between patient and psychotherapist. In Evidence Code section 1024, the Legislature created a specific and limited exception to the psychotherapist-patient privilege: "There is no privilege . . . if the psychotherapist has reasonable cause to believe that the patient is in such mental or emotional condition as to be dangerous to himself or to the person or property of another and that disclosure of the communication is necessary to prevent the threatened danger."

We realize that the open and confidential character of psychotherapeutic dialogue encourages patients to express threats of violence, few of which are ever executed. Certainly a therapist should not be encouraged routinely to reveal such threats; such disclosures could seriously disrupt the patient's relationship with his therapist and with the persons threatened. To the contrary, the therapist's obligations to his patient require that he not disclose a confidence unless such disclosure is necessary to avert danger to others, and even then that he do so discreetly, and in a fashion that would preserve the privacy of his patient to the fullest extent compatible with the prevention of the threatened danger.

The revelation of a communication under the above circumstances is not a breach of trust or a violation of professional ethics; as stated in the Principles of Medical Ethics of the American Medical Association (1957), section 9: "A physician may not reveal the confidence entrusted to him in the course of medical attendance . . . *unless he is required to do so by law or unless it becomes necessary in order to protect the welfare of the individual or of the community."* (Emphasis added.) We conclude that the public policy favoring protection of the confidential character of patient-psychotherapist communications must yield to the extent to which disclosure is essential to avert danger to others. The protective privilege ends where the public peril begins.

Our current crowded and computerized society compels the interdependence of its members. In this risk-infested society we can hardly tolerate the further exposure to danger that would result from a concealed knowledge of the therapist that his patient was lethal. If the exercise of reasonable care to protect the threatened victim requires the therapist to warn the endangered party or those who can reasonably be expected to notify him, we see no sufficient societal interest that would protect and justify concealment. The containment of such risks lies in the public interest.

. . .

Conclusion. For the reasons stated, we conclude that plaintiffs can amend their complaints to state a cause of action against defendant therapists by asserting that the therapists in fact determined that Poddar presented a serious danger of violence to Tatiana, or pursuant to the standards of their profession should have so determined, but nevertheless failed to exercise reasonable care to protect her from that danger.

. . .

MOSK, Justice (concurring and dissenting).

I concur in the result in this instance only because the complaints allege that defendant therapists did in fact predict that Poddar would kill and were therefore negligent in failing to warn of that danger. Thus the issue here is very narrow: we are not concerned with whether the therapists, pursuant to the standards of their profession, "should have" predicted potential violence: they allegedly did so in actuality. Under these limited circumstances I agree that a cause of action can be stated.

Whether plaintiffs can ultimately prevail is problematical at best. As the complaints admit, the therapists *did* notify the police that Poddar was planning to kill a girl identifiable as Tatiana. While I doubt that more should be required, this issue may be raised in defense and its determination is a question of fact.

I cannot concur, however, in the majority's rule that a therapist may be held liable for failing to predict his patient's tendency to violence if other practitioners, pursuant to the "standards of the profession," would have done so. The question is, what standards? Defendants and a responsible amicus curiae, supported by an impressive body of literature discussed at length in our recent opinion . . . demonstrate that psychiatric predictions of violence are inherently unreliable . . . we observed: "In the light of recent studies it is no longer heresy to question the reliability of psychiatric predictions. Psychiatrists themselves would be the first to admit that however desirable an infallible crystal ball might be, it is not among the tools of their profession. It must be conceded that psychiatrists still experience considerable difficulty in confidently and accurately *diagnosing* mental illness. Yet those difficulties are multiplied manyfold when psychiatrists venture from diagnosis to prognosis and undertake to predict the consequences of such illness: 'A diagnosis of mental illness tells us nothing about whether the person so diagnosed is or is not dangerous. Some mental patients are dangerous, some are not. Perhaps the psychiatrist is an expert at deciding whether a person is mentally ill, but is he an expert at predicting which of the persons so diagnosed are dangerous? Sane people, too, are dangerous, and it may legitimately be inquired whether there is anything in the education, training or experience of psychiatrists which renders them particularly adept at predicting dangerous behavior. Predictions of dangerous behavior, no matter who makes them, are incredibly inaccurate, and there is a growing consensus that psychiatrists are not uniquely qualified to predict dangerous behavior and are, in fact, less accurate in their predictions than other professionals.' "

. . .

I would restructure the rule designed by the majority to eliminate all reference to conformity to standards of the profession in predicting violence. If a psychiatrist does in fact predict violence, then a duty to warn arises. The majority's expansion of that rule will take us from the world of reality into the wonderland of clairvoyance.

. . .

CLARK, Justice (dissenting).

Until today's majority opinion, both legal and medical authorities have agreed that confidentiality is essential to effectively treat the mentally ill, and that imposing a duty on doctors to disclose patient threats to potential victims would greatly impair treatment. Further, recognizing that effective treatment and society's safety are necessarily intertwined, the Legislature has already decided effective and confidential treatment is preferred over imposition of a duty to warn.

The issue whether effective treatment for the mentally ill should be sacrificed to a system of warnings, is, in my opinion, properly one for the Legislature, and we are bound by its judgment. Moreover, even in the absence of clear legislative direction, we must reach the same conclusion because imposing the majority's new duty is certain to result in a net increase in violence.

. . .

Generally, a person owes no duty to control the conduct of another. Exceptions are recognized only in limited situations where (1) a special relationship exists between the defendant and the injured party, or (2) a special relationship exists between defendant and the active wrongdoer, imposing a duty on defendant to control the wrongdoer's conduct. The majority does not contend the first exception is appropriate to this case.

Policy generally determines duty. Principal policy considerations include foreseeability of harm, certainty of the plaintiff's injury, proximity of the defendant's conduct to the plaintiff's injury, moral blame attributable to defendant's conduct, prevention of future harm, burden on the defendant, and consequences to the community.

Overwhelming policy considerations weigh against imposing a duty on psychotherapists to warn a potential victim against harm. While offering virtually no benefit to society, such a duty will frustrate psychiatric treatment, invade fundamental patient rights and increase violence.

The importance of psychiatric treatment and its need for confidentiality have been recognized by this court. "It is clearly recognized that the very practice of psychiatry vitally depends upon the reputation in the community that the psychiatrist will not tell."

Assurance of confidentiality is important for three reasons:

Deterrence from Treatment

First, without substantial assurance of confidentiality, those requiring treatment will be deterred from seeking assistance. It remains an unfortunate fact in our society that people seeking psychiatric guidance tend to become stigmatized. Apprehension of such stigma—apparently increased by the propensity of people considering treatment to see themselves in the worst possible light—creates a well-recognized reluctance to seek aid. This reluctance is alleviated by the psychiatrist's assurance of confidentiality.

Full Disclosure

Second, the guarantee of confidentiality is essential in eliciting the full disclosure necessary for effective treatment. The psychiatric patient approaches treatment with conscious and unconscious inhibitions against revealing his innermost thoughts. "Every person, however well-motivated, has to overcome resistances to therapeutic exploration. These resistances seek support from every possible source and the possibility of disclosure would easily be employed in the service of resistance." Until a patient can trust his psychiatrist not to violate their confidential relationship, "the unconscious psychological control mechanism of repression will prevent the recall of past experiences."

Successful Treatment

Third, even if the patient fully discloses his thoughts, assurance that the confidential relationship will not be breached is necessary to maintain his trust in his psychiatrist— the very means by which treatment is effected. "[T]he essence of much psychotherapy is the contribution of trust in the external world and ultimately in the self, modelled upon the trust relationship established during therapy." Patients will be helped only if they can form a trusting relationship with the psychiatrist. All authorities appear to agree that if the trust relationship cannot be developed because of collusive communication between the psychiatrist and others, treatment will be frustrated.

Given the importance of confidentiality to the practice of psychiatry, it becomes clear the duty to warn imposed by the majority will cripple the use and effectiveness of psychiatry. Many people, potentially violent—yet susceptible to treatment—will be deterred from seeking it; those seeking it will be inhibited from making revelations necessary to effective treatment; and, forcing the psychiatrist to violate the patient's trust will destroy the interpersonal relationship by which treatment is effected.

Violence and Civil Commitment

By imposing a duty to warn, the majority contributes to the danger to society of violence by the mentally ill and greatly increases the risk of civil commitment—the total deprivation of liberty—of those who should not be confined. The impairment of treatment and risk of improper commitment resulting from the new duty to warn will not be limited to a few patients but will extend to a large number of the mentally ill. Although under existing psychiatric procedures only a relatively few receiving treatment will ever present a risk of violence, the number making threats is huge, and it is the latter group— not just the former—whose treatment will be impaired and whose risk of commitment will be increased.

Both the legal and psychiatric communities recognize that the process of determining potential violence in a patient is far from exact, being fraught with complexity and uncertainty. In fact precision has not even been attained in predicting who of those having already committed violent acts will again become violent, a task recognized to be of much simpler proportions.

This predictive uncertainty means that the number of disclosures will necessarily be large. As noted above, psychiatric patients are encouraged to discuss all thoughts of violence, and they often express such thoughts. However, unlike this court, the psychiatrist does not enjoy the benefit of overwhelming hindsight in seeing which few, if any, of his patients will ultimately become violent. Now, confronted by the majority's new duty, the psychiatrist must instantaneously calculate potential violence from each patient on each visit. The difficulties researchers have encountered in accurately predicting violence will be heightened for the practicing psychiatrist dealing for brief periods in his office with heretofore nonviolent patients. And, given the decision not to warn or commit must always be made at the psychiatrist's civil peril, one can expect most doubts will be resolved in favor of the psychiatrist protecting himself.

Neither alternative open to the psychiatrist seeking to protect himself is in the public interest. The warning itself is an impairment of the psychiatrist's ability to treat, depriving many patients of adequate treatment. It is to be expected that after disclosing their threats, a significant number of patients, who would not become violent if treated according to existing practices, will engage in violent conduct as a result of unsuccessful treatment. In short, the majority's duty to warn will not only impair treatment of many who would never become violent but worse, will result in a net increase in violence.

The second alternative open to the psychiatrist is to commit his patient rather than to warn. Even in the absence of threat of civil liability, the doubts of psychiatrists as to the seriousness of patient threats have led psychiatrists to overcommit to mental institutions. This overcommitment has been authoritatively documented in both legal and psychiatric studies. This practice is so prevalent that it has been estimated that "as many as twenty harmless persons are incarcerated for every one who will commit a violent act."

Given the incentive to commit created by the majority's duty, this already serious situation will be worsened, contrary to Chief Justice Wright's admonition "that liberty is no less precious because forfeited in a civil proceeding than when taken as a consequence of a criminal conviction."

. . .

NOTES

1. Davidoff, *The Malpractice of Psychiatrist*, 1966 DUKE L.J. 696, 704.
2. Jagim, Wittman, & Noll, *Mental Health Professionals' Attitudes Toward Confidentiality, Privilege, and Third-party Disclosure*, 9 PROFESSIONAL PSYCHOLOGY 458–66 (1978).
3. WIGMORE, 89 EVIDENCE § 2192 at 70, 73 (McNaughton revision, 3rd ed. 1961).
4. *Id.* § 2285 at 527.
5. R. LEMPERT & S. SALTZBURG, A. MODERN APPROACH TO EVIDENCE 615 (1977).
6. Notes, *Nature of the Professional Relationship Required under the Privileged Communication Rule*, 24 IOWA L. REV. 538–58 (1939).
7. State v. Tornquist, 120 N.W. 2d 483 (Iowa 1963).
8. Arnovitz v. Wozar, 222 N.E. 2d 660 (Ohio 1964).
9. FED R. CRIM. P. 26.
10. FED. R. CIV. P. 43(a).
11. Mullen v. U.S., 263 F.2d 275 (D.C. App. 1958).
12. Funk v. U.S., 290 U.S. 371, 383 (1933).
13. Felber v. Foote, 321 F. Supp. 85 (D. Conn. 1970).
14. Michigan, St. 1961, June 9, No. 236 (600.2165).
15. NEV. REV. STAT. 49.291 (1977).
16. S.D. COMP. LAWS ANN. §19–2–5.1 (supp. 1978).
17. MONT. REV. CODES ANN. §93–701–4(6) (1947).
18. R. L. SCHWITZGEBEL & R. K. SCHWITZGEBEL, LAW AND PSYCHOLOGICAL PRACTICE 215, note 9 (1980).
19. S. KNAPP & L. VANDECREEK, PRIVILEGED COMMUNICATIONS IN THE MENTAL HEALTH PROFESSIONS 7 (1987).
20. St. 1967, June 8, Ch. 372 Para. 12.
21. State v. Bednasek, 67 N.W. 2d 815 (Iowa 1966).
22. Tarasoff v. The Regents of the University of California, 551 P.2d 334 (Cal. 1976).
23. *Id.* at 343.
24. *Id.* at 344. The court relied heavily on Fleming & Maximov, *The Patient or His Victim: The Therapist's Dilemma*, 62 CAL. L. REV. 1025 (1974).
25. *Id.* at 345.
26. *Id.* at 345–6.
27. *Id.* at 347.
28. Shaw v. Glickman, 415 A.2d 625 (Md. App. 1980). The case cited MD. CTS. & JUD. PROC. CODE ANN. §9–109(b) (1974).
29. Lipari v. Sears, Roebuck & Co., 497 F. Supp. 185 (D. Neb. 1980).
30. Leedy v. Harnett, 510 F. Supp. 1125 (M.D. Pa. 1981).
31. Marroudis v. Superior Court for County of San Mateo, 162 Cal. Rptr. 724 (App. 1980).
32. Hedlund v. Superior Court of Orange County, 669 P.2d 41 (1983).
33. Peck v. Counseling Serv. of Addison County, 499 A.2d 422 (Vt. 1985).

CHAPTER 3

Liability: Civil and Criminal

OVERVIEW

In our highly litigious society people often are sued in connection with their jobs. Therapists and counselors are no exception, and experience shows that they might find themselves as defendants in civil suits or even in criminal actions. What is the difference between civil and criminal liability? The basic difference is that civil liability arises when one commits a wrong against an *individual*, a wrong that causes damage that can be compensated for with money, whereas criminal liability arises when one commits a crime that is wrong against *society*, in an action forbidden by law. A minor crime is called a misdemeanor; a serious one is a felony. The laws of each state specify which acts constitute felonies and which are misdemeanors.

An action may result in a civil wrong (legally called a *tort*), in a crime, in both, or in neither. For example, if I am sober and I drive down the street in the proper manner, I have committed no wrong. If I drive under the influence of alcohol, weaving down the street and going through red lights, I have violated several laws and thus committed several crimes. However, if I hurt no person or property in this process, I commit no tort. If, on the other hand, while driving under the influence of alcohol I crash into your car, I have committed a crime and I am also liable to you in a tort action for the damages I caused. And finally, if, while sober, I drive negligently and crash into your car, I am liable to you in money damages in an action in tort, but I have committed no crime. In other words, some crimes are also torts, but most of our actions are neither torts nor crimes.

As with the general population, most of the behaviors of therapists and counselors are completely consistent with the law and entail neither civil nor criminal liability. However, experience shows that some counselors, psychologists, and psychiatrists cause damage to their clients through negligent practice, some violate laws and thus incur criminal liability in the form of fines or jail sentences, and some are guilty of both. In this chapter, we examine first the most common areas of negligence in the work of mental health practitioners and then the activities that might lead to possible criminal liability.

What is negligence and how is it related to malpractice?

The law of negligence, which composes a large part of the law of torts, includes various kinds of wrongful actions that result in injury or damages. It excludes damages that result from breaking a contract, which would fall under the law of contracts. For example, if a counselor has a three-year contract with a school district and she is dismissed in the middle of her second year, she could sue for breach of contract but not for negligence. Although money damages might be suffered both through someone's negligent action and for breaking a contract, different legal principles apply to each. But when is a person legally negligent? When can we sue for monetary damages for negligence?

As a general legal principle, civil liability for negligence will accrue if one person causes damages to another through a breach of duty owed to that person. To use our earlier example, when driving a car, I have a duty to you and everyone else on the street to drive it with care so as not to hurt anyone. If I drive carelessly and don't stop at a pedestrian crossing that is occupied, I breach that duty. If my careless driving causes you injury, I am liable for the damages you suffered. Such damages, generally assessed in a lump sum, might include medical expenses and loss of wages, as well as compensation for emotional suffering. The extent of the damages, of course, is determined by a jury or a judge after you present and explain your evidence. These principles apply to the counselor–counselee relationship as well. Thus, to hold a therapist-counselor liable in a tort action for negligence, a court must find the following to be true:

1. A duty was owed by the therapist-counselor to the counselee;
2. The duty owed was breached;
3. There was a sufficient legal causal connection between the breach of duty and counselee's injury;
4. Some injury or damages were suffered by counselee.

What is malpractice?

Malpractice is an area of tort law, one that refers to negligent practice in the rendering of professional services. For example, a physician who leaves a sponge or forceps in the patient's stomach as he closes the wound at the conclusion of surgery is guilty of malpractice. A lawyer who loses a client's case because of carelessness in observing certain deadlines specified by law is liable for money damages in a suit for malpractice. Architects, accountants, and other professionals have been found liable for the negligent practice of their profession.

Similarly, mental health professionals who are negligent in their work could be sued for malpractice. To put it simply, malpractice is the failure to provide reasonably competent service, through ignorance or negligence, that results in injury or damages to a client. Mental health professionals are held to the standards of competent practice accepted by their profession in their geographic region. Thus, the standards for psychiatrists will differ from those applied to social workers or teacher/counselors. In general, however, the legal principles whereby mental health professionals, including counselors, could be held liable for malpractice are not at all clear and certainly not as clear as in medicine, law, architecture, or accounting.

What constitutes malpractice for counselors is not clear for several reasons. First, most counselors do not receive as many years of training as psychiatrists or psychologists, but they are trained more thoroughly than teachers. In most states there are no clear, rigorous licensing laws controlling the practice of counseling similar to the licensing laws governing the professions of psychiatry or clinical psychology. Licensing laws do not specify the areas of responsibility and standards of care that counselors must meet; in the eyes of the law, they work in an ill-defined, ambiguous arena. Thus counselors occupy what is often referred to as a gray, uncertain area in the disciplines related to mental health.

Counselors, in and out of school, work with their clients in individual sessions or in group sessions, or in an emergency, usually referred to as crisis intervention. A claim of malpractice may arise out of each of these settings. However, as we recall the basic elements of negligence, we must ask first whether there was a duty of care owed by the counselor and, if there was, whether he breached such a duty by not living up to expected standards. Furthermore, what level of standards will the law impose on counselors? Counselors can be held liable for failure to exercise "the requisite skill and care,"[1] but how do we decide what that is? As we would expect, the standards of "care" and "skill" differ somewhat for individual counseling and for groups and certainly for crisis intervention. Therefore, we will consider each of these separately.

MALPRACTICE IN INDIVIDUAL COUNSELING

Counselees bring an endless variety of problems to counselors; the more effective the counselor the longer the list of questions and problems he or she is likely to face. These may range from relatively routine matters of program selection and advice concerning colleges or occupational choice, to very complex interpersonal problems, or even health matters and drug abuse.

A teenage boy might seek advice because his girlfriend became pregnant. A 14-year-old girl might seek information about birth control or abortion. A bright student, despondent about his grades and parental pressure, might talk with the counselor about "wanting to end it all." A student, in fear of arrest for drug use, or for helping his friends burglarize a home, may seek help. Teachers and administrators ask the counselor's help to search students' lockers and clothing in an effort to eliminate illegal drug use in school.

In each of these situations, the counselor, as part of the job of counseling, must attempt to help the counselee resolve the problem. At the same time, in our highly litigious society, counselors are concerned with possible malpractice suits that may arise out of each of these relationships. How should the counselor proceed?

It is important to understand that no one is completely free from the possibility of being sued. However, legal actions are expensive, troublesome, and otherwise unpleasant, so most people do not sue frivolously or at the drop of a threat. By understanding some basic principles, the counselor may act with confidence in the proper pursuit of his or her profession.

First, it is clear that, legally, the counselor has a duty to use professionally accepted skill and care in working with counselees. This duty arises from the counseling relationship itself. The governing legal principle is as follows:

> One who undertakes, gratuitously or for consideration, to render services to another which he should recognize as necessary for the protection of the other person or things, is subject to liability to the other for physical harm resulting from his failure to exercise reasonable care to perform his undertaking, if:
> a. His failure to exercise such care increases the risk of harm, or
> b. The harm is suffered because of the other's reliance upon the undertaking.[2]

The counselor, by practicing his or her profession, implies that he or she will conduct him- or herself in a skillful and responsible manner and will be held up to the standards of skill and care generally applied by counselors practicing in the same area. In other words, there is no nationwide uniform standard applied to counselors. It may well be the case that different levels of care and skill will be expected in Palo Alto, California, than in Lorain, Ohio; or the standards applied in Peoria, Illinois, might differ from those in Houston, Texas. There are insufficient cases litigated and reported from which counselors can derive clear guidance concerning the extent of their duty to counselees, and the parents of counselees when working with minors. An often-cited Wisconsin case illustrates this point, together with a more recent California case.

Bogust v. Iverson *(1960).* This case, which eventually reached the Supreme Court of Wisconsin, was filed by the parents of Jane Dunn against the director of student personnel services at Stout State College, who had counseled Jane for approximately half a year. The counselor came to know the young woman's emotional, personal, and social problems, as well as her feelings of conflict and social inadequacy, through personal interviews and aptitude and personality tests. This was consistent with his responsibilities which, according to the court, included counseling and testing for "personal, vocational, educational, scholastic, or other problems," as well as counseling "students torn by conflicting feelings, which cause worry and social ineffectiveness." When the counselor felt that Jane had made all the progress she was likely to make, he terminated their sessions. About five weeks later she committed suicide.

The parents alleged that there was negligence because (a) the educator failed to secure emergency psychiatric treatment after he was aware, or should have been aware, of Jane's incapacity; (b) he failed to advise Jane's parents of her problems; and (c) he failed to provide proper student guidance. Plaintiffs sought $3,500 for funeral expenses, $15,000 for general damages, plus the cost of litigation and attorney fees. (If one considers that this case was adjudicated in 1960, and if one is aware of escalating costs of litigation and jury awards, one realizes that the damages plaintiffs would seek today would be substantially higher.)*

The trial court ruled against the parents and the Wisconsin Supreme Court affirmed its ruling. The court repeatedly referred to the defendant as a teacher and not as a counselor. The defendant, a professor of education with a Ph.D. degree, was director of the college counseling center. The court said, for example, "To hold that a teacher who has no training, education, or experience in medical fields is required to recognize in a student a condition the diagnosis of which is in a specialized and technical medical field, would require a duty beyond reason."[3] Furthermore, the court emphasized the fact that almost six weeks elapsed between the termination of counseling and the act of suicide. It is speculative to suggest, maintained the court, that Jane would not have taken her own life if the parents had been advised of her emotional instability or even if psychiatric help had been secured for her by the defendant.

Thus, the court found no duty on the part of the counselor to warn anybody. Furthermore, even assuming that a duty existed and was violated by the counselor, there is no clear causal connection between the violation of the duty (failure to warn parents or secure psychiatric help) and the suicide. Thus, two elements of the law of torts were missing.

Nally v. Grace Community Church *(1988).*[4] The parents of 24-year-old Kenneth Nally sued the church and its pastors for negligence when their son committed suicide after several years of informal counseling and "discipleship." During these years Kenneth also saw secular psychologists and psychiatrists on brief occasions. After an unsuccessful suicide attempt in March 1979, he and his parents refused to follow the recommendations of a psychiatrist that he commit himself to a psychiatric hospital. A similar recommendation by one of the pastors was also rejected. The pastors continued to give him spiritual advice as well as recommending that he seek therapy. When Nally committed suicide on April 1, 1979, his parents sued, claiming the church and the pastors were negligent. The California Supreme Court ruled in favor of the church and its pastors because it found that there was no *duty of care* that was breached by them and no special relationship that would create such duty. (See pp. 63–70.)

The California court drew an important distinction between nontherapist counselors and professional therapists such as psychiatrists or certified psychologists. The court noted that it has previously imposed a duty of care only on therapists or hospitals with suicidal patients committed in a hospital or other inpatient facility. Since the pastors were nontherapist counselors without the requisite special relationship, the court would not impose the duty of care.

Interestingly enough, two of the justices found that such duty of care existed because the pastors held themselves out to be therapists. However, these justices

---

*Because an important precedent would be established in this case, the American Personnel and Guidance Association, the National Education Association, and the Wisconsin Education Association all requested and received permission from the Wisconsin Supreme Court to submit briefs (legal arguments) presenting their views on how the matter should be decided.

also found that this duty was satisfied by the pastors' various suggestions that Nally seek professional therapy.

Although therapists and counselors will continue to use the *Bogust* and *Nally* cases as precedents in defense of suits for negligence, some cautions must be noted. First, these cases are binding precedents only in their respective states, namely Wisconsin and California. Other states are not bound by them, although they might be used elsewhere to attempt to persuade judges of the merits of their arguments. Furthermore, these cases dealt with a college student and an adult, and some courts might not accept them as precedents for younger students. Furthermore, attorneys for future plaintiffs are likely to bring in the *Tarasoff* [5] case (see Chapter 2) to urge that a counselor has a legal duty arising out of the special relationship with the counselee, and that this duty requires that a warning be given to endangered individuals. In the case of a probable suicide, it is arguable that the warning should go to those who can effectively prevent the counselee from self-destruction. However, we can find no reported cases that have imposed such liability. In *Bellah v. Greenson* [6] a California appellate court specifically refused to extend the *Tarasoff* duty to warn to a case that involved a suicide. The court considered suicide not equivalent to impending danger of violent assault on members of the public. The California court considered confidentiality to be a very important factor in the treatment of suicidal persons, one that outweighs the supposed duty to warn the suicide victim's parents. In the words of the court: "We conclude that *Tarasoff v. Regents* requires only that a therapist disclose the contents of a confidential communication where the risk to be prevented thereby is the danger of violent assault, and not where the risk of harm is self-inflicted harm or merely property damage (citations omitted)." The *Nally* case discussed *Bellah* in detail, refused to impose a duty of care on nontherapist counselors, and would not extend *Tarasoff's* duty to warn to suicide cases in general.

Another case that followed *Tarasoff* held that the "duty requires that the therapist initiate whatever precautions are reasonably necessary to protect the potential victims of his patient." [7] Of course, it is arguable that counselors are not therapists and that the *Tarasoff* case involved a psychologist, and therefore, that case and its progeny should not be applied to counselors or teachers. And the *Nally* case accepted such reasoning.

But what about counselors who are certified psychologists; should *Tarasoff* apply to them? On one hand, it is clear that psychiatrists undergo more extensive training than psychologists or counselors; on the other, counselors aspire to high professional status, and in their code of ethics they impose clear obligation on their practitioners to refer cases to appropriate specialists if they themselves cannot deal with them. [8]

Provisions related to referral of clients by counselors are included in the code of ethics of the American Personnel and Guidance Association (APGA). [9] An effective lawyer could make a strong case for counselors' duty to warn, by weaving together the principles of the *Tarasoff* case with aspirations of professionalism commonly found in APGA literature and the provisions in its *Ethical Principles*.

Although there is no foolproof way to predict the behavior of courts in our complex and changing culture, particularly with 50 different state judicial systems relatively free to follow their own state laws and precedents, some general guidelines may be offered. These guidelines should provide some confidence for counselors in conducting their daily work, but counselors should realize that such general understanding may not suffice if a specific problem arises. In such situations, particularly if a lawsuit is likely to follow, there is no substitute for legal advice.

To summarize, it is clear that counselors have a duty to use reasonable care and skill in their relationship with clients. Psychiatrists will be held to higher standards of care and skill than psychologists and they, in turn, to higher standards than counselors who are not psychologists. If any of these professionals do not perform up to the standards of reasonably competent practitioners in their area *and* if such breach of duty injures the client or a third person endangered by the client, a suit for money damages is likely to succeed.

Among the many issues counselors have faced, two that have occurred often are the suicidal counselee and the counselee who is likely to be dangerous to others. Courts have ruled that if a counselor knew or should have known of the danger to an identified or readily identifiable victim, there is a duty to warn or to take other reasonable measures to prevent the harm. Courts are not as likely to rule similarly in cases of suicidal clients, even if there are indications of self-destructive behavior. Judges do not impose a duty on ordinary school counselors who have no medical or psychological training to recognize subtle signs of serious emotional problems. Foreseeability is an important component of the duty to warn or to take other precautions, and the level of professional training is an important element in determining what a counselor should be expected to predict.

There have been more lawsuits against psychiatrists and psychologists than against school counselors or other nontherapist counselors, such as ordinary social workers (as contrasted with psychiatric social workers), or ministers, pastors, rabbis, and priests who also act as counselors. This reflects the higher standards applied to the former by the public at large, as well as the courts' reluctance to impose unreasonable expectations on school counselors. It might also be reasonable to infer that school counselors, in general, exercise the level of care and skill in individual counseling sessions that is expected of them.

COUNSELORS' RESPONSIBILITY
TO SUPERVISE WITH CARE

The supervision of students is a common responsibility of school counselors, particularly the supervision of "special needs" students. As is true for other school personnel, inadequate supervision by counselors may lead to student injuries and consequent lawsuits. The duty to supervise with care is particularly evident when one realizes that counselors often supervise emotionally disturbed students, those under the influence of drugs, or those otherwise incapacitated.

Any well-trained counselor knows that such students need care and supervision and that they should not go around school or to their home without help. The greater the incapacity of the student, the more careful the counselor must be to provide for his or her safety, either directly or through the help of other responsible persons. If the matter ever came to court, the question to be faced would be, "Did this counselor act in a reasonable manner under the circumstances?" The general principles of law are no different when applied to counselors rather than to teachers, principals, or librarians, except that the specific difficulties of "special-needs" students under a counselor's supervision might call for increased care. One legal scholar expressed it this way in his discussion of tort liability of school personnel:

> If a teacher or administrator contemplates sending a young child home during school hours, she should, as a reasonably prudent person, reflect upon whether she is exposing the child to dangers to which the child would not be exposed if it were dismissed at the normal hour. For instance, if the child would be exposed to a very dangerous crossing when no patrol help was on duty and [he or she] was injured, it would place the teacher in a precarious position as regards liability.[10]

Thus, the rule with regard to supervision is rather straightforward. Counselors must act so that students placed under their care are properly cared for. When the counselee, for whatever reasons, is exposed to danger, the test is one of reasonable prudence on the part of the counselor.

Is the therapist-counselor liable
if the counselee does not improve?

In general, no. The law will not presume negligence from the mere fact that no improvement was made, whether in scholastic achievement, emotional health, or social adjustment. This is the case even when the counselor has made some optimistic predictions and his or her judgment turned out to be wrong. Even the most skillful counselors make such mistakes.[11]

It is generally considered to be professionally unwise for counselors to give an assurance of improvement, but even if such assurance is given and unrealized, courts are not likely to find that malpractice was committed. There are no actual cases in point, but we can argue by analogy from cases involving physicians and psychiatrists, who are all held to higher standards. One court ruled that an unqualified statement by a psychiatrist that shock treatments were perfectly safe constituted a warranty. However, this same court, as well as others, held that a physician's statement that he could cure a disease ordinarily could not be considered a warranty.[12] Although it is arguable that a careless promise by a counselor, guaranteeing improvement, could be construed as a warranty, courts are not likely to so construe it, particularly in light of the ambiguous professional position that counseling occupies in the eyes of the law. In any event, it would make good legal sense for counselors not to make unreasonable promises, either to students or to parents, that might lead to frustrated expectations and thoughts of lawsuits.

Does the counselor have a duty to refer
a client to more competent help?

There may be such a *legal* duty, though no court cases have as yet imposed it. Clearly there is a *professional* duty to refer, if the problem at hand goes beyond the competence of the counselor. Legally, it can be argued that once a counseling relationship has begun, the counselor has a duty to continue it until the problem is resolved or an appropriate referral is made to another competent professional.[13] By accepting the case the counselor, in effect, has created a reliance and discouraged the counselee from seeking help elsewhere. However, professional ethics aside, legally it would be very difficult for a counselee to prove that a counselor's lack of referral was a breach of duty that caused some injury. Thus, it is highly unlikely that an action for negligence would succeed against a counselor on the grounds of lack of referral.

LEGAL ASPECTS OF GROUP COUNSELING

The relatively new technique of group counseling helps counselees understand and communicate with others who have similar or different emotional problems. It is believed that the group session will help one acquire a sense of perspective more effectively than will individual work with a counselor or therapist. Whatever the professional merits of group counseling, there are some new legal questions raised by this technique for which we have no definitive answers as yet, for there is no authoritative case law to guide us.

We have already noted, in Chapter 2, that in all but one state, group sessions are not covered by the privilege of legal confidentiality. Our attention here will focus on questions of tort law as they relate to group counseling and therapy.

Although the legal relationship of counseling to client is the same, in principle, in group sessions as in individual sessions, the factual context is much more complicated. The duty to supervise is increased in proportion to the need, and the need is greater when there are multiple interactions among various members of the group than in the one-to-one interaction between the counselor and a single counselee. Counselors involved in group sessions must constantly evaluate the appropriateness of the group for particular individuals, consider the appropriateness of the size of the group for the particular problems the participants have, and always be prepared to refer individual participants needing special help to competent psychologists or psychiatrists.

In recent years, many counselors have experienced the transformation of group sessions into encounters of various kinds. At times these encounters are deliberate, carefully planned and controlled, and supervised with skill. This, however, is not always the case. Unanticipated encounters occur in group sessions and, due to the unique combination of personalities, can escalate into very complex and explosive situations. Counselors need excellent training and a high degree of skill and maturity to handle such situations without exacerbating the problems of participants. Such situations are fraught with legal problems, particularly potential suits for negligence. It is a dangerous area in which to dabble, and should be practiced only by those who are well trained and certified to conduct and supervise therapy. The typical school counselor is not so qualified and should carefully avoid group-counseling sessions that might turn into encounters, both for professional reasons and to avoid a suit for money damages.

LIABILITY IN CRISIS INTERVENTION

Emergency situations arise wherein a person may be close to serious injury or even death. Counselors might be called upon to avert tragedy, to hold off disaster until systematic help arrives. This is called crisis intervention by some and crisis management by others.

What standard of care does the law require of counselors in such situations? Oliver Wendell Holmes, Jr., while sitting as a justice on the U.S. Supreme Court, said, "Detached reflection cannot be expected in the face of an uplifted knife." What Holmes meant is that, in emergency situations, we cannot expect the same degree of care and thoughtful action that we require in ordinary affairs. The same principle would apply to crisis intervention, where typically the counselor does not have real control over the client or the situation. The guiding legal principle is this: A person is responsible for harm to another only if failure to exercise reasonable care increases the risk of harm to that other person.[14] A failure in crisis intervention would require that the counselor reject the counselee's cry for help in a way that indicated that the counselor did not exercise reasonable care in doing so. If the counselor has so acted, the next legal question would be whether such action by the counselor had increased the risk of harm to the counselee. The following hypothetical situation may help illustrate a crisis-intervention case.[*]

Carey was a teenager who had been having difficulty in school, recently exacerbated by trouble at home, namely, the divorce of her parents. Alienated and without friends with whom to discuss her problems, Carey turned to drugs, specifically barbiturates, to alleviate her anxiety and give her a sense of well-being. Unfortunately, the drugs did not help. The barbiturate dependence she developed caused depression and feelings of diminished self-worth. After an especially heated argument with her mother over her use of drugs, Carey, in a hysterical frenzy, called a crisis-intervention center crying that she planned to kill herself.

The counselor on call, a social studies teacher and counselor for Carey's high school, was aware of Carey's home and school problems. The counselor had strong personal feelings about drug use and felt that Carey was not a helpless individual who was unable to overcome her dependence on barbiturates. At first, the counselor tried to calm her, but Carey, overcome with alienation, depression, and diminished self-worth, did not respond. The counselor tried to help Carey by telling her that he understood her situation because he was a teacher at her school; he suggested a number of ways that she might improve her life. Carey was shocked that the counselor knew her and offended by what she considered preaching on the part of the counselor. She rejected his advice with a disparaging comment. Angry, and not perceiving Carey's desperation, the counselor lashed out at Carey's drug use, blaming it for all her problems. Carey hit back with more disparaging remarks, whereupon the counselor hung up the phone. Carey, feeling severely alienated and rejected by a source of help of last resort, took an overdose of barbiturates and died later that night.

The counselor recorded the conversation with Carey on a worksheet at the crisis-intervention center. On it, he detailed his knowledge of the caller and briefly

---

[*]I am indebted for this example to Ms. Kristin Olsen.

described his response. The next day, feeling guilty about his response to the situation, he called Carey's mother, hoping he might counsel the two of them. Carey's mother was enraged that the counselor had reacted in a way that further added to her daughter's problems. She accused the counselor of "killing" her daughter and filed suit against the crisis-intervention center, claiming negligence that resulted in wrongful death.

The main issue in this case is whether the counselor's failure to respond to Carey's situation with reasonable care increased the risk of harm to Carey. Clearly, a crisis was at hand. Carey was in an extremely distraught emotional state. But still, her emotional state was not sufficiently dangerous that, considered alone, it could be construed as the cause of Carey's death. It can be argued that the last straw for Carey was the counselor's rejection of her final call for help. In that way, the counselor did not merely fail to alleviate an impending crisis, he actually made it worse.

An added factor in the counselor's scope of liability is the fact that he recognized Carey's voice and was aware of her problems. Because he was better informed about her situation than an average counselor on the crisis hot line, he would be held to a higher standard of care. The presumption is that increased knowledge about a situation renders an increased capability to give real assistance. As a result, in such a case, a court might well find that the counselor's actions on the hot line constituted negligence that resulted in wrongful death.

The example used is an unusual one. In the typical crisis-intervention situation, the counselor has no personal knowledge of the counselee and does not react in anger so as to exacerbate the situation. It is most likely that, in an ordinary case, an emergency exists that does not provide the counselor either the time or the requisite knowledge to act with the care necessary to help. Courts will not hold counselors to unreasonable standards in such situations and it would indeed be the rare case where liability would be incurred.

THE MOST COMMON SITUATIONS
IN WHICH MALPRACTICE OCCURS

Although any aspect of counselors' work could lead to claims of negligence and suits for malpractice, certain areas of work are more vulnerable than others. Experience shows that the following activities are the ones most likely to lead to legal problems:

- Prescribing or administering drugs
- Giving birth-control advice
- Giving abortion-related advice
- Making statements that might be defamatory
- Assisting in searches of students' lockers
- Violating the privacy of records

PRESCRIBING OR ADMINISTERING
DRUGS IN SCHOOL

Counselors in schools are at times called on to administer medications or drugs to students. These might be drugs prescribed by physicians, necessary to treat a variety of ailments; in the absence of a school nurse, counselors are often asked to store such drugs and give them out at times prescribed by the physician or the parent. This type of activity has been undertaken by schools for many decades. Toward the end of the 1960s and early 1970s, new types of drugs became widely used in schools. These were drugs to control the behavior of youngsters who otherwise could not sit still long enough nor focus on lessons sufficiently to make effective learning possible. There are various legal issues implicit in these practices, some of which apply to the work of counselors.

Should counselors administer drugs to students?

As a general rule, no. They are not physicians or nurses or otherwise trained in the care and administration of medications. If they make mistakes in the dosage or if, through some confusion or error, one student's medicine is given to another, the counselor is likely to be found liable for injuries suffered by students.

In most schools, as a matter of policy, only school nurses are allowed to dispense medications to students. There are schools, however, without school nurses, or special circumstances may arise where the nurse is not on the premises when the student needs the prescribed medication. In such situations, the counselor or some other administrator is often the backup person for the nurse. In anticipation of such contingencies it is best to have clear, written directions from the physician as well as written permission from the parents. Even these precautions do not protect the *negligent* counselor—for example, the one who, through lack of due care, gives a student a wrong medicine that might cause harm. Parents, by giving written permission for the handing out of prescribed medication, do not thereby authorize counselors to act negligently. Due care is always necessary on the part of all school personnel in order to avoid legal liability.

What drugs are used for "behavior modification"?

The drugs most commonly used to control children's behavior, to make them "behave better" in school, are Ritalin and Dexedrin. They are used in attempts to control hyperactivity or hyperkinesis.

Are hyperkinesis and hyperactivity the same?

Most authors who write on the subject use the terms *hyperkinesis* and *hyperactivity* interchangeably. They claim that the "syndrome of hyperactivity is a medical-social problem which may involve neurological components as well as social and environmental factors."[15] Some authors, however, make a distinction between the two, claiming that hyperkinesis is "organically based behavior," whereas hyperactivity is "environmentally based overactive behavior."[16] Although there is no universal agreement on the meanings of the terms or the ultimate causes of the problem, for our purposes we will consider them the same and accept the major symptoms as (1) inattentiveness, (2) overactivity, (3) learning impediment, and (4) uncontrolled impulsivity.[17]

Is there agreement among educators about which children are hyperactive?

No. Neurologists and trained clinical psychologists are somewhat consistent in their diagnosis, but school officials are not. What one teacher considers to be overactive behavior another teacher in the same school may not. Therefore, whether or not Johnny or Mary is recommended for medication depends on which teacher they happen to have. In general, educators do not have the requisite training to properly identify hyperactive behavior; to accurately diagnose hyperactivity, one needs to observe the child in a variety of settings and apply professional diagnostic techniques.

Given the difficulties of diagnosis, why do schools use these drugs?

Because they seem to work and are easier to use than other techniques of controlling the behavior of children. Some studies showed 50–75 percent improvement in behavior,[18] whereas others showed under 50 percent.[19] Some persons, critical of the use of drugs to control behavior, assert that "certain children are given drugs of unknown therapeutic value to treat a disease imperfectly understood and inaccurately diagnosed."[20]

Are these drugs widely used in schools?

Yes, in certain areas but not in others. It seems to be the case that urban schools make more use of such drugs, particularly Ritalin, than do rural schools. One study indicated that, in some school districts, as high as 15–20 percent of children in grades K–6 were on Ritalin or similar psychoactive medication.[21] These figures were from urban areas, whereas studies in rural schools indicated a 1–6 percent use of the drugs.[22]

Do these drugs produce side effects?

Yes they do, including some very serious ones. Researchers have identified a variety of side effects from the long-term use by children of Ritalin and similar drugs. The most commonly identified side effects are increased heart rate, lowered threshold for epileptic seizures, insomnia, decreased appetite, weight loss, suppressed growth rate, irritability, abdominal pain, headaches, dizziness, nightmares, moodiness, tremor, dry mouth, dazed appearance, nervous tics, and anxiety.[23] Short-term use will also elicit some of these responses, but prolonged use will bring on more of them and may also cause drug dependence.

Why is there a greater reliance on these drugs in urban areas?

Cultural bias in the application of school discipline is probably a major factor. As population density increases, there are a disproportionate number of complaints from teachers and school administrators concerning students' behavior in school.[24] In urban centers, educators—who tend to represent the values and behaviors of the dominant culture—must work with children from subcultures and socioeconomic groups different from their own. These children often have different ideas as to what is and what is not acceptable behavior. Such dissonance leads to discipline problems on a large scale and, therefore, to more reliance by school personnel on behavioral control through medication.[25] In short, racial and ethnic prejudice or misunderstanding might lead to higher frequency of behavior-altering drug use with minority children, particularly with black children, in urban schools:[26] "In rural school districts, where governance is typically local and errors in judgment potentially damaging to school personnel, the administration of drugs may be a less acceptable pattern of corrective therapy."[27]

Have schools been sued because of the use by school personnel of drugs to control student behavior?

Yes, they have been. In Kern County, California, 18 students and their parents signed a settlement in 1980 in a suit against the Taft City School District. The plaintiffs alleged that the schools, their board members, administrators, physicians, nurses, and the school psychologist pressured them to have the children take Ritalin to control what the schools claimed was hyperactive behavior.[28]

Parents alleged that a litany of coercive tactics had been used by the schools. They claimed they were told their children could not possibly succeed without the drug and that their children would have to be removed from regular classes. They were told before a group of educators that they would be "foolish parents" if they didn't use the drug for their children. Parents were told that the drug was harmless and, despite the warnings in the package insert for the drug, they were told nothing of the potentially dangerous side effects. Only superficial medical examinations were done on the children prior to the drug use and there was no follow-up monitoring at all.

After two children experienced their first *grand mal* epileptic seizures while taking the drug, suit was filed on their behalf. Other parents joined the suit when they compared experiences and found their children complaining of insomnia, aches and pains, loss of appetite, moodiness, and other symptoms associated with the use of Ritalin.

In the end, the suit was settled for a lump-sum award of $210,000, allocated by the court to the various plaintiffs according to the evidence of harm suffered.

The settlement also required parental notification concerning the dangers attendant to the use of Ritalin, careful medical monitoring, and in-service training of school personnel involved in its use. School district policies governing the use of any behavior-modification drug were also clarified as part of the settlement.

A recent report by the American Bar Association indicates that lawsuits have been filed alleging the negligent use of Ritalin with hyperactive children in several jurisdictions, including New Hampshire, Massachusetts, Minnesota, Washington, D.C., and Georgia. For example, in *Parker v. American Psychiatric Association* (No. C87–2444A), the association and its doctors are accused of fraud, the doctors of malpractice, and the Gwinnett County (Georgia) Board of Education of depriving children of due process, of fraud, and of negligence. It is too early to predict the outcome of these cases, but the increase in the number of suits should alert potential users to the legal as well as medical problems that might accompany the careless use of Ritalin.[29]

Is there federal legislation to control the use of behavior-modification drugs?

Yes, there is. Public Law 94–142 (the Education of the Handicapped Act) must be considered by schools prior to the use of such drugs. The California case described above was filed before the enactment in 1975 of PL 94–142. Since its enactment, schools that receive federal funds would have to satisfy carefully drafted procedural safeguards, including informed consent by the parents, prior to the use of behavior-modification drugs with hyperactive children.

In sum, counselors should not prescribe and generally should not administer drugs to students. When medications have been prescribed by physicians and there are no school nurses available to dispense them to young children, counselors should do so only with great care and pursuant to written directions of the physician and written consent of parents. Similarly, behavior-modifying drugs should be used in schools only after meticulous adherence to the requirements of PL 94–142.

LIABILITY RELATED TO ABORTION OR BIRTH-CONTROL COUNSELING

According to an official U.S. government report, over one million teenagers become pregnant each year in the United States.[30] These pregnancies result in a variety of medical and social problems, including toxemia, low infant birth weight, high rate of infant mortality, mental retardation, and birth defects of various types, at a much higher rate than among adult mothers. The unwed mother suffers a social stigma along with other psychological effects associated with an unwanted child. Pregnancy is generally believed to be the single most important cause of school dropouts among students from lower socioeconomic classes.

Counselors who work with minors inevitably encounter situations where their clients seek information, advice, and perhaps even assistance, related to procuring contraceptives and abortions. Could counselors find themselves in court, facing civil or criminal liability for helping such minors? Must they inform parents of their children's interest in or activities related to these highly sensitive and controversial matters? In this section, we examine possible dangers of civil liability arising from birth-control counseling; questions about counselors' criminal liability will be explored in a later part of this chapter.

Is counselor liability in the area of birth-control counseling a recent phenomenon?

It is relatively recent, arising primarily from the 1973 U.S. Supreme Court ruling in *Roe v. Wade*[31] legalizing abortion under certain conditions. Prior to that ruling most states prohibited abortion by law; in fact 25 years ago it was illegal in all states, except when necessary to save the life or health of the mother. By contrast, it has been estimated that at least one million abortions have been performed in our country each year in the years since *Roe v. Wade*. The rate of abortions varies from region to region, but it appears that close to 30 percent of all pregnancies nationwide end in abortions, whereas in some areas, for example, New York City and Washington, D.C., there are more abortions than live births.[32] The rate of abortions among teenagers is much higher than in the adult population: "Fifty-eight percent of all pregnancies of girls under age fifteen are aborted. Girls aged fifteen through nineteen terminate forty-three percent of their pregnancies by abortion. Nearly one-third of all abortions performed in the United States are on teenagers."[33] The legalization of abortions, the advances in the technology of contraception, the easy availability of contraceptives to teenagers, and the changes in cultural attitudes toward permissiveness in sexual conduct brought these problems to the counselors' doors. And, although we have experienced massive cultural changes in recent decades, birth control for teenagers and abortion for minors remain highly emotional issues in many households and communities.

Are minors allowed by law to have abortions?

Yes, although states may require parental notification as long as the law provides the alternative of a judicial hearing. In June, 1990, the Supreme Court upheld an Ohio law to that effect and a more restrictive Minnesota law that required notice to both parents with a judicial hearing alternative.*

By what right may minors secure abortions?

The Supreme Court, in a series of decisions beginning with *Roe v. Wade*, has held that the "right of privacy . . . founded in the Fourteenth Amendment's concept of personal liberty and restrictions upon state action, ... is broad enough to encompass a woman's decision whether or not to terminate her pregnancy."[34] Although the Constitution nowhere mentions specifically the right to privacy, the Court, through the years, has made it eminently clear that the concept of "liberty" guaranteed by the due process clause is not limited to the specific guarantees spelled out in the

---

* *Ohio v. Akron Center for Reproductive Health* and *Hodgson v. Minnesota*, the *New York Times*, June 26, 1990, pp. A1; A20.

Constitution. It has ruled, in various decisions, that among the protected liberties is an individual's "freedom of personal choice in matters of marriage and family life."[35]

In effect, the Court ruled in *Roe* that the basic decision concerning whether or not to have an abortion is the individual woman's, with the assistance of her physician if she so desires. As a function of the woman's right to privacy, the physician is protected in assisting her decision and in implementing the decision, should the woman choose abortion.

Is the right to privacy an absolute right?

No. No rights are absolute, except perhaps the right to believe whatever one wants to believe. The Court in *Roe* recognized that the state has some important interests to protect when it comes to abortions. It has an interest in protecting "the potentiality of human life" and "in safeguarding health and . . . maintaining medical standards."

In essence, the *Roe* Court distinguished different stages of pregnancy and held that, during the first trimester, the state may not interfere with a decision made by a woman in consultation with her physician to have an abortion. During the second trimester, the state "may regulate the abortion procedure to the extent that the regulation reasonably relates to the preservation and protection of maternal health."[36] In the third trimester, when "viability" is reached—defined by the Court as that point "at which the fetus [is] potentially able to live outside the mother's womb, albeit with artificial aid"—the state's interest in the potential human life becomes "compelling." This is likely to be at about the 28th week of pregnancy, though it may occur as early as 24 weeks. After viability is reached, according to the Court in *Roe,* the state may proscribe abortion altogether, except when it is necessary to preserve the life and health of the mother. State legislation restricting a woman's right to abortion will be subjected to strict scrutiny and the state must show it has a compelling interest that outweighs the individual's right to privacy. Otherwise the state law will be held unconstitutional.

Do minors have the same privacy rights to abortion as adults?

Not quite the same. Although the Court has repeatedly upheld minors' right to abortion under the right to privacy, it has recently agreed about the constitutionality of requiring parental consent. Missouri, for example, passed a law requiring written consent from a parent or a person *in loco parentis* of any unmarried woman under the age of 18 years who desired an abortion. The Supreme Court held this requirement unconstitutional because it gave an absolute veto power to the parent or third party. The Court said, in the *Danforth* case that involved the Missouri statute, that the state "does not have the constitutional authority to give a third party an absolute, and possibly arbitrary, veto over the decision of the physician and his patient to terminate the patient's pregnancy, regardless of the reason for withholding consent."[37] However, the Court noted that its decision does not mean that "every minor, regardless of age or maturity, may give effective consent for termination of her pregnancy."[38]

A later case considered a Massachusetts law requiring the consent of both parents. If one or both refused to give consent, a court could override their veto "for good cause shown." The Supreme Court declared this statute unconstitutional, but its opinion was highly fragmented.[39] The Court mirrors our society's disagreements on this matter; although eight justices agreed on the result of the case, there was no majority opinion and there was also a dissent. Since the *Danforth* case was decided, Justice Sandra Day O'Connor joined the Court and a new configuration of justices emerged in a 1983 case that arose in Akron, Ohio. This case involved a city ordinance that, among other provisions, prohibits a physician from performing an abortion on an unmarried minor under the age of 15 unless he obtains the informed consent of one of her parents or her legal guardian, or unless the minor obtains an order from a court having jurisdiction over her that the abortion be performed.[40]

In a split decision (6 to 3), the Supreme Court declared the Akron city ordinance unconstitutional. The Court relied on its prior decision in the Massachusetts case and held that there may not be a blanket requirement for the consent of a parent or person *in loco parentis* as a condition for abortion of an unmarried minor. It went on to emphasize its earlier holding that a state law or city ordinance, even when applied to a 15-year-old girl, "must provide an alternative procedure whereby a pregnant minor may demonstrate that she is sufficiently mature to make the abortion decision herself or that, despite her immaturity, an abortion would be in her best interest."[41] The Akron ordinance was too complex and did not protect the minor's confidentiality.

In a strongly worded dissent, Justice O'Connor, the first woman justice to serve on the U.S. Supreme Court, not only disagreed with the majority, but seemed to challenge the soundness of *Roe v. Wade,* decided in 1973. She also claimed that, in her interpretation, the Court had never before decided that the requirement of parental notification is unconstitutional. Justices White and Rehnquist joined Sandra Day O'Connor in the dissent. And, in 1990, with the new composition of the Court, the parental notification requirement was upheld in cases arising in Ohio and Minnesota (*Ohio v. Akron* and *Hodgson v. Minnesota*).

The Supreme Court, in a 1989 decision in *Webster v. Reproductive Health Services,*[42] issued an important ruling that portends major modifications for *Roe v. Wade*. The Court upheld a Missouri law that, among other provisions, (1) prohibits the use of public employees and facilities to perform or assist abortions not necessary to save the mother's life; (2) prohibits the use of public funds, employees, or facilities for the purpose of "encouraging or counseling" a woman to have an abortion not necessary to save her life, and (3) requires that a physician conduct extensive viability tests prior to performing an abortion on any woman whom he or she has reason to believe is 20 or more weeks pregnant. The Court further indicated that each state may enact laws regulating the timing and conditions of abortions since a state may "make a value judgment favoring childbirth over abortion" and implement such judgment by controlling the use of public funds and protecting human life after the point of viability. There are implications in *Webster* that other forms of state restrictions related to abortion are likely to be upheld, short of outright repeal of *Roe v. Wade*.

Since *Webster*, legislation has been introduced in many states proposing new restrictions on abortions, particularly as it relates to minors, on the use of public funds and facilities, and on the quality of the facilities where abortions might be performed. Legal challenges have been mounted against some of these new laws, and it is quite likely that the Supreme Court will create new legal guidelines in this highly controversial area. Counselors must keep abreast of these developments through their professional associations, newsletters, workshops, and professional institutes.

In the meantime, counselors should understand that minors have a right to secure an abortion as part of their constitutional right to privacy. Under current law, states or cities may not impose parental veto over such a right in the form of a required consent, *unless* some alternatives are available to the pregnant minor. These alternatives might be, for example, giving her the option to show she is mature enough to make her own decision, or allowing her to request the court to decide that the abortion would be in her best interest.

May school boards create policy related to abortion counseling?

Yes, as long as such policies are consistent with federal or state law. Some schools refer students with questions in this area to local health clinics, to family physicians, or to their parents. In other schools, counselors discuss these matters with students and give them advice.

May counselors be held liable for giving abortion advice to pregnant minors?

If the counselor gives competent advice or refers the student to the appropriate agency, he or she will not be held liable for any damages. However, if the school has a clear policy prohibiting such counseling and the counselor violates it, he or she might be disciplined for such behavior and, depending on the circumstances, may even be dismissed.

Although there are no cases reported on this point, we can propose a hypothetical situation that might lead some parents to sue for damages. Suppose that your school has a clear policy prohibiting abortion counseling. You knowingly violate it in an honest attempt to help a 15-year-old girl who is desperately afraid of her parents. When she undergoes the abortion, complications develop and the parents sue you and the school, claiming that serious physical and psychological damages were caused to their child as a result of your actions. Would you be liable for damages? Most probably not, if you were careful and gave competent advice consistent with counseling standards in your geographic area. However, you could be fired from your job. In this situation, as in other aspects of a counselor's work, one can be held liable for money damages only if one was negligent, and the violation of a school policy is not automatically proof of negligence.

Under what circumstances might a counselor be held liable for giving abortion advice?

Incompetent advice or advice carelessly given that causes injury could result in courts' awarding damages against counselors. If an immature, emotionally fragile young girl procures an abortion with the help of a counselor, under circumstances where reasonably competent counselors would have notified the parents or would have advised against the abortion, liability for psychological or physical suffering may follow. The specific facts and circumstances must always be considered. The constant criterion is this: How would a reasonably competent counselor behave under these circumstances?

That no court cases have been reported holding counselors liable for giving abortion advice is probably due to the fact that counselors tend to be quite careful in this area. They give well-considered, careful advice and usually succeed in mediating a dialogue between the student and her parents, or else they refer pregnant students to appropriate community agencies. This is not to say that such cases never reach the courts. However, cases filed in state courts generally are not reported, unless they are appealed to higher courts. Thus, no one really knows how many such lawsuits are brought against counselors, who wins them, and to what extent they are settled out of court by insurance companies or school boards. The best advice we can give counselors is to follow their state law and school-district policies and to know the standard of behavior expected of counselors in their geographic area.

May counselors give birth-control information to minors?

Yes, unless there is a specific school policy forbidding this activity. The right to privacy discussed previously applies not only to abortion but also to the use of contraceptives and, of necessity, to information about contraceptives.

Must parents be notified about minors' access to contraception?

As a general rule no. However, some controversies in this area still abound, as we explain in this section. There are distinctions between a minor's right to abortion and a minor's right to contraception; also, there are different requirements for parental notification for abortion and for contraception. Controversies about the requirement of parental notification arose after Congress, in 1975, enacted Title X of the Public Health Service Act.[43] The purpose of the act was to make "comprehensive family planning services readily available to all persons desiring such services." A 1978 amendment required that Title X projects offer a "broad range of acceptable and effective family planning methods and services," including services for adolescents.[44] A further amendment in 1981 added this proviso: "To the extent practical, entities which receive grants or contracts under this subsection shall encourage family participation in projects assisted under this subsection." Subsequently, the secretary of Health and Human Services promulgated regulations requiring all providers of family-planning services that receive Title X funds to notify parents or guardians within 10 working days of prescribing contraceptives to unemancipated minors.

Is the parental notification requirement binding?

No, it is not, ruled courts in three cases that interpreted the law and the regulations.[45] Federal district courts in New York, the District of Columbia, and California ruled that Congress intended to guarantee confidentiality to those receiving services through family-planning projects provided under Title X. Furthermore, there was nothing in the 1978 and 1981 amendments to reverse this assurance of confidentiality.

Although Congress wanted to *encourage* the inclusion of parental or family participation in minors' decision making, it did not *mandate* such participation. Congress has all along recognized that confidentiality is a crucial factor in encouraging teenage use of family planning clinics" and thereby in stemming the epidemic in teenage pregnancies." Therefore, the secretary of Health and Human Services or other government officials may not impose a requirement of parental notification because it "contradicts and subverts the intent of Congress."[46]

Of course, Title X and the foregoing discussion apply only to federally funded family-planning services. School counselors may refer students to such clinics, or to services supported by state funds or local resources. Any institution supported by federal funds would have to respect a minor's constitutional right to privacy and could not *require* parental notification or consent.

A counselor who provides competent information about contraception and family-planning services will not be found negligent by a court. If, however, local school policy forbids such practice by school officials, a counselor who violates such policy may be disciplined by the school board.

COUNSELOR LIABILITY FOR DEFAMATION

Counselors are often placed in situations where they are asked to make evaluative judgments about their clients. This is particularly the case with school counselors who receive requests for evaluations of students from administrators, teachers, colleges and universities, potential employers, and government agencies. Are counselors liable for money damages in civil suits filed against them for defamation if they render negative evaluations in response to such requests? What if they act on their own, placing negative comments in a student's file or informing social-service agencies of situations they consider serious and damaging to a student and his or her family? These are the central concerns in this section.

What is defamation?

It is any type of statement or communication that tends to injure or diminish a person's reputation, that is, diminish the respect, goodwill, esteem, or confidence in which one is held. Defamation is a tort, or civil wrong, the commission of which injures one's interest in a good name or reputation; in order for defamation to occur, some kind of communication to a third person or to others must take place. In law, this is called publication. A face-to-face direct communication when no one else is aware of it, no matter how insulting or derogatory, is not defamation. (Other legal claims might be made in the face of such direct, insulting, or provocative comments, but it is not defamation.) Furthermore, it is not enough that one finds some comments offensive or unpleasant; it is necessary that such statements, communicated to or overheard by third persons, somehow involve the idea of disgrace.[47]

What is the difference between slander and libel?

Slander and libel are the two forms that defamation takes; both are communicated to others and injurious to one's reputation or good name. The key difference is that slander is an oral expression, whereas libel takes a more permanent, usually written, form. Historically, it was assumed that the written word had a more lasting and powerful impact and thus libel provided grounds for a lawsuit by itself, whereas, except for four categories of statements, in cases of slander the plaintiff had to prove that damages were caused by the utterance. The four categories of slander that were considered to be defamatory by themselves are derogatory language related to criminal behavior; to incompetence in one's trade, business, or profession; to having a loathsome disease; or to unchastity in a woman. These historical principles were transplanted from England to the United States along with other aspects of English common law. They influence us today, though many states have changed the common law through legislation to make it more appropriate to our changing culture.

Libel, or written defamation, generally results in some monetary damages, particularly when it involves one of the four categories of slander listed above as defamatory per se. When a case involves other kinds of defamatory statements, most courts require that the plaintiff prove damages suffered.

Are there uniform laws governing libel and slander?

No. Much confusion exists concerning the laws of slander and libel, and the various state courts have come up with differences in interpretation.[48] There is agreement, however, that before there is tort liability for either slander or libel, the defamation must be communicated to someone other than the person defamed. Thus, if a counselor, teacher, or other school official calls a student a "cheater" in a one-to-one conference, that is not defamation. Neither is it defamation when a counselor writes the same thing in his or her informal notes. If the characterization of "cheater" is communicated by the counselor to third parties, in or out of school, the legal requirement of "publication" has been satisfied. We shall see, however, that there might be, and often are, legitimate reasons that will protect the counselor or other educator.

Such "publication" may be oral or written, in gestures, pictures, or even a statue, in a newspaper, a private letter, on radio or television. As long as the receiving person understands the defamatory nature of the communication, it makes no difference that the person was a member of the plaintiff's or defendant's family, a friend, or even a stenographer.

Before one concludes, however, that a counselor's life is very risky and is constantly subject to defamation suits, we should look at some legal principles that protect one who, as part of an occupational role, is expected to render evaluations and communicate them to others.

Does the law protect a counselor who makes negative statements about a client?

In general, it does, provided the counselor acts in good faith and is carrying out the duties assigned to his or her office. The doctrine of privilege or immunity was developed in law, based on the idea that the defendant is acting on behalf of an overriding social interest that should be protected even at the cost of injuring the plaintiff's reputation. Such privilege is absolute when it applies to some communications and qualified in others.

Which communications are absolutely privileged?

Those that occur in judicial proceedings, among legislators and their witnesses during the course of legislative proceedings or hearings, and among executive officers carrying out official functions. Social policy also protects communications between husband and wife, and broadcasters who are required to grant equal time to political candidates, without having the power to censor their speeches. And, clearly, any expression authorized by the plaintiff is absolutely privileged.

Which communications are protected by qualified privilege?

Any publication, oral, written, or in any other form, that was made in a reasonable manner by a person carrying out duties and for a proper purpose is protected by qualified privilege. This principle clearly protects most counselors who, in the course of their daily work, may have to enter negative comments into a student's record or communicate about a student, in what some would consider to be a derogatory manner, with teachers, administrators, parents, or even outside agencies or institutions.

When the counselor and the recipient of the information have a common interest, and the communication is reasonably calculated to advance such interest, a qualified privilege protects it. Typical examples of this would be a counselor communicating with parents, with teachers of the student, or with administrators in the same school. A qualified privilege also protects a parent who complains to a counselor, principal, or teacher about students with whom his or her daughter associates. For example, Mrs. Smith complains to the counselor that Mary X has loose morals and is a bad influence on her daughter, Petunia Smith, particularly because of the closeness of their locker assignments in the gym classes where they are required to shower together three times each week.

For the qualified privilege to apply, it is important that the communicator act in good faith and for a legitimate purpose. If someone is requesting information from the counselor, it is important to ascertain that the person making the request has an apparent, present interest in the information. (Further legal protections related to such information are explained in Chapter 4, where we discuss legal provisions relating to the release of information from student records.)

Is the qualified privilege ever lost?

Yes, it can be lost if the communication is made to persons who have no legitimate reason to receive the information or if the defamatory statements go beyond the common interest involved. For example, counselors might be in trouble if they engage in random chatter in the teachers' room that discloses information damaging to a student's reputation. A counselor goes beyond the qualified privilege when, at a neighborhood barbecue or cocktail party, he or she gossips that Mark X, a high school football star, got two girls pregnant and would not accept responsibility for his actions.

May private individuals complain about counselors?

Such complaints, even those challenging the counselor's competence, conduct, or qualifications, are protected if made in good faith to school board members or other relevant school administrators.[49]

What is abuse of privilege?

If a person with qualified privilege acts with malice, in bad faith, or communicates to persons without legitimate interest, the privilege is abused and immunity may be lost. It is difficult to determine or establish malice. The burden of proof is on the plaintiff claiming that the counselor acted with malice or in bad faith. Courts will look at the motives or purposes behind the actions of the counselor. If he or she acts out of ill will, the action will not be privileged. All the facts and circumstances will be examined to determine the motives involved, particularly the language used by the counselor and the vehemence with which it was expressed.

Clearly, the privilege is lost if the publication is a deliberate lie or if the counselor has no reasonable grounds to believe it to be true. For example, before a counselor enters defamatory statements into a student's records (i.e., he cheats, steals, uses drugs, etc.), reasonable efforts should be made to verify the statements.

Are counselors liable when they notify other social service agencies that there are problems in a family?

No, they are not, if they acted in good faith and had some reasonable grounds for their conclusions. The principles set forth under "qualified privilege" would form an adequate defense for such counselors. A federal district court held, for example, that qualified privilege protected a school counselor whose actions ultimately resulted in commitment proceedings against the parents of a student. Allegations that the parents drank too much and there was a lot of physical violence in the home led to a recommendation of foster-home care for the student. The counselor acted in good faith with a legitimate purpose, and was, therefore, not liable in a defamation suit.[50] In fact, as shown in Chapter 2, in some instances counselors have a legal duty to notify appropriate authorities.

These principles are illustrated in a 1988 case from Nassau County, New York. There, allegations were brought to the attention of a social worker, Caso, suggesting the sexual abuse of a 14-year-old girl by her step-grandfather. Caso, pursuant to state law, filed a written report with the county Department of Child Protective Services and informed the school's internal Committee on the Handicapped, which had "become involved in the student's case due to prior behavioral and academic problems." When the department found the allegations of sexual abuse unjustified, the step-grandfather filed suit alleging libel.

In the final analysis the appeals court of New York held that qualified privilege protected the social worker both in communicating with the department and with the Committee on the Handicapped. According to the court: "A qualified privilege serves to negate any presumption of implied malice or ill will flowing from a defamatory statement. Therefore, the plaintiff bears the burden of proving that the statement was indeed motivated by malice." Furthermore, "such a privilege may attach to a *bona fide* communication upon any subject matter in which the communicating party has an interest or in reference to which he has a duty although the information might otherwise be defamatory. . . . However, for the privilege to attach, the recipient of the communication must have a corresponding interest or duty."

The court found that the social worker had a "moral and social duty" to report both to the department and the Committee on the Handicapped. In the absence of proof of malice or ill will, Caso was protected by the qualified privilege.[51]

Is truth always a defense in a defamation suit?

In general, truth is a good defense in a defamation suit. There are rare instances, however, where one might be held responsible for defamatory statements maliciously made, even if the statements were true. An example might be the one noted earlier (i.e., the counselor who, with malice, spreads the word in the neighborhood that a certain football player got two girls pregnant and would not accept responsibility for his actions).

In sum, a competent counselor who behaves in a reasonable manner and acts as a responsible professional need not worry about suits for slander or libel. He or she has a qualified privilege or immunity that provides protection for functioning on the job. The general principles of tort liability apply and thus one is liable only if his or her action is negligent and such action results in some damage to an individual. Abuse of the qualified privilege would be considered negligence; therefore counselors should be careful in the evaluations they make and to whom they communicate about their clients.

LIABILITY FOR UNAUTHORIZED
DISCLOSURE OF INFORMATION

Although mental health professionals generally accept the principle of confidentiality, there have been various lawsuits based on unauthorized disclosure of information. It is clear that judicially mandated disclosure is absolutely privileged, and that qualified privilege protects disclosure made in good faith to fellow professionals or relevant agencies. Other unauthorized disclosures, however, have been litigated under different legal theories. One theory holds that a therapeutic relationship is a fiduciary one, a relationship of trust based in part on confidentiality. Unauthorized disclosure is a violation of this fiduciary relationship.

Invasion of privacy, through the disclosure of private information, is a legal theory upon which a tort action may be based, even when the facts might not support an action for defamation. Breach of contract is yet another legal theory upon which therapists have been sued. In a therapeutic relationship there is an implied agreement that confidentiality will not be violated. For example, when a therapist wrote a book in which the identity of the patient was but thinly disguised, and the patient did not consent to the writing of the book, the New York court ruled against the therapist on the implied contract theory.[52] It also makes sense for the client to sue on several different legal theories. For example, in Westchester County, New York, a former patient sued the county mental health agency, alleging the unauthorized release of information. While the court ruled against the patient on the implied contract theory, it noted that the case might have been more successful as a tort action.[53]

Thus, it is clear that mental health professionals must use great caution as to when, to whom, and under what circumstances they release confidential information without consent from their clients.

TORT LIABILITY RELATED TO LOCKER
SEARCHES AND SCHOOL RECORDS

Counselors may find themselves in the midst of controversies about the unauthorized search of students' lockers, cars, or even their persons. Legal principles governing possible liability related to student searches, and liability that might arise from improper use of school records or unauthorized disclosure of their content, will be discussed in Chapter 10, as "constitutional torts."

FREQUENCY OF MALPRACTICE SUITS

Codes of ethics of mental health professionals underscore the importance of confidentiality and *declare sexual relationships with clients* to be unethical. Despite the general agreement about these principles, sexual misconduct and violation of confidentiality are among the most frequent grounds of lawsuits against mental health workers. Other frequent grounds for such suits include: legal action related to fee collection, abandonment, failure to supervise properly, failure to warn or protect against a dangerous client, failure to avert suicide, misrepresentation of one's qualifications, failure to refer when the client's needs exceed the therapist's competence, failure to consult, negligent diagnosis or assessment, libel and slander, illegal search, lack of informed consent, unethical research practices, hitting a client in the course of treatment, prescribing or administering drugs improperly, breaching a contract with a client, and failure to keep adequate records.[54]

May counselors incur criminal liability in connection with their work?

Yes, if they are careless and do not pay attention to certain areas of possible danger. These areas include (1) contributing to the delinquency of a minor, (2) being an accessory to a crime before or after the fact, and (3) being a coconspirator in civil disobedience.

What is the crime of contributing to the delinquency of a minor?

Although each state has its own laws about contributing to delinquency, there are some commonalities among them. There is agreement, for example, that the purpose of such laws is to protect children from the evil influence of adults who would lead them astray, and to prevent conduct that would tend to lead to delinquency.[55] A typical law is that of Massachusetts, which provides in part:

> Any person who shall be found to have caused, induced, abetted, encouraged or contributed toward the waywardness or delinquency of a child, or to have acted in any way tending to cause or induce such waywardness or delinquency, may be punished by a fine of not more than five hundred dollars or by imprisonment for not more than one year, or both.[56]

For purposes of delinquency, who is a minor?

Each state defines the meaning of "child" or "minor" for purposes of its own laws. Although there are variations among states, a "minor" is generally defined as a juvenile subject to the control of a parent or guardian, or under a specified age, usually 16. It is safe to consider all children attending subcollegiate schools as minors for purposes of delinquency laws.

Is "immoral" conduct restricted to sexual behavior?

No. The law accepts the ordinary meaning of the term *immoral conduct,* which includes more than sexual conduct. It may mean a wide variety of behaviors inimical to the welfare of the public or to the healthy development of an individual. Consequently, the meaning of "contributing to delinquency" might encompass a wide variety of actions that injure the morals, health, or welfare of children, or encourage their participation in activities that would lead to such injury.

For example, a counselor who chaperoned a school-sponsored weekend trip, and helped the students procure beer and wine for the cookout, found himself in trouble with the law. Similarly, the counselor who chaperoned a Friday evening party, and was aware of several students smoking marijuana but did nothing about it, found herself facing a charge of contributing to delinquency.

Even in this age of sexual permissiveness, a counselor might face a charge of "immoral" conduct for encouraging teenage students to engage in sexual intercourse. It is one thing for counselors to listen to and help students who have become sexually active, but it is quite a different matter for counselors to advise them to become so involved.

In the past, when it was illegal for minors to receive birth-control information or contraceptives, counselors who assisted them in these efforts would run afoul of the laws against contributing to delinquency. As we have seen in this chapter, however, minors now have a constitutionally protected right to birth-control information, contraception, and even abortion. Thus, a counselor who assists students in these matters cannot be charged with contributing to delinquency, if he or she proceeds in a professionally competent manner. However, just because 15-year-olds have a right to contraceptive information and devices and even an abortion if they so desire, does not mean that counselors may *carelessly* advise them in these matters. A counselor may be contributing to delinquency even if the students' right to privacy protects their right to abortions.

Can counselors be found guilty of contributing to delinquency even if they did not intend to commit a crime?

Yes, in some states, but not in others. In general, for one to be guilty of a crime there must be a concurrence of an act and an intent. The law generally requires *mens rea* (guilty intent) for any act to be a crime. Thus, if in a baseball game, a wildly thrown ball hits a runner on the head and kills him, no crime has been committed. However, if it can be proven that the player purposely threw the ball at the runner with the intent to hurt him, that would be a crime.

In cases involving delinquency, some states require proof of guilty intent, for example, Arizona, Indiana, Texas, and Virginia. On the other hand, Alaska, California, Hawaii, Minnesota, New York, Oregon, and some other states do not require the presence of such intent in order for a crime to have taken place. Furthermore, states change their laws over time, and at any one time it is possible to find within a state conflicting interpretations of the laws. Thus, it becomes very important for counselors to know the specific provisions in the laws of their respective states and to stay clear of activities that might be construed by their state courts as contributing to the delinquency of minors.

Can counselors become accessories to the crimes of their clients?

Yes, depending on the facts of the case and the extent of the counselors' information and behavior in helping their clients.

Counselors are in difficult positions when their clients discuss with them either a plan to commit a crime or the crime they have already committed. As we saw in Chapter 2, the law may impose upon counselors a duty to warn probable victims of a crime, and the claim of confidentiality or privilege is generally superseded by the social obligation to warn. Thus, counselors' obligations are fairly clear when the client plans to commit a crime. There is less clarity when a troubled client comes for help after the crime has been committed.

Not all crimes, however, involve danger to persons; some crimes are against property. For example, a troubled student might confide in the counselor a plan to destroy some equipment or building that is related to "war activities." One's mere knowledge that a crime will take place, if one does not have a duty to prevent it, does not make one guilty as a principal. However, were the counselor to take the client to the scene of the crime, with knowledge that a crime probably would be committed, or assist the client in getting away after committing the crime, he or she would become culpable in the eyes of the law. Thus a person, including a counselor, who aids another in the commission of a felony, even if not present when the crime takes place, may be guilty as a principal or as an accessory before the fact, depending on the laws of the particular state.

May counselors be guilty of being accessory after the fact?

Yes, if they are not careful. An accessory after the fact is generally defined as a person who, knowing that a felony was committed, receives, relieves, comforts, or assists the felon or somehow aids the felon in escaping arrest or punishment. Thus, it is necessary that

1. A felony must have been committed;
2. The accessory must know that the principal committed the crime; and
3. The accessory must harbor or protect the principal.[57]

To express this in terms of the counselor–client relationship, if, during the counseling process, the counselor learns that the client committed a felony, and if, thereafter, the counselor helps the client hide or otherwise offers protection from law enforcement authorities or assists the client in getting out of town to escape detection, the counselor is guilty of being an accessory after the fact. It is important to note that at common law there was no accessory to the commission of a misdemeanor. However, states may create such a category. Therefore, it is important, once again, for counselors to check with someone who knows the laws of their particular states.

Could counselors be guilty of conspiracy?

Yes, under certain circumstances. During the 1960s, 1970s, and 1980s, student demonstrations often culminated in sit-ins and other occupations of administrative offices or government buildings. Such demonstrations often exceeded the protected limits of freedom of assembly and constituted illegal trespass, which typically is a misdemeanor.

Counselors who have good relations with student leaders often become involved in informal discussions and even negotiations related to such demonstrations. It is easy for an enthusiastic counselor who sympathizes with the cause of the students to enter the spirit of the demonstration and thus become a coconspirator in the illegal demonstration. Competent counselors keep their own personal views and feelings out of their professional work and avoid the temptation to "join the cause." If they carefully restrict their advice, and help students examine the probable consequences of alternative courses of action, they will not be breaking the law, nor will they violate their own professional ethics.

SUMMARY AND CONCLUSIONS

Our analysis of legal principles and case law leads us to conclude that therapists and counselors should not be seriously inhibited in their work for fear of being held liable in a lawsuit for negligence. As a general rule, one is held liable only if he or she failed to exercise reasonable care in the performance of duties and such negligence caused harm to another. Therapists and counselors who use reasonable care in the performance of their functions will not be held liable in a court of law. Courts will hold them to a standard of care and skill generally accepted by similar professionals in the particular community or area. The more thorough the level of preparation for the particular class of practitioners and the higher their status, the higher the standards they will be expected to meet. Thus, certified psychologists will be held to higher standards of care and skill than typical school counselors and psychiatrists to higher standards than psychologists. The facts of a situation will always be carefully considered by the court, and therapists and counselors are expected to use care appropriate to the situation. The greater the probable danger, the more care one must use. Professionals are not liable simply because a client fails to improve, as long as reasonable efforts were made to assist the client.

Group counseling calls for a greater degree of care due to the increased complexity of the interpersonal relationships involved; the duty to supervise increases commensurate with increased complexity. Group sessions that are likely to become encounters are particularly fraught with the danger of unanticipated consequences. Thus, they call for special training, skill, and maturity on the part of therapists and counselors and should be attempted only by those possessing such training and skill.

A counselor who attempts to help a person in a crisis situation cannot be expected to apply the carefully considered action expected in a noncrisis situation. In emergencies, one generally does not have all the relevant facts at one's disposal and the press of the situation requires action on short notice. Courts understand this and will consider all the emergency factors as part of the circumstances, in deciding whether or not a counselor acted with due care and skill in the particular situation.

In recent years, counselors have been called upon to administer drugs to hyperactive children in order to control their behavior. Along with other problems related to the use of such drugs, there is evidence to suggest that racial and ethnic considerations have played a part in their use. As a general rule, counselors should not participate in either the prescription or the administration of such drugs; these activities belong in the domain of physicians and nurses. If, in special situations, counselors must administer such drugs, they should do so only pursuant to school board policy that makes provision for a physician's prescription and a written informed consent by the parents. Such drug use also should be periodically evaluated by a physician and should meet the requirements of the Education of the Handicapped Act.

Counselors have been sued by parents whose minor daughters have undergone abortions or received birth-control devices with the help of counselors. As a general rule, the constitutional right to privacy extends to minors as well as adults, and protects minors who seek birth-control advice and/or abortion. Counselors who provide competent help in these matters will not be liable in a tort suit for damages. While courts' interpretations in this area continue to be controversial, the right to privacy, as it is currently interpreted, protects the giving of abortion advice and information about contraception. Federal regulations governing publicly supported family-planning services *encourage* family participation; however, such participation cannot be legally *mandated*. Once again, the crucial points to consider are whether or not the counselor acted in a reasonable manner under the circumstances and whether or not the behavior was in accord with generally accepted standards of care and skill in the area. If such standards are met, the counselor need not worry about tort liability. However, in school districts where there are explicit policies prohibiting such counseling, counselors who violate them may be disciplined and even dismissed. Aside from court proceedings or school situations controlled by school board policy, the ethical principles of the profession guide counselors' behavior regarding confidentiality.

Similar principles apply to possible suits for defamation. In an action for slander or for libel, the counselor is protected if he or she acted reasonably in carrying out the duties of the job. The legal principle of qualified privilege protects the counselor who communicates to relevant persons information or evaluations that might be considered negative and damaging to a client. Although laws concerning defamation are in some disarray throughout the country and different states have come up with variations on the law of slander and libel, there is general agreement that qualified privilege protects the counselor carrying out duties in a reasonable manner and for a proper purpose. Idle gossip or the communication of derogatory information to random friends or acquaintances is not protected and may lead to successful lawsuits for damages. Similarly, unauthorized disclosure of confidential information might lead to lawsuits based on invasion of privacy, violation of a fiduciary relationship, or breach of an implied contract. Care must be taken against such disclosure, except when there is a duty to warn, when there is an absolute or qualified privilege, or, as we shall see later, in cases involving child abuse.

From the foregoing, we can see that counselors who act in a reasonable manner, consistent with the standards of care and skill in their profession, should have no serious worries of lawsuits for negligence. This conclusion is supported by the paucity of cases reported in law reporters and is also validated by the very low insurance premiums paid by those counselors who carry insurance protecting them against negligence or malpractice.

Similarly, counselors who act with a reasonable degree of care, consistent with professional standards in their geographic area, should have no worries about criminal liability. This is not to say, however, that all counselors are immune from criminal prosecution. Careless behavior, or even some intentional actions, may constitute contributing to the delinquency of a minor or being an accessory to a crime. The paucity of reported cases indicates that such charges are very seldom brought against pupil personnel workers; thus, by living up to the standards of the profession they can carry out their duties without fear of criminal liability. (See also Chapter 8, "Child Abuse and Neglect.")

NALLY V. GRACE COMMUNITY CHURCH
47 Cal.3d 278 (1988)

LUCAS, Chief Justice.

I. Introduction

On April 1, 1979, 24-year-old Kenneth Nally (hereafter Nally) committed suicide by shooting himself in the head with a shotgun. His parents (hereafter plaintiffs) filed a wrongful death action against Grace Community Church of the Valley (hereafter Church), a Protestant Christian congregation located in Sun Valley, California, and four Church pastors: MacArthur, Thomson, Cory and Rea (hereafter collectively referred to as defendants), alleging "clergyman malpractice," i.e., negligence and outrageous conduct in failing to prevent the suicide. . . . Nally, a member of the Church since 1974, had participated in defendants' pastoral counseling programs prior to his death.

. . .

II. Facts

A. BACKGROUND
In 1973, while attending University of California at Los Angeles (hereafter UCLA), Nally became depressed after breaking up with his girlfriend. He often talked about the absurdity of life, the problems he had with women and his family and he occasionally mentioned suicide to his friends. Though Nally had been raised in a Roman Catholic household, he converted to Protestantism while he was a student at UCLA, and in 1974 he began attending the Church, the largest Protestant church in Los Angeles County. Nally's conversion became a source of controversy between him and his family. During this time, Nally developed a close friendship with defendant Pastor Cory, who was responsible for overseeing the ministry to the collegians attending the Church. On occasion, Nally discussed his problems with Cory, but the two never established a formal counseling relationship. Between 1974 and 1979, Nally was active in defendants' various Church programs and ministries.

Defendants offered pastoral counseling to church members in matters of faith, doctrine and the application of Christian principles. During 1979, defendant Church had approximately 30 counselors on its staff, serving a congregation of more than 10,000 persons. Defendants taught that the Bible is the fundamental Word of God containing truths that must govern Christians in their relationship with God and the world at large, and in their own personal lives. Defendant Church had no professional or clinical counseling ministry, and its pastoral counseling was essentially religious in nature. . . . In essence, defendants held themselves out as *pastoral* counselors able to deal with a variety of problems—not as professional, medical or psychiatric counselors.

In 1975, Nally was seeing a secular psychologist to discuss problems he was having with his girlfriend. After graduating from UCLA in 1976, he spent one semester at Biola College in La Mirada and was enrolled in the Talbot Theological Seminary's extension on defendants' church grounds. During this time, Nally became involved in a relationship with a girlfriend who was a fellow Bible student. In January 1978, he established a "discipling relationship" with Pastor Rea with whom he often discussed girlfriend and family problems. They met five times in early 1978, but when Nally lost interest in "discipling," the meetings were discontinued.

Following the breakup with his girlfriend in December 1978, Nally became increasingly despondent. Pastor Cory encouraged him to seek the counsel of either Pastor Thomson or Rea. The friendship with Cory and the five discipling sessions with Rea in early 1978, constituted the full extent of the "counseling" Nally received from defendants before the spring of 1979.

In February 1979, Nally told his mother he could not "cope." She arranged for him to see Dr. Milestone, a general practitioner, who prescribed Elavil, a strong antidepressant drug, to relieve his depression. Milestone also recommended Nally undergo a series of blood and chemical tests. The record reveals that Milestone never referred Nally to a psychiatrist.

By late February, Nally's depression did not appear to be subsiding, and he was examined by Dr. Oda, a physician, who did not prescribe medication or refer Nally to a psychiatrist, but suggested he undergo a physical examination. Shortly thereafter, Nally spoke briefly in a drop-in counseling session with Pastor Thomson about the marital tensions between his parents and his problems with his current girlfriend. He told Thomson that he considered suicide in 1974 while a student at UCLA. The record shows that Thomson's conversation with Nally focused on their common faith in scripture. During this time, Nally "decided to serve the Lord through law," and was accepted at a Southern California law school for the 1979 fall semester.

B. THE EVENTS PRECEDING NALLY'S SUICIDE

On March 11, 1979, Nally took an overdose of the antidepressant prescribed by Dr. Milestone. Plaintiffs found him the following day and rushed him to a hospital. At the hospital, Dr. Evelyn, Nally's attending physician, advised plaintiffs that because their son "was actually suicidal," she could not authorize his release from the hospital until he had seen a psychiatrist. The record indicates that plaintiffs, concerned about their friends' reactions to their son's suicide attempt, asked Dr. Evelyn to inform other persons that Nally had been hospitalized only for the aspiration pneumonia he suffered after the drug overdose rendered him unconscious.

On the afternoon of March 12, Pastors MacArthur and Rea visited Nally at the hospital. Nally, who was still drowsy from the drug overdose, separately told both pastors that he was sorry he did not succeed in committing suicide. Apparently, MacArthur and Rea assumed the entire hospital staff was aware of Nally's unstable mental condition, and they did not discuss Nally's death-wish comment with anyone else.

Four days later, Dr. Hall, a staff psychiatrist at the hospital, examined Nally and recommended he commit himself to a psychiatric hospital. When both Nally and his father expressed reluctance at the thought of formal commitment, Hall agreed to release

Nally for outpatient treatment, but warned Nally's father that it would not be unusual for a suicidal patient to repeat his suicide attempt. Nally was released from the hospital by Drs. Hall and Evelyn the next day.

On his release from the hospital on March 17, 1979, Nally arranged to stay with Pastor MacArthur, because he did not want to return home. MacArthur encouraged Nally to keep his appointments with Dr. Hall, and arranged for him to see Dr. John Parker, a physician and Church deacon, for a physical examination. Parker's testimony reveals that Nally told him he was depressed, had entertained thoughts of suicide, and had recently taken an overdose of Elavil. After examining Nally, Parker believed he was a continuing threat to himself, and recommended Nally commit himself to a psychiatric hospital. Nally, however, immediately rejected the advice.

Parker testified that after Nally left his office, he telephoned Glendale Adventist Hospital to determine whether any beds were available. He then informed Nally's father that Nally needed acute psychiatric care and that he should contact Glendale Adventist Hospital for information concerning the psychiatric facilities. That same evening, Nally's father telephoned Dr. Hall and told him that Parker had recommended psychiatric hospitalization. Hall offered to come to the Nally residence and arrange for Nally's involuntary commitment; the offer was rejected by plaintiffs. The record shows that Mrs. Nally strongly opposed psychiatric hospitalization for her son, saying, "no, that's a crazy hospital. He's not crazy."

Eleven days before his suicide, Nally met with Pastor Thomson for spiritual counseling. According to the record, Nally asked Thomson whether Christians who commit suicide would nonetheless be "saved." Thomson referred Nally to his training as a seminary student and acknowledged "a person who is once saved is always saved," but told Nally that "it would be wrong to be thinking in such terms." Following their discussion, Thomson made an appointment for Nally to see Dr. Bullock for a physical examination but did not refer Nally to a psychiatrist.

Several days later, Nally moved back home. During his final week of life, he was examined separately by Drs. Bullock and Evelyn. Dr. Bullock testified that he was concerned with Nally's physical symptoms. (Nally complained of headaches and of the fact that his arm was paralyzed because he had slept on it while he was unconscious following the Elavil overdose.) Bullock suggested to Nally that he admit himself to the hospital. Bullock, however, did not refer Nally to a psychiatrist; instead, he subsequently conferred with Dr. Evelyn, and both doctors agreed Nally needed further physical and possibly psychiatric evaluation.

The day after his visit with Bullock, Nally encountered Pastor Thomson in the Church parking lot. Nally told Thomson that he was thinking of seeing a psychologist. Thomson recommended Nally contact Dr. Mohline, director of the Rosemead Graduate School of Professional Psychology. The following day, Nally spent approximately 90 minutes with Mohline, who in turn referred him to the Fullerton Psychological Clinic. Nally and his father went to the clinic the next day, and Nally discussed possible therapy with Mr. Raup, a registered psychologist's assistant. Raup testified he believed that Nally was "shopping for a therapist or counselor or psychologist" and that he was not going to return to the clinic. At the end of the week, Nally met with a former girlfriend. She turned down an apparent marriage proposal by telling Nally, "I can't marry you when you are like this. You have got to pull yourself together. You have got to put God first in your life." The next day, Nally left plaintiffs' home following a family disagreement. Two days later, he was found in a friend's apartment, dead of a self-inflicted gunshot wound.

. . .

Discussion

. . .

B. Cause of Action for Negligent Failure to Prevent Suicide

As stated above, the Court of Appeal characterized the first two counts of plaintiffs' complaint (for clergyman malpractice and negligence) as together stating a cause of action for the "negligent failure [by a nontherapist counselor] to prevent suicide." Conceding that "research [did] not uncover any court decision which has ruled one way or the other specifically on the existence or scope of a *nontherapist counselor's* duty toward suicidal counselees," and that it was venturing "along a largely uncharted path," the Court of Appeal imposed a new and broad duty of care on such counselors without any discussion of causation under the present facts.

. . .

As we explain below, we reject the Court of Appeal's imposition of a broad "duty to refer" on defendants and nontherapist counselors in general.

A) Creation of a Duty of Care

(4) "A tort, whether intentional or negligent, involves a violation of a *legal duty,* imposed by statute, contract or otherwise, owed by the defendant to the person injured. Without such a duty, any injury is 'damnum absque injuria'—injury without wrong. . . . Thus, in order to prove facts sufficient to support a finding of negligence, a plaintiff must show that defendant had a duty to use due care, that he breached that duty, and that the breach was the proximate or legal cause of the resulting injury. . . .

(5) Under traditional tort law principles, one is ordinarily not liable for the actions of another and is under no duty to protect another from harm, in the absence of a special relationship of custody or control. . . . Moreover, in determining the existence of a duty of care in a given case, we must consider several factors, including the "foreseeability of harm to [the injured party], the degree of certainty that [he] suffered injury, the closeness of the connection between [defendants'] conduct and the injury suffered, the moral blame attached to [defendants], the policy of preventing future harm, the extent of the burden to the defendant[s] and consequences to the community of imposing a duty to exercise care with resulting liability for breach, and the availability, cost, and prevalence of insurance for the risk involved." . . . Thus, because liability for negligence turns on whether a duty of care is owed, our first task is to determine whether a duty exists in the present case.

B) Special Relationship

(3b) Although we have not previously addressed the issue presently before us, we have imposed a duty to prevent a foreseeable suicide only when a special relationship existed between the suicidal individual and the defendant or its agents. For example, two cases imposed such a duty in wrongful death actions after plaintiffs proved that the deceased committed suicide in a hospital or other in-patient facility that had accepted the responsibility to care for and attend to the needs of the suicidal patient. . . .

The Court of Appeal here would extend the previously carefully limited precedent, relying initially for the creation of a duty of care (on defendants and other nontherapist counselors) in the . . . *Meier* and *Vistica* cases. Indeed, the Court of Appeal specifically stated that "Logic and policy both dictate the duty announced in those cases applies to non-therapist counselors as well." We disagree. As defendants and amici curiae point out, *Meier* and *Vistica* are readily distinguishable from the facts of the present case and, as we explain, severely circumscribe the duty they create.

Both *Meier* and *Vistica* address the issue of a special relationship, giving rise to a duty to take precautions to prevent suicide, in the limited context of hospital-patient relationships where the suicidal person died while under the care and custody of hospital physicians who were aware of the patient's unstable mental condition. In both cases, the patient committed suicide while confined in a hospital psychiatric ward. Liability was imposed because defendants failed to take precautions to prevent the patient's suicide even though the medical staff in charge of the patient's care knew that the patient was likely to attempt to take his own life.

Neither case suggested extending the duty of care to personal or religious counseling relationships in which one person provided nonprofessional guidance to another seeking advice and the counselor had no control over the environment of the individual being counseled. In sharp contrast, Nally was not involved in a supervised medical relationship with defendants, and he committed suicide well over two weeks after he was released from the hospital against the advice of his attending psychiatrist and physician.

Plaintiffs and the Court of Appeal also rely on *Bellah* v. *Greenson* (1978) . . . as supporting the existence of a special relationship sufficient to impose a duty of care on nontherapist counselors to refer a counselee to a licensed mental health professional once the potential suicide becomes foreseeable. As we explain, the Court of Appeal would unduly extend the *Bellah* holding.

In *Bellah*, two years after their daughter's suicide, plaintiffs brought a wrongful death action against a psychiatrist who had been treating the daughter on an out-patient basis. Plaintiffs alleged the existence of a psychiatrist-patient relationship between defendant and their daughter, knowledge on the part of the defendant that their daughter was likely to attempt suicide, and a failure by defendant to take appropriate preventative measures "consonant with good medical practice in the community." . . . The Court of Appeal affirmed the trial court's order sustaining defendant's demurrer after concluding that the action was barred by the one-year statute of limitations. . . .

In dictum, the *Bellah* court recognized that although plaintiffs' action was time barred, they had stated a traditional medical malpractice cause of action for the breach of a psychiatrist's duty of care to his patient. *Bellah* stated that this duty may be imposed on the treating psychiatrist even though his patient committed suicide outside the confines of a hospital. . . . It is important to recognize, however, that rather than creating a broad duty to refer, the *Bellah* court simply recognized that plaintiffs had stated a "cause of action for the breach by a medical practitioner of the duty of care owed to his patient [which] has long existed in this state." In so doing, *Bellah* distinguished *Meier* . . . and *Vistica*. . . . The court stated: "Obviously, the duty imposed upon those responsible for the care of a patient in an institutional setting differs from that which may be involved in the case of a psychiatrist treating patients on an out-patient basis." . . . Indeed, *Bellah* concluded that licensed medical professionals simply have no duty to disclose to third persons "vague or even specific manifestations of suicidal tendencies on the part of the patient who is being treated in an out-patient setting. . . ."

In a related context, the *Bellah* plaintiffs claimed that *Tarasoff*, . . . "created a duty on the part of the defendant . . . to breach the confidence of a doctor-patient relationship by revealing to them disclosures made by their daughter about conditions which might cause her to commit suicide." . . . The *Bellah* court, however, refused to accept plaintiffs' argument that *Tarasoff* created a new duty on the part of the defendant "to warn others of the likelihood of any and all harm which might be inflicted by a patient. . . ." . . .

Similarly, *Bellah* recognized that creating a duty on the part of a psychiatrist to breach the confidence of a doctor-patient relationship by revealing disclosures made about the suicidal intent of his patient would unduly extend the *Tarasoff* holding, and "could well inhibit psychiatric treatment." . . . *Bellah* reasoned that in *Tarasoff*, we held only that "where a therapist knows that his patient is likely to injure another and where the identity of the likely victim is known or readily discoverable by the therapist, he must use reasonable care to prevent his patient from causing the intended injury. Such care includes, at the least, informing the proper authorities and warning the likely victim. However, [*Tarasoff*] did not hold that such disclosure was required where the danger presented was that of self-inflicted harm or suicide. . . . Instead, [*Tarasoff*] recognized the importance of the confidential relationship which ordinarily obtains between a therapist and his patient, holding that '. . .the therapist's obligations to his patient require that he *not disclose a confidence unless such disclosure is necessary to avert danger to others*. . . .

Rather than create a duty to prevent suicide, *Bellah* (and *Meier* and *Vistica*) recognized that a cause of action may exist for *professional malpractice* when a psychiatrist's (or hospital's) treatment of a suicidal patient falls below the standard of care for the profession, thus giving rise to a traditional malpractice action. . . . With the foregoing in mind, we now turn to other considerations . . . and explain further why we should not impose a duty to prevent suicide on defendants and other nontherapist counselors.

c) The Connection between Defendants' Conduct and Nally's Suicide and the Foreseeability of Harm

Other factors to consider in determining whether to impose a duty of care on defendants include the closeness of the causal connection between defendants' conduct and the injury suffered, and the foreseeability of the particular harm to the injured party. . . .

Plaintiffs argue that Nally's statement to Pastor's Rea and MacArthur (while he was recovering from his suicide attempt at the hospital), "that he was sorry he wasn't successful and that he would attempt suicide after his release from the hospital," were "hidden dangers" that would have affected his prognosis and treatment. Accordingly, plaintiffs reason that Rea and MacArthur should have warned the hospital staff and plaintiffs that Nally was still contemplating suicide after his initial attempt. We disagree.

The closeness of connection between defendants conduct and Nally's suicide was tenuous at best. As defendants observe, Nally was examined by five physicians and a psychiatrist during the weeks following his suicide attempt. Defendants correctly assert that they "arranged or encouraged many of these visits and encouraged Nally to continue to cooperate with all doctors." . . . In addition, as stated above, following Nally's overdose attempt Dr. Evelyn warned plaintiffs that Nally remained suicidal and that they should encourage him to see a psychiatrist on his release from the hospital. Plaintiffs also rejected both Dr. Hall's and Dr. Parker's suggestion that Nally be institutionalized because, according to plaintiffs, their son was "not crazy."

Nevertheless, we are urged that mere knowledge on the part of the defendants that Nally may have been suicidal at various stages in his life should give rise to a duty to refer. Imposition of a duty to refer Nally necessarily would imply a general duty on all nontherapists to refer all potentially suicidal persons to licensed medical practitioners.

One can argue that it is foreseeable that if a nontherapist counselor fails to refer a potentially suicidal individual to professional, licensed therapeutic care, the individual may commit suicide. While under some circumstances counselors may conclude that referring a client to a psychiatrist is prudent and necessary, our past decisions teach that it is inappropriate to impose a duty to refer—which may stifle all gratuitous or religious counseling—based on foreseeability alone. **(6)** Mere foreseeability of the harm or knowledge of the danger, is insufficient to create a legally cognizable special relationship giving rise to a legal duty to prevent harm. . . .

D) PUBLIC POLICY CONSIDERATIONS

Imposing a duty on defendants or other nontherapist counselors to, in the Court of Appeal's words, "insure their counselees [are also] under the care of psychotherapists, psychiatric facilities, or others authorized and equipped to forestall imminent suicide," could have a deleterious effect on counseling in general. . . . Although both plaintiffs and the present Court of Appeal, in dictum, exempt services such as "teen hotlines" which offer only "band aid counseling," from a newly formulated standard of care that would impose a "duty to refer," the indeterminate nature of liability the Court of Appeal imposes on nontherapist counselors could deter those most in need of help from seeking treatment out of fear that their private disclosures could subject them to involuntary commitment to psychiatric facilities.

(3c) As defendants, amici curiae, and the Court of Appeal dissenter observe, neither the Legislature nor the courts have ever imposed a legal obligation on persons to take affirmative steps to prevent the suicide of one who is not under the care of a physician in a hospital. . . .

We also note that the Legislature has exempted the clergy from the licensing requirements applicable to marriage, family, child and domestic counselors . . . and from the operation of statutes regulating psychologists. . . . In so doing, the Legislature has recognized that access to the clergy for counseling should be free from state imposed counseling standards, and that "the secular state is not equipped to ascertain the competence of counseling when performed by those affiliated with religious organizations." . . .

Furthermore, extending liability to voluntary, noncommercial and noncustodial relationships is contrary to the trend in the Legislature to encourage private assistance efforts. . . .

E) CONCLUSION

For the foregoing reasons, we conclude that plaintiffs have not met the threshold requirements for imposing on defendants a duty to prevent suicide. . . . Plaintiffs failed to persuade us that the duty to prevent suicide (heretofore imposed only on psychiatrists and hospitals while caring for a suicidal patient) or the general professional duty of care (heretofore imposed only on psychiatrists when treating a mentally disturbed patient) should be extended to a nontherapist counselor who offers counseling to a potentially suicidal person on secular or spiritual matters.

. . .

We conclude the trial court correctly granted a nonsuit on all causes of action. The suicide of a young man in the prime of his life is a profound tragedy. After considering plaintiffs' arguments and evidence, however, we hold that defendants had no duty to Nally on which to base liability for his unfortunate death.

. . .

KAUFMAN, J.—I concur in the judgment that nonsuit was properly granted, but disagree with the majority's holding that defendants owed no duty of care to the plaintiffs.

. . .

In light of the foregoing factual background, I believe the conclusion is inescapable that defendants owed a duty of care to Nally. That duty, in my view, was simply to recognize the limits of their own competence to treat an individual, such as Nally, who exhibited suicidal tendencies, and once having recognized such symptoms, to advise that individual to seek competent professional medical care. The record further demonstrates, however, and the majority correctly concludes, that defendants neither breached their duty to Nally nor contributed in any legally significant respect to his suicide.

$$\cdots$$

The relation of the nontherapist or pastoral counselor to his counselee contains elements of trust and dependence which closely resemble those that exist in the therapist-patient context. Defendants here patently held themselves out as competent to counsel the mentally ill, and Nally responded to these inducements, placing his psychological and ultimately his physical well-being in defendants' care.

$$\cdots$$

Thus, I am persuaded, on the facts presented, that defendants owed a minimal duty of care to Nally. I am equally persuaded, however, that defendants fulfilled their duty.

$$\cdots$$

I concur in this court's judgment.

NOTES

1. 57 AM. JUR. 2D *Negligence* §1.
2. RESTATEMENT (SECOND) OF TORTS §323.
3. Bogust v. Iverson, 102 N.W. 2d 288 (Wis. 1960).
4. Nally v. Grace Community Church, 47 Cal. 3d 378 (1988).
5. Tarasoff v. Regents of the Univ. of California, 551 P.2d 334 (Cal. 1976).
6. Bellah v. Greenson, 181 Cal. App. 3d 614 (1978).
7. Lipari v. Sears, Roebuck & Co., 497 F. Supp. 185 (D.Neb. 1980).
8. *Ethical Standards of Psychologists,* Principles 2.51–1, 2.51–2, & 2.51–4.
9. *Ethical Principles,* § B, § 6, APGA.
10. R. Zeitz, *Legal Responsibility under Tort Law of School Personnel and School Districts as Regards Negligent Conduct Toward Pupils,* 15 HASTINGS L.J. 495 (1964).
11. 99 A.L.R. 2D 619.
12. Johnston v. Rodis 251 F.2d 917 (D.D.C. 1958).
13. 19 A.L.R. 2D 1206.
14. 57 AM JUR. 2D *Negligence* §33.
15. Singh & Ling, *Amphetamines in the Management of Children's Hyperkinesis,* 31 BULL. NARCOTICS 87 (1979).
16. Murray, *Drugs to Control Classroom Behavior?,* 31 EDUC. LEADERSHIP 21–25 (1973).
17. *Supra* note 14.
18. *Supra* note 15, at 19.
19. *Supra* note 14.
20. Banks, *Drugs, Hyperactivity, and Black School Children,* 45 J. NEGRO EDUCATORS 150–160 (1976).
21. D. DIVOKY & P. SCHRAG, THE MYTH OF THE HYPERACTIVE CHILD (1975).
22. Conway, *An Evaluation of Drugs in the Elementary Schools: Some Geographic Considerations,* 13 PSYCHOLOGY SCHOOLS 442–44 (1976).
23. *Supra* note 14.

24. Address by U. Bronfenbrenner, American Orthopsychiatric Association Meeting (Summer 1975).
25. *Supra* note 19.
26. *Id.*
27. *Supra* note 21, at 443.
28. Benskin v. Taft City School District, 14 CLEARINGHOUSE REV. 529–30 (1980).
29. Debra Cassens Moss, *Ritalin under Fire*, ABA J., November 1, 1988, at 19.
30. HOUSE SELECT COMM. ON POPULATION, 95th CONG., 2D SESS., REPORT ON FERTILITY AND CONTRACEPTION IN THE UNITED STATES (Comm. Print 1978).
31. 410 U.S. 113 (1973).
32. C. RICE, FIFTY QUESTIONS ON ABORTION (1979).
33. Frame, *Parental Notification and Abortion: A Review and Recommendation to West Virginia's Legislature*, 85 W. VA. L. REV. 943–68 (1983).
34. Roe v. Wade, 410 U.S. 113, 153 (1973).
35. *Id.* at 169.
36. *Id.* at 163.
37. Planned Parenthood v. Danforth, 428 U.S. 52, 74 (1976).
38. *Id.* at 75.
39. Bellotti v. Baird, 443 U.S. 622 (1979).
40. City of Akron v. Akron Center For Reproductive Health, Inc. 51 U.S.L.W. 4767 (1983).
41. *Id.* at 4773.
42. Webster v. Reproductive Health Services, 57 U.S.L.W. 5023 (July 3, 1989).
43. 42 U.S.C. §254(c) (1976).
44. 42 U.S.C. §300(a).
45. New York v. Schweiker, 51 U.S.L.W. 2518 (Feb. 14, 1983); Planned Parenthood Fed'n of America, Inc. v. Schweiker, 51 U.S.L.W. 2518 (Feb. 18, 1983); and Planned Parenthood Fed'n of America, Inc. v. Heckler, 52 U.S.L.W. 2028 (July 8, 1983).
46. Planned Parenthood Fed'n of America, Inc. v. Heckler, *supra* note 45.
47. For a thorough discussion, see W.L. PROSSER, LAW OF TORTS, (4th ed. 1971).
48. *Id.*
49. Segall v. Piazza, 260 N.Y.S. 2d 543 (1965).
50. Dick v. Watowan County, 551 F. Supp. 983 (D. Minn. 1982).
51. Dunajewski v. Bellmore-Merrick Cent. High, 526 N.Y.S.2d (A.D.2d Dept. 1988).
52. Doe v. Roe, 400 N.Y.S.2d 668 (Sup. Ct. 1977).
53. Silberstein v. County of Westchester, 459 N.Y.S.2d 838 (App. Div. 1983).
54. B. P. HOPKINS & B. S. ANDERSON, THE COUNSELOR AND THE LAW (2nd ed. 1985). W. H. VAN HOOSE & J. A. KOTTLER, ETHICAL AND LEGAL ISSUES IN COUNSELING AND PSYCHOTHERAPY (2nd ed. 1985).
55. In general, *see* 43 C.J.S. 333–70.
56. Mass. Gen. Laws, ch. 119, §63.
57. For a more thorough discussion, *see* 22 C.J.S. § 85.

CHAPTER 4

Education Records and the Student's Right to Privacy

OVERVIEW

Educational record keeping dates from the nineteenth century, when schools kept simple records of enrollment and attendance. An impressive history of the growth of the record-keeping movement, compiled by Diane Divoky, indicates that it was aided by the twentieth-century centralization and bureaucratization of schools and by an emphasis on "dealing with the 'whole child.' "[1] By 1925, she notes, the National Education Association had recommended that "health, guidance and psychological records" be assembled for all students, and by 1941 the American Council on Education had developed record forms that emphasized the collection of subjective behavioral and evaluative information, in addition to factual information. As a result of the increasingly varied types of information collected about students, one father was able to discover, for example, that his seemingly well-adjusted son "was 'strangely introspective' in the third grade, 'unnaturally interested in girls' in the fifth, and had developed 'peculiar political ideas' by the time he was 12."[2] Despite the obvious usefulness of many educational records, questions eventually were raised about the types of information collected, the purposes for which the information was used, and the procedures and policies controlling its collection, dissemination, and destruction.

Concern among educators and others regarding the use and possible abuse of the information contained in student educational records grew throughout the 1960s, culminating in 1969 in a landmark report from a meeting convened by the Russell Sage Foundation.[3] The participants at the conference, who included school counselors, administrators, and others, concluded that "current practices of schools and school personnel relating to the collection, maintenance, use, and dissemination of information about pupils threaten a desirable balance between the individual's right to privacy and the school's stated need to know."[4] They pointed out that information generally was collected without informed consent, that students and parents did not have a clear idea of what information was available in the records, that regular procedures did not exist to control access to students' records by educational or nonschool personnel, and that there was a lack of procedures and policies to govern destruction of educational records. In addition, a major concern throughout this period was that parents did not usually have access to school records.

A conflict that arose in Ohio in the early 1970s illustrates divergent philosophies regarding the desirability of parental access to educational records. In *State v. Wishner,* a private religious school successfully objected to several of the official minimum standards for Ohio elementary schools because it believed that these standards violated the religious freedom of parents and students. One of these standards stated, "[w]hen a pupil transfers, within a school system or moves to a school outside of the school system, pertinent pupil information is forwarded to the principal of the receiving school. Office records of this nature *are not released to parents and guardians.*"[5] Although the Ohio State Board of Education apparently did not believe it was in the best interest of students to allow parental access to educational records, officials at the private religious school involved in the *Wishner* case believed that parental knowledge was essential to a sound education.

At least prior to the enactment of the Family Educational Rights and Privacy Act (FERPA) in 1974,[6] and despite the pioneering work initiated by the Russell Sage Foundation, students and parents in many states had to seek the help of the judiciary in order to gain access to relevant educational information and to prevent its dissemination to those without a legitimate need to know. But with the enactment of FERPA, an educational philosophy emerged that acknowledged the right of parents (and students 18 or over) to be involved in the educational process by having access to educational records, to challenge the accuracy of those records, and to have some control over their dissemination. The remainder of this chapter focuses on selected provisions of FERPA and related issues, in an effort to illustrate the types of problems the law resolves and those that remain unresolved.

THE FAMILY EDUCATIONAL RIGHTS AND PRIVACY ACT

The Family Educational Rights and Privacy Act (FERPA) guarantees to parents and to "eligible students" (those 18 and over) certain rights with regard to the inspection of "education records" and their dissemination. Because it is a federal law, it applies to all school districts and schools that receive federal financial assistance through the U.S. Department of Education. On the other hand, because state departments of education, at least theoretically, can decide not to accept federal money, the guarantees of FERPA are not really rights at all in the strong sense. As one court noted, FERPA is not necessarily binding on a particular school district, but because federal funding might otherwise be discontinued, the court decided to go along with the spirit of the law.[7] For practical purposes, then, FERPA does create rights for parents and students that most, if not all, schools will be responsible for ensuring.

How are parents and students informed of their rights pertaining to educational records?

Federal regulations enacted pursuant to FERPA require that all educational institutions give parents or eligible students notice on an annual basis of the law, regulations, and local school policy. They also must provide notice of a right to file complaints with the Family Policy and Regulations Office at the Department of Education.[8] Because the regulations make clear that it is the responsibility of the institution to *effectively* notify parents of these provisions, schools may have to identify parents who speak a language other than English in the home and make provisions to notify them in their primary language.[9] Copies of the local school-district policy regarding student records, which is required to be in writing, must be given to any parent or eligible student who requests it.[10]

What should a school's educational records policy contain?

The records policy developed by each school very likely will depend on the types of educational information that school officials collect, the educational philosophy of the district, and the purposes that are considered essential or necessary regarding use of the materials collected. The requirements of FERPA are minimum requirements, and individual schools, school districts, or states may decide to go beyond its requirements. Most high schools, for example, now give students under 18 years of age direct access to their own educational records.[11]

The minimum requirements for schools that receive federal financial assistance include the formulation and adoption of policies and practices that meet the following criteria:

- Inform parents or eligible students of their rights
- Facilitate access to records by parents or eligible students by providing information on the types of educational records that exist and the procedures for gaining access to them
- Permit parents or eligible students to review educational records, request changes, request a hearing if the changes are disallowed, and add their own statement by way of explanation, if necessary
- Ensure that the institution does not give out personally identifiable information without the prior written informed consent of a parent or an eligible student
- Allow parents and eligible students to see the school's record of disclosures[12]

Because the requirements of federal law are quite specific with regard to the minimum requirements of an educational records policy, it is advisable that school districts seek assistance from their state board of education or from the Department of Education in Washington before drafting their policies. The Department of Education has developed a model policy—"Student Records Policies and Procedures for the Alpha School District"—that is included in Appendix E. Employees of the Family Policy and Regulations Staff office are very knowledgeable about federal provisions and are willing to answer specific questions. One should remember, however, that several states have gone beyond the minimal requirements of FERPA, and these provisions also may have to be considered in developing local policy and procedures. In some instances, these state policies predate FERPA and provide very extensive rights to students. For example, in Virginia, all students, even those in elementary school, are guaranteed access to their own educational records.[13] Local school districts also can incorporate tailor-made policies and procedures that are not inconsistent with federal or state law. This would allow districts to grant rights or privileges to parents and students that exceed those already provided by federal or state law.

Must counselors tell parents about information obtained from a student in confidence?

Not necessarily. Although the "education records" that must be made available upon request to parents of students under 18 include a wide variety of materials, some exceptions exist that are especially relevant to the work of school counselors. Probably the most important records not subject to disclosure are those made by educators that remain in "the sole possession of the maker thereof" and are not "accessible or revealed to any other individual except a substitute."[14] The legislative history of FERPA makes clear that educational records do not include the "personal files of psychologists, counselors, or professors if these files are entirely private and not available to other individuals."[15] However, in a recent case illustrating the application of FERPA and an analogous state student records act, a court permitted the release to parents of the raw data from their child's Rorschach test.[16] Although the school district argued that this information (verbatim responses of the student's interpretation of ink blots) consisted of personal notes and was intended for the exclusive use of the psychologist who gave the test, the court disagreed. "If information may be sheltered from disclosure merely by retaining it in the therapist's hands under the guise of exclusive use, then the scheme created by the [state act] would be emasculated."[17] Senator James Buckley, who was largely responsible for the passage of FERPA, further limited the reach of the "memory aids" exception. It was not intended, he said, to allow either regular school personnel or a variety of substitutes to "rotate through courses and classes . . . for the purpose of effectively gaining access to another's notes and evaluations."[18] The FERPA regulations make clear that private records of this type are not to be passed on to a person who permanently takes over the responsibilities of the individual who made the records.

Another narrow exception to the types of records that must be disclosed covers those made by a practicing "physician, psychiatrist, psychologist or other recognized professional or paraprofessional" for the purpose of treating a student *18 years of age or older*.[19] Although it is not likely that this exception would cover records maintained by a school counselor, it sometimes may be necessary for the counselor, as the primary professional link between student and health care professional, to be aware of this exception. As in the case of other essentially private records, these records (created and maintained in the course of treatment) may be made available only to persons who are actively involved in treating the student's disability. The only other person who must be allowed access to these records is a health-care professional of the student's own choosing. It should be noted that records of this type concerning students *under* the age of 18 are included in the definition of "education records" and must be disclosed to parents upon request.

Other notable exceptions to the "education records" that must be made available to parents and eligible students include the private records of a school law enforcement unit.[20] This exception will be lost, however, if these records are used for any purpose other than law enforcement or if the law enforcement unit has access to the educational records of a student. (It seems reasonable to assume that the term "law enforcement" has its usual meaning and would not apply to the normal disciplinary activities of school personnel.) In large urban school districts, where special law enforcement units sometimes exist within a school, this means that school officials will have to determine how they wish to treat law enforcement records. They essentially have two choices: (1) maintain a strict separation between educational records and the records of the law enforcement unit, or (2) allow law enforcement personnel to have access to educational records and/or allow counselors and educators to have access to law enforcement records. If option one is chosen, school officials may *choose* to allow parents to have access to the law enforcement records, but they need not do so. If option two is chosen, the records of the law enforcement unit *must* be made available for parental inspection. In the case of option two, the local school or district policy also should define law enforcement personnel as being among those educational personnel who have a legitimate need to know.

Another exception that makes the management of educational records somewhat easier is the exclusion from the definition of educational records of information relating to the postgraduation accomplishments or activities of former students.[21] When collecting and disseminating information about alumni, therefore, the provisions of FERPA do not apply. However, most information collected prior to graduation would still need to be held in confidence.

Is it necessary to have written permission from parents/eligible students before giving information to other educators, researchers, or judicial officials?

It used to be the case that educational records of students were routinely made available to other educators in the school or local district with virtually no questions asked. Under FERPA, this is no longer allowed. If a school or district wishes to provide for this kind of informational exchange, it must first develop a policy that explicitly states which school officials may have access without parental permission and notes the "legitimate educational interests" that would justify such access. Once this is done, requests in accord with the policy may be honored and no record of disclosure need be kept. Although information from educational records also may be disclosed to state-level education officials (when certain conditions are met), these disclosures generally require that a record be kept of the party requesting the information and the purpose of the request. This record is available to parents or to eligible students.

FERPA allows the transfer of education records to school officials where a student seeks to transfer, without parental permission.[22] However, a reasonable attempt must be made to notify the parent or eligible student of the transfer of information.[23] Although all records generally may be transferred to the new school (including psychological and behavioral records), the educators involved should make certain that no unwarranted publicity is given to the records or else be subject to possible suit for common-law invasion of privacy.[24]

The provision of personal information to those conducting education research raises a more difficult question. Many schools receive requests each year from doctoral students, from professors conducting research, and from educational research organizations, requesting access to the educational records of students. The FERPA regulations appear to say that the only time personal information may be made available without prior consent is when the school itself has initiated a particular study to improve education in some way.[25] It should be remembered that we are talking here about personally identifiable information and not information that may be useful to a researcher that does not identify the students themselves. However, if the school decides to seek the help of an outside organization in conducting research, personally identifiable information may be given out as long as it is kept in confidence by those conducting the research and destroyed when the study is completed.

There are several recorded instances where educational records information was needed in judicial proceedings. The FERPA regulations make clear that the school need not have written permission in order to "comply with a judicial order or lawfully issued subpoena."[26] The school, however, must make every reasonable attempt to notify the parent or eligible student that information has been requested, *before* submitting the information to the court. In one instance of which we have heard, a local judge mandated that information relating to criminal activity by students be routinely turned over to police pursuant to state law. Although such a practice appears to conflict with the spirit of FERPA, school officials would need to comply with the judge's order pending a locally accepted clarification of FERPA's requirements.

In one court case the plaintiffs needed information about the educational progress of particular students in order to try to demonstrate that language-minority students were not being provided adequate instruction in the English language.[27] The court said the plaintiffs could have access to the information after reasonable efforts were made to notify parents (in both English and their primary language) either by mail or by newspaper publication; the notice should inform the parents of what information is needed, why it is needed, and should give them an opportunity to object to its release.

In the face of a judicial order, the burden is on the school or the district to produce the information requested and, if the information is personally identifiable, to notify parents and eligible students. If for any reason the school believes it would be too difficult to provide the information in a manner that is consistent with FERPA, it must ask the court to modify the order.[28]

Courts have generally shown an appreciation of the privacy rights involved in the release of personal information from student records. For example, one court held that before it would order the release of medical and personal records on two students who were allegedly involved in injuring a teacher, it would need to hear from the students.[29]

Although the above exceptions to the rule of prior consent for disclosure are among the most important, the sheer number of provisions and exceptions suggests the need to have at least one person in each school take responsibility for becoming thoroughly familiar with FERPA. Even then, it may sometimes be necessary to seek outside assistance; but many problems likely could be prevented with increased familiarity with the federal law and regulations protecting family privacy.

May a therapist provide information from school records to a student rather than to a parent?

Although nothing in FERPA would prohibit giving information directly to a student if that were deemed necessary or advisable by the therapist, parents also have a right under FERPA to have access to educational records, if their child is under 18 years of age.[30] On the other hand, if the child is 18 years of age or older, the parents generally would not have access unless permission were obtained in writing from the student.[31] A highly relevant exception to this last provision is that there is no need to secure the consent of a student 18 or older in order to release educational records *to his or her parent,* if the student is still a dependent of the parent under the federal tax laws.[32]

The FERPA provisions regarding mandatory parental access to the educational records of students may sometimes present a problem for a counselor who believes that this access would in some way endanger the health or safety of a student. School counselors and therapists are probably the last people who need to be told that some parents do not always act with the best interests of their child in mind. Prudence would suggest, however, that instead of attempting to withhold educational records from parents, professionals should take advantage of special regulations allowing for the disclosure of personally identifiable information to those who would be able to assist in resolving situations that impair or threaten to impair the health or safety of students. This would clearly apply in cases of suspected child abuse and would probably also apply, for example, when there was reason to fear physical retaliation for an unexpected pregnancy.

Schools may thus disclose educational records without securing prior permission "to appropriate parties in connection with an emergency if knowledge of the information is necessary to protect the health or safety of the student or other individual."[33] The threatened harm may be from parents, friends, or other students. For example, it is possible that information might be released from Sarah's record to protect her, or from Linda's record to protect Roberto. Consideration must be given to the seriousness of the emergency, the need for the information, the likelihood that the person given the information will be able to help, and whether or not it is necessary to act immediately. The key provision focuses on the necessity, not just the desirability, of disclosing information in order to prevent harm to someone in an emergency situation. While questions of legal liability are dealt with in Chapter 3, counselors and other school personnel have no reason to fear taking reasonable actions to protect the health and safety of students.

Can married students who are under 18 years of age have complete control over their own educational records?

Probably not. If married students under 18 wanted to prohibit parental access to their educational records, it could present an ethical and legal dilemma for educators. Under the law of most states, and by judicial decision in others, persons who are lawfully married are generally considered "emancipated." (Emancipation also occurs when a parent and child agree that the child should live on his or her own, a procedure that in some states requires the assent and supervision of the court.) An emancipated minor usually accepts certain rights and responsibilities not granted to or imposed upon unemancipated minors. These may include, for example, the right to make contracts and the duty to fulfill the obligations thus created. The problem with emancipation, however, is that it does not necessarily create the same rights and responsibilities that are assumed when the child reaches the age of majority. Emancipated minors are sometimes granted only a few additional rights and responsibilities; and in some cases an emancipated minor might return to the care and custody of his or her parents, thus revoking some of the rights of emancipation.

The guidelines developed at the conference convened by the Russell Sage Foundation in 1969 (before the enactment of FERPA) recommended that married students be afforded complete control over their own educational records, including the right to deny parental access.[34] Referring to the guidelines, the *Congressional Record* contains a notation that FERPA was "closely patterned on the carefully considered recommendations of respected experts and experienced professionals in such fields as law, education, medicine, counseling, school administration, and various academic disciplines."[35] If this is true, it is difficult to understand why FERPA does not deal with the issue of students who are married or otherwise emancipated, unless it was intended not to grant them additional rights.

As for control of educational records by an emancipated minor under 18, it could be argued that a conflict exists between the provisions of FERPA and the student's constitutional right of privacy.[36] Since students do not "shed their constitutional rights . . . at the schoolhouse gate,"[37] it needs to be recognized that a student's constitutional right to privacy could, in a particular case, conflict with the parent's statutory right of access under FERPA. Pending further clarification of this issue, however, it would not be possible under the FERPA regulations as they now stand to deny access to educational records when requested by parents of students under 18. As a matter of educational policy, schools may want to consider providing an explicit right of access to emancipated minors, even if their general policy is to deny student access. Several sections of the FERPA regulations make clear that schools may grant students rights *in addition to* those contained in the regulations themselves;[38] in fact, most schools generally do allow for student access.

Is it necessary to release educational records to a noncustodial parent?

Yes. This often-asked question has been answered definitively in the FERPA regulations and in an interesting New York case. Assuming that the school has not been provided with a court order prohibiting contact between a child and a noncustodial parent, that parent (upon request) is entitled to the same access to the child's educational records as a parent with custody or with joint custody.

In *Page v. Rotterdam-Mohonasen Central School District*,[39] a father sought information about his fifth grade child. Both his oral and written requests were denied by the school district. The court held that, despite the mother's insistence that the father not receive information about his child, the father was entitled to have it: "Educators . . . are charged with a duty to act in the best educational interests of children. . . . Although it may cause some inconvenience, those interests dictate that educational information be made available to both parents of every school child fortunate enough to have two parents interested in his welfare."[40] The court also noted that in the event of the death of the custodial parent, it would be likely that the child would live with the noncustodial parent and therefore it is especially important to have both parents fully informed of the child's educational progress. Federal law also makes clear that school personnel may *assume* that a noncustodial parent has a right to this information, unless they have been given evidence that such access is legally prohibited. Information from educational records must also be given to a guardian or to "an individual acting as a parent" when the child has no parent or legal guardian.[41]

Does the student's right to privacy under FERPA conflict with freedom of information laws?

Not usually. While most states have freedom-of-information laws, they are intended only to facilitate public access to information that is governmental or public in nature—the minutes of a school board meeting, for example. Provisions generally are made in these laws to protect the reasonable expectations of privacy that individuals normally have regarding essentially private matters.

One type of school record that clearly does not involve a freedom of information problem, because it can be generally released from student educational records, is "directory information." This information includes "name, address, telephone number, date and place of birth, major field of study, participation in officially recognized activities and sports, weight and height of members of athletic teams, dates of attendance, degrees and awards received, the most recent previous educational agency or institution attended by the student, and other similar information."[42] However, before the school can disclose directory information, its definition of "directory information" must be publicly announced. Parents or eligible students also must be notified that they have a right to object to the disclosure of this type of "directory information" in the absence of prior written approval. If these procedures are followed, schools may (and in some states must) release "directory information" to anyone who requests it.

A case that illustrates the operation of these provisions occurred when a person requested a listing of the names and addresses of all college students at a particular university.[43] The university denied the request for the information because its students had not expressly agreed to have their names and addresses given out for "political" uses. In resolving the controversy, the court held that FERPA did not prohibit the release of the requested information, because the university had previously given notice to the students that such information was "directory information" and the students had already had an opportunity to object to its disclosure. Thus, the university had to supply the information requested.

In a case not covered by the "directory information" exception, a group of parents tried, under their state's freedom of information law, to get the results of the reading and math test scores of a group of third graders at an elementary school.[44] The court recognized the importance of making information available to the public while, at the same time, protecting the privacy rights of the students involved. Instead of allowing an alphabetical list of the 75 students' scores to be released (without including their names), the court said that the scores should be released in a scrambled order. This would not necessitate preparation of a new record, but would assure that personally identifiable information would not be made available in violation of FERPA. Thus, freedom of information was allowed and privacy rights also were respected.

Although the above approach has been followed in several recent cases,[45] another case illustrates one state's more restrictive approach to the release of records, especially when it involved the *addition* of information.[46] Under the state's open records act, a request for class lists of student test scores was denied. The records contained student names and corresponding test scores (i.e., the information was personally identifiable), but the groups requesting the information asked that the names be deleted and information added to indicate whether each student was Hispanic or Anglo. The court held that there was no implied duty to *alter* records to render them releasable under the open records act.[47]

Another interesting case demonstrates that the FERPA restrictions protecting student privacy are intended to apply only to "educational agencies or institutions."[48] A newspaper sought information, under a state freedom of information act, about how much money had been made available by 10 colleges and universities to student athletes. The information was sought not from the educational institutions themselves but from the statewide intercollegiate athletic association. The court held that the association was not subject to FERPA and must therefore disclose the information requested. Apart from making it clear that personal information given to private associations is not protected from public disclosure, the court suggested that colleges and universities may have been supplying personally identifiable information from student records to the association in violation of FERPA. It is therefore important for schools and colleges to check carefully before joining private regulatory associations, to be sure that the association's rules, regulations, and policies are consistent with the requirements of FERPA. Alternatively, educational institutions might wish to make prior arrangements for the release of necessary information to private associations.

It should be clear from the preceding cases that most courts favor disclosure of information under freedom of information provisions, unless that disclosure is in direct conflict with the principle of family privacy that underlies FERPA. Although schools can generally give out "directory information" and any information that does not personally identify students, when other information is requested it may be necessary to seek legal advice as to whether or not a conflict exists between the principles of privacy and freedom of information.

Can relevant medical or psychological information be disclosed in letters of recommendation written for students by school counselors?

This question troubles many school counselors; in many ways, it is more a question of professional ethics than it is a legal question. A counselor may wish, for example, to explain that a particular student is handicapped by blindness, but her intellectual achievement is nevertheless above average. Or the counselor may wish to explain that an unusually high number of failing grades in a student's sophomore year were likely related to the death of a parent. In addition to professional ethics, what legal provisions must be considered?

A 1979 federal district court case presented a situation where a high school principal confiscated all copies of the last issue of the school newspaper.[49] This action was justified, in part, because the principal claimed that FERPA prohibited the release of personally identifiable information criticizing a certain student government leader. The newspaper mentioned that the student had been suspended—this information was generally known around the school and also was contained in school reports. The court held that the principal could not rely on FERPA to justify his seizure of the newspaper because FERPA does not apply to information gained from personal communication rather than from educational records.

Applying this holding, by analogy, to the above question, it is reasonable to assume that nonconfidential and nondiscriminatory information gained from sources other than school records could be communicated in a letter of recommendation. Of course, another requirement would be that the information be accurate, or the counselor might run the risk of liability for defaming the student in some way. Although the legal issues related to defamation are treated in Chapter 3, professional ethics alone suggest that the only information to be passed on should be that which is gained from personal knowledge or otherwise verified (from a source *other than* school records). The legal issues raised by this type of situation are relatively easy to resolve. The most difficult questions concern the counselor's professional responsibility, which runs not only to the student but to the person or institution receiving the letter of recommendation.

May therapists make audio recordings of their conversations with students, and are such recordings "education records"?

There is nothing in the FERPA regulations that generally would exclude audio recordings from the definition of "education records." An exception would be a recording made by the therapist as a memory aid (*following* a counseling session) and not disclosed to others; then, it would be excluded from the definition and not subject to disclosure to parents or eligible students. A different situation would exist if the audio recording were made during the counseling session itself; it would then be an education record subject to disclosure and could very well present problems concerning confidentiality.

The related question of whether or not it is legal to make a recording of a counseling session in the first instance is more complex. A recent article suggests that the answer depends on the procedure followed, that is, whether all parties to the conversation have given their consent, and the state where the recording is made.[50] About half the states permit such recordings where only one party to the conversation has given consent—for example, the therapist. More than a quarter of the states require the consent of all parties.[51] Apart from the legal and ethical issues involved in making such recordings, their subsequent use must take account of the privacy issues governed by FERPA, must not interfere with other common law or statutory privacy rights, must not contain defamatory material, and should be guided by sound professional considerations.

What can parents or students do if they believe that information contained in school records is incorrect?

Several provisions in the FERPA regulations guarantee the right to challenge information that parents and/or eligible students believe is "inaccurate or misleading or violates the privacy or other rights of the student."[52] If the school declines to change the records there is a further right to a fair hearing, where parents and/or students are allowed to bring a lawyer or any other representative. If, after the hearing, the school still declines to change the record, the complaining party is permitted to add a statement to the record explaining the disagreement. The school is then obliged to give out this explanation any time the part of the record it refers to is disclosed to anyone, including other school personnel.[53]

Are the educational records of students with handicapping conditions treated the same as the educational records of other students?

In dealing with the educational records of handicapped students, school personnel will be required to abide by the requirements of FERPA. In addition, the Education of the Handicapped Act (EHA) contains further procedural protections that pertain to student records. Two major areas of additional protection cover the destruction of records and special rights afforded to handicapped children.

When records are no longer needed in order to provide educational services for handicapped children, parents must be informed of that fact and the school must destroy the records if requested to do so.[54] Unlike FERPA, the EHA may afford privacy rights to children similar to those received by parents. However, the age, level of maturity, and type of disability may be considered in making a determination regarding access and control of records by handicapped students themselves.[55]

When should educational records be destroyed?

Apart from the special provisions of the EHA mentioned previously, educational institutions are largely left to develop their own policies with regard to the destruction of the educational records of students. The major limitation imposed by FERPA regulations is that educational records may *not* be destroyed when there is a current request *by a parent or an eligible student* to see them.[56]

The guidelines developed under the auspices of the Russell Sage Foundation recommend that basic identifying data, records of academic achievement, and attendance records be kept permanently. They further recommend the periodic elimination of information relating to health, family background, intelligence, behavior problems, and so forth. The suggestion is made that this might be appropriate at times of transition from elementary school to junior high school and from junior high school to senior high school. Any data that is not verified and not presently needed for disciplinary, counseling, or other educational reasons should be reviewed on an ongoing basis and destroyed when no longer needed.[57]

For the benefit of the students involved, efforts should be made to assure the accuracy of all records. If unverified information is kept for any reason, it would be highly desirable to note that it is, in fact, unverified. Since this type of information can cause great harm to students, care should be taken to collect it only when necessary and to eliminate it from school records when its usefulness is no longer clear.

Do school counselors generally act in accord with FERPA provisions?

In most cases they probably do. Data from a survey of several hundred high school counselors suggest that access to educational records is routinely provided to school officials who have a legitimate need to know and to the guardian of a student, but not to a potential employer.[58] These disclosures are consistent with FERPA.

School counselors also report that parents are permitted to inspect the discipline record of a student, a student's test results, a student's academic record, and the record of disclosures from their child's educational records. There are other instances, however, where counselors report practices that are not in accord with FERPA and where confusion is suggested as to the requirements of federal law.

What provisions of FERPA do counselors most often violate in practice?

Fully 77 percent of the counselors surveyed in the previously mentioned study said that in their schools a noncustodial parent is not allowed access to the educational records of his or her child.[59] Because both FERPA regulations and judicial decisions have made clear that *both* parents are entitled to be informed about the educational progress of their child (unless the school has been told of a judicial order to the contrary), this is one area that should receive the special attention of school counselors.

Responses to another question in the survey show that a 66 percent majority of high school counselors say their schools do not allow parents to inspect records that are maintained in a separate file exclusively for the use of school personnel. Even though the keeping of special "school only" files was common before FERPA, the FERPA regulations make clear that *all* "education records," no matter where they are stored or how they are labeled, must be made available to parents and eligible students. One should know, however, that private notes (those shared with no one except a substitute) are not considered educational records and therefore may be kept private. Private notes of this type must be distinguished from notes to which two or more counselors, teachers, or administrators have access. The latter are "education records" and therefore are subject to mandatory disclosure upon the request of a parent or eligible student. Eighty-two percent of the counselors surveyed said that parents are not allowed to inspect a principal's private notes that have been shared with a teacher—a practice clearly in violation of federal law, which states that shared notes are no longer private.

What FERPA provisions are the most confusing to counselors?

The responses of the several hundred counselors surveyed suggest that there may be a considerable amount of confusion about the issue of private notes.[60] Although a substantial majority said that parents of students in their schools are not allowed to inspect the private notes of a teacher, principal, or counselor, it is interesting to see that a minority of the respondents (32 percent) said that parents *may* inspect the private notes of a counselor. In contrast, only 11 percent said that such access was allowed to teachers' or principals' private notes. What do these data suggest?

As we noted previously, FERPA does not mandate parental access to private notes. If the information provided by counselors responding to the survey is correct, either schools or individual school personnel (and especially counselors!) are providing greater access to information than is mandated by FERPA. It is not known whether this is being done as a matter of educational policy, out of a mistaken understanding of the requirements of federal law, or for some other reason. But, because federal law allows for discretion in this matter, counselors and others generally will be able to balance the need for full communication with parents against the student's right of privacy in a case where one consideration appears to outweigh the other; that is, they may choose to reveal private notes or not, as they wish.

It appears that confusion also exists as to whether or not parents of students 18 or over should routinely be allowed access to the educational records of their child. Sixty-two percent said that such access is provided; 35 percent said that it is not. Only 1 percent said they did not know.

The federal law on this question is clear but, unfortunately, it may pose practical problems for those seeking to respond appropriately in a given situation. In general, routine access to and control over educational records is transferred to a student 18 years of age or older. This means it is the student who must give written permission for a release of educational records. However, the student's permission need *not* be sought in order to provide *parental* access, *if* the student is still a dependent of the parent for federal tax purposes.

This might not seem to pose a substantial problem for those working in public schools, where most students are very likely dependent upon their parents. But if students who are not dependent on their parents are involved, a safe solution might be to request permission from those few students 18 years of age or older, in all situations where access is requested, with a notation that parental access is allowed by federal law when the student is dependent. If a student over 18 wished to deny his or her parents access to records, it would be incumbent upon the school to verify the student's dependent status before releasing educational records to the parent.

Another question that apparently causes confusion among counselors is whether or not routine access to educational records should be provided to school police or guards and to city or state police officers. A 62 percent majority said that educational records are not routinely provided to city or state police, but only 48 percent said they would deny school police or guards access to the same records (33 percent said they did not know).

The minority of counselors reporting that city or state police officers are routinely provided with information from educational records are reporting a practice that appears to be in clear violation of FERPA. An exception that occasionally may be applicable here is the one allowing release of personally identifiable information "when necessary to protect the health or safety of the student or other individual."[61] Personnel in schools that allow school police or guards access to educational records should remember that such a policy decision means that parents must be permitted access to the records of the law enforcement unit as well.

SUMMARY AND CONCLUSIONS

Legitimate concerns that originated prior to the passage of FERPA about the privacy rights of parents and students have been ameliorated to a great extent in recent years by the development of enlightened local policy and by the implementation of federal requirements. All schools receiving federal monies are now required to provide parents and students 18 years of age and over substantial rights of access to educational records; most schools provide access to students under 18 as well.

Other major advances secured by FERPA include informing parents and students of their rights and providing them the information necessary to effectively exercise these rights; permitting parents and eligible students to request that educational records be corrected or amended; and ensuring that most types of personally identifiable information are not released from educational records without appropriate written consent.

In order to effectively secure the rights guaranteed by FERPA, school districts must develop and disseminate a records policy, and provide procedures to grant appropriate access and ensure against inappropriate access. Probably the best way to start reviewing current school-district policy or developing new policy would be to obtain a copy of the federal regulations themselves. The model policy developed by the FERPA office in Washington may also prove useful (see Appendix E). Because of the detail of the federal regulations, it seems especially appropriate to practice preventive law at this point by securing a knowledgeable review of the policy before implementation. School districts also may want to appoint a coordinating records custodian who, as one facet of his or her work, would make it a point to become thoroughly familiar with FERPA and local school-district policy.

FERPA was designed to correct what were widely considered to be abuses in the collection and dissemination of student records, and, despite the sometimes complex nature of the federal requirements, it is probably fair to say that most educators would support recent advances in protecting family privacy. However, as the previously mentioned survey of counselors indicates, there is still more to be accomplished—*all* parents have the right to see the records of their children; no more "school only" files can be maintained; and informed consent generally must be obtained before releasing educational records to police officials, employers, and institutions of higher education. An effort to apply the provisions of FERPA in good faith should allow for the appropriate advancement of the educational mission while, at the same time, preserving reasonable expectations of privacy.

PAGE V. ROTTERDAM-MOHONASEN CENTRAL SCHOOL DISTRICT
441 N.Y.S.2d 323 (Sup. Ct. 1981)

ROGER J. MINER, Justice.

This is a proceeding . . . wherein petitioner seeks judgment ". . . directing the respondents to allow the petitioner to inspect the records duly maintained by said respondents regarding the petitioner's son, Eric Page, and to discuss said records in periodic conferences with the petitioner and designated employees of the respondent school district."

Petitioner is the natural father of Eric Page, a fifth grade student at the Herman L. Bradt Elementary School. The child was born on December 6, 1969 and resides with his natural mother, Michiko Page, in the Town of Rotterdam, Schenectady County. It appears that the child's parents are living separate and apart under the terms of a separation agreement executed in June of 1979. Although a copy of the agreement has not been furnished to the court, it is uncontroverted that the agreement provides for custody in the mother with rights of visitation to the father. The parents are not divorced and there is no court order affecting custody, visitation or support.

Various requests by petitioner to review his son's school records and to meet with school authorities respecting his son's academic progress have been refused. These requests were made both orally and in writing, commencing at about the time of Eric's enrollment in the Bradt school in September of 1979. On September 15, 1980, Michiko F. Page signed a statement as follows: "I, the undersigned, having legal custody of Eric John Page, persuant (*sic*) to the separation agreement dated June 14, 1979, do not wish to authorize the Mohonasen Central School District to transmit any school records to my former (*sic*) husband, John N. Page, or grant permission in any way to see information or to permit said John N. Page to engage in the educational progress and pursuits such as teacher conferences." It seems clear that the statement was prepared by officials of the school district and signed at their suggestion.

[1–3] It is the contention of respondents that petitioner somehow has "abandoned" any interest he might have in his son's education by agreeing that his wife have custody of the child. While it is true that custody carries the right and obligation to make decisions regarding a child's education, . . . petitioner does not seek to interfere with any decision made by his wife but merely to inform himself of his son's development as a student. It is beyond cavil that a non-custodial parent has not "abandoned" his child simply by reason of non-custody and, ". . . while legal custody may be in one or both of the parents, the fact that it is placed in one does not necessarily terminate the role of the other as a psychological guardian and preceptor. . . ." Moreover, it is well settled that a non-custodial parent presumptively is entitled to custody upon the death of the custodial parent. . . . It would be disastrous for the welfare of a child if an uninformed and ill-prepared parent were suddenly cast into a custodial role upon the occurrence of such a misfortune.

The Family Educational Rights and Privacy Act of 1974 . . . does not support the position taken by respondents. It is specifically provided therein that funds shall not be available to educational agencies which deny to *parents* the right to inspect and review the education records of their children. The regulations implementing the act . . . allow inspection by either parent, without regard to custody, unless such access is barred by state law, court order or legally binding instrument. There is no such bar to petitioner's access here.

Finally, the provisions of the State Education Law, relied upon by respondents to thwart the relief sought by petitioner, have no applicability to the case at bar. Section 3205 deals with requirements for school attendance by minors. Section 3208 pertains to the effect of the mental and physical condition of children upon requirements for attendance. Section 3212 defines the duties of persons "in parental relation" to assure the attendance and proper condition of children for instruction. It is significant that *both* parents are charged with responsibility under the terms of this statutory provision. . . .

[4] Petitioner does not seek to alter custodial rights, as respondents contend; indeed, petitioner seeks no relief which will inequitably affect the rights, duties and obligations of the child's mother. Accordingly, it was not necessary to join Michiko Page as a party in this proceeding. . . . Educators and school districts, including respondents, are charged with the duty to act in the best educational interests of the children committed to their care. Although it may cause some inconvenience, those interests dictate that educational information be made available to both parents of every school child fortunate enough to have two parents interested in his welfare.

Submit judgment for petitioner granting the relief requested in all respects.

NOTES

1. 120 CONG. REC. 27, 36528 (1974).
2. *Id.* at 36529.
3. GUIDELINES FOR THE COLLECTION, MAINTENANCE, AND DISSEMINATION OF PUPIL RECORDS: REPORT OF A CONFERENCE ON THE ETHICAL AND LEGAL ASPECTS OF SCHOOL RECORD KEEPING (Meeting convened by the Russell Sage Foundation, Sterling Forest, New York) (May 25–28, 1969).
4. *Id.*
5. State v. Wishner, 351 N.E.2d 750 (Ohio 1976) (emphasis added).
6. 20 U.S.C. §1232g. (1982).
7. Sauerhof v. City of New York, 438 N.Y.S.2d 982 (Sup. Ct. 1981).
8. The address of the Family Policy and Regulations Staff is: U.S. Dept. of Educ., 400 Maryland Avenue, S.W., Washington, D.C. 20202-4605 (Phone: 202-732-2057).

9. 34 C.F.R. § 99.6.
10. 34 C.F.R. § 99.5(b).
11. Sorenson & Chapman, *School Compliance with Federal Law Concerning the Release of Student Records*, 7 EDUC. EVALUATION AND POLICY ANALYSIS 9 (1985).
12. 34 C.F.R. § 99.5.
13. 120 CONG. REC. 27, 36532 (1974).
14. 34 C.F.R. § 99.3(b)(1).
15. 120 CONG. REC. 27, 36533 (1974).
16. John K. v. Board of Educ., 504 N.E.2d 797 (Ill. App. Ct. 1987).
17. *Id.* at 802–03.
18. 120 CONG. REC. 31, 41381 (1974).
19. 34 C.F.R. § 99.3(b)(4).
20. 34 C.F.R. § 99.3(b)(2).
21. 34 C.F.R. § 99.3(b)(5).
22. 34 C.F.R. § 99.31.
23. 34 C.F.R. § 99.34.
24. *Cf.* Klipa v. Board of Educ., 460 A.2d 601 (Md. Ct. Spec. App. 1983).
25. 34 C.F.R. § 99.31(a)(6).
26. 34 C.F.R. § 99.31(a)(9).
27. Rios v. Reed, 73 F.R.D. 589 (E.D. N.Y. 1977).
28. *See* Mattie T. v. Johnston, 74 F.R.D. 498 (N.D. Miss. 1976).
29. Sauerhof v. City of New York, 438 N.Y.S.2d 982 (Sup. Ct. 1981).
30. 34 C.F.R. § 99.11.
31. *Id.* at § 99.4(a).
32. *Id.* at § 99.31(a)(8).
33. 34 C.F.R. § 99.36(a).
34. *Supra*, note 3.
35. 120 CONG. REC. 27, 36533 (1974).
36. For a fuller discussion of this issue see *A Student Right of Privacy: The Developing School Records of Controversy*, 6 LOYOLA U.L.J. 430 (1975).
37. Tinker v. Des Moines Indep. Community School Dist., 393 U.S. 503 (1969).
38. *See, e.g.,* 34 C.F.R. § 99.4(c).
39. 441 N.Y.S.2d 323 (Sup. Ct. 1981).
40. *Id.* at 325.
41. 34 C.F.R. § 99.3.
42. 34 C.F.R. § 99.3.
43. Kestenbaum v. Michigan State Univ., 294 N.W.2d 228 (Ct. App. Mich. 1980).
44. Kryston v. Board of Educ., 430 N.Y.S.2d 688 (App. Div. 1980).
45. *See, e.g.,* Bowie v. Evanston Community Consol. School Dist. 65, 538 N.E.2d 557 (Ill. 1989) (scrambled test scores must be released).
46. Sargent School Dist. No. RE-33J v. Western Services, Inc., 751 P.2d 56 (Colo. 1988).
47. *Id.* at 61.
48. Arkansas Gazette Co. v. Southern State College, 620 S.W.2d 258 (Sup. Ct. of Ark. 1981).
49. Frasca v. Andrews, 463 F. Supp. 1043 (E.D. N.Y. 1979).
50. Gluckman & Koerner, *Recording Conversations in Schools*, 45 EDUC. LAW RPTR. 19 (1988).
51. *Id.* at 22.
52. 34 C.F.R. § 99.20 9(a).
53. *Id.* at §§99.20–99.22.
54. 34 C.F.R. § 121a.573.

55. 34 C.F.R. § 121a.574.
56. 34 C.F.R. § 99.13.
57. *Supra* note 3, at § 2.0 *et seq.*
58. *See supra* note 11.
59. *Id.*
60. *Id.*
61. 34 C.F.R. § 99.36(a).

CHAPTER 5

Legal Issues Related to the Testing and Grouping of Students

OVERVIEW

Testing for educational purposes began in France near the beginning of the twentieth century. There, Alfred Binet, using an individually administered test of ability, sought to identify "backward" children so that educational programs could be developed to meet their special needs.

In the United States, testing of school children historically has been thought to be a democratic phenomenon—allowing educators to focus their attention on individual characteristics and accomplishments rather than on educationally irrelevant and often prejudicial distinctions. Testing also has been thought to promote greater educational efficiency and effectiveness by permitting curricular programs to be developed that would better serve groups of children with similar needs and abilities.

In the last 15 to 20 years, however, educational testing came under serious attack. There were charges of massive misclassification of students, racial discrimination in testing practices, and bias in the tests themselves. More recently, with the growing popularity of minimum competency testing, have come charges of fruitless and unnecessary stigmatization. Diane Ravitch, a Columbia University historian, has said that the educational use of standardized tests is one of the most "rancorous" issues of recent times.[1]

But despite the many attacks on and defenses of the benefits and validity of testing for a variety of educational purposes, there seems to be general agreement that tests, despite their continued importance, have been overused and sometimes misused in American education. Arthur R. Jensen, a research psychologist at the University of California at Berkeley and a staunch defender of the psychometric validity of many tests, has criticized the educational uses of intelligence tests and minimum competency tests:

> I can see little justification for routinely administering intelligence (or IQ) tests or scholastic aptitude tests of any kind to *all* of the school population.[2]

> [Minimum competency testing] appears to me to be an unnecessary stigmatizing practice, with absolutely no redeeming benefits to individual pupils or to society. . . . I see no utility whatsoever in drawing an arbitrary, imaginary line between "minimal competence" and "incompetence." "Competence" is an entirely relative concept. What is competence for one purpose may be incompetence for another. There can be no single all-purpose demarcation.[3]

Speaking of intelligence tests generally, an educational research associate at Harvard University stated that they have played "enormous and often destructive roles . . . in societies all over the world."[4] And a Yale University professor of psychology perhaps summarized recent discontent with the educational testing movement when he said that "[e]ducators have long searched for a panacea in their attempts to provide high-quality education for all. Tests—old or new—will never be that panacea."[5]

Even though educational testing has been criticized, there are no doubt many (including the psychologists quoted above) who would defend the practice for certain purposes, and, perhaps, some who even would advocate the universal administration of intelligence or minimum competency tests. It is doubtful, however, that many educators or other professionals now believe that testing alone can guarantee the quality education we seek for all students.

Like many other controversial educational issues, most policy decisions regarding the uses of testing for educational purposes will ultimately be made by educators rather than by judges and lawyers. We leave it to therapists, counselors, and other professionals to debate and resolve the policy questions that will continue to arise regarding educational testing and grouping programs, and focus here primarily on problems that have been considered by the judiciary over the last 20 or so years.

In this chapter we consider, more or less chronologically, the main legal issues that have arisen regarding testing programs in the nation's public schools. We deal first with the legality of grouping practices in general, followed by the questions that have been raised about grouping or tracking in school districts undergoing desegregation. We then look at the special questions that have emerged when unusually large numbers of minority students have been assigned to classes for the mentally retarded or mentally handicapped. (Federal regulations regarding the testing and evaluation of children with handicapping conditions are discussed in Chapter 6.) And last, we consider recent challenges to minimum competency tests. It will be apparent that some legal challenges to testing programs have been successful, some have not, and some are still unresolved. Recent years, however, have brought a measure of stability to this once widely litigated subject.

TESTING, GROUPING, AND BIAS

Can schools test students and then group them by "ability" if this results in the placement of greater numbers of minority students in the lower tracks?

In some situations, yes. In one case, *Morales v. Shannon,* standardized test scores, as well as students' grades in junior high school and the recommendations of teachers, were used to group students, which resulted in disproportionate representation of Mexican-American students in the less advanced groups.[6] The court that considered plaintiffs' allegations held that discrimination in grouping decisions could not be inferred from the statistics presented and that ability grouping was not unconstitutional per se: "The record shows no more than the use of a non-discriminatory teaching practice or technique, a matter which is reserved to educators under our system of government."[7] In school situations where ability grouping can be shown to be discriminatory, however, those discriminatory practices can be stopped.

In what is perhaps the most important and best-known case on ability grouping, *Hobson v. Hansen,*[8] a Washington, D.C., federal district court declared in 1967 that the lack of opportunity for remediation and the consequent lack of opportunity for movement between the high- and low-level ability groups had turned a four-track system into a four-rut system. Although the court assumed that ability grouping in general could be "reasonably related to the purposes of public education," the way that it functioned in practice deprived "the poor and the majority of the Negro students in the District of Columbia of their constitutional right to equal educational opportunities."

In contrast to the *Morales* case, where no denial of equal educational opportunity was found, the *Hobson* case makes clear that "any system of ability grouping which, through failure to include and implement the concept of compensatory education for the disadvantaged child or otherwise fails in fact to bring the great majority of children into the mainstream of public education denies the children excluded equal educational opportunity."[9]

What about the legality of "ability grouping" in school districts that have a history of purposeful racial discrimination?

Challenges to ability grouping have been successful when school officials in districts where there had been a judicial determination of prior racial segregation sought to assign students to separate classes or schools on the basis, at least in part, of test results.[10] Although these cases did not determine the legality of ability grouping per se, they signal that grouping decisions generally cannot be implemented until after a school system has been completely desegregated for a reasonable period of time. The implicit assumption in these cases seems to be that such practices—which often result in resegregation—would not be fair because of the negative effects on achievement and motivation fostered by the prior discrimination. In addition, grouping that results in resegregation could be said to deny the overwhelming commitment of our society to eradicate racial separation and prejudice; even the symbolic effects of racial segregation must be overcome.

As recently as 1984, questions were raised about grouping practices in school districts striving to become racially unified. In one case, however, the court said that providing an advanced-placement English class did not constitute "ability grouping" in violation of a prior court order prohibiting grouping.[11] Rather than test students and mandate assignments to particular courses or tracks or schools, this high school had developed a course in which *any* senior who had passed junior English was eligible to enroll. Even if prior achievement did not appear to signal the likelihood of success, and even if a counselor had advised against enrollment, the course was still available to all who chose to attend.

While some might argue that this "voluntary" distinction is without merit, given a history of intentional racial segregation, the symbolism is certainly real and, in practice, the advanced course might permit greater achievement for at least a few students who had been denied equal educational opportunity in the past. The case stands for the proposition that voluntary enrollment in advanced-placement courses is not considered "ability grouping," as that idea normally has been understood. Therefore, such practices are legal in school districts undergoing desegregation.

Can test bias render certain student placement decisions illegal?

Yes. In a case involving Mexican-American students, discrimination was found in the assessment and placement process.[12] The intelligence tests used to determine who would be placed in classes for the educable mentally retarded were given in English, which was not the primary language of the students involved. Upon retesting in their native language, most of the original plaintiffs were found to have been erroneously placed. A settlement agreed to by the plaintiffs and the state required that all further testing be done in the students' native language, that students whose native language was not English and who were in special classes be retested, and that those found to have been erroneously placed be given remedial assistance.

This case demonstrates clear-cut bias in assessment procedures that, if used as the basis for placement decisions, would result in illegal discrimination against ethnic-minority students. The next section deals with the much more complex question of racial or cultural bias in the test items themselves.

Is it legal to use standardized intelligence tests in making determinations that permanently assign black children to classes for the mentally retarded?

Given the enormous complexity of the issues involved in answering this question, and the controversy among psychometricians and psychologists themselves, it is not surprising that courts have come to different conclusions on this question.

In two situations of striking similarity, legal challenges were brought on behalf of black children who had been classified as mentally retarded and placed in special classes.[13] These classes, variously called classes for the educable mentally retarded (EMR) or the educable mentally handicapped (EMH), were special classes in the sense that remediation was thought futile, and so the focus was on socialization and basic vocational training. It is important to note that children assigned to these classes were not expected to move—assignment generally was considered permanent. Black students in these EMR and EMH classes were overrepresented (relative to their numbers in the school population) by approximately 15 to 20 percent, compared with students of other races. In both cases, plaintiffs sought to show that the intelligence tests used in determining placement were biased against black students.

It is necessary to consider at the outset the importance of determining what it is that intelligence tests (IQ tests) measure—necessary at least for those who make educational policy decisions and possibly for the judiciary as well. "The experts testifying . . . agree that IQ tests cannot measure innate intelligence, but they disagree on whether the tests measure the 'mental ability' of children."[14] One of the many experts relied upon in these cases, Leon Kamin, a professor of psychology at Princeton University, said that IQ tests measure nothing more than what the child has learned in the past: "IQ tests measure the degree to which a particular individual who takes the test has experience with a particular piece of information, the particular bits of knowledge, the particular habit and approaches that are tested in these tests."[15]

If the experts cannot agree on what it is these tests measure—ability/aptitude or merely achievement—one might wonder about the fairness of assigning any child of any race to an EMH class on the basis, even in part, of tests results. After all, a basic assumption underlying the creation of many EMH classes is that they will "provide opportunities for pupils whose mental capabilities make it impossible for them to profit from the regular educational program."[16] If the tests measure something other than capability, or if we don't know what they measure, the question of racial or cultural bias in the test items themselves would appear superfluous.

It is possible to look from a slightly different point of view at the issue of policies that determine the ultimate academic placement of students. Another expert in the testing field, Arthur R. Jensen (cited previously in this chapter), has said he believes the individually administered intelligence tests most often used in schools are not biased, because they predict scholastic achievement equally well for both black and white children.[17] We would do well, however, to heed his caution that placement decisions are another issue.[18] That is, whether to place low-achieving students in EMH classes is an educational policy decision. Basically, are these classes educationally suitable for low-achieving students or is there a better way to help them achieve their optimal potential? Do we know enough about what these tests measure, and their relationship to the educational program of EMH classes, to justify possible errors in placement? These are only two of the questions that educators must answer. When reading about the judiciary's response to the question of racial bias, it will be helpful to keep in mind the question of test bias and the separate question of placement.

The* Larry P. *Case. Of the two judges in the two major federal district court cases where cultural and racial bias were considered, it was Chief Judge Peckham, in the case of *Larry P.,*[19] who recognized the importance of the question, "What do

IQ tests actually measure?" Leaving aside the issue of whether particular test items were biased, Judge Peckham initially asked whether the tests were valid in demonstrating the "mental retardation" that made it "impossible" to learn in a regular classroom. If this could not be shown, then placing children in these dead-end classes would mean they would fall further and further behind their age-mates.

Do the tests demonstrate lack of mental capacity? We have already noted, as did Judge Peckham, that the experts could not answer this question. So, rather than attempt to solve the problem, Judge Peckham said, "We need not . . . enter into the controversy. We will assume that the tests can accurately measure the mental ability of white children placed in E.M.R. classes, and ask if the tests as utilized for E.M.R. placement have been validated for black children."[20]

Based upon expert testimony, the judge determined that throughout the entire history of educational testing, the IQ tests (which were developed and standardized for use with white, middle-class children) had only been *assumed* to be valid indicators of mental retardation for black children. Despite the knowledge that a pioneer in developing IQ tests in the United States had said they were not valid for black persons and that certain items were widely considered to be culturally biased, little effort had been made to investigate these issues. Furthermore, bias was not sought out; possible defects in the tests were not corrected; and there was little investigation of why black children consistently scored lower, as a group, than white children.

Relying on court cases concerning testing for employment purposes, Judge Peckham placed on the defendant school officials the burden of showing the validity of IQ tests for their intended use. Because the defendants were not able to show that the tests were valid for the placement of black children (even *assuming* their general validity in determining mental ability), he concluded that their use violated several federal laws and both state and federal guarantees of equal protection.[21]

In fashioning a remedy for the schoolchildren, the judge stopped the use of IQ tests for the identification and placement of black children. Further, all black children then in special classes were to be reevaluated without the use of tests. If erroneous placements were found, an "individual educational plan" for remediation and return to regular classes was to be created.

It should be noted that Judge Peckham did not need to reach the more difficult question of whether or not IQ tests actually measure a type of mental retardation that would make it impossible for children to learn in regular classes. Because the judge found that, for black children, the tests had not been shown to measure fairly whatever it was they measured, there was no need to go further.

As a final note on the *Larry P.* case, the district court, in 1986, directed that student placement evaluations focus on "assessment of the pupil's personal history and development, adaptive behavior, classroom performance, academic achievement, and evaluative instruments designed to point out specific information relative to a pupil's abilities and inabilities in specific skill areas."[22]

The* PASE *Decision. In the *Parents in Action on Special Education* (PASE) case,[23] District Judge Grady also began his analysis of whether IQ tests are culturally biased against black students by asking what the tests measure. While saying that the "current view of most psychologists is that IQ tests measure something which is changeable rather than something which is innate,"[24] the judge also noted the lack of agreement among experts about what the tests actually measure. He quoted those who said the tests measure "current performance," a child's mental strengths and weaknesses, and whether a child shares the "dominant culture." The same lack of agreement had been documented in the *Larry P.* case a year earlier. However, without discussing the importance of this issue, Judge Grady concluded that the expert testimony on this and other issues was not entirely believable: "None of the witnesses in this case has so impressed me with his or her credibility or expertise that I would feel secure in basing a decision simply upon his or her opinion."[25]

Rather than rely on psychometricians, educators, psychologists, and others, Judge Grady decided that the major issue was the possibility of bias in the test questions, and that an "informed decision on the question" could be reached only if he examined the items on the three IQ tests in question himself.

For educators who are interested in Judge Grady's analysis of the Stanford-Binet intelligence test, the Weschler Intelligence Scale for Children (WISC), and the Weschler Intelligence Scale for Children–Revised (WISC–R), it covers 35 pages in the case report.[26] For our purposes, however, it is necessary only to say that the judge found eight biased or suspect items on the WISC and the WISC–R and one on the Stanford-Binet test. He concluded, nevertheless, that these items would not cause an inappropriate placement; this would be prevented by the manner in which the tests were administered and scored, the expertise of the psychologists doing the testing, and the fact that other considerations entered into an EMH placement decision—for example, teacher referral, a multidisciplinary professional assessment, and the recommendation of a psychologist. The judge concluded that "[t]here is no evidence in this record that such misassessments as do occur are the result of racial bias in test items or in any other aspect of the assessment process currently in use."[27]

Why have different decisions been reached in various cases dealing with racial bias in testing?

We believe that the diametrically opposed decisions in the *Larry P.* and *PASE* cases are the result of differences in factual conclusions and the way the two judges framed and handled the issues. First, whereas Judge Peckham determined that the use of IQ tests was "substantial" and possibly the "prime determinant" in the placement process, Judge Grady found that testing was only "one component." This suggests that a policy of identification and referral that includes multiple components and involves a variety of people would be more likely to withstand judicial challenge. Of course, one should remember that Judge Grady found that the tests themselves were not substantially biased. If he had found them to be biased, it is less likely that the existence of other assessment procedures would have led to a decision in favor of school officials.

Another difference in the cases is the two judges' identification and treatment of the major issues. It is interesting to note that Judge Grady referred to Judge Peckham's opinion in the *Larry P.* case; he called it "lengthy and scholarly" but criticized its "relatively little analysis of the threshold question of whether test bias in fact exists. . . . I find reference to specific test items on only one page . . . of the opinion."[28] It appears that Judge Peckham did, in fact, consider bias—ultimately inferring it from the fact that the tests had been standardized on white children. Considering the onerous consequences of misplacement, he put the burden on school officials to show the tests were not discriminatory, rather than take on that burden himself. More importantly, he assumed, in favor of the defendants he eventually ruled against, that the tests actually measured mental retardation—something that was perhaps doubtful and certainly a source of great controversy. On the other hand, Judge Grady did not consider whether the tests measured mental retardation. Moreover, instead of relying on expert testimony, which he found unpersuasive, he undertook his own item-by-item analysis and placed the burden on those representing the *children* to prove that the tests were discriminatory.

Our analysis of the two cases leads us to conclude that no one actually proved that the tests themselves either were or were not discriminatory. Judge Peckham inferred that they were discriminatory because they were not developed for use with culturally diverse populations; and Judge Grady's independent analysis may or may not be correct. Moreover, even if Judge Grady's analysis is psychometrically valid, he did not address the prior question of what the tests actually measure. Even assuming the tests are not culturally biased *and* that they accurately measure "mental ability," this ability is subject to change, and thus we must question the fairness of placing students in dead-end EMH classes, when decisions to do so are based, even in part, on these tests.

When dealing with complexities such as those raised by the *PASE* and *Larry P.* cases, it seems that expert opinion, of necessity, must be utilized and that the burden of proof might more reasonably favor those who stand to suffer severe consequences. These problems, however, must be left to the courts. For the time being, most educators will need to make their own decisions about the propriety of using IQ tests for placement of mentally handicapped students and the role and importance such tests will have.

In the school district involved in the *PASE* controversy, school officials eventually agreed to stop using IQ tests that were not specifically validated for the assessment of black students.[29] The *Larry P.* case was affirmed by the Ninth Circuit Court of Appeals in 1984.[30] Although these controversies are now resolved, educators must continue to deal with some difficult questions: Is current knowledge about the nature of intelligence and its measurement well enough understood to justify the exclusive focus on social and vocational training that is typical of EMH classes? Should the curriculum of the classes be changed? Or is the present curriculum of sufficient benefit to the majority of mentally handicapped students to justify the few erroneous placements that are likely to be made? And finally, shall tests be used in the assessment process and, if so, what role shall they play? Recent evidence suggests that grouping decisions will tend to survive judicial scrutiny, even when disproportionate numbers of minority students are placed in the less advanced tracks, when placement decisions (1) are not made on the basis of standardized tests, and (2) are shown to have educationally beneficial results.[31]

THE MINIMUM COMPETENCY TESTING MOVEMENT

What is minimum competency testing?

In the last decade or so, minimum competency testing has become a nearly universal phenomenon. About half the states now require that students take basic skills tests—primarily in reading and math—for purposes of high school graduation, promotion, and/or remediation. In states where passage of a state or locally created competency test is not a prerequisite to receiving a high school diploma, some school districts have set such requirements as a matter of local policy.

The minimum competency testing phenomenon, and especially its role in certifying high school graduates, has been controversial both within the professional community and in society in general. There are some who think that these testing programs, instituted primarily in response to growing public concern about functionally illiterate high school graduates, assure the quality or value of a high school diploma and provide a motivational goal for students and educators. Concerns have been raised, however, that we may not have the psychometric or educational expertise to develop reasonable testing programs. Additional concerns are that the programs may be discriminatory, may not achieve their intended goals, and may create more problems than they resolve. It is not surprising that some of the controversy surrounding minimum competency testing has reached the courts.

Is there anything constitutionally wrong
with minimum competency testing in general?

Assuming procedural and substantive fairness and lack of discrimination, courts that have considered the issue have found minimum competency testing to be reasonably related to the valid state objectives of improving teaching and learning and ensuring the value of state credentialing systems. One judge, while noting that courts had been called upon to settle a "professional dispute" as well as a legal one, reminded those on both sides of the controversy that courts must decide only what the Constitution *requires*.

> It may not be fair to expect students with differing interests and abilities to learn the same material at the same rate, but is it unconstitutional? Similarly, it may be inequitable that some students, through random selection, are assigned to mediocre teachers while others are given excellent instructors, but does this inequity rise to the level of a constitutional violation?[32]

This insightful comment illustrates, once again, that the judiciary normally attempts to rule on the legality and not the wisdom of educational policy decisions. It should be remembered that a ruling that some program or activity is constitutional does not mean that the judiciary has in any way given its stamp of approval regarding its value.

The **Debra P.** *Case.* A judicial controversy, which lasted more than six years, involving one state's functional literacy test, illustrates three types of legal challenges to minimum competency tests (MCTs), passage of which is a prerequisite to high school graduation. One type of challenge concerns the fairness of requiring black students who have attended often inferior, segregated schools at some point in their school career to pass an MCT. Two additional challenges, affecting all students, relate to procedural fairness and to substantive fairness respectively: Has enough advance notice of the testing requirement been given to allow for appropriate preparation? Does the test measure what actually has been taught in the schools— is it "instructionally valid?" All three of these types of challenges are present in the case of *Debra P. v. Turlington.*[33]

In 1976, the state of Florida enacted a comprehensive accountability measure designed to standardize education throughout the state, so that all public school students would be assured of the education necessary to function adequately in modern society. To achieve this goal, students were required to successfully complete a minimum number of credits, to learn certain basic skills (with the help of remedial education, if necessary), and to pass a functional literacy examination on math and communication skills before graduating from high school. (The required exit examination was added to the accountability plan in 1978.)

A major judicial challenge to the functional literacy test, which was called the State Student Assessment Test, Part II (SSAT–II), was filed in October of 1978 on behalf of all Florida seniors and on behalf of black Florida seniors in particular. In July 1979, a federal district court held that requiring students to pass the SSAT–II violated the black students' right to equal protection and all students' right to procedural due process.[34] Because Florida schools had not been completely desegregated until 1971, and many black students had thus attended integrated schools for only seven years, the court postponed for four years the state's use of the SSAT–II as a graduation requirement. By the school year 1982–1983, all black students would have received their education in desegregated schools and students of all races would have had a fair opportunity to prepare for the test.

In 1981, a federal appeals court generally affirmed the holding of the lower court[35] but, in addition, raised the interesting issue of instructional validity.

If the test covers material not taught the students, it is unfair and violates the Equal Protection and Due Process clauses of the United States Constitution.[36]

Just as a teacher in a particular class gives the final exam on what he or she has taught, so should the state give its final exam on what has been taught in its classrooms.[37]

Because there was not enough evidence to decide whether the test was fair or "fundamentally unfair," the appellate court sent the case back to the lower court to decide that issue. Exactly two years later, on May 4, 1983, the district court held that the SSAT–II was "instructionally valid and therefore constitutional."[38]

What is instructional validity?

The district court in the *Debra P.* case explained that "instructional validity" is an "elusive concept" that, "together with curricular validity, ensures that a test covers matters actually taught."[39] Whereas curricular validity looks to whether or not the curriculum of the schools matches the test content, instructional validity goes beyond that by trying to see if individual students are, in fact, taught the things that would enable them to successfully complete the test. The question of curricular validity was not an issue at this time because the court had found previously that the SSAT–II matched the state's curriculum. The question of instructional validity, however, had not been considered.

Because the court realized that it would be impossible to prove that each student had been taught the skills tested on the SSAT–II, it was necessary to determine whether the "preponderance of the evidence" favored instructional validity. The court said that a series of legislative requirements concerning ongoing state-level oversight and evaluation of local curricular implementation supported the expert opinion testimony that the SSAT–II was instructionally valid. The expert testimony was based on an extensive survey of reports from school districts, teachers, students, and others; it showed that the SSAT–II skills were included in local curricula and that teachers said the skills were being taught. In addition, special remediation programs—focusing specifically on skills needed for the test—were provided for those who failed on any of the five occasions on which the test was given, starting with the tenth grade.

Although it is clear that instructional validity was not proven to everyone's satisfaction and that it will remain a controversial professional and legal issue, the judge in this case believed that the evidence favored instructional validity.

> What is required is that the skills be included in the official curriculum and that the majority of the teachers recognized them as being something they should teach. Once these basic facts are proven, as they have been in this case, the only logical inference is that the teachers are doing the job they are paid to do and are teaching these skills.[40]

After the question of instructional validity was decided in favor of Florida education officials, the SSAT–II testing program was declared constitutional in 1983 and affirmed by the court of appeals in 1984.[41] The appeals court was persuaded of the test's instructional validity by the "[n]inety-nine percent of the students surveyed statewide" who said they had been taught what the test covered, by the "breadth and effectiveness of the state's remedial efforts," and by the fact that most of the test skills were taught in the later school years (i.e., subsequent to the time when everyone knew that students graduating in 1983 would be subjected to a testing requirement).[42] In addition to finding that the "students were actually taught test skills," the court also found that "vestiges of past intentional segregation do not cause the SSAT–II's disproportionate impact on blacks," and that "use of SSAT–II as a diploma sanction would help remedy the vestiges of past segregation."[43]

MINIMUM COMPETENCY TESTING
AND THE HANDICAPPED STUDENT

Can high school diplomas be withheld
from handicapped students who have not passed
a required minimum competency exam?

Yes. Although some people believe it is not fair to require handicapped students to pass a competency exam in order to receive a regular high school diploma, the courts to date have determined that this decision should be left to educators and other state officials. As stated in a 1983 New York court decision,

> [W]e first reject the contention that [state educators] do not have the power to determine educational policy in this State and to establish criteria for high school graduation. Indisputably, control and management of educational affairs is vested in the Board of Regents and Commissioner of Education.[44]

Another court gave the opinion that it was "admirable" for a school district "to insure the value of its diploma by requiring graduating students to attain minimal skills."[45] If the competency test requirement is implemented pursuant to state statutory authority, if modifications in testing procedures are provided to ensure that the test measures achievement and not merely the handicapping condition (e.g., a test in Braille for a blind student), and if handicapped students are given a reasonable amount of notice regarding the requirement, diplomas can be withheld for those who do not pass the test.

How far in advance must notice be given
before a required competency testing program
can be applied to handicapped students?

In answer to this question, one court said that it could not determine how many years would constitute adequate notice, although a year-and-a-half clearly was not enough.[46] Instead, it held that the notice would be adequate if it allowed handicapped students to be "sufficiently exposed to most of the material" on the test or allowed time for a "well-informed decision by parents and teachers" that the educational needs of a student could be better met by focusing on goals other than test-taking.[47] Another court, deferring to legislative judgment, held that three years' notice was sufficient to allow for necessary reprogramming of educational goals in cases where deficiencies were potentially remediable.[48]

Although professional judgment will no doubt differ on the issue of adequate notice (for example, one expert has said that notice give in elementary school would be best),[49] the courts have shown little inclination to disapprove the decision of legislators and state and local education officials. It can be expected that the judiciary will not decide that notice is constitutionally insufficient, unless it appears that educational policy makers are "patently wrong" in their assessments.

Do minimum competency testing programs violate the Education of the Handicapped Act or other federal laws?

No. Courts that have considered this issue have responded that the Education of the Handicapped Act (EHA) was intended to ensure an appropriate education and not in any way to guarantee any particular outcome, such as receipt of a high school diploma.[50] As to whether diploma denial could be considered discrimination in violation of Section 504 of the Rehabilitation Act, which prohibits discrimination against "otherwise qualified individuals with handicaps," the courts have held that those who are not able to meet general requirements are not "otherwise qualified." Standards do not have to be lowered for handicapped students or in any other way substantially modified.[51]

Section 504 would be applicable, however, to students whose physical disabilities make it difficult or impossible for them to complete the test in the ordinary manner. It might be necessary, for example, to allow a student with certain motor problems to take extra time or possibly to record answers in an alternative manner. The point is that, in order to avoid discrimination, steps must be taken to make sure it is the child's knowledge that is being tested and not merely the handicapping condition itself.

Must the content of the test be changed to accurately assess "basic competence" in students with handicapping conditions?

No. Some have argued that tests designed primarily to assess minimum levels of competency in nonhandicapped children will not reflect "basic competency" in handicapped students, but courts have not been persuaded. A minimum competency test constructed so that an average nonhandicapped ninth grader would answer 80 percent correctly was held to be valid with respect to handicapped students.[52] The judge said that the language and math skills tested "would form a part of virtually any acceptable reading or mathematics curriculum," presumably including the curriculum of most handicapped students.

The slightly different question of whether or not it is substantively fair, in the constitutional sense, to relegate those mentally handicapped students who can never be expected to pass minimum competency tests to virtually certain diploma denial has not been addressed by the courts. Thinking back to the issue of instructional validity, is it any more fair to require a student to demonstrate what *cannot* be taught than what *has not* been taught?

Some legislatures have recognized this problem by exempting certain classes of handicapped students from the testing requirements (e.g., those classified as trainable mentally retarded) and have made provision for alternative kinds of recognition, such as a certificate of attendance or completion. Even if that seems educationally and constitutionally defensible, what about handicapped students who are slightly more mentally capable and yet not able to pass the test, thus leaving school with no diploma and no certificate? Although these are primarily educational policy decisions, courts can be expected to intervene if the scheme created is manifestly unfair or in some way denies certain groups of handicapped students equal protection under the fourteenth amendment. To guard against such a possibility, minimum competency testing programs must be reasonable in substance as well as implementation. It can be argued that insufficient attention may have been given to the unique needs of handicapped students in the development of at least some competency testing programs.

SUMMARY AND CONCLUSIONS

The constitutionality of a variety of testing and grouping practices has been widely litigated in American courts. Although these often-related practices have been approved in general, when they operate disproportionately on a particular racial or ethnic minority, courts will look closely for evidence of discrimination. Thus, we have seen that school districts that are still striving to become desegregated generally may not use ability-grouping techniques that would be perfectly permissible in a nonsegregated school system. The same is true for the use of minimum competency testing as a prerequisite to high school graduation. Not until black students have been educated in desegregated schools for their entire school careers can these tests be used as a diploma sanction. On the other hand, grouping that results from students voluntarily choosing to enter advanced-placement programs is not considered "ability grouping," and competency testing for remedial purposes is permissible in school systems in the process of becoming fully integrated. These two practices have been singled out because they do not have the effect of foreclosing future educational opportunities to students who may have been previously disadvantaged. On the contrary, they seek to extend educational options for all students.

Although the issue of racial or cultural bias in IQ tests is far from resolved, it does appear that more and more districts are moving to eliminate the use of these tests for the placement of minority students in classes for the mentally handicapped or to decrease what perhaps has been an overreliance on such tests for placement purposes.

Meanwhile, there is evidence that test makers themselves are seeking to develop culture-free, bias-free assessment instruments—for example, tests that measure information processing and problem solving rather than what a child has already learned. A major issue for professionals, if not for the courts, is to determine what the various IQ tests, in particular, measure and how the tests can be most appropriately and fairly used to increase levels of achievement for all students.

The minimum competency testing movement appears to have taken a secure hold on the educational community in the United States. When used for assessment and remediation, competency tests have been relatively unproblematic; when used as a diploma sanction, they have been extraordinarily controversial. In judicial challenges so far, the courts have not disapproved such programs as long as the tests assess what students have been taught and as long as students have enough advance notice of the requirement to allow for adequate preparation.

In looking at the major judicial disputes surrounding educational testing, it seems that the tests themselves become more controversial as their uses become more intrusive in foreclosing further educational or occupational opportunity. The human cost of a mistake in evaluation when the purpose is remediation, while not insignificant, is far less than when the mistake erroneously deprives a child of the opportunity to be exposed to the ordinary curriculum or to receive a high school diploma. The judiciary has demonstrated that most testing and grouping decisions are not for it to make. Apart from blatant unfairness, which the courts will enjoin, it is educators who must bear the primary responsibility for minimizing errors in judgment—in both policy and practice.

HOBSON V. HANSEN
269 F.Supp. 401 (D.D.C. 1967), **aff'd sub. nom.** *Smuck v. Hobson, 408 F.2d 175 (D.C. Cir. 1969).*

J. SKELLY WRIGHT, Circuit Judge.

. . .

VI. The Track System

Plaintiffs' attack on the track system, Superintendent Hansen's special form of ability grouping, touches yet another phase of the District's administration of the public schools, here the concern being specifically the kind of educational opportunities existing within the classroom. The evidence amassed by both parties with regard to the track system has been reviewed in detail in Part IV of the Findings, where the court has already had occasion to note the critical infirmities of that system. The sum results of those infirmities, when tested by the principles of equal protection and due process, is to deprive the poor and a majority of the Negro students in the District of Columbia of their constitutional right to equal educational opportunities.

At the outset it should be made clear that what is at issue here is not whether defendants are entitled to provide different kinds of students with different kinds of education. Although the equal protection clause is, of course, concerned with classifications which result in disparity of treatment, not all classifications resulting in disparity are unconstitutional. If classification is reasonably related to the purposes of the governmental activity involved and is rationally carried out, the fact that persons are thereby treated differently does not necessarily offend.

Ability grouping is by definition a classification intended to discriminate among students, the basis of that discrimination being a student's capacity to learn. Different kinds of educational opportunities are thus made available to students of differing abilities. Whatever may be said of the concept of ability grouping in general, it has been assumed here that such grouping can be reasonably related to the purposes of public education. Plaintiffs have eschewed taking any position on the contrary. Rather the substance of plaintiffs' complaint is that in practice, if not by design, the track system—as administered in the District of Columbia public schools—has become a system of discrimination founded on socio-economic and racial status rather than ability, resulting in the undereducation of many District students.

As the court's findings have shown, the track system is undeniably an extreme form of ability grouping. Students are early in elementary school sorted into homogeneous groups or tracks (and often into subgroups within a track), thereby being physically separated into different classrooms. Not only is there homogeneity, in terms of supposed levels of ability—the intended result—but as a practical matter there is a distinct sameness in terms of socio-economic status as well. More importantly, each track offers a substantially different kind of education, both in pace of learning and in scope of subject matter. At the bottom there is the slow-paced, basic (and eventually almost purely low-skill vocational) Special Academic Track; at the top is the intense and challenging Honors program for the gifted student. For a student locked into one of the lower tracks, physical separation from those in other tracks is of course complete insofar as classroom relationships are concerned; and the limits on his academic progress, and ultimately the kind of life work he can hope to attain after graduation, are set by the orientation of the lower curricula. Thus those in the lower tracks are, for the most part, molded for various levels of vocational assignments; those in the upper tracks, on the other hand, are given the opportunity to prepare for the higher ranking jobs and, most significantly, for college.

In theory, since tracking is supposed to be kept flexible, relatively few students should actually ever be locked into a single track or curriculum. Yet, in violation of one of its principal tenets, the track system is not flexible at all. Not only are assignments permanent for 90% or more of the students but the vast majority do not even take courses outside their own curriculum. Moreover, another significant failure to implement track theory—and in major part responsible for the inflexibility just noted—is the lack of adequate remedial and compensatory education programs for the students assigned to or left in the lower tracks because of cultural handicaps. Although one of the express reasons for placing such students in these tracks is to facilitate remediation, little is being done to accomplish the task. Consequently, the lower track student, rather than obtaining an enriched educational experience, gets what is essentially a limited or watered-down curriculum.

These are, then, the significant features of the track system: separation of students into rigid curricula, which entails both physical segregation and a disparity of educational opportunity; and, for those consigned to the lower tracks, opportunities decidedly inferior to those available in the higher tracks.

A precipitating cause of the constitutional inquiry in this case is the fact that those who are being consigned to the lower tracks are the poor and the Negroes, whereas the upper tracks are the provinces of the more affluent and the whites. Defendants have not, and indeed could not have, denied that the pattern of grouping correlates remarkably with a student's status, although defendants would have it that the equation is to be stated in terms of income, not race. However, as discussed elsewhere, to focus solely on economics is to oversimplify the matter in the District of Columbia where so many of the poor are in fact the Negroes. And even if race could be ruled out, which it cannot, defendants surely "can no more discriminate on account of poverty than on account of religion, race, or color." . . . As noted before, the law has a special concern for minority groups for whom the judicial branch of government is often the only hope for redressing their legitimate grievances; and a court will not treat lightly a showing that educational opportunities are being allocated according to a pattern that has unmistakable signs of invidious discrimination. Defendants, therefore, have a weighty burden of explaining why the poor and the Negro should be those who populate the lower ranks of the track system.

Since by definition the basis of the track system is to classify students according to their ability to learn, the only explanation defendants can legitimately give for the pattern of classification found in the District schools is that it does reflect students' abilities. If the discriminations being made are founded on anything other than that, then the whole premise of tracking collapses and with it any justification for relegating certain students to curricula designed for those of limited abilities. While government may classify persons and thereby effect disparities in treatment, those included within or excluded from the respective classes should be those for whom the inclusion or exclusion is appropriate; otherwise the classification risks becoming wholly irrational and thus unconstitutionally discriminatory. It is in this regard that the track system is fatally defective, because for many students placement is based on traits other than those on which the classification purports to be based.

The evidence shows that the method by which track assignments are made depends essentially on standardized aptitude tests which, although given on a system-wide basis, are completely inappropriate for use with a large segment of the student body. Because these tests are standardized primarily on and are relevant to a white middle class group of students, they produce inaccurate and misleading test scores when given to lower class and Negro students. As a result, rather than being classified according to ability to learn, these students are in reality being classified according to their socio-economic or racial status, or—more precisely—according to environmental and psychological factors which have nothing to do with innate ability.

Compounding and reinforcing the inaccuracies inherent in test measurements are a host of circumstances which further obscure the true abilities of the poor and the Negro. For example, teachers acting under false assumptions because of low test scores will treat the disadvantaged student in such a way as to make him conform to their low expectations; this acting out process—the self-fulfilling prophecy—makes it appear that the false assumptions were correct, and the student's real talent is wasted. Moreover, almost cynically, many Negro students are either denied or have limited access to the very kinds of programs the track system makes a virtual necessity: kindergartens, Honors programs for the fast-developing Negro student; and remedial and compensatory education programs that will bring the disadvantaged student back into the mainstream of education. Lacking these facilities, the student continues hampered by his cultural handicaps and continues to appear to be of lower ability than he really is. Finally, the track system as an institution cannot escape blame for the error in placements, for it is tracking that places such an emphasis on defining ability, elevating its importance to the point where the whole of a student's education and future are made to turn on his facility in demonstrating his qualifications for the higher levels of opportunity. Aside from the fact that this makes the consequences of misjudgments so much the worse, it also tends to alienate the disadvantaged student who feels unequal to the task of competing in an ethnocentric school system dominated by white middle class values; and alienated students inevitably do not reveal their true abilities—either in school or on tests.

All of these circumstances, and more, destroy the rationality of the class structure that characterizes the track system. Rather than reflecting classifications according to ability, track assignments are for many students placements based on status. Being, therefore, in violation of its own premise, the track system amounts to an unlawful discrimination against those students whose educational opportunities are being limited on the erroneous assumption that they are capable of accepting no more.

Remedy

. . .

As to the remedy with respect to the track system, the track system simply must be abolished. In practice, if not in concept, it discriminates against the disadvantaged child, particularly the Negro. Designed in 1955 as a means of protecting the school system against the ill effects of integrating with white children the Negro victims of *de jure* separate but unequal education, it has survived to stigmatize the disadvantaged child of whatever race relegated to its lower tracks—from which tracks the possibility of switching upward, because of the absence of compensatory education, is remote.

Even in concept the track system is undemocratic and discriminatory. Its creator admits it is designed to prepare some children for white-collar, and other children for blue-collar, jobs. Considering the tests used to determine which children should receive the blue-collar special, and which the white, the danger of children completing their education wearing the wrong color is far too great for this democracy to tolerate. Moreover, any system of ability grouping which, through failure to include and implement the concept of compensatory education for the disadvantaged child or otherwise, fails in fact to bring the great majority of children into the mainstream of public education denies the children excluded equal educational opportunity and thus encounters the constitutional bar.

. . .

Parting Word

It is regrettable, of course, that in deciding this case this court must act in an area so alien to its expertise. It would be far better indeed for these great social and political problems to be resolved in the political arena by other branches of government. But these are social and political problems which seem at times to defy such resolution. In such situations, under our system, the judiciary must bear a hand and accept its responsibility to assist in the solution where constitutional rights hang in the balance. So it was in *Brown v. Board of Education, Bolling v. Sharpe,* and *Baker v. Carr.* So it is in the South where federal courts are making brave attempts to implement the mandate of *Brown.* So it is here.

. . .

Decree

It is FURTHER ORDERED, ADJUDGED and DECREED that the defendants be, and they are hereby, permanently enjoined from operating the track system in the District of Columbia public schools. . . .

NOTES

1. Educ. Daily, Nov. 1, 1983, at 4.
2. A. JENSEN, BIAS IN MENTAL TESTING 716 (1980).
3. *Id.* at 724–25.
4. Gardner, *Assessing Intelligences: A Comment on "Testing Intelligence Without I.Q. Tests,"* 65 PHI DELTA KAPPAN 699, 700 (1984).
5. Sternberg, *Testing Intelligence Without I.Q. Tests,* 65 PHI DELTA KAPPAN 694, 698 (1984).
6. Morales v. Shannon, 516 F.2d 411 (5th Cir. 1975).
7. *Id.* at 414.
8. 269 F.Supp. 401 (D.D.C. 1967), *aff'd sub. nom.* Smuck v. Hobson, 407 F.2d 175 (D.C. Cir. 1969) (en banc).
9. *Id.* at 515.
10. *See, e.g.,* Singleton v. Jackson Mun. Separate School Dist., 419 F.2d 1211, 1219 (5th Cir. 1969), *rev'd on another issue,* 396 U.S. 290 (1970) (per curiam); Lemon v. Bossier Parish School Bd., 444 F.2d 1400 (5th Cir. 1971); Moses v. Washington Parish School Bd., 330 F.Supp. 1340 (E.D. La. 1971), *aff'd,* 456 F.2d 1285 (5th Cir. 1972).
11. Andrews v. City of Monroe, 730 F.2d 1050 (5th Cir. 1984).
12. Diana v. State Bd. of Educ., No. 70–37 (N.D. Cal. 1970), stipulated settlement approved

(9th Cir. June 18, 1973), discussed in Rose & Huefner, *Cultural Bias in Special Education Assessment and Placement*, in SCHOOL LAW UPDATE . . . PREVENTIVE SCHOOL LAW 181–82 (T. Jones & D. Semler eds. 1984).

13. Parents in Action on Special Education (PASE) v. Hannon, 506 F.Supp. 831 (N.D. Ill. 1980); Larry P. v. Riles, 495 F.Supp. 926 (N.D. Cal. 1979); *aff'd in part*, 793 F.2d 969 (9th Cir. 1984) (the court reversed on the constitutional issues).

14. Larry P. v. Riles, 495 F.Supp. at 971.

15. *Id.* at 952.

16. *Id.* at 941.

17. A. JENSEN, STRAIGHT TALK ABOUT MENTAL TESTS 147 (1981).

18. *Id.*

19. 495 F. Supp. 926 (N.D. Cal. 1979).

20. *Id.* at 970.

21. *Id.* at 988.

22. Larry P. v. Riles, EHLR 558:141 (N.D. Cal. 1986).

23. Parents in Action on Special Education v. Hannon, 506 F.Supp. 831 (N.D. Ill. 1980).

24. *Id.* at 835.

25. *Id.* at 836.

26. *Id.* at 837–72.

27. *Id.* at 883.

28. *Id.* at 882–83.

29. Pope, *Judicial Testing of IQ Tests*, 6 WEST'S EDUC. L. REP. 875 (1983).

30. Larry P. v. Riles, 793 F.2d 969 (9th Cir. 1984).

31. *See* NAACP v. Georgia, 775 F.2d 1402 (11th Cir. 1985) (no equally sound educational alternatives shown that would decrease racial disproportionality; S-1 v. Turlington, 646 F.Supp. 1179 (S.D. Fla. 1986) (racially disproportionate placements not discriminatory). *See also* McNeal v. Tate County School Dist., 508 F.2d 1017 (5th Cir. 1975) (assignments cannot be a result of past segregation or must increase educational attainment).

32. Debra P. v. Turlington, 564 F.Supp. 177, 183 (M.D. Fla. 1983), *aff'd*, 730 F.2d 1405 (11th Cir. 1984).

33. 474 F.Supp. 244 (M.D. Fla. 1979), *aff'd in part, vacated and remanded in part*, 644 F.2d 397 (5th Cir. 1981), *reconsidered*, 564 F.Supp. 177 (M.D. Fla. 1983), *aff'd*, 730 F.2d 1405 (11th Cir. 1984).

34. Debra P., 474 F.Supp. 244.

35. Debra P., 644 F.2d 397.

36. *Id.* at 402.

37. *Id.* at 406.

38. Debra P., 564 F.Supp. at 186.

39. The term "instructional validity" was developed by Merle McClung and by Diana Pullin, one of the lawyers representing the plaintiffs in the *Debra P*. case, because the professional literature did not address the match between test and instruction. McClung, *Competency Testing Programs: Legal and Educational Issues,* 47 FORDHAM L. REV. 651, 682 n. 153 (1979). This article provides an extensive review of the legal and educational issues involved in competency testing up to its date of publication.

40. Debra P., 564 F.Supp. at 186; *See also* Anderson v. Banks, 540 F.Supp. 761, 765 (S.D. Ga. 1982) (proof that every teacher taught every lesson is too burdensome).

41. Debra P., 730 F.2d 1405 (11th Cir. 1984).

42. *Id.* at 1411.

43. *Id.* at 1416–17.

44. Bd. of Educ. of Northport-East, Northport Unified School Dist. v. Ambach, 458

N.Y.S.2d 680, 683–84 (App. Div. 1982) (citations omitted), *aff'd,* 469 N.Y.S.2d 669 (1983), *cert. denied,* 465 U.S. 1101 (1984).

45. Brookhart v. Ill. State Bd. of Educ., 697 F.2d 179, 182 (7th Cir. 1983).
46. *Id.*
47. *Id.* at 187–88.
48. Bd. of Educ. of Northport, 458 N.Y.S.2d 680.
49. Bd. of Educ. of Northport, 436 N.Y.S.2d 564, 574 (Sup. Ct. 1981).
50. *See, e.g.,* Brookhart v. Illinois State Bd. of Educ., 697 F.2d 179 (7th Cir. 1983), Bd. of Educ. of Northport, 458 N.Y.S.2d 680 (App. Div. 1982), *aff'd,* 469 N.Y.S.2d 669 (1983).
51. *Id.*
52. Bd. of Educ. of Northport, 458 N.Y.S.2d at 688.

CHAPTER 6

Students with Special Educational Needs

OVERVIEW

The contemporary emphasis on providing educational resources to meet the unique and special needs of various groups of students began in the mid-1960s with the passage of the Elementary and Secondary Education Act (ESEA).[1] Much of the federal money made available under that program was to be spent to supplement the needs of children who, although not necessarily poor themselves, lived in areas with concentrations of low-income families. These children were considered "educationally deprived" and were therefore provided with a variety of compensatory educational programs.

In the late 1960s and early 1970s, judicial and legislative action began to coalesce around the notion that the more than three million handicapped children living in the United States should no longer be discriminated against or excluded from school, actually or functionally. In 1975, the Education for All Handicapped Children Act (EAHCA) (PL 94–142) was passed, as an amendment to the Education of the Handicapped Act (EHA),[2] to provide additional federal funding for those states agreeing to give a free and appropriate education to children with handicapping conditions. Just two years earlier, a major judicial controversy was settled, protecting the rights of students with limited English-speaking ability to an education that would enhance their English-language skills;[3] and in 1978, the Bilingual Education Act of a decade earlier was reauthorized, providing federal financial assistance for programs to aid limited-English-speaking children.[4]

At the same time that the special needs of handicapped and limited-English-speaking children were beginning to be fully recognized, the first federal funds were made available for gifted students. This effort was significantly expanded in 1978 with the passage of the Gifted and Talented Children's Education Act of 1978.[5] To date, however, the special needs of these children have received relatively less attention than the needs of other special students, perhaps because their needs seem less compelling in the short run.

As educators know, the current scope of activity at the federal, state, and local levels aimed at providing services and programs to meet unique student needs is unprecedented in American history. Federal funding for fiscal 1984 included $3.5 billion for disadvantaged children, $1.2 billion for the handicapped, and $139 million for language-minority programs; funds for gifted students came from a $479 million educational block grant that merged approximately 30 separate educational programs.[6]

We have chosen in this chapter to deal only with basic legislation and judicial provisions and pronouncements, with an emphasis on emerging issues. We begin with the legal issues affecting educationally deprived children; we then discuss issues having an impact on children with handicapping conditions and those with a limited ability to speak English; we conclude with those legal issues relevant to children with special gifts and talents. Problems related to the testing and grouping of handicapped students are dealt with in Chapter 5, and discipline of the handicapped is considered in Chapter 7.

EDUCATIONALLY DISADVANTAGED CHILDREN

Where does aid for the educationally disadvantaged come from and how is it used?

Originally, federal monies were made available to state and local school officials through Title I of the ESEA, which is now called Chapter I. The money is to be used to supplement the special educational needs of the more than five million children who are educationally deprived, no matter where they attend school. Services comparable to those provided in public schools are provided to children who attend private and parochial schools in areas with high concentrations of low-income families. If the money is not spent exclusively for educating the targeted populations, the federal government may recover misused funds from the states involved.[7] However, where 75% or more of students are from low-income families, Chapter I funds can be used in schoolwide projects.

Does providing federal money to educate disadvantaged students attending religious schools violate the establishment clause of the first amendment?

Although aid to parochial school students has been challenged as violating the constitutional provision regarding separation of church and state, it appears that the obstacles to obtaining such aid are not insurmountable. One federal district court said that, although government monies "could conceivably engender a program that did not satisfy establishment standards," there was no problem in the case under consideration[8] because there was a secular legislative purpose in aiding disadvantaged children, the program's primary effect was to benefit the children and not the religious school, and there was no excessive administrative or political entanglement between church and state.

The Supreme Court also has looked favorably on legislative schemes that seek to aid society in general by advancing the educational achievement of all students.[9] However, a 1985 case placed substantial limits on the methods that could be used to deliver Chapter I services to educationally deprived students attending parochial schools. The Supreme Court, in *Aguilar v. Felton* (see Appendix D), ruled that teachers, guidance counselors, psychologists, psychiatrists, and social workers employed by the public schools could no longer provide remedial education and guidance services within parochial school buildings.[10] Even though publicly paid personnel were to limit their contact with parochial school personnel and to remove religious items and materials from the classrooms, the Court determined that the program, as implemented, excessively entangled church and state in violation of the first amendment's establishment clause. Oversight by field supervisors and coordinators, and extensive administrative cooperation between public and parochial educators, violated the policy of governmental neutrality toward religion that is implicit in the first amendment.

The *Aguilar* decision has significantly altered the way Chapter I services are delivered to parochial school students and further has affected the delivery of services for the handicapped and other special-needs students as well. Whether the use of mobile classrooms, computers, shared-time programs, and other methods are as effective as on-site instruction is a matter of considerable debate. Nevertheless, the Supreme Court continues to be particularly sensitive to questions of possible religious indoctrination and entanglement when it comes to elementary and secondary school students, and can be expected to closely scrutinize methods for providing these types of services in the future.

An interesting additional question, related by analogy to the one presented here, involves the placement of handicapped children in parochial schools by public officials who believe those placements to be educationally appropriate. While parents certainly may choose a parochial school placement for their children, legal scholars have provided convincing arguments against such placements at the behest of public officials.[11]

EDUCATION OF THE HANDICAPPED

What are the major federal laws protecting students with handicapping conditions?

Section 504. A major federal provision protecting all handicapped persons, including students, is Section 504 of the Rehabilitation Act of 1973.[12] Section 504 says that no "otherwise qualified" individual with a handicap can be discriminated against in any federally assisted program or activity "solely by reason of his handicap." In addition to protecting handicapped students from discrimination, Section 504 applies to teachers, administrators, and others as well, and requires that reasonable accommodation be made to the handicapping condition; it also applies widely to education, employment, and federally aided social service programs such as housing and transportation. Although no federal money is given under this law, states that receive any type of federal financial assistance (which includes all states) must comply with its provisions against discrimination or risk losing aid.

In response to a controversy over whether or not a woman with a serious hearing impairment would be admitted to a professional educational program that trained nurses, the Supreme Court said that "[a]n otherwise qualified person is one who is able to meet all of a program's requirements in spite of his handicap."[13] If reasonable accommodation cannot be made that would allow a person to function efficiently and safely in an educational program and in the occupational capacity for which the person is being educated, it is not discriminatory to deny admission.

In the elementary and secondary education context, Section 504 requires that handicapped students be provided with an appropriate education in an environment with as many nonhandicapped peers as possible; however, courts may reach a different opinion in cases concerning some types of extracurricular activities. In a case where a severely physically handicapped high school junior wanted to attend a school-sponsored trip to Spain, it was held that she was not "otherwise qualified" within the meaning of Section 504.[14] The student's diminutive size (3½ feet) and severe congenital limb deficiencies made it necessary for her to be transported to school in a special van and to receive the assistance of an aide while in school. After examining the activities that were contemplated for the trip to Spain, the court found that the girl would not be capable of keeping up with the group on her own and that the activities would pose a substantial danger to her well-being. Because school officials had originally said she could go, if accompanied by an aide to assist her, it can be inferred that the court did not believe Section 504 required such affirmative accommodations on the part of the school.

The EHA. A more detailed and focused federal statutory scheme to provide education to handicapped children was enacted in 1975—and is now called the Education of the Handicapped Act (EHA).[15] Pursuant to the EHA, handicapped students who live in states accepting money under the act (as all states now do) must be evaluated and provided with a free, appropriate education and related services in the least restrictive environment. Although Section 504 requires that the individual needs of students be considered, the EHA generally requires the development of an individualized educational plan (IEP) for all children between ages 3 and 21. The IEP must include the following information: the child's present level of performance; a statement of goals; a statement of what particular kinds of special education and related services are to be provided; a statement about the degree of mainstreaming that will be provided; and a plan for evaluation, which must be done at least once a year. To help ensure that state policies and plans for education of the handicapped are implemented, a number of rights are afforded to the parents of handicapped children. These include the right to be involved in the initial placement decision and any subsequent changes in placement, the right to an impartial hearing if controversy arises, the right of access to school records and to an independent evaluation of their child, and the right of appeal to state education officials or courts, if necessary, regarding educational decisions affecting their child.

Apart from the philosophy of "mainstreaming" (placing as many handicapped children as possible in programs with nonhandicapped age-mates), perhaps the most important provision of the EHA involves the collective creation and annual review of the IEP. The IEP defines the education and related services the child is to receive, and therefore represents an opportunity for all concerned to create a program suited to the special needs of a particular child.

In 1986, the EHA was amended by the Handicapped Children's Protection Act,[16] which significantly enhanced the rights of handicapped children. An important part of the EHA now authorizes the award of "reasonable attorneys' fees as part of the costs to the parents or guardian of a handicapped child or youth who is the prevailing party" in most disputes regarding identification, placement, or services.[17] It is now reasonably clear that parents who prevail on a significant issue—*if* they have not rejected a more favorable offer or unreasonably protracted the dispute[18]— may recover fees and costs from the losing party in all administrative and judicial proceedings.[19] The potential for recovery under the amendment was made retroactive to cases brought or pending after July 3, 1984, which artificially increased litigation on this issue for some time after 1986. A federal court of appeals has ruled recently, however, that "where the plaintiff achieved only limited success, the district court should award only that amount of fees that is reasonable in relation to the results obtained."[20]

The EHA was amended again, in the same year, by the Education of the Handicapped Amendments of 1986.[21] This amendment was intended to encourage the development by states of comprehensive interagency programs to provide early intervention for handicapped infants and toddlers and their families. "Handicapped" in this context includes young children who are developmentally delayed or have a mental or physical condition that is likely to result in developmental delay. This renewed emphasis on individual needs in a public education system that has historically favored efficiency is perhaps nowhere more necessary than when dealing with the handicapped. (See Appendix C for excerpts from the EHA.)

Section 1983. An important protection for all individuals, and not just those who are handicapped, Section 1983 authorizes suit in federal or state court to vindicate constitutional or federal statutory rights that have been compromised by persons acting under color of state law.[22] As a practical matter, Section 1983 probably will be used to remedy pervasive or large-scale violations of fourteenth amendment equal protection or due process rights or to enforce the guarantees of the EHA itself—for example, where the state or local district is not identifying and placing handicapped students or is doing so in an untimely or discriminatory manner. Compensatory relief and attorneys' fees may be awarded to prevailing parties.

Although the EHA likely will be the major avenue of redress for aggrieved handicapped students, a recent amendment to the EHA has made clear that the EHA does not limit other available remedies.[23] Therefore, Section 1983 remedies are available, as long as state administrative appeals have been pursued (where relief *also* is available under the EHA) and such appeals would not be futile.

Are children with AIDS (Acquired Immunodeficiency Syndrome) considered handicapped under federal law?

The answer to this question is "yes and no," so it requires a bit of explanation. The EHA defines handicapped children, in relevant part, as those who are "other health impaired" and who "*by reason thereof* require special education and related services."[24] Therefore, many children who have AIDS (or test positive for the AIDS virus), while "other health impaired," may *not* need special education and therefore would not be protected by the EHA. Section 504, however, has a different definition of "handicapped"; it is one that includes persons with handicapping conditions, those who have had an impairment in the past, and those who are "regarded as having an impairment."[25] It should be readily apparent that children with AIDS are "handicapped" under Section 504,[26] because they are regarded as having an impairment, so it is not surprising that many relevant court cases (including cases concerning other contagious diseases) deal with this statute rather than the EHA.

The case of a 5-year-old California boy, who was excluded from kindergarten following a biting incident, illustrates the application of Section 504 to a child whose only handicap was infection with the AIDS virus, a result of contaminated blood he received in a transfusion as an infant.[27] The court issued a permanent injunction mandating the child's admission to school, concluding that he was "handicapped" under Section 504 and was "otherwise qualified" to attend. According to the court, and despite the biting incident, the boy was qualified:

> The best available medical evidence shows that the AIDS virus is not spread in the air by infected droplets. . . . The virus is fragile and is killed by most household disinfectants. The virus is transmitted from one person to another only by infected blood, semen or vaginal fluids (and, possibly, mother's milk). Transmission by either semen or blood accounts for virtually all reported cases.
> There are no reported cases of the transmission of the AIDS virus in a school setting. The CDC has stated that "[n]one of the identified cases of [AIDS] infection in the United States are known to have been transmitted in the school, day-care, or foster-care setting or through casual person-to-person contact."
> The overwhelming weight of medical evidence is that the AIDS virus is not transmitted by human bites, even bites that break the skin. . . . Any theoretical risk of transmission of the AIDS virus . . . in connection with . . . attendance in regular kindergarten class is so remote that it cannot form the basis for any exclusionary action. . . .[28]

A relatively recent case illustrating the application of the EHA and Section 504 concerns a trainable mentally handicapped (TMH) 7-year-old who, because of blood transfusions, also had AIDS.[29] The child was not toilet trained, had a disease that can cause blood to appear in the saliva, and sucked her thumb. A federal court of appeals ruled that under the EHA an appropriate placement for the child was the district's TMH class and that "a 'remote theoretical possibility' of transmission with respect to tears, saliva, and urine" did not "rise to the 'significant' risk level" required for exclusion from the TMH class.[30] This case, like the last one discussed, suggests that theoretical possibilities will not be considered in the face of overwhelming medical evidence that AIDS is not transmitted in schools.

What is an "appropriate education"?

The **Amy Rowley** *Case.* The Supreme Court first began to define "appropriate education" in the case of *Board of Education v. Rowley.*[31] (See Appendix D.) Rejecting previous judicial interpretations that the EHA required states to "maximize the potential of each handicapped child commensurate with the opportunity provided nonhandicapped children,"[32] the Supreme Court held that educators must provide "personalized instruction with sufficient support services to permit the child to benefit educationally from the instruction."[33]

The *Rowley* case involved a young hearing-impaired student, Amy Rowley, who was being educated in a regular elementary school classroom. She was assisted by a hearing aid and, in addition, attended speech-therapy sessions three hours a week and a special tutorial one hour a day. Amy's parents approved of the educational plan for their daughter, but they also wanted her to have a sign-language interpreter, despite the fact that when an interpreter had been used experimentally the year before, Amy seemed not to need the special help. After much consultation, the parents' request for an interpreter was denied.

A series of appeals by Amy's parents followed, resulting in a 1982 decision by the Supreme Court. Applying the definition of an "appropriate education" to Amy, the court found that she was receiving "personalized instruction and related services," was "advancing easily from grade to grade," and was performing "better than the average child in her classes." Because all the procedural requirements of the EHA had been followed and because the facts supported the conclusion that Amy's education was "adequate," the Court held that the EHA had not been violated in this case.

Although the *Rowley* decision does not in any way preclude individual states or local school districts from attempting to maximize the potential of a handicapped child (and indeed some states have set higher standards by legislation), it does signal that federal law sets only two major requirements: (1) that states comply with the procedural requirements of the EHA regarding the creation of policies, general plans, and IEPs for educating handicapped students, and (2) that the IEPs developed enable students to *benefit* educationally. This is the "basic floor of opportunity" required by federal law.

What "related services" must be provided to students with handicapping conditions?

Federal law defines "related services" as "transportation, and such developmental, corrective, and other support services . . . as may be required to assist a handicapped child to benefit from special education."[34] Included are "speech pathology and audiology, psychological services, physical and occupational therapy, recreation, and medical and counseling services, except that such medical services shall be for diagnostic and evaluative purposes only."[35] Related services need not be provided to students not needing special education, even though the student may have a handicapping condition (e.g., an orthopedic handicap), and only need to be provided to special education students when necessary to help them get an education.

In the case of Amy Rowley it was not disputed that a sign-language interpreter was a related service. The only question was whether or not that service was needed to enable Amy to benefit educationally. One can imagine a variety of related services that, although expensive, might be necessary for particular children with particular handicaps to benefit—a sign-language interpreter among them. Questions of a different sort have arisen, however, regarding certain aspects of the federal definition of "related services."

It is immediately clear, on reading the law, that problems were inevitable regarding the definition of "medical services" and which of these are *not* included among "related services." Is periodic catheterization to allow a child to urinate normally during school hours a covered related service or an excluded medical service? Is psychotherapy (which in some states can be provided only by a physician) a covered psychological or counseling service or an excluded medical service?

A federal court of appeals affirmed in 1983 that when a child needs a life support service such as catheterization, which must be performed during school hours by a qualified person, such service is a related service.[36] The court, using an instrument analysis, noted that without the service the child, who had spina bifida, could not benefit from her education because she would not be able to attend school at all.

In the arguments the Supreme Court heard in this case in 1984, the child's attorney said that a related service is one that allows a child meaningful access to education. The school district's attorney argued that catheterization is a medical service not done for purposes of diagnosis or evaluation and therefore is not covered under the EHA.[37] In its second interpretation of EHA provisions, the Court ruled in July 1984, in the case of *Irving Independent School District v. Tatro*,[38] that the school must provide the necessary catheterization twice a day. The Court said that services permitting a handicapped child to "remain at school during the day are no less related to the effort to educate than are services that enable the child to reach, enter, or exit school." Catheterization, which is a simple procedure taking only an hour to learn and five minutes to administer, is a "related service" in the same way that dispensing necessary medicine and administering emergency injections pursuant to medical authorization are related services.

Whether or not psychotherapy is a related service has been answered in the affirmative.[39] When a private mental-health program in which a child had been placed by virtue of public authority sought to recover the costs of psychotherapy from the parents of an emotionally disturbed boy, the court ruled that such services are "related" within the meaning of the EHA. The court reasoned that providing psychotherapy is consistent with the intent of Congress, as inferred from the specific authorization of psychological and counseling services. Although it is relatively clear that psychotherapy provided by persons who are not physicians would be considered a related service, the Supreme Court's decision in the *Tatro* case suggests that psychotherapy provided by a physician generally would not be covered under the "related services" provision of the EHA.

More recently, courts have been faced with parental requests to include extensive, in-school nursing services among the EHA's related services. In the case of a 7-year-old child named Bevin, who had severe, multiple handicaps requiring the constant attention of a specially trained nurse, it had to be determined if such care was a covered related service or a nondiagnostic medical service excluded from EHA's coverage.[40] There was no question that the service was necessary to allow Bevin to attend school and there was no dispute about Bevin's placement in a class with six handicapped students, one teacher, and two aides. Expenses for the nurse were $1850 a month, in 1984–1985, which did not include up to $1,000 of additional expenses for Bevin's needs outside of school. Unlike clean intermittent catheterization and tracheostomy care, which previously had been held to be related services,[41] the services in the *Bevin H.* case were "varied and intensive," "time-consuming and expensive," and necessary to prevent a "life-threatening" situation. Case law precedent, and the EHA and attendant regulations, convinced the court that classifying these extensive services as related services did "not appear to be consistent with the Act and the regulations."

Although Bevin did not have to be hospitalized, she had fetal face syndrome, was profoundly mentally handicapped, suffered from spastic quadriplegia and a seizure disorder, among other things, and was legally blind. She also breathed through a tracheostomy tube and was fed and given medicine through a gastrostomy tube. She made "inconsistent and minimal" progress in a program designed to "improve [her] awareness of and interaction with the world around her." It is perhaps this type of situation that has led the courts to search for a definition of related services that is "within reason" and, more recently, has raised the question that follows.

Are there limits to a state's responsibility under the EHA to educate severely and profoundly handicapped individuals?

Probably not. Despite ever-increasing burdens on the educational system resulting from medical advances that permit more and more severely handicapped children to survive, the overwhelming majority of states and districts have attempted to educate *all* children, even those whose potential for education, in the broadest sense, has appeared extremely limited.[42] It was widely assumed throughout the early to mid-1980s and beyond that the EHA's mandate to educate *all* handicapped children meant what it said, that is, that it implemented a zero-reject policy. A 1988 federal district court decision, however, brought that assumption into question.[43] The court, sitting in New Hampshire, ruled that where a child, Timothy W., was so severely physically and mentally handicapped as to have no potential for learning, the school district was not obligated to provide services.

Perhaps not surprisingly, the *Timothy W.* case was reversed in 1989 by the First

Circuit Court of Appeals.[44] The appeals court, after a lengthy review of the EHA, its legislative history, and pertinent case law, concluded that Congress unequivocally intended the act to apply to all children; in fact, the most severely handicapped children were to be given priority. The court discovered no evidence to suggest that an ability to benefit from education was a prerequisite to obtaining services under the act.

While the appellate decision above appears completely correct on the law, commentary following the district court's decision in the *Timothy W.* case suggests that Congress's policy decision may be creating untenable problems for public school systems and that we may not have heard the last of this issue. One writer said that the public schools "possess neither the financial nor the professional expertise to provide or oversee the services that children like Timothy need. Requiring them to do so is an unrealistic diversion of resources and attention. Our public-education system, already severely overstrained, should not be expected to make up for the shortfalls in our social-services system."[45] To remedy such a situation, another legal scholar has suggested a need for cooperation between various state agencies so that school districts will not be totally responsible for services that may well be beyond their competence to deliver, both in terms of cost and expertise.[46]

Must states provide a full-year educational program to handicapped children rather than the normal 180 days?

In some cases, yes. When a child's educational, social, emotional, or physical development would suffer if only the traditional 9- or 10-month period of education were provided, it may be necessary under the EHA to make services available for a longer duration. Lower federal courts that have considered the issue of regression, particularly among profoundly or severely mentally retarded individuals, have unanimously ruled that policies limiting education to 180 days or precluding the consideration of individual needs violate the EHA.[47] Relying heavily on the EHA's mandate of an individually tailored educational plan, the lower federal courts have struck down any policy that would preclude consideration of unique educational needs:

> The Act requires the state to treat each child as an individual, a human whose unique qualities and needs can be evaluated and served only by a plan designed with wisdom, care and educational expertise. Its grand design does not tolerate policies that impose a rigid pattern on the education of children. Each IEP must be prepared on the basis of an individual evaluation of a particular boy or girl. The child and his or her parents and guardians can exact no more. The state must provide no less.[48]

Although action by the Supreme Court in 1984 cast some doubt on the above reasoning,[49] lower federal courts have continued to approve full-year placements, including transportation and other support services, when necessary for the child to avoid regression.[50]

What if the parents of a handicapped child prefer a local, mainstreamed placement and the school district a distant, specialized one, or vice versa?

Federal law provides that, in order to receive funding, states must establish

> procedures to assure that, to the maximum extent appropriate, handicapped children, . . . are educated with children who are not handicapped, and that special classes, separate schooling, or other removal of handicapped children from the regular educational environment occurs only when the nature or severity of the handicap is such that education in regular classes with the use of supplementary aids and services cannot be achieved satisfactorily.[51]

As a matter of federal educational policy, then, "mainstreaming" (education in a regular classroom to the extent possible) or education in the "least restrictive environment" is a necessary consideration in all placement determinations for handicapped children. In other words, for an education to be appropriate, it must not only enable a child to *benefit* educationally, but it must be provided in the *least restrictive environment*. Also, placements must be made in the school the child would attend if not handicapped, if possible, or as close as practicable to the child's home. Given the federal policy favoring mainstreaming, it was inevitable that challenges would arise where one party (either the parent or the school district) would prefer a less restrictive environment.

In a case where an 18-year-old mentally retarded girl's IEP called for placement in a special classroom in a regular public school (with the addition of a special summer program), her parents sought placement in a private, year-long day school.[52] They believed that, because their daughter had been attending the day school for several years before moving into the new school district, a change would cause her to regress psychologically and developmentally. Although it was conceded that both programs would benefit the girl, the court relied on the EHA's mainstreaming philosophy to conclude that placement in the regular public school was "satisfactory" and might even be of "greater benefit" than remaining in the private school.

Affirmation of mainstreaming can also be seen in a case where the parents of a hearing-impaired child preferred a placement within the local school district (with support services) rather than at a distant state school for the deaf.[53] Even though the court determined that the school for the deaf would be the better placement, it concluded that the local school placement would be both appropriate and less restrictive.

These cases clearly demonstrate that once it is determined that two alternative placements are satisfactory, in the sense that both would benefit the child, courts will uphold the federal preference for placement in the less restrictive environment. In most instances this will result in the child being placed in a school situation in or near the school the child would have attended if not handicapped. On the other hand, there are times when mainstreaming simply is not appropriate, as in the case of a blind, hearing-impaired boy with emotional problems whose placement in a state school was affirmed despite parental objection.[54] Thus, proximity is a relevant consideration in placement decisions, but it is not of such importance that it can override other considerations of appropriateness; only part of what makes a placement appropriate is the extent to which it is less restrictive than other placements. The notion that mainstreaming is the preferred placement permeates federal law.[55] Only in that context can proximity become part of the decision-making process.

Does providing an education in the least restrictive environment mean that educators must provide specialized services in every school in which a need for them exists?

Not necessarily. In a case where all parties agreed that a child with learning disabilities and emotional problems needed to be placed in a "self-contained" learning disabilities program for at least three hours a day, a controversy arose over where that placement would be.[56] The local school district determined that the child should be placed in the only self-contained program in the country, a centrally located program that served approximately 10 students. The child's parents, however, asked that a self-contained program be established at their child's local school, which was a half-hour closer to home by bus.

Although the court noted that federal regulations require placement "as close as possible to the child's home" and, if possible, in the school the child would normally attend, it also noted an exception in those cases where a child's IEP called for a different placement. Regarding the state's role in determining how to spend educational dollars, the court said,

> It hardly needs to be stated that educational funding is not unlimited. It follows, therefore, that competing interests must be balanced to reach a reasonable accommodation. On the one hand are the undeniably important personal needs of the individual handicapped child, on the other, the realities of limited funding and the necessity of assisting in the education of all handicapped children. These competing interests must be considered. Indeed, failure to consider them would ultimately work to circumvent congressional intention to educate *all* handicapped children as best as practicable.[57]

The court held that the school district had reached a "reasonable accommodation" in making available a centrally located self-contained program to meet the needs of the few students who needed it. It should be noted that there was no disagreement about the appropriateness of the program; it is doubtful that financial considerations would prove as persuasive in a situation where a school district made no provision at all for necessary educational services.

Who is responsible for paying the costs associated with special education?

Although money for special-education programs comes from the federal government under the EHA and is used, in most states, in combination with state and local funding, a federal district court has recently clarified that the ultimate responsibility for such matters rests with the state.[58] In a controversy over who would pay the costs of the private residential placements of a number of students, the court said,

> It is the court's opinion and ruling that the State of Oregon's receipt of federal funds for assistance in educating these plaintiffs requires the State of Oregon to comply with its part of the bargain—namely, to provide sufficient funds to cover the cost of their educations. Budgetary constraints do not excuse the State of Oregon from the obligations arising from the acceptance of federal funds.[59]

Thus, it appears that states must pass legislation that will assure funding to meet their contractual obligations—from state and/or local sources—or provide sufficient funding from state treasuries to complement the money received under the EHA.

When must a handicapped child be provided with a residential placement?

Surely the most expensive type of educational program is the intensive, structured, 24-hour-a-day residential placement, which may be necessary in order for some handicapped children to obtain educational benefits. Federal law defines "special education" as "specially designed instruction, at no cost to parents or guardians, to meet the unique needs of a handicapped child, including classroom instruction, instruction in physical education, home instruction, and instruction in hospitals and institutions."[60]

One case that illustrates the need for a residential placement involved a severely retarded 16-year-old boy whose mental age was under 4 years old.[61] He was unable to speak, could not care for himself at all, was unable to apprehend danger, and was seriously emotionally disturbed. The boy was described as a "truly 'atypical child' for whom learning is extraordinarily difficult."[62]

The issue confronted by the judiciary was whether it was necessary for this handicapped boy to be provided with "more continual instruction and reinforcement" than was available in the day program proposed by his school district. Although it noted that the EHA "does not authorize residential care merely to enhance an *otherwise sufficient* day program" or to "remedy a poor home setting," the court found, in this case, that a more comprehensive and structured program was essential to allow for "*any* educational progress."[63] When the school district argued that residential care was custodial and not educational, the court embraced the notion that the term "education" as applied to severely or profoundly retarded children must be broadly construed to include the basic skills of living and self-preservation. A decision as to whether or not educational benefit could be achieved in an institutional placement or a group home was left to educators; the court reaffirmed only that some educational benefit be provided. In another case, where a child suffered from chronic, undifferentiated schizophrenia, the court upheld reimbursement to parents for the cost of a residential placement.[64] "As long as the child is properly educable only through a residential placement [in this case, a psychiatric hospital], when the medical, social or emotional problems that require hospitalization create or are intertwined with the educational problem, the states remain responsible for the costs of the placement [excluding purely medical costs]."[65]

As is clear from the *Rowley* case discussed previously, placements under the EHA need not provide the best possible education for a handicapped child. However, when a child is not able to benefit from anything other than education in a structured residential environment, the state or local school district must provide and pay for education and normal attendant services, including room and board. And while these costs may be substantial, as evidenced by a 1984 placement costing $88,000 a year,[66] "cost considerations are only relevant when choosing between several [appropriate] options. . . ."[67]

A partial solution to the cost problem associated with residential placements may be in recognizing the need for additional placement options for seriously emotionally disturbed (SED) students. At times, parents and/or schools prefer that the SED child be classified as learning disabled (LD) (because of the stigma of an SED label or inadequate facilities for SED students), virtually assuring inappropriate educational and supportive services. Furthermore, SED students, particularly those that are unclassified or misclassified, become troublemakers, drop out, or get expelled from school, and remain unaided during those years when help should be available. Although psychiatric hospitals are one option for some of these students, their greatest needs as a group appear to be accurate identification, earlier intervention, and a full range of educational options and supportive services.

May parents unilaterally transfer their handicapped child to a private school and then recover their costs from the local school district?

Only if the school district's proposed placement is judicially determined to be inappropriate and that of the parents appropriate. The Supreme Court, in the 1985 case of *Burlington School Committee v. Department of Education*,[68] ruled that despite the EHA's stay-put provision (requiring that the child remain in the current placement pending administrative or judicial review of a placement controversy), parents could recover in unusual circumstances. Although parents act at their own financial risk, and will not recover if the district's proposed placement meets minimal standards of appropriateness,[69] recovery was necessary to assure the child's right to an appropriate education. Subsequent cases have followed *Burlington*[70] and clarified that the parents' chosen placement must be appropriate (e.g., it must be a state-approved special-education placement)[71] and that the schools will lose if they neglect to provide for optimal mainstreaming.[72]

Can compensatory education be awarded beyond age 21 to students who have been denied an appropriate education?

Although this question is not entirely settled, recent federal courts of appeals decisions have approved awards of compensatory education.[73] In a case where a private school for blind and retarded students closed, leaving a 20-year-old with no educational placement during a protracted hearing process, the court affirmed the award of a year-and-a-half compensatory education beyond age 21.[74] The hearing officer, whose decision is mandated within 45 days, took 13 months to make a decision; and, there was an additional three-month delay attributable to other state administrative irregularities. "Obviously the federal regulations were grossly violated in this case."[75]

Relying on the Supreme Court's decision in *Burlington* (see previous section), the court noted that "equitable considerations are relevant in fashioning a remedy." Believing that Congress did not intend to create a right with no remedy, and that the student's entitlement to an education should not depend upon the parents' ability to fund a placement and then seek to recover their costs, the court awarded the prospective relief.

LANGUAGE BARRIERS AND EDUCATION

Must educators take affirmative steps to overcome the educational problems encountered by students whose native language is not English?

Yes. In a landmark decision in 1974, *Lau v. Nichols*,[76] the Supreme Court found that there was "no equality of treatment" where more than half the students of Chinese descent in San Francisco received no instruction to overcome English-language deficiencies. When the state requires, as a prerequisite to high school graduation, that children attend school and become proficient in English, it is not enough to provide nonnative speakers with the "same facilities, textbooks, teachers, and curriculum" that native speakers receive. Such treatment, the Court noted, was not equal, because "students who do not understand English are effectively foreclosed from any meaningful education. . . ."

> Basic English skills are at the very core of what these public schools teach. Imposition of a requirement that, before a child can effectively participate in the educational program, he must already have acquired those basic skills is to make a mockery of public education.[77]

The Chinese students did not seek any particular remedy and the Court did not impose one. Allowing educators to make the final policy decision regarding the method to be used to overcome the identified inequalities, the Court merely said, "Teaching English to the students of Chinese ancestry who do not speak the language is one choice. Giving instructions to this group in Chinese is another. There may be others."[78]

Although the particular federal statute[79] relied upon by the Court in *Lau* might not be applied in the same way today, it is clear that the *result* would be the same.[80] Under the Equal Educational Opportunities Act of 1974 (EEOA), states may not "deny equal educational opportunity to an individual" because of "the failure by an educational agency to take appropriate action to overcome language barriers that impede equal participation by its students."[81] As one court has recently said,

[T]he essential holdings of *Lau*, i.e., that schools are not free to ignore the need of limited English speaking children for language assistance to enable them to participate in the instructional program of the district, has now been legislated by Congress, acting pursuant to its power to enforce the [equal protection clause of the] fourteenth amendment.[82]

If the EEOA provision continues to be strictly applied, schools will have an obligation to provide language assistance to each nonnative speaker who demonstrates such a need, an obligation that has become increasingly important in the last decade as the numbers of refugee and immigrant children have grown.

Are school districts required to provide bilingual instruction to nonnative speakers of English?

Not unless state law requires it. But, in order to answer this question appropriately, it is first necessary to define "bilingual" education, along with the other possible methods of instruction.

For many years there has been great controversy over the best method for educating nonnative speakers of English. The only approach that is definitively disallowed at the present time is the "sink-or-swim" approach illustrated by *Lau*. It simply is not appropriate to provide no special help at all to those who demonstrate a compelling need for language assistance. Unless state law requires a particular approach, as some state laws do, schools may choose to offer instruction in English as a Second Language (ESL) for several hours each day or week. This is essentially a pull-out approach, where students needing help receive special English-language instruction but otherwise attend regular classes.

Another approach that has been widely used is that of transitional bilingual education, where students are given English-language instruction but are taught the regular curriculum (e.g., math, history, science) in their native language. This procedure is intended to be "transitional," in the sense that it is expected that the students eventually will be able to pursue all of their usual studies in English.

Another form of bilingual education is not intended to be transitional. In these types of programs, sometimes called "maintenance programs," students continue to learn in both English and their native languages throughout their school years. Both types of bilingual education have majority support among Hispanics, the largest language minority in the country, and among non-Hispanics as well.[83] Only a minority of non-Hispanics, however, favor bilingual instruction in situations where students already speak English. Other, lesser-used models combine language instruction with linguistic and cultural enrichment and include programs to improve native language skills, bilingual–bicultural education (where two languages and cultures are studied), and multilingual–multicultural education.

It is a virtual certainty that debate will continue over the best educational method for use with nonnative speakers of English. Some persons argue that bilingual education, for example, can be "ineffective and even harmful,"[84] and others argue that it promotes social and political integration of both students and their families.[85]

Still others believe that there is no one best method and that educators should be free to try a variety of approaches in different situations. As one court has said, "We think Congress' use of the less specific term, 'appropriate action,' rather than 'bilingual education,' indicates that Congress intended to leave state and local educational authorities a substantial amount of latitude in choosing the programs and techniques they would use to meet their obligations under [federal law]."[86]

Although congressional and popular support for bilingual education grew throughout the 1970s and into the 1980s, moderated to some degree during the Reagan administration, and picked up in the early years of the Bush administration, no one method is universally required by law. A federal district court ruled in 1989, for example, that a program that relied heavily on ESL and "sheltered English" approaches did not violate federal law.[87] However, advocates for limited-English-proficient (LEP) students continued to suggest that bilingual programs would more easily satisfy the federal requirement for appropriate programs.[88] In 1989, both the U.S. secretary of education and the head of the office of bilingual education and minority-language affairs voiced continued support for native-language instruction for LEP students.[89]

Must educators take steps to overcome language barriers encountered by students who speak nonstandard English?

In some situations, yes. Section 1703(f) of the Equal Educational Opportunities Act of 1974[90] covers all language barriers that limit a student's access to educational benefits on account of race, color, sex, or national origin. In the case of *Martin Luther King Junior Elementary School Children v. Ann Arbor School District Board*,[91] a federal district court went beyond providing protections for students whose native language was other than English and ruled that school districts must also aid those who speak nonstandard American English.

> The art of communication among the people of the country in all aspects of people's lives is a basic building block in the development of each individual. Children need to learn to speak and understand and to read and write the language used by society to carry on its business, to develop its science, arts and culture, and to carry on its professional and governmental functions.[92]

At the time of the foregoing litigation, Martin Luther King Junior Elementary School, a school in Ann Arbor, Michigan, with over 500 students, was a modern school with a black student population of approximately 13 percent. Most of the black students who attended the school lived in the Green Road Housing Project, came from single-parent families, and were less affluent than their school-age peers.[93] They spoke a variety of nonstandard English, often referred to as "black English," that did not cause oral communication problems at home or in school but did appear to impede their ability to read standard American English. An example of black English that illustrates the characteristic use of the word "be" as a verb can be seen in the following statement of one of the plaintiff children: "That teacher, he too mean. He be hollin at us and stuff."[94]

The use of black English by these children, although not a language barrier in and of itself, was found by the court to be implicated in the students' learning difficulties. The court found it necessary for the teachers, many of whom were white, to learn more about black English and to use that knowledge in devising better methods of teaching reading to the students involved. In this way, the court hoped that the students would be effectively instructed in a manner that would ensure their equal participation in the educational program of the school.

Although it is not yet clear how widely the federal mandate to overcome language barriers will be applied by the judiciary, school districts should take action to deal with the barriers that result from students' greater knowledge of a foreign language than of English, from black English, and probably from native American Indian languages as well.[95] In keeping with the spirit of federal law, school districts might also wish to consider learning problems that may be associated with those who speak other identified vernaculars, such as rural-Appalachian, poor-southern-white, or working-class English. The art of "communication" is a "basic building block" for all of us—and, as the judiciary has noted, its importance is societal as well as individual.

EDUCATION OF THE GIFTED AND TALENTED

Who are the gifted and talented students?

According to legislation passed in 1988,[96] "gifted and talented students" refers to

> children and youth who give evidence of high performance capability in areas such as intellectual, creative, artistic, or leadership capacity, or in specific academic fields, and who require services or activities not ordinarily provided by the school in order to fully develop such capabilities.

It should be noted that the definition in this act, like other contemporary concepts of "gifted and talented," goes beyond the popular conception of the "academically" talented or the high-IQ student to include those with special leadership, creative, artistic, and other abilities.

For most of the twentieth century it has been thought that, in addition to possessing unique individual potentialities, gifted and talented students represent an important national resource. Many educators and many advocates for the gifted believe that these children have special needs that are every bit as important as the special needs of handicapped and language-minority children, and some people feel that this group is being denied a right to equal educational opportunity. But whatever their legal rights, it is clear that the gifted and talented have not been favored, as a matter of educational policy or law, among those students who require individualized educational attention if they are to receive an appropriate education.

Does federal law require that gifted and talented students be provided with educational services to meet their unique needs?

No. Although federal government funds have been used from the late-1950s post-Sputnik era to the present to fund a variety of special educational programs for the gifted, receipt of these relatively small amounts by the states has never been conditioned on identifying and serving all gifted and talented children.[97] Furthermore, the federal commitment to gifted education, which reached relatively high levels in the 1970s, declined in the 1980s, and only recently has been revived. The federal Office of Gifted and Talented, which was created subsequent to a comprehensive 1972 federal study of the needs of gifted children,[98] was abolished in the early 1980s, leaving no one in the federal government to assume an official leadership role for gifted children.[99]

What has the federal government done to support special programs for the gifted and talented?

The first federal categorical funds for improving the educational opportunities of gifted and talented children were provided by Congress in 1974.[100] This effort was expanded with the passage of the Gifted and Talented Children's Education Act of 1978,[101] which allowed the federal government to share in the cost of identifying and meeting the educational needs of gifted children in both public and private schools.

After the act was repealed in October of 1982, gifted education had to compete for funds with over 30 separate educational programs that became part of the Elementary and Secondary Education Block Grant Program of the Reagan administration.[102] By 1986, only 13 percent of school districts used any of the Block Grant funds for education of gifted and talented students,[103] setting the stage for new legislation.

The Jacob K. Javits Gifted and Talented Students Education Act of 1988,[104] authorized $20 million for fiscal 1989 to be used for research, demonstration projects, and personnel training, with highest priority directed toward the identification and education of gifted students who were economically disadvantaged, limited English proficient, and/or handicapped. The legislation also authorized the creation of a federally funded National Center for Research and Development in the Education of Gifted and Talented Children and Youth, an additional indication of a renewed federal government presence in the gifted education movement.

What have the states done to encourage the appropriate education of gifted students?

As of the 1981–1982 school year, all but 13 states provided an average of approximately $100 to $1,500 per year to meet the special needs of each identified gifted child.[105] Most of these states provided funds as part of their special education budget or as a separate categorical grant to aid gifted education, but only 14 states mandated the identification and education of these students.[106]

Just as all states have not made efforts to educate the gifted and talented, not all of these students receive special services—even in the states where these services are available. Although it has been estimated that up to 15 percent of the school-age population may be gifted or talented—including many handicapped, language-minority, and poor children—the states serving these students in 1983 provided special services or programs for only 2.6 percent of the student population.[107] Among the states that serve more gifted and talented students than the national average are the populous states of New York, Texas, and California.[108]

In Pennsylvania, which has been a leader in the education of gifted students, "exceptional" children are defined by state law to include children who are gifted as well as those with handicapping conditions. All exceptional children must be provided with an appropriate educational program that meets their individual needs. A 1985 Pennsylvania Supreme Court opinion, which affirmed the necessity of individualized instruction for a student with exceptional math and reading abilities, made clear that gifted students were entitled to specially tailored programs.[109] However, the court noted that the law did not require "individual tutors or exclusive individual programs outside or beyond the district's existing regular and special education curricular offerings."[110] Despite Pennsylvania's leadership, the latter statement reflects a general attitude to strictly construe the relatively limited entitlements of gifted students.

In contrast to Pennsylvania's mandatory program, gifted education in New York State, for example, is permissive. Although local school districts are encouraged to develop special programs for gifted students, they need not do so and, when programs are available, not all gifted students need be served.[111]

Probably because of the general judicial deference to educational decision making, coupled with a perception that identification or selection for gifted programs carries lesser consequences than for programs for the handicapped, courts have tended not to look closely at identification and selection practices. Gifted education has not become a high federal or state priority, in general; so, it is not surprising that IQ scores, standing alone, and lotteries to select a portion of the eligible gifted students for a special program, have appeared reasonable to legislatures and courts.[112]

It seems clear that programs for the gifted and talented could benefit from additional legislative and funding initiatives at the state level. Although it is generally thought that the states have held firm in recent years in their commitments to the gifted and talented, the reduced federal presence in gifted education could have a negative effect at the state level if not reversed.

SUMMARY AND CONCLUSIONS

From the mid-1960s to the present, the attention of the federal government has been focused as never before on the special needs of students in public and private schools. Motivated in large part by external events and by pressure from special advocacy groups, in recent years Congress has provided financial support for education in excess of $15 billion per year. The major beneficiaries of this increased funding have been educationally disadvantaged children from low-income areas and children with handicapping conditions. Funds to aid children encountering language barriers and to provide special programs and services to gifted children have been lesser by comparison.

Federal monies to supplement the education provided by the states to disadvantaged children has been continuously available for over 25 years. It is likely that the federal mandate to provide comparable educational services to disadvantaged students attending private and parochial schools will not encounter prohibitive constitutional barriers, although the services may no longer be provided within parochial schools by publicly paid teachers.

Handicapped students are provided comprehensive educational services and procedural protections by the EHA in all states that receive federal dollars under the act. In the event that a state chose not to participate in the program, it is generally thought that Section 504 of the Rehabilitation Act nevertheless would afford handicapped children similar educational guarantees.

The EHA requires the provision of a free, appropriate public education—one that will allow all handicapped children to benefit meaningfully from their studies. It also requires that students be provided those "related services" that are necessary in order for them to realize educational benefits; these include necessary technological devices, transportation, school health services, psychological help and guidance, and other support services.

The procedural guarantees of the EHA help to ensure that placement decisions made pursuant to the act will be appropriate. Although these decisions have generated a substantial amount of controversy, if a school district can show that its placement decision will permit the child to benefit educationally in the least restrictive environment *for that child,* it is likely that the decision will stand. Federal law does not require the *best* placement, but only one that will allow educational opportunity to be meaningful.

Federal law also requires meaningful educational opportunity for nonnative speakers of English and for others who encounter language barriers on account of race, color, sex, or national origin. Even though bilingual education is favored by Hispanics (the largest language minority in the country) and by non-Hispanics as well, recent governmental and judicial actions appear to favor allowing questions of method to be determined at the state or local level. In this way, it is hoped that a variety of approaches will be tried (adding to our understanding of how to overcome language barriers) and that unique applications will develop to meet unique circumstances and needs.

Gifted and talented students are increasingly being recognized as "special" students who may underachieve or even drop out of school entirely if not educationally challenged. Thousands of children with special gifts and talents can be found throughout the school population—among the poor and educationally disadvantaged, among the handicapped, among limited-English-speaking children, and among those who are not noticed for any other "special" reason. Although these students, when identified early enough, have been among the indirect and direct beneficiaries of federal financial assistance, there has not yet been an effective, concerted, and coordinated national effort to identify and serve all gifted and talented students. These students, like other students with special needs, deserve to receive an education that is meaningful to them; and, when they do, society also will benefit—economically, politically, and socially. Gifted and talented students are indeed "special," but they cannot be recognized by race, color, creed, sex, national origin, or handicap. To aid them in realizing their educational potential is to aid all special groups.

IRVING INDEPENDENT SCHOOL DISTRICT V. TATRO
468 U.S. 883

CHIEF JUSTICE BURGER delivered the opinion of the Court.

We granted certiorari to determine whether the Education of the Handicapped Act or the Rehabilitation Act of 1973 requires a school district to provide a handicapped child with clean intermittent catheterization during school hours.

I

Amber Tatro is an 8-year-old girl born with a defect known as spina bifida. As a result, she suffers from orthopedic and speech impairments and a neurogenic bladder, which prevents her from emptying her bladder voluntarily. Consequently, she must be catheterized every three or four hours to avoid injury to her kidneys. In accordance with accepted medical practice, clean intermittent catheterization (CIC), a procedure involving the insertion of a catheter into the urethra to drain the bladder, has been prescribed. The procedure is a simple one that may be performed in a few minutes by a layperson with less than an hour's training. Amber's parents, babysitter, and teenage brother are all qualified to administer CIC, and Amber soon will be able to perform this procedure herself.

In 1979 petitioner Irving Independent School District agreed to provide special education for Amber, who was then three and one-half years old. In consultation with her parents, who are respondents here, petitioner developed an individualized education program for Amber. . . . The individualized education program provided that Amber would attend early childhood development classes and receive special services such as physical and occupational therapy. That program, however, made no provision for school personnel to administer CIC.

Respondents unsuccessfully pursued administrative remedies to secure CIC services for Amber during school hours. In October 1979 respondents brought the present action in District Court against petitioner, the State Board of Education, and others. . . . They sought an injunction ordering petitioner to provide Amber with CIC and sought damages and attorney's fees. First, respondents invoked the Education of the Handicapped Act. Because Texas received funding under that statute, petitioner was required to provide Amber with a "free appropriate public education," . . . which is defined to include "related services." Respondents argued that CIC is one such "related service." Second, respondents invoked § 504 of the Rehabilitation Act of 1973 . . . which forbids an individual, by reason of a handicap, to be "excluded from the participation in, be denied the benefits of, or be subjected to discrimination under" any program receiving federal aid.

. . .

We granted certiorari, 464 U.S.———(1983), and we affirm in part and reverse in part.

II

This case poses two separate issues. The first is whether the Education of the Handicapped Act requires petitioner to provide CIC services to Amber. The second is whether § 504 of the Rehabilitation Act creates such an obligation. We first turn to the claim presented under the Education of the Handicapped Act.

States receiving funds under the Act are obliged to satisfy certain conditions. A primary condition is that the state implement a policy "that assures all handicapped children the right to a free appropriate public education.". . .Each educational agency applying to a state for funding must provide assurances in turn that its program aims to provide "a free appropriate public education to all handicapped children.". . .

A "free appropriate public education" is explicitly defined as "special education and related services.". . . The term "special education" means

> specially designed instruction, at no cost to parents or guardians, to meet the unique needs of a handicapped child, including classroom instruction, instruction in physical education, home instruction, and instruction in hospitals and institutions. . . .

"Related services" are defined as

> transportation, and such developmental, corrective, and other *supportive services (including* speech pathology and audiology, psychological services, physical and occupational therapy, recreation, and *medical* and counselling *services, except that such medical services shall be for diagnostic and evaluation purposes only) as may be required to assist a handicapped child to benefit from special education,* and includes the early identification and assessment of handicapping conditions in children. . . .(emphasis added).

The issue in this case is whether CIC is a "related service" that petitioner is obliged to provide to Amber. We must answer two questions: first, whether CIC is a "supportive servic[e] . . . required to assist a handicapped child to benefit from special education"; and second, whether CIC is excluded from this definition as a "medical servic[e]" serving purposes other than diagnosis or evaluation.

A

The Court of Appeals was clearly correct in holding that CIC is a "supportive servic[e] . . . required to assist a handicapped child to benefit from special education." It is clear on this record that, without having CIC services available during the school day, Amber cannot attend school and thereby "benefit from special education." CIC services therefore fall squarely within the definition of a "supportive service."

As we have stated before, "Congress sought primarily to make public education available to handicapped children" and "to make such access meaningful." *Board of Education of Hendrick Hudson Central School District v. Rowley,* 458 U.S. 176, 192 (1982). A service that enables a handicapped child to remain at school during the day is an important means of providing the child with the meaningful access to education that Congress envisioned. The Act makes specific provision for services, like transportation, for example, that do no more than enable a child to be physically present in class . . . and the Act specifically authorizes grants for schools to alter buildings and equipment to make them accessible to the handicapped. . . . Services like CIC that permit a child to remain at school during the day are no less related to the effort to educate than are services that enable the child to reach, enter, or exit the school.

We hold that CIC services in this case qualify as a "supportive servic[e] . . . required to assist a handicapped child to benefit from special education."

B

We also agree with the Court of Appeals that provision of CIC is not a "medical servic[e]," which a school is required to provide only for purposes of diagnosis or evaluation. . . . We begin with the regulations of the Department of Education, which are entitled to deference. . . . The regulations define "related services" for handicapped children to include "school health services,". . .which are defined in turn as "services provided by a qualified school nurse or other qualified person.". . ."Medical services" are defined as "services provided by a licensed physician." . . . Thus, the Secretary has determined that the services of a school nurse otherwise qualifying as a "related service" are not subject to exclusion as a "medical service," but that the services of a physician are excludable as such.

This definition of "medical services" is a reasonable interpretation of congressional intent. Although Congress devoted little discussion to the "medical services" exclusion, the Secretary could reasonably have concluded that it was designed to spare schools from an obligation to provide a service that might well prove unduly expensive and beyond the range of their competence. From this understanding of congressional purpose, the Secretary could reasonably have concluded that Congress intended to impose the obligation to provide school nursing services.

Congress plainly required schools to hire various specially trained personnel to help handicapped children, such as "trained occupational therapists, speech therapists, psychologists, social workers and other appropriately trained personnel." . . . School nurses have long been a part of the educational system, and the Secretary could therefore reasonably conclude that school nursing services are not the sort of burden that Congress intended to exclude as a "medical service." By limiting the "medical services" exclusion to the services of a physician or hospital, both far more expensive, the Secretary has given a permissible construction to the provision.

. . .

To keep in perspective the obligation to provide services that relate to both the health and educational needs of handicapped students, we note several limitations that should minimize the burden petitioner fears. First, to be entitled to related services, a child must be handicapped so as to require special education. . . . In the absence of a handicap that requires special education, the need for what otherwise might qualify as a related service does not create an obligation under the Act. . . . Second, only those services necessary to aid a handicapped child to benefit from special education must be provided, regardless how easily a school nurse or layperson could furnish them. For example, if a particular medication or treatment may appropriately be administered to a handicapped child other than during the school day, a school is not required to provide nursing services to administer it.

Third, the regulations state that school nursing services must be provided only if they can be performed by a nurse or other qualified person, not if they must be performed by a physician. . . . It bears mentioning that here not even the services of a nurse are required; as is conceded, a layperson with minimal training is qualified to provide CIC. . . .

Finally, we note that respondents are not asking petitioner to provide *equipment* that Amber needs for CIC. . . . They seek only the *services* of a qualified person at the school.

We conclude that provision of CIC to Amber is not subject to exclusion as a "medical service," and we affirm the Court of Appeals' holding that CIC is a "related service" under the Education of the Handicapped Act.

III

Respondents sought relief not only under the Education of the Handicapped Act but under § 504 of the Rehabilitation Act as well. After finding petitioner liable to provide CIC under the former, the District Court proceeded to hold that petitioner was similarly liable under § 504 and that respondents were therefore entitled to attorney's fees under § 505 of the Rehabilitation Act. . . . We hold today, in *Smith v. Robinson,* ———— U.S.————(1984), that § 504 is inapplicable when relief is available under the Education of the Handicapped Act to remedy a denial of educational services. Respondents are therefore not entitled to relief under § 504. In all other respects, the judgment of the Court of Appeals is affirmed.

It is so ordered.

NOTES

1. Elementary and Secondary Education Act, 20 U.S.C. § 2701 *et seq.* (1982).
2. 20 U.S.C. § 1400 *et seq.* (1982).
3. Lau v. Nichols, 414 U.S. 563 (1974).
4. Bilingual Education Act (Title VII of the ESEA), 20 U.S.C. § 3321 *et seq.* (1982).
5. 20 U.S.C. § 3311 *et seq.* (Supp. V 1981) (repealed 1982). For a comprehensive review of education for the gifted, see Comments, *Equal Educational Opportunity for the Gifted and Talented: Is It Illusory Without the Right to a Free Appropriate Public Education?,* 1980 DET. C. OF L. REV. 957 (1980).
6. EDUC. DAILY, Apr. 27, 1984, at 1.
7. *See* Bell v. New Jersey, 103 S. Ct. 2107 (1983).
8. National Coalition for Pub. Educ. and Religious Liberty v. Harris, 489 F.Supp. 1248 (S.D. N.Y. 1980).
9. *See* Mueller v. Allen, 103 S. Ct. 3062 (1983) (educational tax deduction for parents of all children does not violate establishment clause).
10. Aguilar v. Felton, 473 U.S. 402 (1985).
11. Murakami & Pullin, *Establishment Clause Challenges to the Provision of Special Education Programs and Services,* 34 E.L.R. 639 (1986).
12. 29 U.S.C. § 794 (1982).
13. Southeastern Community College v. Davis, 442 U.S. 397, 406 (1979).
14. Wolf v. South Colonie Cent. School Dist., 534 F.Supp. 758 (N.D.N.Y. 1982).
15. *See supra* note 2.
16. Pub. L. No. 99–372, 100 Stat. 796.
17. 20 U.S.C. § 1415(e)(3)(b).
18. 20 U.S.C. § 1415(e)(3)(f).
19. *See, e.g.,* Mitten v. Muscogee County School Dist., 877 F.2d 932 (11th Cir. 1989); *but see,* Moore v. District of Columbia, 886 F.2d 335 (D.C. Cir. 1989). *See also* Mr. D. v. Glocester School Comm., 711 F.Supp. 66 (D. R.I. 1989) (attorneys fees awarded for work done leading to settlement).
20. Muth v. Central Bucks School Dist., 839 F.2d 113 (3rd Cir. 1988), *quoting* Hensley v. Eckerhart, 461 U.S. 424 (1983). The Supreme Court in *Hensley* also noted that "prevailing parties" are those who "succeed on any significant issue in litigation which achieves some of the benefits the parties sought. . . ." *Id.* at 433.

21. *See especially,* 20 U.S.C. §§ 1471–85.
22. 42 U.S.C. § 1983.
23. 20 U.S.C. § 1415(f).
24. 20 U.S.C. § 1401(a)(1).
25. 34 C.F.R. 104.3(j)(1).
26. *See, e.g.,* School Bd. v. Arline, 107 S.Ct. 1123 (1987) (person with contagious disease is handicapped under Sec. 504); Doe v. Belleville Pub. School Dist. No. 118, 673 F.Supp. 342 (S.D. Ill. 1987) (child with AIDS not handicapped under EHA and no exhaustion of administrative remedies required for Sec. 504 action).
27. Thomas v. Atascadero Unified School Dist., 662 F.Supp. 376 (C.D. Cal. 1987).
28. *Id.* at 380.
29. Martinez v. School Bd., 861 F.2d 1502 (11th Cir. 1988), *on remand,* 711 F.Supp. 1066 (M.D. Fla. 1989) (plaintiff ordered admitted).
30. *Id.* at 1506.
31. 102 S. Ct. 3034 (1982).
32. *Id.* at 3048.
33. *Id.* at 3049.
34. 20 U.S.C. § 1401(17) (1982).
35. *Id.*
36. Tatro v. Texas, 703 F.2d 830 (5th Cir. 1983), *aff'd in part and rev'd in part sub. nom.* Irving Indep. School Dist. v. Tatro, 468 U.S. 883 (1984).
37. Irving Indep. School Dist. v. Tatro, 468 U.S. 883 (1984).
38. *Id.,* 468 U.S. 883.
39. T. G. and P. G. v. Bd. of Educ., 576 F.Supp. 420 (D. N.J. 1983); *cf.,* Max M. v. Thompson, 592 F.Supp. 1437 (N.D. Ill. 1984). In the *Max M.* case, the plaintiff was allowed reimbursement for psychiatric services comparable to what a social worker, psychologist, or guidance counselor would have charged, where bad faith procedural violations were shown.
40. Bevin H. v. Wright, 666 F.Supp. 71 (W.D. Pa. 1987); *see also,* Detsel v. Board of Educ., 637 F.Supp. 1022 (N.D. N.Y. 1986), *aff'd per curiam,* 820 F.2d 587 (2d Cir. 1987).
41. *See, e.g.,* Irving Indep. School Dist. v. Tatro, 468 U.S. 883 (1984) and Katherine D., 727 F.2d 809 (9th Cir. 1983).
42. *See, e.g.,* Battle v. Commonwealth, 629 F.2d 269 (3rd Cir. 1980), *cert. denied,* 452 U.S. 986 (1981).
43. Timothy W. v. Rochester School Dist., No. C-84-733-L (D. N.H. 1988). *See also* Parks v. Pavkovic, 753 F.2d 1397 (7th Cir. 1985), *cert. denied,* 474 U.S. 918 (1985) (dicta suggesting unconscious child would be uneducable and thus beyond the EHA's responsibility).
44. Timothy W. v. Rochester School Dist., 875 F.2d 954 (1st Cir. 1989).
45. Rosenfeld, Educ. Week, Feb. 8, 1989, at 32.
46. McCarthy, *The Public School's Responsibility to Serve Severely Handicapped Children,* 49 ED. LAW REP. 453 (1988).
47. *See, e.g.,* Battle v. Pennsylvania, 629 F.2d 269 (3d Cir. 1980); Georgia Assn. of Retarded Citizens v. McDaniel, 511 F.Supp. 1263 (N.D. Ga. 1981), *aff'd,* 715 F.2d 1565 (11th Cir. 1983), *vacated* 52 U.S.L.W. 3932 (1984); Bucks County Pub. Schools v. Commonwealth, 529 A.2d 1201 (Pa. Commw. Ct. 1987).
48. Crawford v. Pittman, 708 F.2d 1028, 1030 (5th Cir. 1983).
49. In July 1984, the Supreme Court vacated the judgment of a federal court of appeals that disallowed a 180-day limitation on education for handicapped children. No reasoning was given. *See* Georgia Assn. of Retarded Citizens, 52 U.S.L.W. 3932 (1984).

50. *See, e.g.,* Alamo Hts. Indep. School Dist. v. State Bd. of Educ., 790 F.2d 1153 (5th Cir. 1986).
51. 20 U.S.C. § 1412.5 (1982).
52. Lang v. Braintree School Comm., 545 F.Supp. 1221 (D. Mass. 1982).
53. Springdale School Dist. v. Grace, 494 F.Supp. 266 (W.D. Ark. 1980), *aff'd.* 963 F.2d 41 (1982).
54. Bailey v. Unified School Dist. No. 345, 664 P.2d 1379 (Kan. 1983).
55. *See, e.g.,* Roncker v. Walter, 700 F.2d 1058, 1063 (6th Cir. 1983).
56. Pinkerton v. Moye, 509 F.Supp. 107 (W.D. Va. 1981).
57. *Id.* at 112–13.
58. Kerr Center Parents Assoc. v. Charles, 581 F.Supp. 166 (D. Ore. 1983).
59. *Id.* at 168.
60. 20 U.S.C § 1401.16 (1982).
61. Abrahamson v. Hershman, 701 F.2d 223 (1st Cir. 1983).
62. *Id.* at 224.
63. *Id.* at 227.
64. Vander Malle v. Ambach, 667 F.Supp. 1015 (S.D. N.Y. 1987).
65. *Id.* at 1039.
66. Clevenger v. Oak Ridge School Bd., 744 F.2d 514 (6th Cir. 1984).
67. *Id.* at 517.
68. 471 U.S. 359 (1985).
69. *See, e.g.,* Cain v. Yukon Pub. Schools, Dist. I-27, 775 F.2d 15 (10th Cir. 1985).
70. *See, e.g.,* Eugene B. Jr. v. Great Neck Union Free School Dist., 635 F.Supp. 753 (E.D. N.Y. 1986).
71. *See, e.g.,* Schimmel v. Spillane, 819 F.2d 477 (4th Cir. 1987); Tucker v. Bay Shore Union Free School Dist., 873 F.2d 563 (2d Cir. 1989).
72. Briggs v. Board of Educ., 707 F.Supp. 623 (D. Conn. 1988).
73. Burr v. Ambach, 863 F.2d 1071 (2d Cir. 1988); Miner v. Missouri, 800 F.2d 749 (8th Cir. 1986).
74. Burr v. Ambach, 863 F.2d 1071 (2d Cir. 1988).
75. *Id.* at 1075.
76. 414. U.S. 563 (1974).
77. *Id.*
78. *Id.*
79. Sec. 601 of the Civil Rights Act of 1964, 42 U.S.C. § 2000(d) (1982).
80. *See* Castenada v. Pickard, 648 F.2d 989 (5th Cir. 1981).
81. 20 U.S.C. § 1703(f) (1982).
82. Castenada, 648 F.2d at 1008.
83. 4 NATL. CLEARINGHOUSE FOR BILINGUAL EDUC. FORUM 1 (1983).
84. Baker & deKanter, *Response to "Evaluation and Incrementalism: The AIR Report and ESEA Title VII"*, 6 EDUC. EVALUATION & POL. ANALYSIS 189, 189 (1984).
85. *See supra* note 83 at 3.
86. Castenada, 648 F.2d at 1009.
87. Theresa P. v. Berkeley Unified School Dist., Education Week, Feb. 22, 1989, at 1, col. 1.
88. Educ. Week, Feb. 22, 1989, at 1, col. 1.
89. Educ. Week, May 24, 1989, at 1, col. 2.
90. *See supra* note 81 and accompanying text.
91. 473 F.Supp. 1371 (E.D. Mich. 1979).
92. *Id.* at 1372.
93. Lewis & Bates, *The Who, What, Why, When and How of the Ann Arbor Black English*

Case (or what it be like?), in THE ANN ARBOR BLACK ENGLISH CASE 3 (A. Brown ed. 1980).

94. Smitherman, *Talkin and Testifyin on Ann Arbor's Green Road,* in *id.* at 26.

95. *See* Heavy Runner v. Bremner, 522 F.Supp. 162 (D. Mont. 1981), where dicta suggest that educators must address Indian students' English language deficiencies.

96. Jacob K. Javits Gifted and Talented Students Education Act of 1988, 20 U.S.C. sec. 3061 *et seq.*

97. For an excellent historical, comparative, and philosophical view of the gifted education movement see *Comments, Equal Educational Opportunity for the Gifted and Talented: Is It Illusory Without the Right to a Free Appropriate Public Education?,* 1980 DET. C. L. REV. 957 (1980).

98. U.S. COMMISSIONER OF EDUCATION, 92D CONG., 2D SESS., REPORT ON EDUCATION OF THE GIFTED AND TALENTED (the Marland Report) (1972).

99. 130 CONG. REC. E1925–26 (daily ed. May 3, 1984) (remarks of Rep. Murphy).

100. Education Amendments of 1974, 20 U.S.C. § 1863 (1976).

101. Gifted and Talented Children's Educ. Act of 1978, 20 U.S.C. 3311 (repealed 1982).

102. 20 U.S.C. § 3801 *et seq.* (1982).

103. 1988 U.S. Code Cong. & Ad. News 135.

104. *Supra* note 96.

105. C. Kane, Gifted and Talented Education Funding Study: A Look at the Fifty States (July 1982) (unpublished manuscript).

106. *Id.*

107. THE CONDITION OF EDUCATION 33 (1983 ed.) (U.S. Government Printing Office).

108. *Id.*

109. Centennial School Dist. v. Commonwealth, 539 A.2d 785 (Pa. 1988).

110. *Id.* at 791.

111. Bennet v. City School Dist., 497 N.Y.S.2d 72 (N.Y. App. Div. 1985).

112. *See, e.g., id.*

CHAPTER 7

Behavior Control and Student Discipline

OVERVIEW

The time is long past when the guidance counselor's nearly exclusive responsibility was academic and vocational counseling. Along with the changing structure of the family, increased geographic mobility, financial insecurity, the weakening of traditional values, and other societal changes, an unprecedented variety of disciplinary and behavioral problems has appeared in the nation's public schools. Although the idealized role of the guidance counselor may not necessarily encompass behavioral control and student discipline, one of the nontraditional functions that many counselors have had to assume in recent years is that of disciplinarian.

This chapter begins with a consideration of fourth amendment issues related to search and seizure and their application to the search of students, their lockers, and possessions. It continues with an overview of the constitutional principles applicable to determining what type of procedural due process is necessary in various types of disciplinary situations, and proceeds to an examination of a variety of methods used to discipline students, ranging from the minimally intrusive in-school suspension or detention to more onerous forms of punishment including expulsion and corporal punishment. In addition to the general legal problems encountered, special limitations applicable to the discipline of students with handicapping conditions are considered, as are the legal implications of the disproportionate exclusion from school of minority students.

Major constitutional provisions related to the issues discussed in this chapter include the due process and equal protection principles of the fifth and fourteenth amendments, the fourth amendment prohibition against unreasonable searches, and the eighth amendment proscription against "cruel and unusual punishments." The major federal statutes of relevance are the Education of the Handicapped Act and

139

Section 504 of the Rehabilitation Act. The applicability of typical state statutory provisions is also mentioned.

THE PROHIBITION AGAINST UNREASONABLE SEARCHES

As you consider the questions that follow, imagine that you, as head of counseling at an area high school, are asked to serve on a committee, consisting of three teachers, the vice principal, two students, and yourself, to develop schoolwide policy on student discipline and due process. The development of this policy is mandated by the state and will be submitted to the state education department, along with the names of the committee members, after it has been approved by the school board. Because there has been an increasing number of reported drug sales at the high school, the policy is expected to have practical as well as theoretical benefits. The vice principal admits she is woefully ignorant of school law, and you suspect the same may be true of most of the other committee members. What advice will you be able to give in the course of the committee's deliberations?

What is a search?

The Supreme Court has developed the notion that if something illegal is in "plain view," it can be confiscated by a law enforcement officer and the Court will hold that no search has taken place. Because a search involves an intrusion on a person's reasonable expectation of privacy, there can be no reasonable expectation that a marijuana plant grown in a window facing a public street or carried along the sidewalk will be a private matter. On the other hand, because the fourth amendment protects people rather than places, there may well be an expectation of privacy when a person places a phone call in a public phone booth, just as there would be if the call were made from a private home telephone. A search, then, involves an intrusion by public officials on the privacy of an individual, with the greatest protection extending to bodily intrusions.

In the context of the public school, what is an "unreasonable search"?

The reasonableness of a search depends upon several contextual factors including the level of expectation of privacy, the degree of intrusiveness, and the necessity of obtaining the information or thing being sought. It can be assumed that people who deposit contraband in publicly owned lockers or relinquish control of their luggage to a common carrier have a lesser expectation of privacy. On the other hand, intrusive searches that involve blood samples, stomach pumping, strip searches, and the like require unusually high levels of justification. The necessity of the search also will vary with the nature of the materials being sought (e.g., a five-dollar bill versus a cache of illicit drugs) and with the location, (e.g., a person's house versus a school).

The **T.L.O.** *Case.* In 1985, the Supreme Court decided its first case concerning search and seizure in public schools. In *New Jersey v. T.L.O.*[1] (see Appendix D), the Court made clear not only that public school officials must not invade students' right to be free from unreasonable searches but that what is reasonable and unreasonable depends on the "context within which a search takes place." Students' legitimate expectations of privacy, the Court said, must be balanced against the need for the search. The Court put forth a twofold reasonableness test: (1) was the search justified at its inception, and (2) was it reasonable in scope? For a search to be justified, there must be reason to assume the search will uncover evidence of a violation of law or school rules. The scope of the search must be related to the objectives of the search and not excessively intrusive considering the type of infraction and the student's age and sex.

Is it necessary for school personnel to have a search warrant before conducting a search?

Years ago it was thought that public school officials could act *in loco parentis* (in place of the parents or in the same way that parents might act) in all disciplinary matters arising in schools. Parents always have been able to search their own children or their rooms, if they believed it desirable or necessary, so school administrators and counselors used to do likewise. *T.L.O.* has changed all that. Although police officers must have "probable cause," meaning specific evidence that contraband will be discovered in a search, and usually must also secure a search warrant, *T.L.O.* has made clear that the standard for student searches is *reasonableness.* As many lower courts had said in the past, a student search requires only "reasonable suspicion" or "reasonable cause to believe" that particular stolen goods, dangerous substances, and so on will be found. No search warrant is required if school officials act on their own, but there is substantial authority that the probable cause standard and a warrant would be necessary if police officers conducted the search or if the search were done at the behest of the police.[2] Because of the importance of maintaining a safe environment for the many students school officials must protect, the ordinary probable cause and warrant standard has been relaxed for public school personnel. However, administrators, counselors, and others should be aware that they are considered state officials and, as the Court said in *T.L.O.*, "cannot claim the [p]arents' immunity from the strictures of the fourth amendment."

Can trained dogs be used to search students, lockers, and cars for drugs?

The **Goosecreek** *Case.* School officials in Goosecreek, Texas, adopted a drug-detection program whereby trained Doberman pinschers and German shepherds were brought to elementary and secondary schools to sniff students, lockers, and cars for the presence of contraband.[3] After the dogs showed signs of alert to the substances they had been trained to recognize, the cars, the lockers, and the clothing of students were searched. The plaintiffs in the case were students who had been searched by school officials, a search that yielded nothing more incriminating than a bottle of perfume. They claimed that the fourth amendment right of students at Goosecreek High School to be free from unreasonable searches had been violated. The federal district court held that the sniffing by dogs was not an unreasonable search, but the Federal Court of Appeals for the Fifth Circuit disagreed with regard to the sniffing of the students themselves.

The court of appeals first considered whether the sniffing of objects and people by dogs constituted a search. Reasoning by analogy from cases that had allowed for sniffing of luggage, storage lockers, and the like, the court said that dogs could be used to sniff *objects* because they were in the public space, so to speak. A "public smell," as the court called it, was analogous to seeing something in "plain view," and therefore simply was not, in a constitutional sense, a search at all. The court also said that it would be necessary to show that the dogs were reasonably reliable in their ability to detect the presence of drugs or other contraband before even lockers or cars could be opened.

Having determined that the sniff of a car or locker was not a search, but that it might lead to a "reasonable suspicion" that opening the objects would uncover contraband and therefore be reasonable, the court turned to the question of whether the sniff of a person constituted a search. Because the fourth amendment is especially intended to protect individuals from intrusive invasions of their privacy, the court held that close sniffing of students by dogs was indeed a search within the meaning of that amendment. The next question to determine was whether or not such a search was reasonable, given the importance of maintaining a safe school environment for all students.

By balancing the intrusiveness of a search against the importance of discovering whatever is being searched for, magnomoter searches at airports have been upheld, as have so-called stop-and-frisk searches of persons suspected of engaging in criminal activity. Although the court in *Goosecreek* recognized the important duty of school officials to maintain a safe learning environment and the broad disciplinary authority of educators in general, it also stressed the special importance of protecting the constitutional rights of students. While educators need not have the kind of evidence that would constitute "probable cause" in order to search a student for dangerous instrumentalities, it is necessary that they have reasonable cause to believe that something prohibited will be found. This means that they must not only be acting in good faith but on the basis of evidence. The court in the *Goosecreek* case held that searching students could be done only when there was an "individualized suspicion" that a particular student possessed drugs or alcohol.

It should be noted that the *Goosecreek* court considered and rejected a much criticized Seventh Circuit case that held that a 2½–3 hour inspection by six teams of school personnel and police accompanied by trained dogs was *not* a search and therefore not subject to constitutional limitation.[4] In *Doe*, the dogs sniffed 2,780 junior and senior high school students, alerting 50 times; 11 students, including one 13-year-old girl who had been playing with her dog the morning of the search, were strip searched; other searches revealed that 17 students possessed beer, drug paraphernalia, or marijuana. The Seventh Circuit held that only the body searches were unreasonable. Although the full Supreme Court did not consider this case, Justice Brennan expressed the following opinion:

> I cannot agree that the Fourth Amendment authorizes local school and police officials to detain every junior and senior high school student present in a town's public schools and then, using drug-detecting, police-trained German shepherds, to conduct a warrantless, student-by-student dragnet inspection "to see if there were any drugs present."[5]

> I cannot agree that the . . . school officials' use of the trained police dogs did not constitute a search.[6]

The weight of opinion in these types of cases strongly favors Justice Brennan's analysis and that of the court in the *Goosecreek* case.[7] Justice Brennan has pointed out that the lesson school officials teach by organizing and conducting mass searches of students may well be that the fourth amendment does not grant protection against unreasonable searches:

> Schools cannot expect their students to learn the lessons of good citizenship when the school authorities themselves disregard the fundamental principles underpinning our constitutional freedoms.[8]

If lockers are school property, can they be searched at any time?

Although some courts have held in the past that lockers can be searched either because they are school property or because the student has given implicit consent in advance, school personnel generally should have reasonable cause to believe that someone has concealed something dangerous or illegal in a particular place before conducting a search, as the court pointed out in the *Goosecreek* case.[9] In circumstances of grave danger, however, as in the hypothetical example of a bomb threat, evidence of the threat itself and the possible danger to students would be sufficient to override considerations of privacy and intrusiveness.

What type of evidence constitutes "reasonable cause"?

Evidence constituting "reasonable cause" or "reasonable suspicion" will most often be based on observations by school district employees or on information received from student informants. In some instances, both types of evidence will be present. In one 1983 case, two administrators saw David, a high school junior, passing and smoking a "cigarette" and exchanging a plastic bag and money with another student.[10] Later, the administrators smelled the odor of marijuana on David's breath. Although this information probably would have been sufficient to justify the subsequent search, the administrators also learned from another student that David had sold marijuana.

In the court proceeding that followed these events, David argued that the search was done without his consent. Although any search made pursuant to truly voluntary consent would not violate the fourth amendment, the court did not have to resolve that dispute in this case. The court held that even assuming David did not give his consent, the available evidence indicated that the school officials acted with reasonable cause in conducting the search.

Another interesting case involved a high school where several students had been exploding "party-popper" firecrackers.[11] Several different students said they had gotten the firecrackers from a particular freshman girl. Although the girl refused to allow school officials to search her purse and was therefore suspended for five days without being searched, the court noted that the suspension was justified because the requested search had been justified. The request was based upon reasonable suspicion and even probable cause, according to the court. Although all situations will not be based on such conclusive evidence, the important point is that there must be some reliable information, not just a subjective belief that a search is needed.

An example of judicially determined lack of reasonable grounds for a search can be seen in a Michigan case where a 15-year-old high school girl was seen ducking behind a car in the parking lot at a time when she should have been in class; she subsequently gave a false name to the security guard who questioned her and was taken to the office of the vice principal.[12] Suspecting drug possession, the vice principal directed that a strip search take place, a search that was conducted by one female employee and witnessed by another. Illustrating the application of *T.L.O.*, the court stated:

> It is clear that plaintiff's conduct created reasonable grounds for suspecting that some school rule or law had been violated. However, it does not create a reasonable suspicion that a search would turn up evidence of drug usage. Plaintiff's conduct was clearly ambiguous. It could have indicated that she was truant, or that she was stealing hubcaps, or that she had left class to meet a boyfriend. . . . This court does not read TLO so broadly as to allow [such a search]. Rather, the burden is on the administrator to establish that the student's conduct is such that it creates a reasonable suspicion that a specific rule or law has been violated and that a search could reasonably be expected to produce evidence of that violation.[13]

May students be given urine tests in order to detect and prevent drug abuse?

Probably not. Although there are few reported cases, one court has ruled that yearly urine tests for the purpose of detecting drug or alcohol use would violate students' reasonable expectations of privacy.[14] Furthermore, such testing would not have been reasonably related in scope to a problem that appeared from the evidence to be limited. In a more recent case, however, a federal court of appeals upheld a random urine testing program applicable only to high school interscholastic athletes and cheerleaders.[15] The program to test for use of controlled substances or performance-enhancing drugs contained protections to limit the necessary invasion of privacy, to double-check results and allow them to be challenged, and to protect the confidentiality of the information obtained. Student sanctions were limited to denial of the right to participate in sports activities. The court concluded that

[t]he convergence of several important factors convinces us that the searches involved here take place in one of the relatively unusual environments in which suspicionless searches are permissible: interscholastic athletes have diminished expectations of privacy, and have voluntarily chosen to participate in an activity which subjects them to pervasive regulation of off-campus behavior; the school's interest in preserving a drug-free athletic program is substantial, and cannot adequately be furthered by less intrusive measures; the [school district] program adequately limits the discretion of the officials performing the search; and the information sought is intended to be used solely for noncriminal educational and rehabilitative purposes.[16]

May counselors and administrators be deputized, in order to deal more effectively with severe student disciplinary problems?

Just as some schools hire local police officers as guards to protect the school environment, it has been suggested that school personnel could be deputized in order to help solve school drug problems. Although no case has concerned this precise issue, it is possible that deputized school personnel would be held to the higher probable cause standard and would generally need to have a warrant in order to conduct a search in a school. Because police officers are held to this higher standard whenever they conduct searches, if school personnel were to become police officers, they might well lose the broader authority they generally possess to conduct school searches without a warrant and with only reasonable grounds to believe something prohibited would be discovered.

In one California case,[17] a school security agent saw bulges that looked like knives in a student's pockets. Knowing that the student had a history of disciplinary problems and was a member of a gang, the security agent conducted a "pat-down" of the student's outer clothing. After the agent felt a knife in each pocket, he retrieved them. A major issue in the case was whether the search was reasonable under the fourth amendment.

The court noted that despite the fact that "peace officer" status had been granted to the security agent under California law, he did not have general police powers. The court did not actually decide whether the security agent was a police officer, which would make him subject to the higher probable cause standard under the fourth amendment; its conclusion was that the security agent acted within the law in any case. The implication from the court's decision is that, even if he were a police officer, he acted appropriately—that is, with probable cause. Since he satisfied that standard, he also satisfied the lesser standard of conducting a school search on the basis of reasonable suspicion. The more important implication is this: if the security agent actually were a police officer, he might have been subjected to the higher standard, thus removing some of the discretion normally afforded school personnel to maintain a safe learning environment. This possibility should be distinguished, however, from situations where an off-duty police officer is merely working a second job as a school security guard. In such cases, the higher probable cause standard would not apply.[18]

"DUE PROCESS" FOR STUDENTS

Most educators probably are now familiar with the major holding of the Supreme Court in the 1975 case of *Goss v. Lopez:*[19] "Due process requires, in connection with a suspension of 10 days or less, that the student be given oral or written notice of the charges against him and, if he denies them, an explanation of the evidence the authorities have and an opportunity to present his side of the story."[20] It is important to review the *Goss* case for a number of reasons. First, the case is a reminder of the lack of procedural fairness in student discipline prior to the mid-1970s. In addition, it defines the precise nature of due process and gives important clues to the types of procedures that might be necessary in a variety of disciplinary situations.

What is due process and what process is due?

Goss v. Lopez. In the early 1970s, Ohio law allowed school principals to suspend students for up to 10 days or to expel them, requiring only that parents be notified of the action and given reasons within 24 hours. Students who were expelled could appeal the decision, but there was no appeal for students who were suspended. In February and March of 1971, demonstrations, disruptions, and disturbances broke out in several schools throughout a large city school system. One student was accused of disrupting a class, another of assaulting a police officer at a demonstration in the school auditorium, and others of causing physical damage to school property. In some instances it was not clear from the record what misbehavior had been alleged or, indeed, if any misbehavior had actually occurred. At least two of the students said they were not involved in the disturbances that occasioned their suspensions, but they were never given a chance to explain their version of the incidents. Another student was given two 10-day suspensions, to run consecutively, for alleged misbehavior occurring at two different times, again without being questioned about her role in the incidents. Nine students from several public junior and senior high schools eventually sought judicial review of their suspensions, claiming that the right to an education had been unfairly denied.

The Supreme Court explained that the fourteenth amendment prohibits state officials, including school personnel, from denying to students "liberty" or "property" without due process of law. Students have a liberty interest in their reputation and a property interest in receiving whatever education the state has chosen to provide. If no liberty or property right were involved, as would be the case with a *de minimus* punishment such as an after-school detention, students would not be entitled to due process. In this case, however, the Court concluded that suspension for any longer than a "trivial period" is a "serious event in the life of the suspended child."[21] Therefore, fundamentally fair due process procedures must be provided as a matter of constitutional law.

The court next turned to the question of "what process is due." Noting that due process is a flexible concept, the Court made clear that the "timing and content of the notice" and the "nature of the hearing" will vary depending upon the severity of the punishment involved and the educational interests to be preserved. In the usual suspension situations, the notice and opportunity to be heard will be provided in an informal discussion between a school administrator and the student. And, although "as a general rule notice and hearing should precede removal of the student from school,"[22] the Court made clear that students posing a danger to others or likely to disrupt the educational process can be immediately suspended, with the hearing following "as soon as practicable."

In keeping with the idea that due process procedures should be flexible, the Supreme Court suggested that short-term suspensions where the facts are in dispute, long-term suspensions, and expulsions might require "more formal procedures." Whereas the usual short-term suspension would not require representation by an attorney or the opportunity to cross-examine witnesses, more onerous punishments might require such formality. The important point is to provide whatever is necessary to ensure fairness to all involved.

Is it necessary to provide students with due process in all situations where punishment is imposed?

No. It is important to remember that when the Supreme Court decided *Goss v. Lopez,*[23] it was dealing with a situation in which students were being deprived of their state-created right to an education. Although the court did not give examples of the *de minimus* punishments that would not require due process procedures, it is probable that they would include after-school detention, "time-out" periods, periods of school probation, and temporary exclusion from participation in extracurricular activities.

In 1982, a federal court held that a student who was placed on "school probation" after returning from a disciplinary expulsion was not denied any liberty or property interest, making due process inapplicable.[24] Another court gave the opinion that hockey team members who had been suspended from team membership for six weeks for a violation of training rules (smoking marijuana and drinking beer after an away game) also were not deprived of any property interest.[25] Although the court did not actually have to decide whether due process was applicable, because the students involved had admitted their misbehavior and had been given an opportunity to explain, it did say that participation in sports was a privilege and not a property right. Because due process generally is not applicable unless it can be said that the person involved is *entitled* to some particular benefit, the court was suggesting the possible inapplicability of due process in this situation.

There is reason to believe, however, that the right/privilege distinction that some courts have made with regard to athletics will not long endure. At the college level, participation in athletics has sometimes been considered a property right;[26] at the high school level, some courts have assumed that athletic participation is protected under the due process clause of the fourteenth amendment.[27] Although it is clear that students have a property right to education in general, the situation with regard to participation in athletics and other extracurricular activities is not yet clear.

Why shouldn't students have at least the same due process rights as those accused of a crime?

In the years since the *Goss* case was decided by the Supreme Court, lower state and federal courts have had to deal with a number of school disciplinary situations where students claimed that they were denied their "Miranda warnings,"[28] that they had a right to have their parents present at their hearing, that they had a right to have the names of the witnesses against them, and that they had a right not to have hearsay evidence presented against them. Because the nature of due process varies, it would be difficult to say for sure that these things would never be required. On the other hand, in most school disciplinary situations, the courts have not been eager to inject trial-like procedures into the school disciplinary context. In this regard they are following the advice of the Supreme Court in *Goss*, which expressed sensitivity to the possibility that to do so would be too costly and might fundamentally change the educational nature of school discipline.

In one interesting case, the director of pupil personnel was called on to describe an incident where a ring had been stolen and where most of the evidence presented was based on hearsay.[29] The student whose ring was stolen did not testify at the expulsion hearing of the student who allegedly stole the ring. The court reviewed a number of due process cases, beginning with *Goss*, and rejected technical rules of evidence in favor of fundamental fairness in procedures: "[A] student's right to due process is satisfied even though some of the testimony presented was hearsay given by members of the school staff."[30] A considerable amount of judicial opinion suggests that hearsay evidence, which is prohibited in criminal trials, is permitted in school disciplinary hearings.[31] This approach is necessary in public schools because their primary mission is education and not punishment; it is reasonable because punishments imposed in school disciplinary procedures are less onerous than those in criminal trials, and the long-term effects of such punishments are less severe.

In another case, a 14-year-old eighth grader brought a switchblade knife to school, knowing that it was against school rules to have it.[32] When he protested his school-year suspension, arguing that he was not given the names of the witnesses against him and a report of their testimony, the court held that there was no violation of the student's due process rights because he had never denied that he had the knife in school. The court noted that the nature of the hearing varies according to the circumstances of the case. Thus, in a situation where the student does not deny his misbehavior, there is no risk that the wrong person will be punished, and a corresponding lessening of the procedural safeguards that must be provided is reasonable.

Perhaps as a result of watching television, students have become aware of many of the procedural protections that are afforded in the criminal law context. For example, in one school discipline case a student who had been questioned for over an hour regarding the use of marijuana on school premises and later was expelled for the rest of the semester claimed that his "Miranda rights" had been violated.

In *Miranda v. Arizona*, the Supreme Court held that the fifth amendment privilege against self-incrimination in a criminal context applies to periods of custodial interrogation.[33] When an individual is "deprived of his freedom of action in any significant way" he must be informed of his right to remain silent, that anything he says may be used against him in a court of law, and that he has a right to the assistance of a lawyer.

In the school disciplinary context, however, the court that reviewed the case of the student suspected of smoking marijuana said that the *Miranda* rule was not needed in public schools. Students can be detained for questioning, and they have no right to have their parents present. The court's ruling seems correct, because the *Miranda* rule derives from the fifth amendment provision that a person shall not be "compelled in any *criminal case* to be a witness against himself."[34] Judicial opinion, from *Goss* to the present, is firmly opposed to an unreasonable extension of criminal procedural protections to the very different context of public education.

How can school personnel know if the punishments imposed will violate due process?

It is never possible to know for sure; but if school personnel remember that the touchstone of due process is fairness, in the procedures involved as well as in the type of punishment meted out, there should be very little possibility of violating the due process rights of students. The concept of due process actually involves two somewhat different ideas—that procedures must be fair, (called "procedural due process") and that the punishment itself must be fair (called "substantive due process"). If no hearing is provided before a student is suspended, there has been a violation of procedural due process. If the student is suspended for an indefinite period, there may be a violation of substantive due process. Some examples may help to make the two different types of due process clear.

In one case, where there was a violation of both types of due process, two high school students who seriously vandalized the school were suspended pending an investigation of the incident.[35] The suspension actually turned into an expulsion for the rest of the school year—which the court called a *de facto* expulsion. The court ruled that school officials had violated the students' procedural due process rights by not providing an expulsion hearing and written notice of the charges against the students. The students' substantive due process rights also had been violated because school officials never determined when the "suspension" would end, which was unfair to the students. The case is interesting for suggesting that there may be limits to the use of indefinite suspensions. It may be fair to suspend students "indefinitely" for the purpose of investigating an alleged incident of misbehavior, but care must be taken to assure that the suspension does not become a *de facto* expulsion.

Another situation illustrating substantive unfairness in punishment involved the suspension of *students* because their *parents* did not pay school textbook fees.[36] Although the court held that the students had been treated unequally in violation of the fourteenth amendment's equal protection provision, it also could have based its decision on a denial of substantive due process. It is obviously unfair to punish a student for parental behavior over which the student has no control.

A situation where the substantive unfairness is somewhat less obvious involved the mandatory expulsion for one semester of a number of students who left school during the school day and returned intoxicated.[37] The justification for the mandatory expulsion was a drug policy that specifically exempted alcohol from its provisions. The court held that using the policy to expel students who had consumed alcohol violated their right to substantive due process. Presumably, the court thought it was unfair to automatically apply a policy created for one type of situation to an incident that possibly was less serious.

It should be noted, however, that courts generally will not disturb the judgments of school personnel who have followed due process procedures in arriving at a punishment, even if the court believes that the punishment is too severe. In one case illustrating that serious punishments can be legally imposed by school personnel, a group of students drank alcoholic beverages on a school-sponsored band trip in September. They initially were suspended (following a conference), and later expelled (after a hearing) for the rest of the semester. In addition, they were deprived until the following year of the opportunity to participate in extracurricular activities. These actions were upheld by a court of appeals in Kentucky, despite the fact that the trial court believed other factors should have been considered, including the students' previous behavior, their academic standing, the probability that the misbehavior would be repeated, and the possibility of alternative punishments. Even if the trial court was correct, from an educational policy point of view, judges generally try to avoid policy issues, preferring to apply legal principles in a relatively objective manner to the disputes that come before them. Discretionary decisions related to school discipline will not be overturned unless the penalty is arbitrary, capricious, or completely unfair.[38]

ACADEMIC PENALTIES FOR DISCIPLINARY PROBLEMS

May certificates of completion or diplomas be withheld as a disciplinary measure?

No. When a student has completed all of the requirements for promotion or graduation, school officials must issue diplomas as a matter of law.[39] It has been clear for many years that in the absence of fraud in the completion of the requirements themselves, students have a right to receive the appropriate diploma.

May school officials deny students the opportunity to participate in graduation ceremonies, as a means of discipline?

Generally, they cannot. However, students who do not agree to wear the type of clothing that may be prescribed by those in charge of the ceremony, or who do not agree to abide by other reasonable and pertinent requirements, may be barred from participation.[40] It is probable that this limitation on participation would be applicable, for example, to a student who chose to wear a Mickey Mouse cap instead of the more traditional graduation attire, but probably not to a student who decided to wear an armband in symbolic protest. For more information on the free speech rights of students, see Chapter 9.

The threat of present disruption of graduation ceremonies, however, needs to be distinguished from the situation where a student is being punished for past misconduct. At least one court has held that a student who has completed graduation requirements and did not threaten to disrupt the ceremony could not be barred from participation for misbehavior that had occurred in the past.[41] In this case, a black high school senior named Anna had been disciplined for her part in a disruption that had involved both black and white students at a particular school. Among other disciplinary measures, she was suspended for 22 school days and barred from the graduation ceremony.

Considering the graduation ceremony to be a "significant educational land-mark," the court strictly construed state statutes granting the power to suspend "from required attendance upon instruction"[42] and found that graduation ceremonies, being optional, were not covered. The court further explained that although school authorities have the power to discipline for educational purposes, in this case the "justice of the situation favors graduation attendance."[43] The student had completed requirements, had not been in trouble previously, and had been accepted to college. "It would indeed be a distortion of our educational process . . . to snatch from a young woman at the point of educational fruition the savoring of her educational success."[44]

It thus appears that the authority to deprive a student of the opportunity to participate in graduation ceremonies is valid only to the extent that it directly relates to probable disruption of the ceremony itself. When used as punishment for past behavior, it may be held invalid.

May academic penalties, such as grade reductions or denials of credit, be imposed for misbehavior or truancy?

It depends. Although case law in this area is sparse, it appears that some state statutes evidence an intent that additional penalties, such as grade reductions or denial of credit, not be given for suspensions or expulsions (whether labeled excused or unexcused absences).[45] In other words, some state legislatures have decided that the punishments of suspension and expulsion, along with the inevitable problems encountered in making up missed classwork, are penalty enough. Therefore, some local districts may not add additional burdens to the exclusion penalty.

Imposing additional penalties, however, should be distinguished from a situation where credit is lost *as a consequence* of a legitimate exclusion from school for serious misbehavior. In the latter case, no direct academic penalty has actually been imposed. In one controversy, for example, where a 15-year-old girl was suspended for a trimester because she took drugs at school and nearly died, the court held that neither the suspension nor the eventual loss of credit violated her right to due process.[46] That is, there was no substantive unfairness. Although the court felt the punishment was justified (from a constitutional point of view), in part because it would deter such conduct by other students, it did express sympathy for the severity of the consequences: "The loss of credit was undoubtedly a bitter pill for plaintiff to swallow; the court does not find it a particularly therapeutic dose of justice."[47] Nevertheless, this court did not substitute its judgment for that of school officials.

If state law does not preclude, either explicitly or implicitly, the imposition of a grade-reduction penalty when a student is suspended for misconduct, it is possible that a court would approve such a policy. Although some counselors might feel that this "double penalty" is unfair and might argue that it violates substantive due process, at least one court has held to the contrary. The case involved two high school seniors who were suspended for three days each for consuming alcohol on school property.[48] In addition, they received zeros for all graded classwork for the three days and a deduction of nine points from their six-weeks grades.

Relying on a state attorney general's opinion generally approving of grade penalties, the court held that the double penalty did not deprive the students of due process, because it did not have an adverse impact on their right to an education nor on their liberty right to a good reputation. The court was thus favorably disposed to find at least relatively minor academic penalties for misbehavior legally unobjectionable.

Another court approved a grade reduction as a penalty for truancy;[49] although not a "double penalty," this punishment might nevertheless be thought unfair by some. Insofar as grades are thought to reflect academic achievement and not deportment, a grade reduction for truancy makes the meaning of a grade ambiguous. Over a strong dissent saying that a letter-grade reduction imposed on a senior-level boy for one quarter of the school year as punishment for two days of truancy was a violation of substantive due process (i.e., arbitrary, capricious, and unfair), one court nevertheless approved such action.[50] According to the court, it was rational to grade truants more harshly, because grading can be thought to reflect both academic achievement and behavior.

It must be emphasized that there are few reported cases on the question of using academic penalties for disciplinary problems. Given the fact that courts hesitate to interfere with the broad discretion generally afforded state and local school officials to govern schools and discipline students, it is possible that only the most severe cases of academic deprivation or unequal treatment would invoke judicial response favorable to students. If students are treated fairly and there is some legitimate educational reason for the disciplinary penalties imposed, courts will not lightly disregard professional judgment. Whether or not academic penalties may be used to correct or punish misbehavior must be determined, at the present time, by carefully reviewing state statutes and local school board policies. The wisdom of such policies also is largely a local matter. Judges often say that it is not their job to determine the best policy or action; that difficult decision is left to educators.

THE PROBLEM OF CORPORAL PUNISHMENT

Corporal punishment of schoolchildren, unfortunately, is more than a philosophical problem for many counselors. Despite theoretical arguments against allowing school counselors to serve in disciplinary roles, it is well known that they are often drawn into situations where they must officially witness corporal punishment or where their advice is sought with regard to its actual administration. It is important, therefore, that counselors be aware of the educational and psychological as well as the legal aspects of various types of discipline. We focus on the legal issues here, on the assumption that the other issues are adequately addressed during the preservice and in-service education of counselors.

Corporal punishment of children, whether by parents or by school officials, has a long and controversial history in American society. Given this history, it is not surprising that policies and procedures vary widely from state to state, and sometimes from district to district, with regard to the corporal punishment of students. It is also not surprising that questions have arisen regarding the constitutionality of corporal punishment in the educational context. The following case represents the Supreme Court's most thorough examination of that issue.

Does the Constitution prohibit corporal punishment?

The **Ingraham** *Case.* The leading Supreme Court case on corporal punishment is *Ingraham v. Wright,* decided in 1977.[51] The incident that resulted in the suit occurred in Florida, in 1970, when two junior high school boys were paddled with a wooden paddle, causing injuries that lasted from several days to a week. The issues presented to the Supreme Court involved whether or not the eighth amendment's prohibition of "cruel and unusual punishments" applied to corporal punishment in public schools and, if it did not, whether the due process clause of the fourteenth amendment granted any procedural protections to the students before punishment was administered.

With regard to the first issue, the Court reviewed the historical "common-law" tradition allowing reasonable corporal punishment of schoolchildren and the fact that the eighth amendment, prohibiting "cruel and unusual punishment," traditionally had been applied only to criminals. It concluded that the eighth amendment was not applicable in school disciplinary situations. The comparatively open nature of the public school environment, combined with the traditional legal constraint that corporal punishment be reasonable lest it result in criminal or civil liability, convinced the Court that students had "little need for the protection of the eighth amendment." The Court apparently felt that the behavior of school officials would be supervised by the community and that reasonable punishment was assured because of the possibility that school personnel could be charged with a crime or held liable for money damages by parents.

Regarding the due process issue, the Court determined that restraint and punishment did indeed implicate a student's fourteenth amendment liberty right. But, because there was little likelihood of erroneous punishment and because it would be difficult to formulate a due process rule that would not unduly burden school officials, the Court determined that the common-law limitations of reasonableness and the availability of civil and criminal remedies were enough to guarantee due process to students.

Although the Supreme Court recognized that the practice of corporal punishment has been widely criticized "for more than a century," it also noted that corporal punishment was allowed in most states in 1977. The *Ingraham* case itself, a 5–4 decision, may well reflect the societal division on the issue of corporal punishment. The dissenting justices (White, Brennan, Marshall, and Stevens) believed that the eighth amendment was meant to protect all persons from abusive treatment. They also felt that the simple give-and-take of *Goss*-type due process procedures was the minimum that should be required before corporal punishment, which is "final and irrevocable," could be administered.

There is now evidence that more and more states and individual school districts are disallowing the practice of corporal punishment entirely or are granting greater protections to schoolchildren than those required by the Constitution.[52] This is, of course, perfectly permissible. The Constitution is not necessarily meant to establish maximal protections for individual liberties but only to guarantee the preservation of certain basic and fundamental societal values.

Are there other constitutional protections that might be granted to students who are subjected to excessive corporal punishment?

Although students do not have any federal constitutional right to procedural due process, that is, to notice and a "hearing," before corporal punishment is administered, they may be able to claim a violation of "substantive due process" (fundamental fairness) if the corporal punishment is exceptionally severe.[53] Although the Supreme Court did not consider substantive due process in the *Ingraham* case, a lower-court judge suggested the possibility that the students' right to substantive due process might have been violated.[54]

Relying on cases that have held that individuals have a right to be "free of state intrusions into realms of personal privacy and bodily security through means so brutal, demeaning, and harmful as literally to shock the conscience,"[55] another court said that students should receive no less protection than do those held in custody for a criminal offense.[56] In this case, it had been alleged that a grade school student was injured so severely by a teacher that she had to be hospitalized for 10 days and may have sustained permanent injuries to her lower back and spine. More recently, a federal court of appeals remanded a case for trial where an elementary school student was given two beatings (one while being held upside down by the ankles), resulting in bleeding, severe bruises, and a cut that left a permanent scar.[57]

It is important to realize that the type of punishment that would amount to a fourteenth amendment substantive due process violation would, in some cases, be even more severe than that which would be considered assault and battery under the criminal and civil laws of a state. It would have to be inspired by malice and be so excessive as to be shocking. But, because there is really no way to adequately compensate for corporal punishment that causes severe or permanent injury to a child, when corporal punishment *is* used, it should be administered fairly, reasonably, and, in most cases, after the student has had a chance to explain his or her behavior.

Do parental objections to corporal punishment control its use?

Not usually. Assuming that the parents do not live in states such as Hawaii, Massachusetts, and New Jersey, where corporal punishment of students is statutorily disallowed,[58] it generally is not necessary that school officials have parental permission before administering corporal punishment.[59] As one court said, "[W]e cannot allow the wishes of a parent to restrict school officials' discretion in deciding the methods to be used in accomplishing the not just legitimate, but essential purpose of maintaining discipline."[60] It should be noted however, that in some states that allow corporal punishment, it is nevertheless mandatory or permissible for local districts to require parental approval or notification before corporal punishment can be administered.[61]

What types of procedures must be followed when corporal punishment is administered?

Assuming that corporal punishment is allowed, which is very much a matter of state law and/or local school board policy, a variety of procedures may be mandated. A typical school board policy on corporal punishment would define corporal punishment in a way that makes clear the policy is intended to apply to disciplinary situations and is not intended to limit action in situations of necessary self-defense or defense of another. It would usually specify how corporal punishment is to be effected and that it be administered in a reasonable manner. Other provisions might include the following stipulations: that corporal punishment be used as a last resort, that the student have advance notice of the types of behavior that would occasion its use, that some opportunity be provided for the student to explain his or her behavior, that another school official be present when corporal punishment is administered, and that a complete record of the incident be kept.[62]

When a state has neither disallowed nor specifically provided for correction by corporal punishment, courts generally have held that reasonable corporal punishment is permissible under general statutes relating to the control of education; such holdings have also relied on the common-law doctrine of *parens patriae*, which allows the state to act for its own good, or the common-law doctrine of *in loco parentis*, which allows school personnel to act in place of the parent. At least one court, however, going substantially beyond the reasoning of the *Ingraham* case, has said that reasonable corporal punishment under the *in loco parentis* doctrine "cannot be interpreted as permitting corporal punishment of public school children by means of a paddle, whip, stick, or other mechanical devices."[63] The court also required "minimal due process procedures," including giving the student an opportunity to explain, and required that another adult be present. Even where corporal punishment is permitted, however, school personnel who excessively or otherwise improperly administer corporal punishment may be subject to dismissal or may be judged guilty of child abuse.[64]

DISCIPLINE AND THE HANDICAPPED STUDENT

Is it true that handicapped students cannot be expelled from school?

No. While there is substantial authority to the effect that educational services for handicapped students cannot be completely discontinued, these students can be "expelled" or "excluded" from school if their misbehavior is not a result of the handicapping condition and if federally mandated procedural protections are afforded.[65] The Education of the Handicapped Act (EHA),[66] along with the complementary provisions of Section 504 of the Rehabilitation Act,[67] provides procedural protections in the identification, evaluation, placement, and change of placement of handicapped children, in order to assure them a free and appropriate education.

It has been argued that the special procedural protections afforded to handicapped students create, in a sense, a double standard with regard to the discipline of handicapped students as compared with nonhandicapped students. Although this is not true, in the sense that both groups *can* be disciplined, long-term suspension and expulsion is considered to be a change in educational placement for handicapped students, and can be accomplished only upon the recommendation of the district's committee on the handicapped. In a case of expulsion, it also must be determined that the student's behavior was not caused by the handicap.[68] Of course, because all children suffer educationally as a result of lengthy absences from school, school districts would be free to implement complementary procedural protections for all children facing long-term suspension or expulsion. In the case of handicapped children, however, the procedures are especially necessary in order to guarantee an appropriate education to a category of students who, historically, had been actually or effectively excluded from school.

What can be done on a short-term basis to discipline a handicapped student?

There is nothing in the federal law or regulations governing the disciplinary treatment of children with handicapping conditions that would prohibit short-term suspensions, when necessary to deal with disruptive behavior or in an emergency situation. If they are long-term suspensions or take on the character of an expulsion, as would be the case with an indefinite suspension, they become equivalent to a change in placement, invoking the procedural protection of federal law.[69]

In one case, an eleventh grade learning-disabled student used abusive language in objecting to a detention imposed by his teacher. When his five-day suspension was subsequently challenged in court, the judge remarked that "there was no expulsion from, or termination of special education here, but rather a five-day disciplinary interruption for a flagrant offense."[70] In the judge's opinion, this "interruption" did not constitute a "termination of educational services" and therefore could be effected in the same way as any other short-term suspension. This means that the learning-disabled student needed only to be informed of the behavior leading to the suspension and asked to give his side of the story. For a five-day suspension, he could be treated just like a nonhandicapped student.

May students whose handicap has resulted in dangerous behavior be given summary long-term suspensions?

The **Honig** *Case.* No. The Supreme Court has ruled that an exclusion from school for more than 10 days is equivalent to a change in placement that cannot be accomplished in summary fashion, even for dangerous behavior. In the 1988 case of *Honig v. Doe* (see Appendix D,)[71] the Court ruled that the EHA's "stay-put" provision was "very much meant to strip schools of the *unilateral* authority they had traditionally employed to exclude disabled students, particularly emotionally disturbed students, from school."[72] This means that unless school officials and parents or guardians agree otherwise, the handicapped child must remain in the current placement until proper procedures have been followed. Meanwhile, school officials can use their normal disciplinary procedures, including "study carrels, time-outs, detention, or the restriction of privileges"; temporary suspensions of up to 10 days (following the *Goss* due process procedures); or an interim placement with parental approval. If the parents decline a suggested interim placement, "the 10-day respite gives school officials an opportunity to invoke the aid of the courts," to sanction the proposed placement.

The *Honig* case, in refusing to approve a "dangerousness exception" to the stay-put rule, has clarified not only what schools may do in the short run but what they must do in order to effect a more restrictive placement: They must follow the procedures outlined in the EHA (beginning with a meeting of the multidisciplinary placement team), as complemented by any applicable state regulations.

SUMMARY AND CONCLUSIONS

Recent Supreme Court action has confirmed that school personnel are permitted to conduct searches when they have reasonable cause to believe that particular students possess illegal or dangerous items or that the students have violated school rules; the higher probable cause standard is not generally applicable to school searches unless the police are involved.

In the school situation, reasonable cause most often will be based on observation or information received from other students or from teachers; and, although an anonymous tip would not generally be considered reliable, school officials may be forced to act pursuant to such information when the possibility of danger to persons within the school is great. Reasonable cause thus depends, to some extent, on particular circumstances.

In addition to the fourth amendment right to be free from unreasonable searches, students in public schools also are entitled to fourteenth amendment procedural due process protections before being deprived of their state-created right to attend school.

For a suspension of 10 days or less, which is considered a short-term suspension in many states, the Constitution requires that the student be informed of the reason for the suspension and allowed to provide pertinent information—especially if the student denies have misbehaved. These procedures would likely be required for any suspension in which the child is actually sent home from school. In situations where more onerous punishments are imposed, such as long-term suspension or expulsion, students will need to be afforded correspondingly more thorough and formal procedural due process protections.

In states and districts where corporal punishment is permitted, procedural due process is not constitutionally required before corporal punishment is administered. However, as a matter of educational policy, many school districts do require that certain procedures be followed, which means that a careful examination of state and local law is necessary before such punishment is considered.

Students with handicapping conditions may be disciplined, if appropriate consideration is given to the nature of their handicapping condition and whether or not their misbehavior might have been a result of their handicap. At least in the case of long-term suspension (more than 10 days) or expulsion, handicapped students must be afforded the procedural protections applicable under federal law to a change in placement. However, there is now considerable authority to the effect that federal law prohibits the complete termination of educational services for these children, so that expulsion in the traditional sense is not a placement option. (See Chapter 6 for a discussion of placement decisions for handicapped students.)

We know of no reported cases dealing with the corporal punishment of a handicapped child, but it stands to reason that the nature and extent of the handicapping condition should be evaluated if this type of punishment is considered. As always, constitutional and federal statutory limitations are only a beginning; it is therefore necessary to consider whether additional protections have been provided to students by virtue of state authority.

GOSS V. LOPEZ
419 U.S. 565 (1975)

Mr. Justice WHITE delivered the opinion of the Court.

This appeal by various administrators of the Columbus, Ohio, Public School System ("CPSS") challenges the judgment of a three-judge federal court, declaring that appellees—various high school students in the CPSS—were denied due process of law contrary to the command of the Fourteenth Amendment in that they were temporarily suspended from their high schools without a hearing either prior to suspension or within a reasonable time thereafter, and enjoining the administrators to remove all reference to such suspensions from the students' records. . . .

Two named plaintiffs, Dwight Lopez and Betty Crome, were students at the Central High School and McGuffey Junior High School, respectively. The former was suspended in connection with a disturbance in the lunchroom which involved some physical damage to school property. Lopez testified that at least 75 other students were suspended from his school on the same day. He also testified below that he was not a party to the destructive conduct but was instead an innocent bystander. Because no one from the school testified with regard to this incident, there is no evidence in the record indicating the official basis for concluding otherwise. Lopez *never had a hearing.*

Betty Crome was present at a demonstration at a high school different from the one she was attending. There she was arrested together with others, taken to the police station, and released without being formally charged. Before she went to school on the following day, she was notified that she had been suspended for a 10-day period. Because no one from the school testified with respect to this incident, the record does not disclose how the McGuffey Junior High School principal went about making the decision to suspend Betty Crome nor does it disclose on what information the decision was based. It is clear from the record that *no hearing* was ever held. . . .

II

At the outset, appellants contend that because there is no constitutional right to an education at public expense, the Due Process Clause does not protect against expulsions from the public school system. This position misconceives the nature of the issue and is refuted by prior decisions. The Fourteenth Amendment forbids the State to deprive any person of life, liberty or property without due process of law. Protected interests in property are normally "not created by the Constitution. Rather, they are created and their dimensions are defined" by an independent source such as state statutes or rules entitling the citizen to certain benefits. Having chosen to extend the right to an education to people of appellees' class generally, Ohio may not withdraw that right on grounds of misconduct absent fundamentally fair procedures to determine whether the misconduct has occurred. The authority possessed by the State to prescribe and enforce standards of conduct in its schools, although concededly very broad, must be exercised consistently with constitutional safeguards. Among other things, the State is constrained to recognize a student's legitimate entitlement to a public education as a property interest which is protected by the Due Process Clause and which may not be taken away for misconduct without adherence to the minimum procedures required by that clause.

The Due Process Clause also forbids arbitrary deprivations of liberty. "Where a person's good name, reputation, honor, or integrity is at stake because of what the government is doing to him," the minimal requirements of the clause must be satisfied. School authorities here suspended appellees from school for periods of up to 10 days based on charge of misconduct. If sustained and recorded, those charges could seriously damage the students' standing with their fellow pupils and their teachers as well as interfere with later opportunities for higher education and employment. It is apparent that the claimed right of the State to determine unilaterally and without process whether that misconduct has occurred immediately collides with the requirements of the Constitution.

Appellants proceed to argue that even if there is a right to a public education protected by the Due Process Clause generally, the clause comes into play only when the State subjects a student to a "severe detriment or grievous loss." The loss of 10 days, it is said, is neither severe nor grievous and the Due Process Clause is therefore of no relevance. Appellee's argument is again refuted by our prior decisions; for in determining "whether due process requirements apply in the first place, we must look not to the 'weight' but to the *nature* of the interest at stake.". . .

A short suspension is of course a far milder deprivation than expulsion. But, "education is perhaps the most important function of state and local governments.". . .and the total exclusion from the educational process for more than a trivial period, and certainly if the suspension is for 10 days, is a serious event in the life of the suspended child. Neither the property interest in educational benefits temporarily denied nor the liberty interest in reputation, which is also implicated, is so insubstantial that suspensions may constitutionally be imposed by any procedure the school chooses, no matter how arbitrary.

III

"Once it is determined that due process applies, the question remains what process is due." At the very minimum, therefore, students facing suspension and the consequent interference with a protected property interest must be given *some* kind of notice and afforded *some* kind of hearing." Parties whose rights are to be affected are entitled to be heard; and in order that they may enjoy that right they must first be notified."

The student's interest is to avoid unfair or mistaken exclusion from the educational process, with all of its unfortunate consequences. The Due Process Clause will not shield him from suspensions properly imposed, but it disserves both his interest and the interest of the State if his suspension is in fact unwarranted. The concern would be mostly academic if the disciplinary process were a totally accurate, unerring process, never mistaken and never unfair. Unfortunately, that is not the case, and no one suggests that it is. Disciplinarians, although proceeding in utmost good faith, frequently act on the reports and advice of others; and the controlling facts and the nature of the conduct under challenge are often disputed. The risk of error is not at all trivial, and it should be guarded against if that may be done without prohibitive cost or interference with the educational process.

The difficulty is that our schools are vast and complex. Some modicum of discipline and order is essential if the educational function is to be performed. Events calling for discipline are frequent occurrences and sometimes require immediate, effective action. Suspension is considered not only to be a necessary tool to maintain order but a valuable educational device. The prospect of imposing elaborate hearing requirements in every suspension case is viewed with great concern, and many school authorities may well prefer the untrammeled power to act unilaterally, unhampered by rules about notice and hearing. But it would be a strange disciplinary system in an educational institution if no communication was sought by the disciplinarian with the student in an effort to inform him of his defalcation and to let him tell his side of the story in order to make sure that an injustice is not done. . . .

We do not believe that school authorities must be totally free from notice and hearing requirements if their schools are to operate with acceptable efficiency. Students facing temporary suspension have interests qualifying for protection of the Due Process Clause, and due process requires, in connection with a suspension of 10 days or less, that the student be given oral or written notice of the charges against him and, if he denies them, an explanation of the evidence the authorities have and an opportunity to present his side of the story. The clause requires at least these rudimentary precautions against unfair or mistaken findings of misconduct and arbitrary exclusion from school.

There need be no delay between the time "notice" is given and the time of the hearing. In the great majority of cases the disciplinarian may informally discuss the alleged misconduct with the student minutes after it has occurred. We hold only that, in being given an opportunity to explain his version of the facts at this discussion, the student first be told what he is accused of doing and what the basis of the accusation is. . . .

Since the hearing may occur almost immediately following the misconduct, it follows that as a general rule notice and hearing should precede removal of the student from school. We agree with the District Court, however, that there are recurring situations in which prior notice and hearing cannot be insisted upon. Students whose presence poses a continuing danger to persons or property or an ongoing threat of disrupting the academic process may be immediately removed from school. In such cases, the necessary notice and rudimentary hearing should follow as soon as practicable, as the District Court indicated.

In holding as we do, we do not believe that we have imposed procedures on school disciplinarians which are inappropriate in a classroom setting. Instead we have imposed requirements which are, if anything, less than a fair-minded school principal would impose upon himself in order to avoid unfair suspensions. . . .

We stop short of construing the Due Process Clause to require, country-wide, that hearings in connection with short suspensions must afford the student the opportunity to secure counsel, to confront and cross-examine witnesses to verify his version of the incident. Brief disciplinary suspensions are almost countless. To impose in each such case even truncated trial type procedures might well overwhelm administrative facilities in many places and, by diverting resources, cost more than it would save in educational effectiveness. Moreover, further formalizing the suspension process and escalating its formality and adversary nature may not only make it too costly as a regular disciplinary tool but also destroy its effectiveness as part of the teaching process.

On the other hand, requiring effective notice and informal hearing permitting the student to give his version of the events will provide a meaningful hedge against erroneous action. At least the disciplinarian will be alerted to the existence of disputes about facts and arguments about cause and effect. He may then determine himself to summon the accuser, permit cross-examination and allow the student to present his own witnesses. In more difficult cases, he may permit counsel. In any event, his discretion will be more informed and we think the risk of error substantially reduced.

Requiring that there be at least an informal give-and-take between student and disciplinarian, preferably prior to the suspension, will add little to the fact-finding function where the disciplinarian has himself witnessed the conduct forming the basis for the charge. But things are not always as they seem to be, and the student will at least have the opportunity to characterize his conduct and put it in what he deems the proper context.

We should also make it clear that we have addressed ourselves solely to the short suspension, not exceeding 10 days. Longer suspensions or expulsions for the remainder of the school term, or permanently, may require more formal procedures. Nor do we put aside the possibility that in unusual situations, although involving only a short suspension, something more than the rudimentary procedures will be required.

IV

The District Court found each of the suspensions involved here to have occurred without a hearing, either before or after the suspension, and that each suspension was therefore invalid and the statute unconstitutional insofar as it permits such suspensions without notice or hearing. Accordingly, the judgment is *Affirmed.*

NOTES

1. 469 U.S. 325 (1985).
2. *See, e.g.,* Doe v. Renfrow, 451 U.S. 1002 (1982) (Brennan, J. dissenting from denial of certiorari). *See also* Cason v. Cook, 810 F.2d 188 (8th Cir. 1987); Martens v. School Dist. No. 220, 620 F.Supp. 29 (N.D. Ill. 1985).
3. Horton v. Goosecreek Indep. School Dist., 690 F.2d 470 (1982), *cert. denied,* 463 U.S. 1207 (1983).

4. Doe v. Renfrow, 631 F.2d 91 (7th Cir. 1980), *cert. denied*, 451 U.S. 1022 (1981).
5. *Id.*, 451 U.S. at 1022.
6. *Id.* at 1025.
7. *See, e.g.*, Doe v. Renfrow, 635 F.2d 582 (7th Cir. 1980) (Swygert, et al., J., dissenting from denial of rehearing); and Jones v. Latexo Indep. School Dist. 449 F.Supp. 223 (E.D. Tex. 1960).
8. 451 U.S. at 1027–28 (1981).
9. *See, e.g.*, State v. Brooks, 718 P.2d 837 (Wash. Ct. App. 1986); R.D.L. v. State, 499 So.2d 31 (Fla. Dist. Ct. App. 1986).
10. Tarter v. Raybuck, 556 F.Supp. 625 (N.D. Ohio 1983).
11. Bahr v. Jenkins, 539 F.Supp. 483 (E.D. Ky. 1982).
12. Cales v. Howell Pub. Schools, 635 F.Supp. 454 (E.D. Mich. 1985).
13. *Id.* at 457. *See also* T. J. v. State, 538 So.2d 1320 (Fla. Ct. App. 1989) (reasonable suspicion of drug possession did not arise in course of weapon search).
14. Odenheim v. Carlestadt-East Rutherford Regional School Dist., 510 A.2d 709 (N.J. Super. Ct. Ch. Div. 1985).
15. Schaill v. Tippecanoe School Corp., 864 F.2d 1309 (7th Cir. 1988).
16. *Id.* at 1322.
17. *In re* Guillermo M., 181 Cal. Rptr. 856 (Ct. App. 1982).
18. *See In re* Reynaldo R., 196 Cal. Rptr. 238 (Cal. App. 1983).
19. 419 U.S. 565 (1975).
20. *Id.* at 581.
21. *Id.* at 576.
22. *Id.* at 582.
23. 419 U.S. 565 (1975).
24. Boynton v. Casey, 543 F.Supp. 995 (D. Me. 1982).
25. Buhlman v. Bd. of Educ., 436 N.Y.S.2d 192 (Sup. Ct. 1981) (dicta).
26. *See, e.g.*, Regents of Univ. of Minnesota v. NCAA, 422 F.Supp. 1158 (D. Minn. 1976), *rev'd on other grounds*, 560 F.2d 352 (8th Cir. 1977).
27. *See, e.g.*, Breasch v. DePasquale, 265 N.W.2d 842 (Neb. 1978), *cert. denied*, 439 U.S. 1068 (1979).
28. *See infra* note 33 and accompanying text.
29. Racine Unified School Dist. v. Thompson, 321 N.W.2d 334 (Ct. App. Wisc. 1982).
30. *Id.* at 335.
31. *See, e.g.*, Boykins v. Fairfield Bd. of Educ., 492 F.2d 697 (5th Cir. 1974), *cert. denied*, 420 U.S. 962 (1975).
32. McClain v. Lafayette County Bd. of Educ., 637 F.2d 106 (5th Cir. 1982).
33. Miranda v. Arizona, 384 U.S. 463 (1966).
34. U.S. CONST., amend. V, emphasis added.
35. Darby v. School Superintendent, 544 F.Supp. 428 (W.D. Mich. 1982).
36. Carder v. Michigan City School Corp., 552 F.Supp. 869 (N.D. Ind. 1982).
37. McCuskey v. Bd. of Educ., 662 F.2d 1263 (8th Cir. 1981).
38. *See, e.g.*, Hogan v. Bd. of Educ. of North Colonie Central School Dist., 442 N.Y.S.2d 623 (App. Div. 1981).
39. *See* State v. Wilson, 297 S.W. 419 (Ct. App. Mo. 1927); Ryan v. Bd. of Educ., 257 P.2d 945 (Kan. 1927).
40. *See* Fowler v. Williamson, 448 F.Supp. 497 (W.D. N.C. 1978); Valentine v. Indep. School Dist. of Casey, 183 N.W. 434 (Iowa 1921).
41. Ladson v. Bd. of Educ., 323 N.Y.S.2s 545 (Sup. Ct. 1971).
42. *Id.* at 549.

43. *Id.* at 550.
44. *Id.*
45. Gutierrez v. School Dist. R-1, 585 P.2d 935 (Colo. App. 1987); Dorsey v. Bale, 521 S.W.2d 76 (Ky. App. 1975).
46. Fisher v. Burkburnett Indep. School Dist., 419 F.Supp. 1200 (N.D. Tex. 1976).
47. *Id.* at 1205.
48. New Braunfels Indep. School Dist. v. Armke, 658 S.W.2d 330 (Tex. App. 1983).
49. Knight v. Bd. of Educ., 348 N.E.2d 299 (Ill. App. 1976).
50. *Id.*
51. 430 U.S. 651 (1977).
52. The state of Virginia recently became the first southern state to prohibit corporal punishment of public school children. Educ. Week, Mar. 1, 1989, at 8, col. 3. A total of 19 states have banned the practice and the national PTA has called for a federal ban. Educ. Week, Oct. 18, 1989, at 2, col. 2.
53. *See, e.g.,* Hall v. Towney, 621 F.2d 607, 611 (4th Cir. 1980).
54. Ingraham v. Wright, 525 F.2d 909, 921 (5th Cir. 1976) (Godbold, J., dissenting), *aff'd on other grounds,* 430 U.S. 651 (1977).
55. Hall v. Towney, 621 F.2d 607, 613 (4th Cir. 1980).
56. *Id.*
57. Garcia v. Miera, 817 F.2d 650 (10th Cir. 1987), *cert. denied,* 108 S.Ct. 1220 (1988).
58. HAWAII REV. STAT. § 296-16; MASS. GEN. LAWS ANN. ch. 71, § 37G; N.J. STAT. ANN. § 18A:6-1.
59. *See* Ingraham v. Wright, 430 U.S. 651, 662 n.22 (1977); Hall v. Tawney, 621 F.2d 607 (4th Cir. 1980); Baker v. Owen, 395 F.Supp. 294 (M.D. N.C.), *aff'd* 423 U.S. 907 (1975).
60. Baker v. Owen, 395 F.Supp. at 301.
61. *See, e.g.,* CAL. EDUC. CODE §§ 4900–4901 (approval required); MONT. REV. CODES ANN. § 75-6109 (notification required); Donaldson v. Bd. of Educ., 424 N.E.2d 737 (Ill. App. Ct. 1981) (approval required per local policy).
62. *See, e.g.,* Rhodus v. Dumiller, 552 F.Supp. 425 (M.D. La. 1982).
63. Smith v. W. Va. State Bd. of Educ., 295 S.E. 680, 687 (W. Va. 1982); *cf.* Ingraham v. Wright, 430 U.S. 658 (1977) (by implication).
64. *See, e.g.,* Gane v. Ambach, 522 N.Y.Supp.2d 736 (N.Y. App. Div., 1987); Educ. Week, April 12, 1989, at 2, col. 4.
65. *See, e.g.,* S-1 v. Turlington, 635 F.2d 343 (5th Cir. 1981), *cert. denied,* 445 U.S. 1030 (1981).
66. 20 U.S.C. § 1400 *et seq.* (1982).
67. 29 U.S.C. § 794 (1982).
68. For a case summarizing the leading judicial opinions on this issue *see* Kaelin v. Grubbs, 682 F.2d 595 (6th Cir. 1982).
69. *See* Sherry v. New York State Educ. Dept., 479 F.Supp. 1328 (W.D. N.Y. 1979).
70. Bd. of Educ. v. Ill. State Bd. of Educ., 531 F.Supp. 148, 150 (C.D. Ill. 1982).
71. 484 U.S. 305 (1988).
72. *Id.* at 323.

CHAPTER 8

Child Abuse and Neglect

OVERVIEW

Any scholarly account of the history of childhood tells us that children have been subjected to various kinds of abuse throughout the ages. Some historians trace such abuse back to biblical references, others to Greek and Roman antiquity.[1] There is ample historical evidence that, during every age, children have been grossly mistreated, abused, often whipped, sacrificed for various causes, burned, disfigured, and killed. In Western law, they were often treated as chattel, completely at the disposal of their owners. It has only been in recent years, however, that the general public has become aware and concerned about this phenomenon. One bit of evidence about the interest the general public in America has recently developed in the subject is the fact that approximately 60 million viewers watched an ABC-TV movie on the subject of child abuse when it was aired in January 1984.

We have no reliable statistics on the extent of child abuse and neglect. This uncertainty is caused by inconsistencies in definitions of abuse and neglect, variations in reporting laws from state to state, and the different methods of data collection. Nonetheless, it has been estimated that during 1982 and 1983, close to one million cases of child abuse and neglect were reported to child welfare agencies each year.[2]

Various professionals are legally responsible for reporting suspected cases of child abuse. Are therapists and counselors among them? If yes, to whom do they report and how? What are the obligations and liabilities involved in such reporting? And just what is child abuse? These are some questions considered in this chapter.

What is child abuse?

There is no single, authoritative definition of child abuse. The National Committee for the Prevention of Child Abuse defines it as a nonaccidental injury or pattern of injuries to a child for which there is no "reasonable" explanation. This might be a place to start, but for our purposes it is too vague. We shall look at a definition provided by federal law as well as some variations in state laws.

In 1974, Congress enacted the National Child Abuse Prevention and Treatment Act (PL 93–247), which defines child abuse and neglect as follows:

> Physical or mental injury, sexual abuse or exploitation, negligent treatment, or maltreatment of a child under the age of eighteen or the age specified by the child protection law of the state in question, by a person who is responsible for the child's welfare, under circumstances which indicate that the child's health or welfare is harmed or threatened thereby.

Because child abuse is not a federal crime, the federal law did no more than make money available to the states that met its reporting guidelines and other qualifications, and set reporting standards. The act also provided help to local agencies concerned with child abuse and neglect and established a central registry that lists substantiated cases of child abuse.

In the Child Abuse Prevention, Adoption, and Family Services Act of 1988, Congress buttressed the federal involvement in this area by appropriating $48 million through 1991. The act also created the position of a permanent director and professional staff for the National Center on Child Abuse and Neglect, an advisory board, and an interagency task force. The center provides technical assistance as well as conducts research on the causes, prevention, and treatment of child abuse and neglect.[3]

Because child abuse is a state crime, state definitions become very important. Although there are variations among state statutory definitions, we list two that are somewhat typical:

> Child abuse or neglect means the physical injury or neglect, sexual abuse, sexual exploitation, or maltreatment of a child under the age of eighteen by a person who is responsible for the child's welfare under circumstances which indicate that the child's health or welfare is harmed or threatened. (Alaska).[4]

> "Abused or neglected child" means a child whose physical or mental health or welfare is harmed or threatened with harm by acts or omissions of his parent or other person responsible for his welfare. (Vermont).[5]

Although state laws vary, they all use a combination of two or more of the following elements in defining abuse and neglect: (1) physical injury, (2) mental or emotional injury, (3) sexual molestation or exploitation.[6]

Is it important to be able to distinguish between abuse and neglect?

No. Whereas some states define them as a single concept, others have separate definitions for them. In 1977, the U.S. Department of Health, Education, and Welfare created the Model Child Protection Act with Commentary, which does not require the reporter to know or to be certain whether it is abuse or neglect to which a child has been subjected. State laws are similar to this act in not requiring a person to know whether it is abuse or neglect that is being reported.[7]

> The time and effort spent in trying to distinguish between abuse and neglect serves no useful purpose. A child may suffer serious or permanent harm and even death as a result of neglect. Therefore, the same reasons that justify the mandatory reporting of abuse require the mandatory reporting of child neglect.[8]

Which states require reporting of child abuse or neglect?

All of them do, if the abuse or neglect results in physical injury. The states that do not require the reporting of emotional or mental injury are Georgia, Indiana, Iowa, Maryland, Minnesota, Oregon, and Wisconsin; those that do not explicitly require the reporting of sexual abuse are New Mexico, South Dakota, Tennessee, and Texas.[9] This picture, however, can be expected to change through the years as state legislatures amend their laws. For example, Maryland included sexual abuse in its laws in 1978; Florida so acted in 1979, also including in its broad definition the procuring or use of children in photographs, motion pictures, or other presentations depicting sexual conduct.[10] Therefore, educators must check periodically with appropriate state agencies in order to keep up to date with the law in their respective states.

How certain must you be that abuse or neglect is taking place?

No state requires that you be absolutely certain, before you file a report, that abuse is taking place. It is sufficient that you have "reason to believe" or "reasonable cause to believe or suspect" that a child is subject to abuse or neglect. As in many other areas of the law, the standard applied is what the reasonable person would believe under similar circumstances. Because abuse very seldom occurs in front of witnesses, and because the protection of children is the main purpose of reporting laws, the reporters are not held to unduly rigorous standards as long as they act in good faith. In fact, there are some states that even require one to report when he or she "observes the child being subjected to conditions or circumstances which would reasonably result in child abuse or neglect."[11]

What symptoms should alert you to child abuse or neglect?

There are various symptoms that should alert educators that some form of abuse or neglect is taking place. Educators in general and counselors in particular are trained observers of children. Through formal education and their work experience they have become sensitive to the range of normal behavior expected of children in their school and classes and are quick to notice deviations or exceptional behavior. They often observe the same children day after day over long periods of time; thus they are in key positions to notice signs of abuse or neglect. With a little training that focuses on the most common symptoms, they can become the most reliable reporters of such damage or danger to children.

We list, in chart form, the most common indicators of abuse or neglect (see Table 8.1). The list, however, is neither exhaustive nor definitive. Not all indicators are included in the chart, nor does the presence of a single indicator assure us that abuse or neglect exists. These are, however, some of the major indicators that should alert one to the possibility that abuse or neglect is taking place and should be investigated. Clearly, if several indicators are present, or if they occur repeatedly, the probability of maltreatment is greater.

Even in the absence of the specific symptoms or indicators listed in Table 8.1, educators might recognize some general signs of abuse and/or neglect. These can be either academic or psychological clues. Sudden changes in academic performance or sudden loss of interest in schoolwork should alert the observer to the possibility of mistreatment of a student. Studies indicate that there is a significant relationship between child abuse/neglect and learning difficulties. Delayed language development and motor development is found in high proportion among such children. Also, the emotional stress placed on families with special-needs children can bring on abuse or neglect. Educators experienced with special-needs children know that family neglect may lead to failure to provide the child with a hearing aid or glasses, which in turn impedes academic progress. Similarly, sudden changes in a child's emotional tone may be a clue to abuse or neglect. A previously outgoing, happy child who becomes angry, withdrawn, or sullen may be signaling serious changes in his or her home life. Children who are very passive and uncommunicative should alert us to the possibility that problems exist in the life of the family. Clearly, there is not a one-to-one correlation between academic problems and abuse or neglect, but alert and knowledgeable educators can gather clues from a variety of sources in the process of identifying problems in their schools.

All these signs, of course, are only indicators that should alert reasonable educators to the *possibility* of abuse or neglect. They do not *prove* that abuse or neglect exist. Through conversations with the parents or with the child, further clues may be gathered that will confirm suspicions of abuse or neglect, or provide other satisfactory explanations for the child's condition.[12]

Do laws require counselors to report child abuse or neglect?

Yes. Some state statutes explicitly name "school counselors" among the mandatory reporters of child abuse or neglect. Others include them among "educators," "other school personnel," or "employees or officials of any public or private school." Still others have catch-all provisions that require reporting by "any person" who works with children and has "reasonable cause to believe" that abuse or neglect is going on. Such general requirements would clearly include therapists and counselors who work with children.

TABLE 8.1 PHYSICAL AND BEHAVIORAL INDICATORS OF CHILD ABUSE AND NEGLECT

Type of CA/N	Physical Indicators	Behavioral Indicators
PHYSICAL ABUSE	Unexplained Bruises and Welts: —on face, lips, mouth —on torso, back, buttocks, thighs —in various stages of healing —clustered, forming regular patterns —reflecting shape of article used to inflict (electric cord, belt buckle) —on several different surface areas —regularly appear after absence, weekend, or vacation Unexplained Burns: —cigar, cigarette burns, especially on soles, palms, back, or buttocks —immersion burns (sock-like, glove-like, doughnut shaped on buttocks or genitalia) —patterned like electric burner, iron, etc. —rope burns on arms, legs, neck, or torso Unexplained Fractures: —to skull, nose, facial structure —in various stages of healing —multiple or spiral fractures Unexplained Lacerations or Abrasions: —to mouth, lips, gums, eyes —to external genitalia	Wary of Adult Contacts Apprehensive When Other Children Cry Behavioral Extremes: —aggressiveness, or —withdrawal Frightened of Parents Afraid to Go Home Reports Injury by Parents
PHYSICAL NEGLECT	Consistent Hunger, Poor Hygiene, Inappropriate Dress Consistent Lack of Supervision, Especially in Dangerous Activities or Long Periods Unattended Physical Problems or Medical Needs Abandonment	Begging, Stealing Food Extended Stays at School (early arrival and late departure) Constant Fatigue, Listlessness, or Falling Asleep in Class Alcohol or Drug Abuse Delinquency (e.g., thefts) States There Is No Caretaker

Type of CA/N	Physical Indicators	Behavioral Indicators
SEXUAL ABUSE	Difficulty in Walking or Sitting	Unwilling to Change for Gym or Participate in Physical Education Class
	Torn, Stained, or Bloody Underclothing	
	Pain or Itching in Genital Area	Withdrawal, Fantasy, or Infantile Behavior
	Bruises or Bleeding in External Genitalia, Vaginal, or Anal Areas	Bizarre, Sophisticated, or Unusual Sexual Behavior or Knowledge
	Veneral Disease, Especially in Preteens	Poor Peer Relationships
	Pregnancy	Delinquent or Run-Away
		Reports Sexual Assault by Caretaker
EMOTIONAL MALTREATMENT	Speech Disorders	Habit Disorders (sucking, biting, rocking, etc.)
	Lags in Physical Development	
	Failure to Thrive	Conduct Disorders (antisocial, destructive, etc.)
		Neurotic Traits (sleep disorders, inhibition of play)
		Psychoneurotic Reactions (hysteria, obsession, compulsion, phobias, hypochondria)
		Behavior Extremes: —compliant, passive —aggressive, demanding
		Overly Adaptive Behavior: —inappropriately adult —inappropriately infant
		Developmental Lags (mental, emotional)
		Attempted Suicide

SOURCE: Diane D. Broadhurst, The Educator's Role in the Prevention and Treatment of Child Abuse and Neglect, *National Center on Child Abuse and Neglect, U.S. Department of Health, Education and Welfare, Publ. No. 79-30172 (1979).*

Is the reporter of child abuse or neglect protected from lawsuits?

Yes. Every state provides immunity by law from civil suit and criminal prosecution that might arise from the reporting of suspected child abuse or neglect. Such immunity applies to all mandatory or permissible reporters who act "in good faith."

In many states, good faith is presumed; therefore, the person suing the reporter has the burden to prove that the reporter acted in bad faith. Clearly, any educator, therapist, or counselor who acts in good faith and is mandated by law to report suspected cases of abuse or neglect is immune from suit.

In order to be eligible for federal funds under the Child Abuse Prevention, Adoption, and Family Service Act, states must grant immunity to reporters. All states have complied with this requirement. The expressed intent of immunity legislation is to encourage reporting without fear of civil or criminal liability.

Should counselors violate privileged communication by reporting suspected cases of abuse or neglect?

Yes, in fact they must. First of all, most states deny such privilege to counselors in any legal proceeding. Second, as a matter of public policy it is more important to require the reporting than to respect the privilege. And finally, because counselors are among those who must report, the legal requirement of reporting overrides any claim to privilege or confidential communication.

Do religious beliefs provide exemption from liability for child abuse?

Yes, in most states, although this matter continues to be a subject of controversy. Because there are some religions that believe in nonmedical spiritual healing, most states provide special laws pertaining to them. Typical is the Missouri statute, which makes the following provision:

> A child who does not receive specific medical treatment by reason of the legitimate practice of the religious belief of said child's parents, guardians, or others legally responsible for said child, for that reason alone, shall not be considered to be an abused or neglected child.[13]

Although 44 states have similar statutes, some of them explicitly authorize courts to order medical treatment when the child's health requires it. Furthermore, courts may have such power even without explicit statutory authorization.[14]

Is there a penalty for failure to report suspected child abuse or neglect?

Yes. At this writing, in all but six states (Idaho, Illinois, Maryland, Mississippi, Montana, and Wyoming) mandated reporters are criminally liable for failure to report a suspected case of child abuse or neglect. Failure to report is a misdemeanor in most states. The penalty might range from a 5- to 30-day jail sentence and/or a fine of $10 to $100 to as high as a fine of $1000 and a year in jail.

However, there are no *reported* cases of a criminal prosecution for failure to report a case of child abuse or neglect. Why? Because state laws usually require a "knowing" or "willful" failure to report. It is extremely difficult to prove, beyond all reasonable doubt, that someone "knowingly" or "willfully" failed to report; therefore, cases are not prosecuted. Perhaps a more likely route of enforcement is the threat of civil liability.

Some states already have enacted laws that impose civil liability (liability in money damages) for failure to report. However, different state laws require differing degrees of proof. For example, in Arkansas, Colorado, Iowa, and New York, proof of willful misconduct is required, whereas Michigan and Montana use a lesser standard for establishing liability, namely the standard of negligence.[15] Various scholars believe that civil liability for not reporting will be the trend of the future and will help increase the number of abuse and neglect cases reported.[16]

At this writing, there are no reported cases imposing civil liability on teachers or counselors for failure to report, but with the increase in the number of states imposing such liability by statute, such cases are likely to arise. Currently, the best-known cases seeking money damages for failure to report child abuse and neglect have been filed against physicians and hospitals. The landmark case of *Landeros v. Flood* established the principle that a physician could be held liable in money damages for failure to report a case of child abuse.[17] Reasoning by analogy, courts could hold educators, including counselors, liable for money damages for violating their mandated duty to report. Such liability will be all the more possible in states that explicitly impose liability by statute, for example, Michigan and Montana.

There are cases, however, where counselors or psychologists have been disciplined for failure to promptly report a suspected case of child abuse. One controversial case arose in Illinois, where Dr. Rosario C. Pesce, a tenured teacher school psychologist was suspended without pay for five days and demoted from "school psychologist" to "school psychologist for the behavior disorders program." The state law required school psychologists to *immediately* report suspected cases of abuse or neglect. When information first came to Dr. Pesce about the probability of abuse, he consulted with his attorney and a psychologist and chose not to report for 10 days, at which time he became more certain of the actual abuse. The facts indicated probable sexual involvement of the student with his male teacher as well as threats of suicide. When Dr. Pesce challenged the administrative action, claiming it to violate his constitutional right to due process as well as his federal right to confidentiality, the U.S. district court and the court of appeals ruled against him. (An edited version of the case appears at the end of this chapter.)[18]

How does one report child abuse or neglect?

Each state statute that mandates reporting of child abuse or neglect specifies the procedures reporters are required to follow (see Appendix F). As indicated on the chart, most states require an oral report, within a reasonable period of time (24–72 hours, though some allow up to seven days), followed by a more detailed written report. A number of states have set up to 24-hour toll-free "hot lines" to facilitate reporting.

Most states require that the reporter include in the report, if known, the names and addresses of the child, the nature and extent of the injury or condition observed, and the reporter's name and address. The reporting form often has a general request for "any other information that the person making the report believes may be helpful in establishing the cause of the injury . . . and protecting the child." Some states and some school districts provide a reporting form in order to facilitate the making of written reports (see Appendix F). The absence of such forms, however, does not excuse one from reporting; any piece of paper may be used as long as the required information is provided.

Is a social service agency liable for failure to protect the child after the abuse has been reported?

No, ruled a divided Supreme Court in the 1989 *DeShaney* case.[19] Joshua DeShaney was beaten by his father to the point of abuse, repeatedly, from the time he was 1 year old until the age of 4, when he landed in the hospital with life-threatening coma, and after brain surgery was expected to live as a profoundly retarded person. His father was convicted of child abuse.

Suit was filed in a federal court on behalf of Joshua and his mother alleging that the county Department of Social Services deprived him of "his liberty without due process of law" by failing to intervene to protect him after they knew or should have known of the risk of violence at his father's hands.

Although the Supreme Court acknowledged that "the facts of this case are undeniably tragic" and that the social service worker was fully cognizant of the brutality of the beatings and did not intervene except to take notes, the majority of six justices held that the fourteenth amendment was not violated. The purpose of the amendment, according to the majority, is to protect people from the state and not from each other or from private actors. Thus, the social worker or the Department of Social Services was under no duty to protect Joshua. If there is to be such duty placed on them, reasoned the Court, the state legislature has to create the obligation; it is not for the courts to impose it.

A minority of three justices disagreed. They would have held that once the state intervened and the Department of Social Services moved in to document and report the abuse, a duty was created to protect Joshua. (See Appendix D for an edited version of this case.)

SUMMARY AND CONCLUSIONS

Although child abuse and neglect is an age-old phenomenon, it has become a matter of concern to the general public only in recent decades. California, in 1962, was the first state to require by law the reporting of child abuse. By 1964, 20 states had followed suit. Today all states, the District of Columbia, Puerto Rico, the Virgin Islands, and American Samoa have such laws.

Laws, however much they may help, do not prevent child abuse and neglect from occurring each year. During recent years, over one million such cases per year have been brought to the attention of the National Center on Child Abuse and

Neglect. This is probably only the tip of the iceberg, for it is generally believed that a very large number of child abuse and neglect cases never get reported.

Counselors, among others, are mandated by law to report cases of suspected or known abuse. If one has reasonable grounds to suspect abuse or neglect, the law requires a report under penalty of a fine and/or jail term. Furthermore, a suit for money damages may be filed against one who fails to report. States are increasingly enacting laws imposing liability for failure to report on those mandated to file child abuse reports. State laws also grant immunity for those who are mandated to report; thus individuals need not fear lawsuits for invasion of privacy, defamation, or some other cause of action.

Federal funds are available to states that meet certain requirements for reporting cases of abuse or neglect. The ultimate purpose of all these laws, federal and state, is to increase the reporting of children in danger of abuse or neglect and to provide more comprehensive services for those children and their families. Counselors and educators are in key positions to assist in these efforts and they have the duty to do so.

PESCE V. J. STERLING MORTON HIGH SCHOOL DISTRICT 201
830 F.2d 789 (7th Cir. 1987)

CUDAHY, Circuit Judge.

Dr. Rosario C. Pesce was disciplined by a public school for his delay in reporting suspected child abuse by a public school teacher. Pesce claims that his federal constitutional rights of due process and privacy were thereby violated. The district court dismissed the complaint, . . . We affirm.

I

. . .

Pesce was a tenured teacher and school psychologist at Morton East High School. On the morning of February 26, 1986, a female student ("C.R.") provided Pesce with a note written to her by a male friend ("J.D."). The note included statements apparently made by J.D. expressing guilt and confusion about his sexual preference and possible hints of suicide. C.R. also informed Pesce that J.D. had visited the home of a male faculty member where "something sexual" had occurred between them. Pesce urged C.R. to have J.D. get in touch with Pesce to discuss these matters; Pesce also asked C.R. to pass along to J.D. the name and phone number of a professional therapist. Pesce did not notify anyone else of C.R.'s communications at that time.

Later the same day, J.D. visited Pesce in his office at school. Pesce assured J.D. of the confidentiality of any information divulged and questioned him about the issues raised by the letter. J.D. denied having any current suicidal intentions and denied that any sexual acts had occurred between the male teacher and him, but stated that the teacher had once shown him "pictures" when he visited the teacher's home. J.D. also expressed a desire to have help in addressing his confusion over sexual preference. Pesce arranged for J.D. to see a therapist.

Pesce reached a professional judgment that it was in J.D.'s best interest for Pesce to honor their confidential relationship and not to inform school authorities about J.D.'s communications without his consent. Pesce considered the legal and psychological implications before choosing this course of action; he consulted with his attorney and a psychologist and considered relevant state laws, school regulations and guidelines of the American Psychological Association. After due consideration and in good faith Pesce chose not to notify any school officials of the rumored sexual activity or the suicidal tendencies.

During the following week J.D. kept two appointments with the therapist whom Pesce had recommended, but on March 5, 1986, Pesce learned that J.D. had cancelled an appointment. On March 7, Pesce met with J.D. and the therapist and discussed the advantages and disadvantages of disclosing to school officials the information about the male teacher. During that discussion J.D. revealed that in fact he and the male teacher had engaged in a sexual act. J.D. then agreed with Pesce that it would be best to reveal the information to school authorities. Pesce promptly did so.

The school superintendent asked Pesce to submit a written report of the incident; Pesce filed the report on March 13. The superintendent subsequently informed Pesce that he would recommend to the school board that Pesce be suspended without pay for five days for failure promptly to report J.D.'s possible suicidal tendencies and the alleged sexual misconduct of the male teacher. The superintendent also informed Pesce of his right to a hearing before the school board.

Pesce and his attorney requested a hearing; on May 5 they appeared at a hearing before the school board and presented a defense of Pesce's actions including documentary evidence. After the hearing was concluded, the board requested and received from Pesce's attorney a statement of supporting authorities. On May 24 the school board voted to impose a five-day suspension without pay. Pesce served the suspension beginning May 28, and upon his return to work was "demoted" from "School Psychologist" to "School Psychologist for the Behavior Disorders Program."

Pesce filed this action on August 20, 1986, alleging that the school district, acting under color of state law, violated his federal constitutional rights, . . . and his rights "under Illinois public policy," . . .

The district court concluded that, under Illinois law, as a tenured teacher, Pesce had a property interest in his employment and that Pesce could claim a liberty interest in his professional reputation. The court determined, however, that it was evident from Pesce's complaint that he received whatever process was due when he was given notice of the reasons for his possible suspension, a presuspension hearing with counsel and certain post-hearing procedures. . . . The court concluded that Pesce failed adequately to allege a violation of either substantive or procedural due process.

. . .

Because much of this case turns on the requirements of several Illinois laws, a brief outline of these various provisions is necessary. The Abused and Neglected Child Reporting Act, III.Rev.Stat. ch. 23, ¶¶2051 *et seq.* (the "Reporting Act"), requires that certain described individuals report suspected child abuse or neglect to the Illinois Department of Children and Family Services. The reporting requirement mandates:

> Any . . . school personnel . . . [or] registered psychologist . . . having reasonable cause to believe a child known to them in their professional or official capacity may be an abused or a neglected child shall immediately report or cause a report to be made to the Department [of Children and Family Services].

III.Rev.Stat. ch. 23, ¶2054. As a school psychologist Pesce is subject to this reporting requirement. Ultimately it also was evident that J.D. was an "abused child" as defined in the Reporting Act.* Two other provisions of the same paragraph are relevant here. First:

> Whenever such person is required to report under this Act in his capacity as a member of the staff of a . . . school . . . he *shall* make report immediately to the Department . . . and *may* also notify the person in charge of such . . . school . . . or his designated agent that such report has been made.

Id. (emphasis supplied). And second:

> The privileged quality of communication between any professional person required to report and his patient or client shall not apply to situations involving abused or neglected children and shall not constitute grounds for failure to report as required by this Act.

Id. The Reporting Act establishes administrative bodies to receive and act upon reports of child abuse or neglect and insures against the improper release of reports to the public. The Reporting Act also grants immunity to everyone who reports in good faith under the act:

> Any person . . . under this Act, participating in good faith in the making of a report . . . shall have immunity from any liability, civil, criminal or that otherwise might result by reason of such actions. For the purpose of any proceedings, civil or criminal . . . good faith . . . shall be presumed.

Id. ¶2059.

The Mental Health and Developmental Disabilities Confidentiality Act, Ill.Rev.Stat. ch. 91½, ¶¶801 *et seq.* (the "Confidentiality Act"), is also relevant. The Confidentiality Act provides generally that all communications between a psychologist and a patient made in connection with the provision of mental health services are confidential and shall not be disclosed except pursuant to the Confidentiality Act. *Id.* ¶803. The Confidentiality Act permits disclosure of confidential communications of a minor between the ages of twelve and eighteen if a parent or guardian of the minor consents and either the minor consents or the therapist finds disclosure to be in the best interest of the minor. *Id.* ¶805. The Confidentiality Act also specifically permits disclosure of confidential communications in accordance with the Reporting Act and repeats the immunity provisions of that act. *Id.* ¶811. However, the Confidentiality Act imposes a criminal penalty for any knowing violation of its provisions. *Id.* ¶816.

The State of Illinois requires that psychological services be available, in appropriate degree, to all children in the state system. . . . Pesce was a school psychologist employed to provide such counseling for students at Morton East High School. As a school psychologist, Pesce looked to professional guidelines for standards of behavior; the American Psychological Association adopted guidelines for school psychologists indicating:

> The school psychologist conforms to current laws and regulations with respect to release of confidential information. As a general rule, however, the school psychologist does not release confidential information, except with the written consent of the parent or, where appropriate, the student directly involved. . . .

---

*The Reporting Act defines an "abused child" as including a child under 18 years of age who is a victim of a sex offense. See Ill.Rev.Stat. ch. 38, ¶¶11–1 *et seq.* Pesce does not argue that J.D. was not in fact an abused child under this definition.

When there is a conflict with the force of law, or with a court order, the school psychologist seeks a resolution to the conflict that is both ethically and legally feasible and appropriate. . . .

And finally, Pesce was a party to an employment contract with the school district that permitted suspension without pay for "misconduct," which was defined to include:

Any act or failure to act occurring during the course of an employee's duties which jeopardizes the health, safety and welfare of any person, student, parent or school employee.

. . .

Any act or failure to act which constitutes a violation or an attempt to violate any federal or state law or regulation or municipal ordinance and which relates to the employee's duties.

Employee Suspension Policy, J. Sterling Morton High School District 201. . . . The defendants claim that Pesce's failure to report his information about J.D. to school authorities constituted misconduct that justified imposition of a penalty of suspension without pay.

II

A. PROCEDURAL DUE PROCESS

[1] Pesce contends on appeal that his procedural due process rights were violated because he was temporarily suspended from his position for violating standards of which he had inadequate prior notice. As noted above, Pesce's employment agreement contemplated possible suspension for any action that "jeopardize[d] the health, safety and welfare" of a student. Pesce argues both that this standard is too vague to comport with due process requirements and that he complied with the standard by acting in the best interests of the student, J.D. According to Pesce, factual questions are raised that render a trial necessary.

Viewing the facts in the light most favorable to Pesce, it is clear that he received written notice of the proposed disciplinary action and the reasons supporting the action, that he was granted a hearing to present argument and evidence with the assistance of an attorney and that he received a written statement from the school board explaining the rationale for its decision. We believe that these formal procedures adequately protected Pesce's right to procedural due process before being suspended. . . . Pesce does not argue that the hearing itself was inadequate.

The essence of Pesce's procedural due process claim seems to be that he was punished for violating a standard too vague to be enforced, or for actually complying with the standard. As to the first issue we cannot agree that the standard applied by the school board was unconstitutionally vague. Admittedly, the requirement is broad; the teacher shall not jeopardize a student's health, safety or welfare. However, Pesce has not alleged that the requirement gave him no prior notice of requirements. Illinois law establishes that teachers stand in the relation of parents to the students in their charges, and the school board has chosen to require its employees always to act in the best interests of their charges. The requirement is not arbitrary and the board's decision cannot be construed as a change in policy. . . .

We cannot agree with Pesce that he was punished for *obeying* school board requirements thus violating procedural due process. . . . Pesce's complaint makes clear that he received a letter indicating that a male student, J.D., possibly was suicidal, and was informed by another student that a male teacher had engaged in sexual activity with J.D.

Even though Pesce alleges that in his judgment nondisclosure was in J.D.'s best interest, we cannot agree that the school board conclusion to the contrary that Pesce's actions "jeopardized the health, safety and welfare" of students was unconstitutional. Such a conclusion was within the discretion of the board rationally to reach.

B. SUBSTANTIVE DUE PROCESS

[2] In his argument to this court, Pesce acknowledges that his substantive due process claim depends on a rather "exceptional" and narrow doctrine, but he stresses that the facts as alleged do comprise an exceptional array. Essentially Pesce contends that he has been punished by one arm of the State of Illinois—the school board—for obeying the requirements of another arm—the legislature. According to Pesce, he conscientiously and scrupulously followed the dictates of state law (including the Confidentiality Act and the Reporting Act) when he decided not to inform his supervisors of allegations about and by J.D.; nonetheless, he was punished by the state for not following other inconsistent requirements.

The defendants argue that Pesce's interpretation of his legal obligations was "patently erroneous," that in fact no conflicting obligations confronted Pesce: "It could not be any clearer that state law and professional ethics *did not* require or suggest that plaintiff withhold such information from school officials until he obtained the student's consent." . . . The defendants contend that, even if Pesce faced some conflict between his obligations as a psychologist and the school board's demands, the interest of the board is substantial and compelling in protecting students from sexual abuse and self-destruction. According to the defendants, Pesce's interest is therefore far outweighed by the school board's interest in protecting the student.

Neither the litigants' nor our own research has disclosed a case upholding a similar substantive due process claim founded on an allegation that the state has acted in a conflicting or inconsistent manner toward an individual. . . . Nonetheless, Pesce's claim raises substantial questions. The crux of the issue must be whether the state imposed truly inconsistent obligations in such a fashion that an individual could not avoid punishment. Perhaps the starkest example of this sort of conflict might be posed by a state employer that discharged a state employee for failing to violate a state criminal statute. The citizen in such a situation would presumably face a choice between violating a state criminal statute and being deprived of a property interest in a job. We believe that such a dilemma posed by a state might work a violation of substantive due process in some circumstances.

Pesce, however, does not face such a stark choice, at least under Illinois law as we construe it. Pesce argues in considerable detail that he followed the letter and spirit of all applicable state laws and regulations. The general outline of his argument is as follows: Communications between a patient and his psychologist are protected by a state law privilege, with limited exceptions. Pesce's discussions with J.D. were in connection with mental health counseling and therefore are protected by this privilege. The only possibly relevant exception to this privilege permits nonconsensual disclosure of information pursuant to the Reporting Act. However, Pesce did not have reasonable cause to believe that J.D. was an abused child—J.D. denied the fact and only unreliable evidence supported it. Even if reasonable cause existed, Pesce could report his suspicions only to the Department of Children and Family Services and could notify his supervisors only of the *fact* of making the report, not the substance of the report. Finally, Pesce's supervisors cannot claim that he violated the Reporting Act because they themselves apparently did not believe the fact warranted a report—they never reported any abuse to the state department.

The defendants just as vehemently contend that state laws and regulations require that Pesce notify others of his information about J.D. and the teacher; thus the school requirement that he notify his supervisors was not inconsistent with state law. As the defendants would have it: First, Pesce's information was not at any time confidential under state law, because he received much of it from C.R., a friend of J.D. Second, no privilege applied because the Reporting Act requires disclosure of information that a child has been abused. Third, guidelines for school psychologists permit disclosure where, as here, not to disclose would result in clear danger to the patient or to others. Fourth, any person who makes a good faith report of suspected child abuse is protected by statute with immunity from civil or criminal liability, so the school could require Pesce to make all good faith disclosures.

Without a doubt there are factual issues in dispute between the parties. There are also crucial questions of Illinois law in dispute. This latter state of affairs convinces us that Pesce has not stated a violation of substantive due process because he has not alleged that the state has imposed on him clearly inconsistent demands that leave him no safe harbor. There might in principle be some merit to Pesce's general contention—the State of Illinois has applied arguably inconsistent policies to him: on the one hand, he is to protect professional confidences, but on the other, he is to inform his supervisors at school about all threats to the safety and welfare of the students. But state laws or policies are occasionally, if not frequently, at loggerheads. Unless the inconsistency of legal demands is so stark as to force a citizen to bring down the wrath of the state regardless of the decision made, the federal doctrine of substantive due process does not seem applicable.

Here, in light especially of the broad immunity granted to a citizen who in good faith reports suspected instances of child abuse, we cannot say that Illinois has placed such inconsistent demands on Pesce as to violate substantive due process.

C. Privacy Right

Pesce argues that the school board's decision to discipline him for failing to disclose information he received in a confidential discussion with his patient J.D. violated Pesce's federal constitutional right of confidentiality, which purportedly derives from J.D.'s right to privacy. The district court rejected this argument summarily:

> Aside from the fact that it is by no means clear that plaintiff has standing to assert any such [privacy] right derivatively, plaintiff has not shown how the alleged privacy violation gives rise to a cause of action under § 1983. . . .

We think the district court reached the correct result.

[3] As a first step, Pesce's claim here does not even implicate the law of Illinois with respect to privacy. As noted, issues of state law certainly could arise in a federal substantive due process analysis, but Pesce cannot claim any section 1983 violation based solely on an alleged violation of state privacy rights. It may well be that Pesce can claim protection under the aegis of Illinois privacy law, but not in a § 1983 claim. *Cf.* Ill. Const. art. I § 6 ("The people shall have the right to be secure in their persons, houses, papers and other possessions against unreasonable . . . invasions of privacy. . . ."); . . . (suggesting that Illinois Constitution protects right to confidentiality). The question raised by Pesce's claim is whether Illinois has so invaded the relationship between psychologist and patient as to deprive Pesce and J.D. of federal rights.

[4] The federal Constitution does, of course, protect certain rights of privacy including a right of confidentiality in certain types of information. . . .

We recognize that the federal right of confidentiality might in some circumstances be implicated when a state conditions continued employment on the disclosure of private information. But we cannot agree that Pesce has alleged such circumstances in the present case. Instead we conclude . . . that the state statutory scheme does not "pose a sufficiently grievous threat" to any right of confidentiality as to rise to a constitutional violation. . . .

We do not necessarily agree with the district court that, as a matter of pleading, Pesce failed adequately to allege standing to assert a federal right of confidentiality. It is far from clear that the right of confidentiality protects one party to a psychologist-patient relationship more than the other party. Indeed, significant authority suggests that the constitutional right of privacy as relevant to doctor-patient relationships applies equally to doctor and to patient. . . . As a school psychologist, Pesce may well be able to claim a right to confidentiality in his professional relationships with his patients. *Cf.* Smith, *Constitutional Privacy in Psychotherapy,* 49 Geo.Wash.L.Rev. 1 (1980).

However, a constitutional right to confidentiality does not protect against any and every compelled disclosure nor does it federalize every state professional privilege. . . . And while it may not be settled what standard of review governs a claim of abridgment of a right to confidentiality, we conclude in the circumstances of this case that Pesce has not adequately alleged a violation of any federal right to confidentiality.

Even if there is here a federal right to confidentiality that can be infringed only to further a compelling state interest, we conclude that such an interest is present in the present circumstances. Of critical importance here is the fact that the state is acting to protect one of the most pitiable and helpless classes in society—abused children. The Supreme Court has recognized the substantial interest of a state in protecting all children. . . . A state serves a compelling interest in protecting abused children. Illinois, like other states, has adopted measures seeking to uncover instances of child abuse in order to protect children from subsequent abuse. The compelling interest of the state reflects several characteristics special to abused children: they often may be unaware of their own abuse or injury; they may often be unable to report abuse; the effects of abuse may be invisible to third parties; abused children can carry physical and emotional scars for a lifetime; and of course the state bears a special responsibility to protect children who are considered unable voluntarily to choose their own course of action. . . . In light of the unique problems of child abuse, we find that the Illinois requirement that Pesce and others in similar positions of responsibility promptly report child abuse to a state agency does not unconstitutionally infringe any federal right of confidentiality. Pesce may have some sort of privilege under Illinois law, but that is not a matter we need address.

We of course do not purport to define the contours of any federal right to confidentiality in matters other than the one before us. In the unique circumstances of child abuse, Illinois may constitutionally require that psychologists report to an agency of the state suspected instances of present abuse. In addition, Pesce has not contended that psychologists' reports would be too widely disseminated by the state, so we need not evaluate the adequacy of the recordkeeping procedures employed by the state. . . .

III

We conclude that Pesce failed adequately to allege a violation of his federal rights to procedural due process, substantive due process or confidentiality. Accordingly the judgment of the district court is *Affirmed.*

NOTES

1. Friedman, *Unequal and Inadequate Protection Under the Law: State Child Abuse Statutes,* 50 GEO. WASH. L. REV. 243–74 (1982).

2. *See* generally U.S. Department of Health and Human Services, Report by the National Center on Child Abuse and Neglect (1983).

3. For more information, see Child Abuse Prevention, Adoption, and Family Services Act of 1988, §§ 101–401. PL 100–294, 42 U.S.C. § 5101 (1988).

4. Alaska Stat. ch. 17 § 47.17.010.

5. Vt. Stat. Ann. tit. 13, §§ 1351–1356 (Supp. 1981–82).

6. Frazier, *A Glance at the Past, A Gaze at the Present, A Glimpse at the Future: A Critical Analysis of the Development of Child Abuse Reporting Statutes*, 54 Chi.-Kent L. Rev. 641, 643 (1978).

7. U.S. Department of Health, Education and Welfare Child Abuse & Neglect; State Reporting Laws (Special Report from the National Center on Child Abuse and Neglect) DHHS Publication No. (OHDS) 80–30265 at 3.

8. *Id.* at 5.

9. *Supra* note 1 at 254.

10. Md. CODE ANN. art. 27, § 35A(b)(8)(Cum. Supp. 1978); Fla. Stat. Ann. § 827.07(1)(b) (Supp. 1979).

11. Such laws are found in Arkansas, Colorado, Idaho, Maine, Utah, West Virginia, American Samoa, and the Virgin Islands. *See supra* note 7 at 3.

12. For an excellent guide to the use of such clues and interviews, see *id.* at 20–27.

13. Mo. Rev. Stat. § 210.115(3)(supp. 1979).

14. *See, e.g., In re* Sampson, 278 N.E. 2d 919 (1972). For a list of states granting religious immunity as well as modified immunity, see *supra* note 7 at 15.

15. Aaron, *Civil Liability for Teachers' Negligent Failure to Report Suspected Child Abuse*, 28 Wayne L. Rev. 183–213 (1981).

16. *Id.*

17. Landeros v. Flood, 551 P.2d 389 (1976); Robinson v. Wical, No. 37607 (Cal. Sup. Ct., San Louis Obispo, filed Sept. 4, 1970); Leach v. Chemung, No. 75–2652 (Chemung City Sup. Ct. N.Y., filed May 18, 1976).

18. Pesce v. J. Sterling Morton High School, 830F.2d 789 (7th Cir. 1987).

19. DeShaney v. Winnebago County Dept. of Social Services, 57 U.S.L.W. 4218 (1989).

CHAPTER 9

Rights Related
to Schooling: Part I

OVERVIEW

During recent decades there has been a veritable explosion of litigation relating to schooling. Much of this litigation has been in the area of rights related to schooling, with a heavy emphasis on the constitutional rights of students, teachers, and parents. This flood of lawsuits can be best understood when viewed in a more comprehensive, cultural context, with special emphasis on the civil rights movement of the 1960s, the rise of the counterculture, and the increased militancy of organized teachers.

Historically, no one spoke of the application of the national Constitution to schools, except in matters related to religion and academic freedom. Schooling was considered to be a function of the state pursuant to the tenth amendment of the Constitution, which reserves to the states all powers not specifically granted to the federal government. We all know that this is no longer the case. Although schooling is still primarily a state function, with states delegating much of their power to local communities, it is clear today that schools must function consistently within the "basic law of the land," the Constitution. This chapter explains these developments and highlights the current state of the law in relation to constitutional rights and the public schools.*

Not all rights related to schooling are discussed in Chapters 9 and 10. Rights related to student discipline, including due process, are analyzed in Chapter 7, those related to special needs students are discussed in Chapter 6, and rights related to

---

*It is important to note that private schools need not abide by constitutional law, because they are not organs of the state and their actions are not considered to be "state action," whereas public schools are arms of the state, and thus their actions are considered to be "state actions" for purposes of constitutional law.

testing and bilingual students are covered in Chapter 5. Our emphasis in this chapter is primarily, but not exclusively, on rights related to the first and fourteenth amendments of the Constitution. Furthermore, due to its length, the topic is divided into two chapters, the second of which presents materials related to legal issues of equal protection.

Why should counselors know the rights of students, teachers, and parents?

We need not dwell at length on why counselors should know their own rights; it is almost self-evident. As professionals they want to know how the laws apply to them so they can function more intelligently and with more confidence in their relations with school administrators, teachers, students, and parents. As we shall see, the rights of counselors are the same as those of teachers, with certain exceptions that we shall highlight. However, counselors are often sought out for advice by administrators, teachers, students, and parents. Such advice often relates to highly controversial matters that can be resolved or understood only if one considers the relevant educational, social-psychological, and legal issues involved. Furthermore, many school counselors are also part-time teachers. Because it is impractical for counselors to consult lawyers constantly, it becomes important for them at least to be aware of the relevant legal issues as well as the general guidelines we can derive from important court decisions. Such knowledge should also enable the counselor to know when an attorney should be consulted and thus to practice preventive law.

FREEDOM OF EXPRESSION

Private schools, as well as private business and industry, may dismiss or otherwise discipline employees for publicly criticizing their policies, practices, and products. Do employees of public schools have more freedom than employees in the private sector? Should teachers and counselors be restricted to official channels for expressing their criticisms? What are the limits, if any, to teachers and students expressing themselves orally or in writing in schools and through school publications? These and related issues are considered in this section.

May teachers publicly criticize school board policy?

Yes, the Supreme Court ruled in 1968.[1] The case involved Marvin Pickering, a high school teacher in Illinois, who published a long, sarcastic letter in a newspaper, criticizing the superintendent and the school board. The school board wanted to fire Pickering for "damaging the professional reputation of school administrators and the board" and for making statements "detrimental to the efficient operation and administration of the schools." Pickering, believing that he had the right, under the first amendment, to express himself and criticize school policies, filed suit challenging his dismissal.

Although he lost in the courts of Illinois, Pickering ultimately prevailed in the Supreme Court of the United States. In what became a landmark decision, the Court upheld teachers' freedom of expression away from school, even if it involved criticism of school policies. The Court, noting that school policies are public policies, stated that on such issues

> free and open debate is vital to informed decision making by the electorate. Teachers are, as a class, the members of a community most likely to have informed and definite opinions as to how funds allocated to the operation of the schools should be spent. Accordingly, it is essential that they be able to speak out freely on such questions without fear of retaliatory dismissal.

The Court also held that the teacher's criticism need not be completely accurate; innocent or unintentional errors will not vitiate the right to free expression. To require complete accuracy would inhibit people from speaking out and thus have a "chilling effect" on their first amendment rights. On the other hand, false statements made knowingly or recklessly will not be protected.

May school boards ever restrict teachers' rights to publicize their views?

Yes. In *Pickering*, the Court said that "it is possible to conceive of some positions in public employment in which the need for confidentiality is so great that even completely correct public statements might furnish a permissible ground for dismissal." This would be the case, for example, if a teacher or counselor publicly revealed the content of confidential interviews or the contents of students' files without permission. Similarly, a teacher who disseminated to the news media charges about a local principal's negligence found himself in trouble.[2] When he claimed to be exercising his freedom of speech, the court ruled against him and distinguished the case from *Pickering*. The *Pickering* case involved open criticism of public policy, to be resolved by majority vote; the possible removal of a principal is not a matter of public policy, it is a personnel decision to be made by the school board. Publicizing such matters before they are thoroughly investigated, ruled the court, can "interfere with the orderly operation of the school system."

Similarly, in 1983 the Supreme Court had occasion to consider the application to employment situations of the first amendment's provision for freedom of expression. In *Connick v. Myers*[3] the Court emphasized the distinction between matters of public concern and grievances related to internal personnel decisions. Expressions related to public concerns receive the protection of the first amendment, whereas ordinary employee grievances (in this case the circulation within an office of a petition related to the functioning of the office) are to be handled by the appropriate administrative agencies, without involving the federal courts.

More recent cases continued the distinction between public criticism of policy, which is protected, and public criticism or complaining about internal school matters. For example, in a 1988 decision a federal appeals court ruled that "sarcastic, unprofessional, and insulting" memoranda written by a teacher to various school officials were not protected by the first amendment.[4] The teacher was articulating his private disagreement with policies and procedures that he had either failed to apply or refused to follow. He was not speaking out as a citizen concerned with problems facing the school district. Public complaints about classroom materials, teacher aids, scheduling, or the adequacy of laboratory equipment are similarly not protected.[5] "To hold otherwise," wrote the court, "would be to transform every personal grievance into protected speech."

A very important restriction on counselors' freedom of expression can be derived from *Pickering*. There, Justice Marshall wrote that "certain forms of public criticisms of the superior by the subordinate would obviously undermine the effectiveness of the working relationship between them" and thus justify discipline. Although the typical relationship between principal and teacher is not a close one and thus would not be seriously impaired by the public criticism of school policy, courts might well conclude otherwise if counselors were to publish such criticisms. This would be the case *if in fact,* in the particular situation, there were a close working relationship between the counselor and the principal. Often this is the case, and such a relationship could be seriously impaired by public criticism.

The right of assistant football coaches to participate in a public debate concerning corporal punishment imposed on students by the head coach was protected by the courts. When school officials wanted to impose involuntary transfers on the assistant coaches, a federal court held that they could not be punished for their exercise of first amendment rights. They were able to keep their positions and also received an award of attorney fees.[6]

Thus, critical remarks of teachers receive more protection than those of counselors, vice principals, assistant superintendents, or others in close, subordinate administrative positions, whose public comments about their superiors might make it difficult to continue the somewhat intimate daily working relationship. Courts attempt to balance the competing interests involved—the individual's interest in freedom of expression, on one hand, and the community's interest in the effective and efficient operation of the school, on the other. As a general rule, because freedom of expression is one of the "fundamental rights" guaranteed by the Constitution, courts go far to protect it, and its restriction will be tolerated only if there is "material and substantial" interference in the operation of the schools.

Is circulating a petition a protected expression?

Yes, ruled a federal appeals court. Two nontenured teachers filed suit alleging that the school board's nonrenewal of their contract was in retaliation for their circulating a petition, with a letter addressed to the state superintendent of education, questioning administrative use of certain school funds. The evidence showed that their nonrenewal was based on their drafting and circulating of the petition. Although the trial court found a violation of their rights, it would not reinstate them, for fear that such action would "breed difficult working conditions." The court of appeals overruled this judgment, stating that "although the district court's concerns are understandable, they do not justify the court's refusal to grant reinstatement."[7]

May counselors be transferred for publicly criticizing a school program?

No, not when such transfer is made as retaliation for the exercise of protected speech. Such a case arose in Arizona, where a counselor publicly criticized the placement of Mexican-American children in classes for the mentally retarded. She suggested that parents could sue to stop the practice of testing children in English even though they spoke little or no English at all. When she was transferred to a school in a wealthy area with very few Mexican-American children, she went to court and challenged what she considered to be a disciplinary transfer.[8]

The case went as high as a federal appeals court, which ruled in her favor. The court agreed with the school board that the counselor's assignment to work with Mexican-American children was not a protected legal right. However, once she was so assigned, the administrators could not transfer her as a disciplinary measure for her public criticism of school policies or programs.

May counselors express their criticisms in private?

Yes. There are no reported cases involving counselors who criticized their principals in the privacy of an office, but at least one case of this type, involving a teacher, reached the Supreme Court.[9] In this case, Bessie Givhan, a teacher of English, was dismissed after a series of private encounters with the principal wherein, according to the principal, Givhan made "petty and unreasonable demands" in an "insulting, loud and hostile" manner. The trial court determined that her demands were not petty or unreasonable, because they involved racial discrimination in the school. Although the lower courts ruled against the teacher on the grounds that private complaints are not protected by the Constitution, the Supreme Court disagreed and extended the *Pickering* principle to apply to private as well as public criticism.

The Court emphasized that a teacher's freedom of speech is not diminished when she communicates privately with her employer, rather than choosing to spread her views before the public. On the other hand, the limits of freedom of expression are reached where such expression interferes with classroom duties or the operation of the schools. To decide whether or not a confrontation is protected expression, the Court ruled in *Givhan*, judges must consider the "manner, time, and place" of the confrontation when attempting to reach the proper balance between the rights in conflict.

Arguing by analogy from the *Givhan* case as well as cases from lower courts, it is highly probable that counselors' criticisms, expressed in the privacy of the principal's office, are protected expressions, as long as the focus is on legitimate school-related matters that pertain to public policy. The "manner, time, and place" criteria will be applied by the courts in light of the working relationships within the particular school. The closer the working relationship between the counselor and the principal, the more sensitive the counselor has to be in the expression of such criticism. On the other hand, freedom of expression receives powerful protection from the courts and counselors don't lose this freedom when they enter the principal's office.

Do whistle-blowing statutes protect counselors?

They do in 35 states that, as of 1989, had laws covering teachers and other employees who in good faith report a violation of law, gross waste of public funds, or specific dangers to public health, safety, or welfare.*

Those statutes protect counselors who make such reports against discharge, coercion, or retaliation and thus supplement rights protected by the first amendment.[10]

If a teacher who is dismissed for exercising the right to free expression sues for reinstatement, will he or she be reinstated?

Not necessarily. Such cases involve at least a two-stage analysis. First, the burden of proof is on the teacher to show that the conduct was constitutionally protected and that it was a "substantial or motivating" factor in the dismissal. Then the burden of proof shifts and the school board has an opportunity to show that it had sufficient other grounds to dismiss the teacher. If the board meets this burden of proof, the teacher will be dismissed; if it does not, the teacher will be reinstated and might even be entitled to money damages. In the words of the Supreme Court,

> A borderline or marginal candidate should not have the employment question resolved against him because of constitutionally protected conduct. But the same candidate ought not to be able, by engaging in such conduct, to prevent his employer from assessing his performance record and reaching a decision not to rehire on the basis of that record, simply because the protected conduct makes the employer more certain of the correctness of its decision.[11]

Is academic freedom protected by freedom of expression?

Yes. Courts have held that academic freedom is protected by the first amendment of the Constitution. Although the exact boundaries of academic freedom are yet to be determined, it is clear that included within those boundaries are the rights of teachers to express themselves about the subjects they teach, the right to select appropriate teaching methods and materials, and the right to experiment with new ideas and teaching methods.

---

*States with whistle-blowing statutes are Alaska, Arizona, Arkansas, California, Colorado, Connecticut, Delaware, Florida, Hawaii, Illinois, Indiana, Iowa, Kansas, Kentucky, Louisiana, Maine, Maryland, Michigan, Minnesota, Missouri, Nebraska, New Hampshire, New Jersey, New York, North Carolina, Ohio, Oregon, Pennsylvania, Rhode Island, South Carolina, Texas, Utah, Washington, West Virginia, and Wisconsin.

Does academic freedom protect teachers' use of controversial printed materials?

In general, it does, as long as the materials are relevant to a legitimate teaching objective, are appropriate to the age, maturity, and experience of the students, and do not cause disruption of the educational process.

However, school boards have broad discretion in the selection of texts, instructional materials, and library books, as long as their selections are not arbitrary or based on religion, race, ethnicity, gender, or other forms of discrimination. Even literary classics are not immune to board action. This was illustrated in a 1989 case that arose in Florida, when a school board removed Aristophanes' *Lysistrata* and Chaucer's *The Miller's Tale* from the curriculum of an elective high school humanities course, because of their "sexuality and excessively vulgar language." The court emphasized that it did not endorse the board's decision; it only ruled that the books' removal was not unconstitutional. The board's action reasonably related to legitimate educational concerns, although the judges noted: "We seriously question how young persons just below the age of maturity can be harmed by these masterpieces of Western Literature."[12]

Are teachers free to use vulgar or offensive language in the classroom?

The answer depends on the specific facts of the situation. It is clear that random, careless, or casual use of such language is not protected by academic freedom. Courts have held that it is legitimate for local school authorities to expect high standards in the verbal behavior of teachers so as to provide desirable "language models" for students. That does not mean, however, that teachers are never protected in the use of "dirty" or vulgar language. The *Keefe*[13] case is a good illustration of this principle.

Robert Keefe, a high school English teacher in a Massachusetts community, assigned an article from *Atlantic* magazine while attempting to teach about contemporary writing. The article discussed the counterculture of the 1960s, including social protest, dissent, and revolt. It contained the word "motherfucker," repeated a number of times. Although there was no disruption of the learning process and there were no negative student reactions, several parents objected to the presence of a "dirty" word in the classroom and complained to the school board. When the board asked Keefe to agree to never again use the word or article in class, he refused as a matter of conscience, and was fired. In a lawsuit that followed, Keefe ultimately prevailed.

The federal appeals court found the article to be relevant to a legitimate course objective, as well as "scholarly, thoughtful and thought-provoking." In the view of the judge, the article was not an "incitement to libidinous conduct" and its reference to incest was "not to suggest it but to condemn it," for the word was used "as a superlative of opprobrium." The court also considered the age of the students and concluded that the students in this particular case, high school seniors, would not be shocked by a "dirty" word that was in current use. Although some parents might be shocked by such vulgarism, the court emphasized that the sensibilities of offended parents "are not the full measure of what is proper in education."

Keefe and other cases lead us to conclude that the use by teachers of controversial written or oral language will be protected, if such use meets the criteria listed in the preceding paragraphs. Although there are no reported cases involving counselors, there is no apparent reason why they would be treated any differently than teachers by the courts. There are educators who try to achieve "instant rapport" with some students by adopting the students' "street language," including a sprinkling of vulgar expressions. Such behavior is not protected by the courts, and communities have the right to impose higher standards of language usage on teachers and counselors than on students. It is also difficult to argue that the random use of vulgar language by educators serves any first amendment purpose.

Does the first amendment's right of freedom of expression apply to students in school?

As a general principle, yes. However, because no freedom is absolute, the courts have recognized that reasonable restrictions may be placed on student freedom of expression.

The *Tinker* case[14] became the legal landmark in this area during America's involvement in the Vietnam War. When a group of students in Des Moines, Iowa, planned to publicize their antiwar views by wearing black armbands in school, the principals of the school district established a policy prohibiting the armbands, in order to prevent possible disturbance. Several students wore the armbands in contravention of the policy; they were suspended. The students went to court and argued that they had a constitutional right to express their views through the symbol of the armband. The controversy that arose in 1965 ultimately reached the Supreme Court, which ruled in 1969 in favor of the students.

The Court, while recognizing the authority of school officials to control student conduct, held that neither teachers nor students "shed their constitutional rights to freedom of speech or expression at the schoolhouse gate." The Court was quite concerned with citizenship education when it said that school boards should scrupulously protect the "constitutional freedoms of the individual, if we are not to strangle the free mind at its source and teach youth to discount important principles of our government as mere platitudes."

Thus, the Court protected symbolic speech as well as actual expression. Either one can be restricted or prohibited only if there is evidence that it would "materially and substantially" interfere with the work of the school. Even if the principals of Des Moines honestly feared possible disruption, that would not have justified the restriction, because, in the words of the Court, "undifferentiated fear or apprehension of disturbance is not enough to overcome the right to freedom of expression."

Can school officials punish students for offensive or lewd speech?

Yes, ruled the U.S. Supreme Court in a 1986 decision. The case involved Matthew Fraser, a high school senior in Bethel, Washington, who gave a nominating speech at a school assembly that described his candidate using terms of "an elaborate, graphic, and explicit sexual metaphor."[15] The Court held that such speech could be punished even if it was not legally obscene and caused no disruption. Furthermore, ruled the court, school officials have discretion to determine "what manner of speech" is vulgar and offensive in classrooms, assemblies, and other school-sponsored educational activities. The Court, however, confirmed its support for the *Tinker* decision that protects speech related to political, religious, educational, or other controversial public policy issues. Such speech, actual and symbolic, is still protected unless it causes substantial disruption or interferes with the rights of others.

To restrict students' freedom of expression, must school officials wait until disruption actually occurs?

No. Courts held that school administrators may take preventive action and restrict student freedom of expression where there is enough evidence for a reasonable person to conclude that substantial disorder is likely to take place.[16] This, of course, places a burden on school administrators; they must not act prematurely, yet they have a duty to keep order in the school. In fact, the first duty of the administrator is to protect students' right to express themselves, as long as they do it in a peaceful and orderly manner and at the appropriate time and place. Administrators and teachers should control the would-be hecklers or those who would begin the disturbance in order to protect other students' freedom of expression from the "hecklers' veto."

Are demonstrations by students protected expressions?

They can be, depending on where they take place and how they are conducted. Schools may forbid demonstrations on or near school grounds at times when they are likely to disturb classes. In a case that upheld the constitutionality of such a regulation, the Supreme Court said that "the crucial question is whether the manner of expression is basically compatible with the normal activity of a particular place at a particular time."[17] Thus, demonstrations, as forms of expression, can be prohibited if they substantially and materially interfere with the processes of schooling.

Is the use of insulting, provocative words protected by the first amendment?

Not if they amount to "fighting words," the Supreme Court held in one case, in which it stated that some words in certain contexts, by their very utterance, inflict injury.[18] Such "fighting words" serve no first amendment purposes and therefore do not receive its protection. In a Pennsylvania case,[19] a high school student loudly said to a friend, off campus, that his teacher was "a prick." When he was to be punished for such behavior, he claimed the protection of the first amendment and lost. The federal district court said that his conduct was an invasion of the right of the teacher "to be free from being loudly insulted in a public place."

Do students have academic freedom?

It depends on what one means by student academic freedom and, also, on the jurisdiction in which the question arises. Clearly, students do not have the right to determine either course content or methods and materials used in class. When there was disagreement among the federal courts, however, concerning the removal of books from a school library, the Supreme Court ruled on the matter in a 1982 case. The *Pico* case[20] involved the removal of nine books from the school library. The school board claimed that its action to remove the books was based on its judgment that they were vulgar, immoral, in bad taste, and irrelevant, thus educationally unsuitable for junior and senior high school students. The evidence, however, showed that the board did not follow its normal objective procedures in reviewing the books, and that they were removed because of the undue influence and pressure of an organization of conservative parents.

The Supreme Court, in a highly fragmented opinion, ruled against the school board. The Court recognized that, as a general rule, local boards have power over the curriculum and may choose to promote "respect for authority and traditional values be they social, moral, or political." However, boards may not so exercise their discretion as to "strangle the free mind" and limit students in acquiring important information. The Court made motivation the critical issue in the *Pico* case. If members of the board were motivated to suppress certain ideas with which they disagreed, their action was unconstitutional. If, on the other hand, they intended to remove vulgar, obscene, meaningless books they considered to be educationally unsuitable for students, no constitutional rights were violated. Thus, in this analysis, the evidence of conservative pressure on board members and their reaction to such pressure became a controlling issue in the Court's decision.

Do student newspapers receive first amendment protection?

Yes. Courts have ruled repeatedly that school newspapers, both official and unofficial (underground) papers, are protected by the first amendment.[21] In their papers students may express strong criticism of school policies, programs, methods, and even individual administrators and teachers.

First amendment rights of student newspapers, however, are not the same as newspapers in general. This was made explicit by the Supreme Court in the *Hazelwood* case, discussed on page 192.

May student newspapers publish defamatory statements?

Defamation is not protected by freedom of the press. Students may be punished for publishing libelous statements and, in most jurisdictions, school officials are allowed to screen student publications for nonprotected matter prior to distribution.[22] However, such prior screening must be based on clearly stated objective standards with timely review available to appeal negative decisions.

May schools prevent the publishing of vulgar, "dirty" language in student publications?

Yes, if such language is legally obscene. There is a significant difference between what is vulgar and offensive and what is legally obscene. The legal test for obscenity developed by the Supreme Court requires that the published material must meet each of the following three criteria: (1) it must appeal to the prurient interest of minors; (2) it must describe sexual conduct in a way that is patently offensive to community standards; and (3) taken as a whole, it "must lack serious literary, artistic, political or scientific value."[23]

This three-part test is a demanding one and, furthermore, is not completely clear. We do know, however, that just because an article in a student publication might contain four-letter words or other matter that might be offensive to parents, teachers, or administrators, that does not mean the Supreme Court test for obscenity has been met.

The first amendment protects more than the cognitive content of speech; it protects the emotional content as well. It protects both the medium and the message, to the extent that they are separable in expression. This principle was well expressed by Justice Harlan in *Cohen v. California*. In that case, Cohen was convicted for disturbing the peace when he entered a courthouse wearing a jacket inscribed "Fuck the Draft." The Supreme Court reversed his conviction, declaring that

> [m]uch linguistic expression serves a dual communicative function: it conveys not only ideas capable of relatively precise, detached explication, but otherwise inexpressible emotions as well. In fact, words are often chosen as much for their emotive as their cognitive force. We cannot sanction the view that the Constitution, while solicitous of the cognitive content of individual speech, has little or no regard for that emotive function which, practically speaking, may often be the more important element of the overall message sought to be communicated.[24]

A similar expression by a student in school received different treatment in the appeals court of California.[25] A high school student was suspended when he refused for several days to remove a 1 1/2" badge that said "Fuck the Draft." The student claimed the protection of the first amendment as well as that of the California Education Code Section 48916, which provides, in part, that "students of the public schools have the right to exercise freedom of speech . . . including . . . the wearing of buttons, badges and other insignia, . . . except that expression shall be prohibited which is obscene, libelous or slanderous."

The court also considered California Education Code Section 48900, to the effect that "[a] pupil shall not be suspended from school . . . unless the principal determines that the pupil has . . . committed an obscene act or engaged in habitual profanity or vulgarity."

The court concluded that the button was not legally obscene, but that the student's continued display of it and his refusal to remove it constituted engaging in habitual vulgarities. However, is the statute authorizing suspension of students for habitual vulgarity itself unconstitutional? No it is not, ruled the court. The court's analysis showed that the conduct of students in school may be regulated more than that of citizens in general and found the regulation entailed in Section 48900(g) a valid exercise of power by school authorities. However, at least one dissenting judge saw no difference between this case and *Cohen v. California,* where the vulgar insignia was protected when worn in a courthouse.

In 1988, the U.S. Supreme Court in the *Hazelwood* case gave broader powers to school officials to regulate student publications that are part of the curriculum.[26] The case involved the censoring of two articles in a newspaper published by a journalism class. In the opinion of the principal, the references to sexuality were inappropriate to younger students in high school; some students might be identifiable from the wording of one of the articles, while the second article about divorce included a complaint about a student's father without giving the father an opportunity to respond. In the final analysis the Court gave school officials substantial control over school-sponsored activities, including publications or dramatic productions that are part of the curriculum, "whether or not they occur in a traditional classroom setting." This ruling gave broad powers to educators as long as their actions are justifiable on educational grounds. At this time, only "underground" student publications are free from such control by school officials. Those can be restricted only if they are libelous, obscene, or liable to cause substantial disruptions.

May schools regulate the distribution of student publications?

Yes, within reason. Schools may regulate the "time, place, and manner" of distribution of both official and "underground" publications, in order to prevent significant disruption of the work of the school. Unreasonable restrictions, however, are not permitted, because they can be used to stifle readership, which is an indirect way of abridging freedom of the press.

FREEDOM OF ASSOCIATION

Freedom of association is nowhere explicitly granted in the Constitution. Nonetheless, we value it as a very important attribute of a free society, and the Supreme Court has recognized it as implicit in freedom of speech, assembly, and petition." Among the rights protected by the first amendment is the right of individuals to associate to further their personal beliefs," wrote Justice Powell in *Healey v. James.*[27] It is well known that, in the past, the rights of teachers and students to join controversial organizations and even political parties was often limited. In recent years the rights of teachers have been increasingly recognized by the courts, whereas students' rights of association continue to be more strictly controlled.

Must counselors sign loyalty oaths as a condition of employment in public schools?

It depends on the wording of the oath. There are basically two kinds of loyalty oaths administered by states to public employees: affirmative oaths and negative (disclaimer) oaths.

Courts have held simple affirmative oaths to be constitutional as long as they are clear, unambiguous, and not overbroad. Such oaths typically ask public employees to swear or affirm support for the state and federal constitutions and laws and, at times, a pledge to uphold professional standards.[28] Negative oaths, on the other hand, typically ask the subscriber to affirm that he or she "is not now nor has ever been" a member of a "subversive" or "revolutionary" organization, without ever specifying the meaning of such highly charged, ambiguous terms. The Supreme Court, in *Baggett v. Bullitt*, struck down such a law required by the state of Washington[29] and, later, a similar Maryland statute. The Court warned that "the continued surveillance which this type of law places on teachers is hostile to academic freedom," and its overbreadth makes possible "oppressive or capricious applications as regimes change."[30]

How clear and precise must a loyalty oath be?

That depends on the court interpreting it. Because there is no ultimate objective standard for judicial review, the judge hearing the case and, in the final analysis, the composition of the Supreme Court will influence the outcome of the case. The Court that ruled in 1964 on the *Baggett* case required the oath to be "narrowly drawn" and the conduct prohibited to be "defined specifically," so that reasonably intelligent educators could know what behavior is expected of them. By contrast, the Burger Court in 1972 upheld a Massachusetts loyalty oath that seemed as vague and ambiguous as the Washington oath struck down above.[31]

In part, the Massachusetts oath requires state employees to swear to "oppose the overthrow" of the state and federal government "by force, violence, or by any illegal or unconstitutional method." Critics of the oath argued that this places on teachers and other public employees "vague, undefinable responsibilities actively to combat a potential overthrow of the government." Chief Justice Burger, writing on behalf of the Court, disagreed. In upholding the oath, he criticized the state legislature for the awkward language of the oath, but went on to assert that its purpose "was not to create specific responsibilities but to assure that those in positions of public trust were willing to commit themselves to live by the constitutional processes of our system." He further indicated that the oath merely requires a commitment not to use illegal force to change the government. Thus it seems that an oath that is too vague or overbroad for one court might be acceptable to another.

May counselors be dismissed for belonging to controversial organizations?

No, they may not be fired for mere membership, whether the organization be the Communist or Nazi party, the Black Panthers, the Ku Klux Klan, or others. So ruled the Supreme Court in the *Keyishian* case,[32] when New York passed a law requiring teachers to sign a certificate stating that they are not a member of a subversive organization. The Court distinguished between mere membership in such organizations, which is protected, and engaging in its illegal activities, which is not. In the words of the Court, "a law which applies to membership, without the specific intent to further the illegal aims of the organization, infringes unnecessarily on protected freedoms. It rests on the doctrine of guilt by association which has no place here."

May counselors engage in partisan political activities?

Yes, as long as they do not commingle such activity with their work at school. It is clear that teachers and other educators should not use their positions in public schools to promote political candidates,[33] but they may wear partisan buttons, badges, or other symbols.[34] The mature behavior we should expect from professionals would exclude partisan activities such as passing out a candidate's buttons or bumper stickers, or sending literature to the students' homes.

School boards may prohibit political activity that interferes with schooling, but a ban enacted in a Texas community on all political activity on the part of teachers was struck down as unconstitutional.[35] Such a ban threatens popular government, wrote the judge, not only "because it injures the individuals muzzled, but also because of its harmful effects on the community" that result from depriving it of the political participation of educators.

Can a counselor be prohibited from marrying an administrator?

Yes, or the school district might transfer or dismiss the administrator who marries the counselor. Such power is given to school boards as a way to reduce or eliminate conflicts of interest, or favoritism. A Minnesota case so held in 1975[36] and a 1988 New York case ruled similarly to avoid the "perception of favoritism on the part of other members of the teaching faculty,[37] upholding the transfer of a teacher who married the assistant principal. However, service in the state legislature and voting on education laws is not a substantial conflict of interest, just because one's spouse is a teacher. Remote, insubstantial conflicts of interest should not be prohibited for such an "interest is so small" that it "could not reasonably be expected to influence . . . judgement."[38]

May counselors be prohibited from running for public office?

There is no uniform law on this issue. Some courts have held it unreasonable to require the educator to resign before campaigning for public office, whereas others consider such a general prohibition to be unconstitutional because it is overly broad and vague. Some courts have been concerned that the political office might entail a conflict of interest for the educator and some emphasize that the demands of a campaign are likely to interfere with the educator's duties.[39] By contrast, a case in Oregon struck down as unconstitutional a law barring public employees from running for any political office.[40] The Oregon law, which prohibited public employees from running for state, federal, or nonpartisan office, was declared "unconstitutional because of overbreadth."

Thus, a counselor interested in running for public office should examine the laws and cases of his or her particular state. Some require educators who are elected to take a leave of absence, or even resign, as a way of avoiding conflict of interest.[41]

May counselors be dismissed for engaging in union activity?

No. Although the reported cases concern teachers, there is no apparent reason why counselors would be treated differently by courts. When evidence shows that teachers are dismissed because of union activity, courts will order their reinstatement with back pay. Activity on behalf of unions is protected as part of the freedom of association guaranteed implicitly by the first amendment.[42] The right to engage in union activities, of course, does not include the right to strike, unless the laws of the particular state specifically provide for it.

Are the associational rights of students the same as those granted to teachers and counselors?

No. Courts have recognized that the differences in social roles of teachers and students, as well as the differences in their age, maturity, and experience, makes it reasonable to treat them differently for purposes of constitutional law.

May schools ban students' secret societies?

Yes, because such organizations are inconsistent with the purposes of public schools, which attempt to develop a commitment to democracy on the part of students. Courts have interpreted the word "secret" to include exclusive social clubs that tend to perpetuate themselves through secret voting and "blackballing" by their own members. Since the turn of the century, when some states passed legislation against such clubs, to recent times, courts have upheld laws or school board policies prohibiting such practices.[43] Today more than half of our states make it unlawful for public school students to join secret clubs.

Do students have the right to form controversial organizations?

It depends on the nature of the organization. Public schools are not required to have extracurricular activities, clubs, or organizations. But once they proceed to recognize some, they may not arbitrarily turn down others. For example, if they recognize as clubs the Young Republicans or Young Democrats, they may not deny recognition to the Young Socialists or the Young Black Panthers simply because they might be more controversial. On the other hand, schools may refuse recognition to proposed organizations if there is evidence that they are going to be disruptive, break rules, or substantially interfere with schooling.[44]

May schools regulate student organizations?

Yes, as long as such regulations are reasonable and do not discriminate against certain groups. They may require, for example, that the group secure a faculty sponsor to meet with the group at regularly scheduled meetings. They may require that membership lists be filed with the school administration and that the time and place of meetings be publicly announced by the school to assure equitable access to school facilities. Other reasonable rules may be promulgated for school-related organizations.

Are students' religious groups entitled to recognition?

That depends on whether or not the particular secondary school allows noncurricular student groups to meet on campus. Congress passed the Equal Access Act in 1984, which prohibits discrimination against student groups on the basis of their political, religious, or philosophic ideas. This issue is discussed in a later part of this chapter.

Are gay-student groups entitled to recognition?

There are no authoritative court decisions on this issue. Groups of gay students seeking recognition at the college level have generally prevailed. Courts have ruled that they had the right to meet and discuss common problems as long as they did not engage in illegal activities or advocate such activities.[45] However, in this area, as in some others, courts may well differentiate between college and high school students on the basis of their maturity and experience, and because students attend college voluntarily, whereas students below that level are in school by compulsion. The courts are likely to grant administrators more or less discretion to recognize or deny recognition to such groups, depending on the social and emotional development of the students involved.

FREEDOM OF PERSONAL APPEARANCE

Historically, schools often regulated the personal appearance of both students and teachers. Such regulation took place through formal dress and grooming codes in some schools. Other schools accomplished the same ends by invoking the power of tradition; students and teachers who violated accepted traditions would be brought into line with peer pressure or a warning of disciplinary action by school administration. Beginning with the countercultural revolution of the 1960s, one dimension of which was a rejection of middle-class styles in dress and grooming, teachers and students often have challenged local tradition in these areas and have sought the protection of the Constitution for what might be called the "freedom of personal appearance."

May schools require male counselors to be clean shaven?

That depends on where the counselor works. When this question first arose courts tended to protect the teachers, and some even ruled that a beard is "symbolic expression" and thus merits constitutional protection. In a California case,[46] for example, an appeals court ruled that teachers' beards "cannot constitutionally be banned from the classroom" unless school officials can show adverse consequences to the educational process. Similarly, a Massachusetts court protected a teacher who did not shave his beard after the superintendent told him that the school district had an unwritten policy against beards.[47] Without deciding whether or not the teacher had a constitutional right to have a beard, the court ruled that he could not be dismissed for having the beard, without due process. Such due process, according to this court, would require that (1) there be a clear school policy forbidding beards, (2) teachers be given adequate notice of the policy and the consequences of not adhering to it, and (3) teachers be given the right to a hearing if there is a dispute over facts.

More recently, however, the trend of decisions seems to be against granting constitutional protection to teachers' beards, mustaches, and hair length. Although courts continue to be divided on this issue, in several recent cases judges refused to elevate teachers' grooming to an issue of constitutional magnitude. An Illinois case held that "dress and hair styles [are] matters of relatively trivial importance on any scale of values in appraising the qualifications of a teacher."[48] Similarly, the Tennessee Supreme Court upheld school board discretion in regulating the grooming of teachers. It said: "The grooming of one person is of concern not only to himself but to all others with whom he comes in contact; we have to look at each other whether we like it or not. It is for this reason that society sets certain limits upon the freedom of individuals to choose his own grooming."[49]

Are students free to choose their grooming styles?

Yes or no, depending on the jurisdiction in which they live. Approximately half the jurisdictions in the United States protect students' rights to determine their own style of grooming. They do so under a variety of constitutional principles.

Some courts have held that students' choice of hair length constitutes symbolic speech and is therefore protected by the first amendment.[50] Others have invoked the fourteenth amendment's concept of "liberty," which cannot be abridged by the state without good reason.[51] Still others have relied on the equal protection clause of the fourteenth amendment when schools required short hair for boys but not for girls, allegedly for reasons of health and safety in the gym, the swimming pool, and in laboratories.[52] Still other courts have upheld students' rights to determine their own hair length by recognizing that "the Constitution guarantees rights other than those specifically enumerated, and that the right to govern one's personal appearance is one of those guaranteed rights."[53]

Courts that uphold the right of school boards to regulate the hair length and other grooming choices of students do not accept the preceding argument. They are likely to say that not all freedoms are of equal importance and that we ought not give equal weight to freedoms such as speech and religion, on one hand, and personal grooming, on the other. They argue that we should recognize a continuum of importance, at one end of which are our "greater liberties" while at the other are the "lesser liberties" that might be curtailed by proper state authorities acting in a reasonable manner.[54]

What is the law on student grooming in my state?[*]

The federal appeals courts have decided that grooming is a constitutional right in the First Circuit (Maine, Massachusetts, New Hampshire, Rhode Island), the Fourth Circuit (Maryland, North Carolina, South Carolina, Virginia, West Virginia), the Seventh Circuit (Illinois, Indiana, Wisconsin), the Eighth Circuit (Arkansas, Iowa, Minnesota, Missouri, Nebraska, North Dakota, South Dakota), and probably the Second Circuit (Connecticut, New York, Vermont).[†] In these states, courts will hold grooming regulations unconstitutional unless school officials present convincing evidence that they are fair, reasonable, and necessary to carry out a legitimate educational purpose.

The law is different in the Fifth Circuit (Alabama, Florida, Georgia, Louisiana, Mississippi, Texas), the Sixth Circuit (Kentucky, Michigan, Ohio, Tennessee), the Ninth Circuit (Alaska, Arizona, California, Hawaii, Idaho, Montana, Nevada, Oregon, Washington), the Tenth Circuit (Colorado, Kansas, Oklahoma, New Mexico, Utah, Wyoming), and probably in the Third Circuit (Delaware, New Jersey, Pennsylvania)[‡] and the Eleventh Circuit (the District of Columbia).[§] In these states, the circuit courts have decided that grooming is not a significant constitutional issue

---

[*]The answer to this question is taken substantially from Louis Fischer, David Schimmel, and Cynthia Kelly, *Teachers and the Law*, 3rd. Ed. (New York: Longman Inc., 1990).

[†]In 1973, the Second Circuit clearly ruled that hair-length regulations raised a "substantial constitutional issue."[55] Although the U.S. Supreme Court overruled that decision as it applied to policemen,[56] the Second Circuit would probably reaffirm its decision as applied to students, because of the important differences between regulating the appearance of students and of policemen and the refusal of the Supreme Court to rule on student hair-length cases.

[‡]Although the Third Circuit held that civilian employees of the National Guard could challenge the Guard's hair-length regulations,[57] this court clearly ruled in 1975 that "the federal courts should not intrude" in the area of school regulation of student hair length and that it would no longer consider school-grooming cases.[58]

[§]The D.C. Court of Appeals has not ruled directly on the issue of school grooming regulations, but in a related case it indicated that it agreed with the U.S. Supreme Court and "sees no federal question in this area,"[59] that grooming is not a significant constitutional issue, and that federal courts should not judge the wisdom of codes regulating hair length or style. This does not necessarily mean that there is no legal remedy if a student is disciplined for violating school grooming regulations. It only means that federal courts will generally not consider these cases. Such grooming restrictions may still be challenged in state courts.

and that federal courts should not judge the wisdom of codes regulating hair length or style.

Has the Supreme Court ever ruled on the issue of student grooming?

No, and therefore the disagreements among lower courts are likely to continue. The Court has a very busy schedule and has repeatedly refused to accept this issue for review, because it does not consider it to be a question of national significance.

May schools have dress codes for counselors?

Yes, as long as such codes are reasonable and not extreme or arbitrary, and counselors receive clear and timely notice. Even courts that protect a teacher's right to have a beard will uphold reasonable dress regulations established by administrators, because such restrictions are temporary. Teachers and counselors can change right after school hours into their favorite leisure outfits, miniskirts, or jeans, each of which can be excluded in a dress code.[60]

In a 1977 Connecticut case, a teacher of English argued that his choice of clothing was a form of symbolic expression protected by the first amendment.[61] The federal court upheld the power of the school administration to require that male teachers wear a coat and tie, and refused to extend the protection of the first amendment "to include a teacher's sartorial choice." The court warned that if we extend the protection of the Constitution to "trivial activities," we "trivialize the Constitution."

Currently, most school systems address questions of grooming and attire for teachers either through collective bargaining contracts or through informal agreements between teachers and administrators.

May schools have dress codes for students?

Yes, as long as such codes are clear and reasonable and students are properly notified. However, such general principles are not always easily applied. For example, students challenged a rule in New Hampshire that prohibited the wearing of blue jeans and dungarees.[62] In this case the school officials claimed that jeans and dungarees "detract from discipline and a proper educational climate," but presented no evidence to support their claim. Recognizing the right of schools to "exclude persons who are unsanitary, obscenely or scantily clad," or who are wearing clothing that is dirty or otherwise unhealthy, the judge nonetheless struck down the no-jeans rule as arbitrary and unrelated to the educational process.

Clothing with controversial messages might be prohibited, depending on the nature of the message. A federal district court so held in a 1987 case in Idaho, where a high school senior was sent home for wearing a T-shirt with caricatures of school administrators drinking alcoholic beverages and acting drunk.[63] The court would not accept the student's free speech argument, saying that he could not "articulate the expression which was in danger of suppression" and there was no political protest or school policy being expressed. Furthermore, the T-shirt falsely accused the administrators of committing a misdemeanor—drinking alcohol on school property. Since the Supreme Court has previously upheld the authority of schools to discipline students for "lewd, indecent or offensive speech and conduct," that precedent applies to this case.[64]

May schools require girls to wear skirts or dresses?

No. A New York dress code that prohibited girls from wearing slacks was struck down as an arbitrary regulation of style and taste unrelated to concerns for order, safety, and discipline.[65] Schools may, however, prohibit the wearing of distracting clothing such as "excessively tight skirts or pants or dresses more than six inches above the knee," wrote an Arkansas judge,[66] for such clothing is likely to distract students and interfere with learning.

In sum, there is no uniform law in the area of personal appearance. It is very important for counselors to know how courts have ruled in their particular jurisdiction and what the trend of judicial decisions might be. The current trend in the federal courts seems to be to let state courts adjudicate personal appearance cases and to reserve their calendars for what they consider to be more important issues.

FREEDOM OF RELIGION

Certain issues arise from time to time throughout the history of a people. The appropriate relationship, if any, between religion and the state (and therefore public schools) is one of these perennial issues in American life. The twin clauses of the first amendment seem to be clear enough at first glance: "Congress shall make no law respecting the establishment of religion, or prohibiting the free exercise thereof." However, the interpretation and proper application of these clauses in the daily life of the schools have been quite problematic. As we know by now, although the amendment seems to restrict only Congress, the same restrictions apply to all governmental action—including actions of school officials—because the fourteenth amendment has incorporated the first and thus applies it to any and all "state action."

Issues related to religion tend to be highly charged emotionally. Bitter controversy about such issues has divided many communities throughout the country. There is no reason to expect these controversies to disappear in the foreseeable future; thus it is important for counselors and other educators to understand them and to help students and parents understand the relevant constitutional principles involved and the key decisions of the courts interpreting these principles. Not all school-related issues involving religion can be discussed here; we have selected those of greatest relevance to daily life in schools and, therefore, to counselors.

May counselors be excused from saluting the flag?

Yes, if they object to saluting the flag on the basis of religion, conscience, or strongly held belief. Although there are no reported cases of counselors involved in such a controversy, courts have so ruled in cases involving teachers, and there are no legal reasons why courts would treat counselors any differently on this issue. When a teacher in New York was fired for refusing to participate in the daily flag salute, she filed suit in the federal court in which she stated that she objected to participating as a matter of conscience.[67]

The court of appeals, upholding her right to remain silent, said, "[W]e ought not impugn the loyalty of a citizen . . . merely for refusing to pledge allegiance, any more than we ought necessarily to praise the loyalty of a citizen who without conviction or meaning, and with mental reservation, recites the pledge by rote every morning."

Teachers or counselors may stand silently and respectfully while the flag ceremony is conducted by other teachers, administrators, or even students. They don't have the right to disrupt or in any way demean such ceremonies.

May students be excused from saluting the flag?

Yes, if they base their objections on their religious beliefs, ruled the Supreme Court in 1943 in *West Virginia v. Barnette*.[68] This case involved children of Jehovah's Witnesses who refused to recite the official pledge, but offered instead to recite their own religious pledge. When school administrators insisted that they participate like everyone else, the students went to court and eventually they prevailed. In the words of the Court, "We think the action of local authorities in compelling the flag salute and pledge transcends constitutional limitations on their power and invades the sphere of intellect and spirit which it is the purpose of the first amendment to reserve from all official control."

In this case, the majority of the Court emphasized that under our Constitution, freedom of religion is a *preferred* or *fundamental freedom*. Such freedoms can be restricted or regulated only if the state can demonstrate a *compelling* need to do so. This is unlike the case of *ordinary freedoms*, such as the freedom to drive a car, which can be regulated if the government has legitimate reason to do so (e.g., to control traffic flow or reduce pollution). There was no compelling state interest that required Jehovah's Witnesses' children to salute the flag, for no public interest was jeopardized by their refusal; therefore, their fundamental freedom prevailed. The Court requires a similar analysis when other fundamental rights, such as freedom of speech, press, or assembly, are threatened by state action and these rights may be restricted only when there is a compelling state need to protect something of great public value.

Historically, objections to participating in the flag salute had to be based on *religious* convictions. More recently, however, courts have held that a sincerely based *conscientious objection* will receive the same legal protection. An objecting student who refused to stand during the pledge was protected by the court on the grounds that "standing is an integral part of the pledge ceremony and is no less a gesture of acceptance and respect than is the salute or the utterance of words of allegiance."[69] Furthermore, nonparticipating students may not be asked to leave the room but may remain quietly there even if other students might emulate them,[70] because "the First Amendment protects successful dissent as well as ineffective protest."

May public schools begin the day
with prayers or Bible reading?

No, ruled the Supreme Court in 1963,[71] and various courts have followed this ruling consistently ever since. The Court held that such practices violate the establishment clause of the first amendment, and that it makes no difference whether prayer or Bible reading is compulsory or voluntary if these activities are conducted under the supervision of the schools.

This does not mean, however, that religion must be completely excluded from public schools. In this same case, in which the Court declared prayers and Bible reading unconstitutional, the Court also made it abundantly clear that studying *about* religion is perfectly legal. Consequently there are many schools that teach the history of religion, comparative religion, and the contribution of religion to music, art, and literature.

May students be released from school
for religious purposes?

Yes. "Release time" religious education may complicate scheduling of classes and may highlight religious differences among students; however, as long as this education takes place away from school, is not paid for from public funds, and is not conducted by public-school personnel, it is not unconstitutional.[72]

Is silent meditation allowed in public schools?

That depends on the wording of the law or regulation that provides for it, and on the intent of the legislative body that enacted the law. If it is clear that the intention of the legislators was to encourage religion, the law is unconstitutional as a violation of the establishment clause. The Supreme Court so ruled in 1985 when it voided an Alabama law because it had no secular purpose and was a government "endorsement" of prayer.[73] Justice Rehnquist wrote a strong dissent in the case, indicating his readiness to abandon the idea of "separation of church and state." His views, together with those of Justices O'Connor, Scalia, Kennedy, and White, gleaned from several cases, suggest that the Court is changing toward a position of "accommodation" between church and state. Such a position, yet to be announced in some authoritative decision, would differ from the principle of separation dominant for the past several decades.

What principles guide judges in making decisions
about the legality of religious activities in the public schools?

It is generally accepted that, in the United States, the government must not advance or support religion nor be hostile to it. Its stance of neutrality toward religion was expressed by Thomas Jefferson, in correspondence with John Adams, as carrying out the intent to create a "wall of separation between Church and State." Historically, this wall was never too high or impregnable, and thus the separation never was absolute. Although we don't seem to worry too much about religious slogans on our coins, the presence of chaplains in the armed forces, or religious invocations in Congress, at athletic events, and at graduation ceremonies, concerns escalate when it comes to the daily life of our elementary and secondary schools.

Until approximately 1970, the Supreme Court used a two-step test to determine whether a particular school policy or practice was religiously neutral. It inquired, first, whether the intention behind the law, policy, or practice was to aid religion and, second, whether the principal or primary effect would either advance or inhibit religion. In 1971 the Court developed a three-prong test in *Lemon v. Kurtzman*[74] to determine (1) purpose or intent, (2) effect or consequences, and (3) if there is excessive entanglement of government and religion. A violation of any one of these three criteria would invalidate the particular law, policy, or practice.

Some questions about the solidity or reliability of the *Lemon* test were raised in 1984, in the case of *Lynch v. Donnelly*,[75] where a religions scene (a creche) was used in a display on public property. The case created much public controversy; although it protects the religious display as being primarily secular, with no significant religious components, Chief Justice Burger did indicate that the three-prong test established in *Lemon* is not the only analytic tool the Court has used in cases that focus on the establishment clause of the first amendment. At this point, however, as we may await guidance from the Court in future cases, the three-prong test set down in *Lemon* is our most reliable guide. In the near future the Court may issue a possible new criterion of "accommodation" referred to in the previous section, under the conservative majority of the "Rehnquist Court."

May students hold religious meetings in schools?

Yes, they can under certain circumstances. The Supreme Court upheld the right of *college* students to have access to public college buildings for voluntary religious programs.[76] The Court considered a college campus to be a public forum with all groups, including religious groups, having a right to equal access. Efforts to apply this logic to subcollegiate schooling, however, have failed in federal appeals courts.[77] These cases distinguished high schools from colleges and universities and rejected the idea that high schools are public forums where religious views can be freely aired. The Supreme Court refused to review these cases, thus, by implication, accepting the distinction between high schools and colleges.

This question was raised anew in two recent cases that reached seemingly inconsistent results. The U.S. Court of Appeals for the Eighth Circuit ruled in the Mergens case that in high schools that have "limited open forums," students may organize Bible study clubs.[78] This ruling is based on the Equal Access Act, a law passed by Congress in 1984 that provides that:

> It shall be unlawful for any public secondary school which receives Federal financial assistance and which has a limited open forum to deny equal access or a fair opportunity to, or discriminate against, any students who wish to conduct a meeting within that limited open forum on the basis of the religious, political, philosophical, or other content of the speech at such meetings.

The act defines "limited open forum" as follows:

> A public secondary school has a limited open forum whenever such school grants an offering to or opportunity for one or more noncurriculum related student groups to meet on school premises during noninstructional time.

By contrast, the Ninth Circuit Court of Appeals ruled against the students who, in the state of Washington, requested classroom use for a "non-denominational Christian group." The school denied their request, claiming it had no "limited open forum," since all its clubs were "co-curricular," related to specific courses or programs.[79] In light of disagreements among lower courts, the Supreme Court accepted the Mergens case for review and upheld the constitutionality of the Equal Access Act and ruled in favor of students' right to religious meetings along with other extracurricular activities.*

Should students be exempt for religious reasons from certain courses?

Yes, within limits, if there is a genuine religious objection to participating in the specific course. For example, some students have a genuine religious objection to dancing and thus have a right to be excused from physical education classes that incorporate folk dancing.[80] Similarly, at least one case ruled in favor of a student who objected on religious grounds to participating in required ROTC training[81] in lieu of physical education.

In recent years, objections have been raised to participation in sex-education classes. One California court ruled that such courses do not violate freedom of religion, particularly if individual students may be excused from participation.[82] The New Jersey commissioner of education went further and ruled that even a required course on family living, in which some sex-education materials were included, would not violate freedom of religion.[83]

And a federal appeals court ruled against fundamentalist Christian families who objected to a reading series and to stories such as the *Wizard of Oz, Rumpelstiltskin*, and *Macbeth*. They objected to materials that exposed their children to witchcraft, pacifism, feminism, vegetarianism, and situational ethics.[84] The Supreme Court let stand this decision. In all likelihood, public schools can require student participation in the curriculum that is related to some compelling state interest, for example the three Rs and courses in citizenship.

May students be exempt, on grounds of religion, from public school attendance?

Yes, if they otherwise satisfy their states' laws mandating school attendance. This principle was established in 1925 in the *Pierce* case,[85] when the state of Oregon passed a law requiring all children between the ages of 8 and 16 to attend public

---

The New York Times, June 5, 1990, A-1.

schools. The Court, in upholding the property right of the religious order to conduct its school, also negated "any general power of the state to standardize its children by forcing them to accept instruction from public teachers only."

Thus, it is clear that compulsory attendance laws may be satisfied by attending schools that are public *or* private, religious or secular. They can also be satisfied through "home schooling" if a parent's home-schooling arrangement meets the criteria of his or her respective state. Some states allow for home instruction through the wording of their constitution, some do it by statute, and some do not provide for it at all.[86]

In a landmark case that is probably unique, the Supreme Court ruled in favor of Amish parents who refused to allow their children to attend public school beyond the eighth grade, in violation of the state laws of Wisconsin.[87] Strong evidence was presented in this case to show that the curriculum of the high school was inconsistent with the religious beliefs of the Amish. It was also argued that schooling beyond the eighth grade was likely to destroy the Amish community's close-knit, religion-centered life. Furthermore, Amish children at the conclusion of the eighth grade were quite competent in the three Rs and would continue learning the tasks required for farming; their delinquency rate was very low and they were not burdens on the community. In exempting the Amish children from high school attendance, the Court considered the long history of the Amish religion, and, balancing the interests of the state on one hand and those of the parents on the other, came down on the side of the parents' freedom of religion.

May public schools provide services for students attending private religious schools?

That depends on what the services are. The rendering of some services, such as transportation, has been upheld by the Supreme Court, based on the theory that communities may pay the fares of all pupils attending schools.[88] Thus the "child benefit theory" was born. The limits of this theory are still being tested, and the Court draws the line at the point where services rendered the children bring on excessive entanglement between the church and the public schools. For example, in the *Wolman v. Walter* case in Ohio, the Court ruled that reimbursement for the cost of religious- school field trips is unconstitutional, because to ascertain that such trips were made for secular purposes would require close supervision that, in turn, would foster excessive entanglement.[89]

In the *Wolman* case, the Court ruled acceptable the provision of standardized tests and scoring devices for all students, whether attending public or private schools; again, its decision was based on the child-benefit theory. Similarly, it upheld the provision of speech and hearing diagnostic services as well as diagnostic and therapeutic services, when such services were provided away from the premises of the religious school.

By contrast, the loan of materials and equipment by public institutions to religious schools has been struck down as impermissible aid to religion. Because such materials can be used for either secular or sectarian instruction, any effective supervision of its use would lead to excessive entanglement between church and state.[90]

May schools teach "creationism" as an alternative to scientific evolutionary explanations of human origins?

No. In recent years, various states and local school boards have attempted to mandate by law or policy equal time in the curriculum for biblical explanation of the creation of human beings along with scientific evolutionary explanations, but courts have struck down such efforts as being religiously motivated[91] and thus in violation of the establishment clause of the first amendment.

May counselors take religious leaves of absence?

Yes. Whether or not they have a right to be paid during such leaves is a more complicated question. Once again, we must draw our examples from reported cases involving teachers.

When analyzing these cases, as well as others related to teachers, one must consider not only the first amendment's clauses on religion but also Title VII[92] of the Civil Rights Act of 1964, which prohibits any employer from discriminating against anyone because of religion. The 1972 amendment to the act provides the following guidelines: "The term religion includes all aspects of religious observance and practice, as well as belief, unless an employer demonstrates that he is unable to reasonably accommodate an employee's or prospective employee's religious observance or practice without undue hardship on the conduct of the employer's business."

A South Dakota teacher relied on this federal law when his request for a seven-day leave to attend a religious festival was denied. He attended despite the denial, but he first carefully prepared lesson plans and materials and consulted with his substitute about the plans.[93] He was fired by the board of education, which claimed that because no qualified teacher could be found as a substitute, a guidance counselor had substituted for him instead. Evidence showed that the classes went well and that the board's claim of undue hardship did not materialize. The federal district court ruled in the teacher's favor under Title VII.

Similarly, in the *Pinsker* case,[94] a Jewish teacher requested a leave beyond the two personal leave days provided in the district's collective bargaining contract. The teacher pointed out that the school calendar was constructed so as to accommodate the religion of Christian teachers, but that the school board was forcing her to choose between her religion and her employment. The court ruled in her favor under Title VII and she was allowed to take a leave without pay to observe her religious holidays.

Whether or not local school systems pay for religious leaves of absence is within the discretion of the school board. So ruled a California court in the case of a teacher who requested a "personal-necessity leave" to observe Rosh Hashanah, a Jewish holiday.[95] A New Jersey court went further when it ruled that a collective-bargaining agreement providing for paid leaves of absence for religious purposes violated the establishment clause of the first amendment.[96] The court held that the *Lemon* test was violated, because the agreement had no secular purpose—it benefitted religious individuals only and even encouraged religious participation.

Other issues in the general area of the church–state relationship as it applies to schooling include the use of school buildings; loans of public funds for capital improvements of church schools; tax exemption; tuition and tax benefits; and others. Although each of these is important in itself and involves complex issues of law and public policy, we selected only those we considered most important for counselors to understand. We encourage interested readers to pursue these issues in the rich literature available on this topic.

FREEDOM IN PERSONAL LIFE

Until recently, educators, counselors among them, were expected to conform closely to the standards of the local community in all aspects of their personal lives. Moral codes were strictly enforced against them; in fact, communities wanted them to be models for the young and therefore held them to higher standards of conduct than the population at large. In recent years there has been a dissolution of our national consensus on morality, and diversity in personal behavior is now increasingly accepted in most communities. The Supreme Court of California is not alone in asserting that "[t]oday's morals may be tomorrow's ancient and absurd customs."

Although educators increasingly insist that their personal behavior away from school is their own business, not all communities agree with such a clean separation. The "educator as a role model" theory is not completely dead. Educators and counselors continue to find their jobs in jeopardy when they are accused of being drunk, using illegal drugs, advocating homosexuality, engaging in adultery, becoming pregnant while unmarried, and other violations of traditional morality. In this section, we examine what constitutes immoral conduct for educators and how courts have ruled when such conflicts were presented to them.

May counselors be dismissed for immoral conduct?

Yes, even though there is no general agreement on what immoral conduct is. Immorality as grounds for dismissal has been challenged in various courts as unconstitutional because it is too vague, but courts tend to uphold the concept, particularly when it relates to fitness to teach or counsel students. When school officials wish to discipline someone on the grounds of immorality, they generally have the burden of showing that there is a connection between the alleged immorality and the professional work of the individual.

Although sexual misconduct is the most often cited example of immorality, other behaviors that offend local morals and serve as bad models for youth will also fall under its purview. For example, a teacher who attended a conference, after being denied a paid personal leave to do so, filed for sick leave. When she was dismissed for immoral conduct the court upheld the dismissal and said, in part, "Questions of morality are not limited to sexual conduct, but may include lying."[97]

However, not all lies are of the same magnitude. Thus, when a California court considered the case of a teacher who was dismissed for dishonesty for misusing her sick leave, the judge noted that "dishonest conduct may range from the smallest fib to the most flagrant lie." Therefore, the court ruled, the judges must weigh the seriousness of the dishonesty in each case and consider factors such as the likelihood of its recurrence, extenuating or aggravating circumstances, motivation, the extent of publicity, its likely effect on students, and the proximity or remoteness of the conduct. Consequently, "not every falsehood will constitute 'dishonesty' as a ground for dismissal."[98]

Is homosexuality considered to be immoral conduct sufficient for dismissal?

Not necessarily. The California Supreme Court ruled in the *Morrison* case[99] that terms such as "immoral" or "unprofessional" may be interpreted too broadly. Some people include laziness, selfishness, gluttony, and cowardice under "immorality." In order to discipline a teacher for immoral conduct, according to this court, the board of education must show that the objectionable conduct is clearly related to the individual's professional work. In the words of the court, "An individual can be removed from the teaching profession only upon a showing that his retention in the profession poses a significant danger of harm to either students, school employees, or others who might be affected by his actions as a teacher."

When can educators be dismissed for homosexual behavior?

There is no uniform law on this question. The facts of the *Morrison* case indicated that the homosexual acts took place between consenting adults in private and completely independent of any school relationship. As a general rule, if any of these conditions are violated, namely, consent, adulthood, privacy, and independence from work, the courts will not protect the individual.

In another California case, for example, the courts would not protect a teacher who pleaded guilty to a criminal charge based on homosexual advances made on a public beach.[100] The law in this area is still changing and developing; because there are no Supreme Court decisions to guide us, it becomes important for counselors to check the law in their particular state. A federal judge in Oregon, for example, struck down, as unconstitutionally vague, a state law empowering school boards to dismiss teachers for immorality, because it did not define "immorality."[101] In this case, a teacher acknowledged that she was a "practicing homosexual," yet the judge ruled in her favor because the state law (1) failed to give warning of what conduct was prohibited, (2) permitted erratic and prejudicial exercise of authority, and (3) did not require a connection between the alleged conduct and teaching.

Four years later, the state supreme court upheld the firing of a high school teacher, in the neighboring state of Washington, after he admitted to his vice principal that he was homosexual.[102] The evidence in this case indicated that some parents, teachers, administrators, and at least one student objected to this teacher remaining on the staff after he voluntarily disclosed his homosexuality. The state supreme court upheld the school board's claim that the facts warranted its conclusion—that, under these circumstances, retention of the teacher would result in confusion, fear, and parental concern sufficient to impair this man's effectiveness as a teacher. When the teacher argued that he should not be dismissed, because it was school administrators, not himself, who had publicized his homosexuality, the court disagreed; it noted that the vice principal was duty-bound to report the information to his superiors, and that school administrators need not wait for specific homosexual acts before they act to prevent them, for that would be taking an unacceptable risk in discharging their responsibilities.

In 1988, a Nebraska high school teacher was dismissed for making a homosexual advance to a typewriter salesman in a teacher's lounge. When he argued that his teaching effectiveness was in no way impaired by this incident, the state court upheld his dismissal on the ground that such sexual advances in school are "a clear departure from moral behavior and professional standards" and indicate "unfitness to teach." In all likelihood this court would treat counselors the same way.[103]

There is a difference between homosexual activity, on one hand, and the advocacy of homosexuality, on the other. The latter is protected under the first amendment in the same way that other forms of expression are protected. So ruled the Tenth Circuit Court of Appeals when members of the National Gay Task Force challenged an Oklahoma statute that proscribed both "public homosexual activity" and "public homosexual conduct" and also provided for the dismissal of teachers found in violation of the statute.[104] The statute defined "public homosexual conduct" as "advocating, soliciting, imposing, encouraging or promoting public or private homosexual activity in a manner that creates a substantial risk that such conduct will come to the attention of school children or school employees."

The court declared the statute to be an overly broad effort to regulate "pure speech" and thus a violation of the first amendment, which protects advocacy of illegal as well as legal conduct as long as such advocacy does not incite imminent lawless action.

May counselors be dismissed for heterosexual activity?

Yes, if such activity involves students, or even adults connected to the school if the activity causes notoriety. Furthermore, heterosexual activities that outrage public decency, even away from school, can be grounds for dismissal or other disciplinary action.

In a Colorado case, a tenured teacher with an excellent reputation became involved with some female students in what he characterized as "good natured horseplay" while they were on a field trip. Evidence showed that he tickled and touched them on various parts of their bodies, including between their legs, and that he watched television in a motel room while lying on the bed with a female student. The Colorado court upheld his dismissal, on the grounds of immorality and evident unfitness to be a teacher.[105] Similarly, an Illinois court upheld the dismissal of a male teacher who was discovered partially undressed playing strip poker in his automobile with a female high school student.[106]

A teacher's sexual involvement with a minor can be grounds for dismissal, even when the minor is not a student in the teacher's school. A Washington court so ruled, concluding that such conduct "is inherently harmful to the teacher–student relation, and thus to the school district."[107]

Unusual heterosexual practices may land one in trouble even where consenting adults are involved. This was the ruling of a California court in the case of a teacher with many years of successful teaching experience. The teacher and her husband joined a private club whose members observed her in several separate acts of oral copulation. After an undercover police officer arrested her and she pleaded guilty to a charge of "outraging public decency" the state revoked her teaching certificate. Although her behavior did not directly affect the school, the court seemed to be outraged at the semipublic atmosphere where strangers witnessed her unorthodox sexual behavior. To the court, her behavior "reflected a total lack of concern for privacy, decorum or preservation of her dignity and reputation" and indicated "a serious defect of moral character, normal prudence and good common sense."[108]

Are there other examples of controversial or unprofessional conduct for which educators may be disciplined?

Yes. In New Jersey, a court upheld the dismissal of a male music teacher who underwent "sex-reassignment" surgery. The operation changed Paul Monroe Grossman's external anatomy to that of a female, and she wanted to continue teaching as Paula Miriam Grossman. The school board met with the teacher and proposed, among other alternatives, that she teach elective courses at the high school for a year and then resign. When she rejected the options, the board dismissed her. Although there was conflicting psychiatric evidence about the probable impact on the students, the court upheld the dismissal because of the "potential psychological harm to students."[109]

A different type of controversial conduct is exemplified in a Maryland case, where a federal court upheld the dismissal of a teacher for misrepresentation, because he intentionally omitted from his application that he had been a member of the Homophiles.[110] Although he had the right to join the Homophiles and to urge public acceptance of homosexuality, and although he had the right to challenge some of the questions on the application, he had no right to certify it as complete and accurate "when he knew that it contained a significant omission." Because he purposely misled the school officials, he was precluded from arguing that the questions on the application were unconstitutional.

Behavior that might go unnoticed or that is acceptable, in the anonymity of a city, might be objectionable in some tradition-bound rural communities. This is exemplified by the case of a female teacher in a small rural community in South Dakota, whose boyfriend moved in with her shortly after she began teaching there. When several persons expressed their dismay to members of the board of education, administrators spoke with the teacher, who insisted that her living arrangements were her private business. Her dismissal was upheld by a federal court, which ruled that the school board, as an arm of the state, is entitled to maintain a "properly moral scholastic environment," and that, under these circumstances, it acted properly within its discretion.[111] In this case, the court specifically rejected the teacher's claim to a constitutional right to privacy, noting that the scope and limits of the "newly evolving constitutional right to privacy" are not clear. Thus, we can expect different courts to reach different conclusions on whether "the right of a couple to live together without benefit of matrimony" falls within the scope of the right to privacy.

Is pregnancy out of wedlock a proper ground for dismissal?

In general, no. In the past, no court would interfere with school board action dismissing unmarried teachers who were pregnant, but evolving cultural conditions and new laws and interpretations of constitutional principles have changed all this. For example, a federal appeals court overturned a school board decision dismissing an unmarried, pregnant, elementary school teacher. The board claimed such a condition to be inherently immoral and, when it offered no other evidence to support its decision to dismiss her, the court held that the board action violated her right to equal protection under the Constitution.[112] In other cases, courts protected such pregnant teachers when they were shown that other unmarried pregnant teachers were not dismissed by the district[113] and when the school board could not show that the alleged immorality affected the teacher's competency or fitness to teach.[114]

A strong statement by an Illinois court in 1986 illustrates the trend of decisions. When a teacher was dismissed for being unmarried and pregnant and deciding to raise the child as a single parent, the judge wrote: "Under the overwhelming weight of authority, it is beyond question that [the teacher] had a substantive due process right to conceive and raise her child out of wedlock without unwarranted . . . School Board intrusion."[115]

Thus, in the preceding two sections we have seen some curious conclusions that courts reach in a culture undergoing profound transition from one set of morals to an as-yet-undefined new morality. There are courts that uphold the dismissal of an unmarried teacher living with a member of the opposite sex, whereas other courts protected unmarried pregnant teachers from dismissal. It is difficult not to be confused in light of such judicial inconsistencies. It helps to know that we have not one judicial system but 51 (one federal and 50 state systems) and that some matters are controlled by federal law although most school-related conflicts are resolved in state courts (see Chapter 1 and Appendix A). Furthermore, even within the same state or within the same federal jurisdiction, courts might reach different results, based on the unique facts of a case and the social context surrounding the facts. One obvious example of this is the difference between teaching in a thriving metropolis, on one hand, and in a closely knit small town, on the other. Certain activities of teachers who are protected by the anonymity of the metropolis would be on public display in a small town and might well affect their teaching. School boards as well as courts consider such factors in their deliberations. Thus, although we all live under the same Constitution, the *application* of constitutional principles will always take the social context into consideration.

May counselors be dismissed for excessive drinking?

Yes, if the consequences of such drinking affect the welfare of other individuals or the common good. Even the issuance of a teaching certificate can be denied to applicants with repeated convictions of drunkenness in public, because such convictions can be proof of an individual's immorality and evident unfitness to teach.[116]

Various cases have upheld school board dismissals of teachers who were drunk while in school[117] or who were convicted of disturbing the peace while under the influence of alcohol.[118] Once again, however, courts do not rule uniformly on such matters. Since these cases are generally decided by state courts, we can expect some differences in their conclusions. The Supreme Court of Montana, for example, ruled that even a third conviction for "driving under the influence," was not tantamount to immorality. To sustain a dismissal this court would require evidence that the convictions would adversely affect the teacher's professional performance.[119]

May counselors be dismissed for using illegal drugs?

That depends on the circumstances and the laws of the particular state. Courts tend to uphold the dismissal of teachers if they are convicted of drug use that amounts to a felony, although even in such cases we find exceptions. When a California teacher was convicted of and dismissed for cultivating a marijuana plant, the state appeals court thought the punishment too severe. In this case, however, there were strong extenuating circumstances favoring the teacher. Evidence indicated that he was not likely to repeat the crime, that he cultivated only a single plant that he found while taking a walk, and that his return to teaching would have no negative effect on the school. The court noted that "a felony conviction, standing by itself, is not a ground for discipline in the absence of moral turpitude" and that, considering today's morals, offenses involving marijuana are not always crimes of moral turpitude.[120] By contrast, a Florida court upheld the revocation of the teaching certificates of two teachers convicted for growing 52 marijuana plants in a greenhouse. Much publicity accompanied their arrest and conviction and the court held that such immorality and the attendant publicity would significantly impair their effectiveness as teachers.[121]

A Georgia teacher was dismissed when she pleaded guilty to charges of possessing cocaine, glutethimide, and marijuana, in violation of the state's Controlled Substances Act.[122] The state appeals court upheld the discharge based on immorality and concluded that immorality "may be inferred, even in the absence of criminal purpose or intent." Selling of "controlled substances" will generally receive no protection from the courts and neither will behavior by educators that in any way encourages students to possess, use, or sell alcohol or illegal drugs.[123] In general, if local school boards wish to discipline educators for the possession, use, or sale of illegal drugs, courts will support such actions, but will scrutinize the disciplinary action to ensure that the penalty is appropriate and is not meted out in a discriminatory fashion.

Furthermore, no court is likely to protect a teacher or counselor who allows under-age students to use drugs in their presence or while under their care, either at school, or even "during the summer . . . and in the privacy of their own apartment."[124] A Kentucky court that ruled on such a case labeled such behavior "serious misconduct of an immoral and criminal nature" and indicated that there was a direct connection between the off-campus misconduct and the teacher's in-school role "as a moral example for the students."

May convictions for other types of crimes be grounds for dismissal?

Yes, particularly if the crime is a felony. We saw earlier that not all felonies involve moral turpitude and that the commission of such felonies, in the view of some courts, is not sufficient grounds for dismissal. However, felonies that involve the use or threat of serious bodily harm will generally lead to dismissal, supported by courts. An example of this is a Delaware case in which an industrial-arts teacher pleaded guilty to charges of theft and aggravated assault with a gun.[125] The court upheld the dismissal even though expert testimony indicated that such behavior was most unlikely to recur and in spite of the defendant's long record of successful teaching. The court considered such a serious crime to be "unquestionably immoral" and adequate grounds for termination. Similarly, a Florida court upheld the dismissal of a teacher who pleaded guilty to the charge of manslaughter after killing her husband with a shotgun.[126]

May misdemeanors lead to dismissal?

Yes, depending on the nature of the offense. School boards or courts will not dismiss a teacher or counselor for occasional minor traffic violations, which are misdemeanors. On the other hand, when a school board dismissed a teacher charged with theft, assault and battery, and fleeing a police officer (all misdemeanors in the state where the case occurred), the court upheld the dismissal and confirmed the widely held view that a teacher's conduct away from school may bear a "reasonable relation to his qualifications for employment."[127]

In an unusual case in West Virginia, a high school counselor was dismissed for immorality and fined $100 after he pled *nolo contendere* (he does not contest the charge) to a charge of misdemeanor petty theft. When he fought the dismissal, the state supreme court ruled in his favor. The court held that there must be a "rational nexus between the conduct and the teacher's ability to perform duties" and that a plea of "*nolo contendere* to a misdemeanor charge of shoplifting did not show the requisite nexus."[128]

In sum, it is clear that the private and personal lives of teachers are no longer as restricted as they were in the past. It is equally clear that their lives away from school may still be considered by school officials in determining whether or not they are fit to teach and thus to be "models for the young." Courts increasingly require that, before educators can be dismissed for immoral conduct, there must be credible evidence that such conduct is likely to impair their teaching effectiveness. The size and sophistication of the community as well as the notoriety resulting from the controversial behavior are important factors to consider along with the criminality of the act.

COUNSELORS' RIGHT TO DUE PROCESS

It is said among lawyers that procedure is to law what the scientific method is to science. Because rights without adequate procedures to protect them are no rights at all, the framers of the Constitution inserted the right to due process of law in both the fifth and fourteenth amendments. Our focus here will be on the fourteenth amendment's provision that no state shall "deprive any person of life, liberty or property, without due process of law." As we have seen earlier, public schools are instruments of the state, therefore actions of public school officials and board members are state actions for purposes of constitutional law. Counselors in private schools must seek their rights through the contractual arrangements they have made with their private employers, rather than through constitutional law.

It is useful to think of due process as "fair procedures," rather than as some highly technical set of requirements imposed by a mysterious legal system. In civil actions, which are the only kind we focus on in this chapter, the courts rely on principles of due process to remedy governmental action that is arbitrary and unreasonable and to ensure that fair procedures are followed when anyone's "life, liberty or property" is in jeopardy.

Do counselors have a property or liberty interest in their jobs?

That may depend on whether or not they are tenured. There are significant differences in the protections afforded tenured as opposed to probationary counselors and teachers. A tenured educator may reasonably expect continuity in employment. Such a "continuous contract," one that need not be annually renewed, gives one a sufficient "property" right to bring it within the protection of the fourteenth amendment. Probationary teachers have such a property right only to fulfill their temporary contract and have no legally recognized reasonable expectation of continuous employment beyond that period.

In public schools, tenure is generally conferred by the laws of the particular state, which also specify the grounds on which such tenure can be broken. Such grounds are usually very limited and typically include incompetence, immorality, and financial exigency.

Can't it be argued, however, that if a probationary teacher or counselor is not rehired, his reputation will have been sufficiently tainted to make it difficult to secure another position and, thus, his "liberty" interest will have been diminished? Just such an argument was made in the *Roth* case[129] decided by the Supreme Court in 1972.

When David Roth was informed, during his probationary period, that he would not be rehired for the subsequent year, he filed suit.* He alleged that he never received a notice or hearing concerning the reasons for the nonrenewal of his contract and that such failure deprived him of his "liberty" and "property" rights, without due process of law.

Upon appeal, the Supreme Court disagreed with Roth. The Court, reconsidering Roth's claim that his property rights were violated, made it clear that a probationary employee would have a right to due process if terminated *during* the term of his contract. There is an important distinction, however, between termination and nonrenewal. The probationary employee has no right to a renewal of the contract beyond its original term and the employer is not required by the Constitution to give notice, provide for a hearing, or specify reasons for the nonrenewal. The very meaning of a probationary period, according to the Court, is that there is no right to a renewal of the contract and, therefore, an ordinary nonrenewal violates no property rights. Therein lies one crucial distinction between the probationary and the tenured status.

Roth also argued that his "liberty" interests were seriously impaired by a nonrenewal. Addressing this issue, the Court noted that although it

> has not attempted to define with exactness the liberty . . . guaranteed [by the fourteenth amendment], the term has received much consideration, and some of the included things have been definitely stated. Without doubt, it denotes not merely freedom from bodily restraint but also the right of the individual to contract, to engage in any of the common occupations of life, to acquire useful knowledge, to marry, establish a home and bring up children, to worship God according to the dictates of his own conscience, and generally to enjoy those privileges long recognized . . . as essential to the orderly pursuit of happiness by free men.[130]

According to the Court, there might be circumstances where even probationary teachers would have a right to a hearing. Such would be the case if school officials, in the process of nonrenewal, made stigmatizing statements against the educator that would seriously damage his or her possibilities for future employment. What kinds of statements are stigmatizing? Statements, made in connection with the nonrenewal, that would damage one's "good name, reputation, honor or integrity." Thus, if one were accused of being incompetent, racist or sexist, or mentally or morally unfit, adequate notice and hearing would be warranted, in which the validity of such charges could be examined and refuted.[131]

Absent such stigmatizing allegations, there is no *constitutional* right to due

---

*Roth was a college professor. However, the legal principles of his case apply with equal force to public school teachers and counselors at the elementary and high school levels.

process when the contract of a probationary counselor is not renewed. The counselor, however, should also examine provisions of the state law, local district policies, and any collective bargaining agreements extant in his or her school district. The Constitution provides the basic framework for our legal system, but it does not preclude states and local communities from providing rights not guaranteed in the Constitution; they may not deny rights guaranteed by it, but they may go beyond the minimum assured by the Constitution. There are state laws as well as local policies and contracts that provide some modicum of due process for probationary educators, although typically they are nothing more than a right to a statement of reasons for the nonrenewal. In some instances, however, even probationary employees can be nonrenewed only "for cause." Where laws, policies, or contracts make such provisions, probationary employees have a right to due process; in such cases the burden of proof is on the employer to establish adequate "cause" for its action.

Although the preceding answers apply only to public schools, many private schools also grant tenure. They do so pursuant to the policy of the governing board; the terms of the policy, together with the traditions or past practices of the institution, will determine the legal significance of its terms for granting tenure.

May tenure be acquired by custom?

Yes. In the usual situation tenure is either provided or proscribed by law, policy, or contract, but that is not always the case. There are situations where school policies and practices are such that, even in the absence of formal provisions, a reasonable teacher might infer the existence of tenure from the circumstances of employment.

Such was the situation in the *Sindermann* case.[132] Robert Sindermann had been employed by Odessa Junior College in Texas for several years, when, after a public disagreement with the Board of Trustees over a union matter, his contract was not renewed. Sindermann requested a due process hearing and claimed a property right based on "de facto" tenure. Although Odessa had no formal tenure, its official faculty guide for many years contained the following provision:

> *Teacher Tenure:* Odessa College has no tenure system. The Administration of the College wishes the faculty member to feel that he has permanent tenure as long as his teaching services are satisfactory and as long as he displays a cooperative attitude toward his co-workers and his superiors, and as long as he is happy in his work.

The Court held that, with such a policy, Sindermann "might be able to show from the circumstances of this service—and from other relevant facts—that he has a legitimate claim of entitlement to job tenure." Such proof, of course, would not automatically entitle him to a contract renewal, but it would obligate school officials to grant him a hearing wherein they would have to establish the grounds for the nonrenewal.

May school officials decline to renew the contract of a probationary counselor for any reasons they might choose?

No. Even probationary public school employees may exercise their constitutional rights, such as freedom of speech; nonrenewal as punishment for their exercise of such rights is impermissible. For example, three probationary teachers in Missouri won reinstatement when the court found that their nonrenewals were motivated by their exercise of first amendment rights.[133] There are also many reported cases of retaliation against teachers involved in unionizing activities. In one such case, school officials argued, unsuccessfully, that there is no right to public employment and, therefore, the board may deny renewal of a contract at will.[134] The federal appeals court rejected this argument:

> The right sought to be vindicated is *not* a contractual one, nor could it be since no right to reemployment existed. What is at stake is the vindication of constitutional rights—the right not to be punished by the state or to suffer retaliation at its hand because a public employee persists in the exercise of First Amendment rights.

May probationary employees be nonrenewed if there are mixed reasons to do so?

That depends on the situation. The *Mt. Healthy* case[135] presented just such a situation. The teacher claimed that his nonrenewal was based on his union activities and his presidency of the teachers' association. The evidence presented by school officials showed that he got into arguments with cafeteria workers over the amount of spaghetti served him, that he referred to students as "sons of bitches," and that he had made obscene gestures at two girls in the cafeteria who disobeyed him. The case ultimately found its way to the Supreme Court.

The Court recognized that the claims of a probationary teacher to his constitutional rights "are not defeated by the fact that he did not have tenure." Attempting to balance the rights of the individual, on one hand, and the interests of the community, on the other, the Court used a two-step analysis. First, the burden of proof is on the individual to show that his constitutionally protected activities constituted a "substantial factor" or a "motivating factor" in the board's decision not to renew the contract. If he could prove this, he'd have a right to be reinstated, *unless* the school officials could prove that there were ample nonprotected reasons to not reemploy him.

Is a hearing by a school board an impartial hearing?

It could be, ruled the Supreme Court.[136] Teachers often have complained that due process requires an impartial tribunal, but that a hearing before a school board cannot meet this criterion because school administrators and school boards are on the same side of the controversy. Upholding the legitimacy of the school board acting as a tribunal, the Court noted that strict legal procedures need not be used at such administrative hearings; if its procedures are fair, the board is not disqualified. Its proceedings must be orderly but technical rules of evidence need not be followed.

In sum, although tenured counselors have much more protection than probationary employees, the latter are not completely defenseless in the face of administrative action. Insofar as administrators try to balance the competing interests involved when they are making decisions to renew or not renew probationary employees, their administrative discretion is protected. In the final analysis, that is a key function of administrators and also the meaning of the probationary period. On the other hand, the constitutional rights of probationary employees in public schools are protected from arbitrary and capricious actions by school officials. For an analysis of due process rights of students, please consult Chapter 7.

SUMMARY AND CONCLUSIONS

In recent years, significant gains have been made by educators toward the full recognition of their constitutional rights. Their freedom of expression outside of school is substantially the same as that of other citizens. If they criticize school matters outside of school, however, they are protected only if they speak on matters of policy that concern the general community, and are not protected if they criticize internal administrative, personnel, procedural, or technical matters. The Supreme Court has also ruled that neither teachers nor students lose their constitutional rights when they enter a public school. Thus, academic freedom, which is an aspect of freedom of expression, protects the use of controversial materials, books, and expressions, as long as they are relevant to legitimate teaching objectives, appropriate to the age and experience of students, and do not disrupt the processes of schooling. Students' freedom of the press is also protected, as long as the published materials do not contain defamation or obscenity.

Recent Supreme Court decisions, however, gave school officials broad discretion to control student speech and press at school functions or in activities related to the curriculum, to ensure that the expression is not sexually offensive or sensitive for portions of the student body, and that the materials are not inconsistent with the legitimate educational objectives of the school. Schools may create reasonable rules regulating the time, place, and manner of distributing student publications; both expression and publication may be restricted if there is a likelihood of substantial and material disruption of the processes of schooling.

Educators' freedom of association also receives constitutional protection; they may belong to controversial organizations of various types; but there is a difference between mere membership, which is protected, and engaging in illegal activities, which is not. Loyalty oaths have been upheld by courts when they are affirmations of support for the constitution and the laws of the land, but struck down when they are negative (disclaimer) oaths.

Courts uphold school restrictions on students' freedom of association when students want to belong to "secret" societies that control their own membership through closed rituals. Such organizations are inconsistent with the goals of public schooling.

In the area of personal appearance there is no uniform law. Most courts tend to protect the right of male teachers to wear a beard and mustache if these are neat and well groomed. However, some state courts will uphold school board policy that requires teachers to be clean shaven and wear short hair. Reasonable dress codes are upheld by all courts, on the ground that such codes are minimal incursions on educators' liberty, particularly because such restrictions are in effect only during school hours. Most school districts address this matter in collective bargaining agreements with their teachers and, increasingly, it is the arbitrators rather than the courts that resolve conflicts involving personal appearance.

There is greater controversy concerning grooming regulations for students; there are great variations between different jurisdictions in the degree of protection afforded students' choice, on one hand, and school regulation, on the other. Dress code for students are likely to be upheld, as long as they are reasonable and are made available to all students sufficiently in advance to allow them to comply.

Efforts to keep schools neutral toward religion continue to be controversial. Significant gains have been made in recent years toward achieving a separation between church and state in our public schools, but disagreements flare up from time to time. Prayers, Bible reading, and other religious exercises are unconstitutional in public schools, but teaching *about* religion is acceptable. Both students and educators are exempt from saluting the flag if they object as a matter of religion, conscience, or strongly held belief. And certain services, such as transportation, textbooks, and diagnostic testing may be made available to students attending religious schools, if this can be done without "excessive entanglement" between the public school and the religious institution.

Educators may take leaves of absence for religious purposes as long as such leaves place no burden on their schools. Whether or not schools must pay for such leaves is left to the discretion of local school districts.

Dramatic gains have been made by educators in asserting their freedom to choose their lifestyles. The historic demands for conformity to some idealized adult model are no longer enforceable and, in most respects, when away from school, educators may lead private lives like anyone else. Their jobs, however, may still be in jeopardy for immoral conduct, particularly if such conduct in any way relates to students or to the schools. Publicity about such conduct may also prove very damaging. Homosexual behavior and the use of illegal drugs are two highly controversial areas that have led to dismissals in recent years.

Educators with tenure have a right to due process before they can be dismissed or disciplined in some other way. This is so because tenure confers a continuous contract, which has been interpreted to be a property right that is protected by the fourteenth amendment. On the other hand, a probationary educator has no such property right. Thus, he or she has a right to due process only if dismissed *during* the term of the contract, but not if there is a mere nonrenewal of the contract. There are only two circumstances under which probationary teachers have a constitutional right to due process: (1) if the reasons given for the nonrenewal are stigmatizing and thus damaging to their possibility of finding future employment, and (2) if the reason for the nonrenewal is retaliation for their exercise of a constitutional right (such as freedom of speech), or for unionizing activity. Of course, state constitutions, state laws, or local policies and contracts may always expand such due process rights, even though they may not abridge them.

TINKER V. DES MOINES INDEPENDENT COMMUNITY SCHOOL DISTRICT
393 U.S. 503 (1969)

Mr. Justice FORTAS delivered the opinion of the Court.

Petitioner John F. Tinker, 15 years old, and petitioner Christopher Eckhardt, 16 years old, attended high schools in Des Moines, Iowa. Petitioner Mary Beth Tinker, John's sister, was a 13-year-old student in junior high school.

In December 1965, a group of adults and students in Des Moines held a meeting at the Eckhardt home. The group determined to publicize their objections to the hostilities in Vietnam and their support for a truce by wearing black armbands during the holiday season and by fasting on December 16 and New Year's Eve. Petitioners and their parents had previously engaged in similar activities, and they decided to participate in the program.

The principals of the Des Moines school became aware of the plan to wear armbands. On December 14, 1965, they met and adopted a policy that any student wearing an armband to school would be asked to remove it, and if he refused he would be suspended until he returned without the armband. Petitioners were aware of the regulation that the school authorities adopted.

On December 16, Mary Beth and Christopher wore black armbands to their schools. John Tinker wore his armband the next day. They were all sent home and suspended from school until they would come back without their armbands. They did not return to school until after the planned period for wearing armbands had expired—that is, until after New Year's Day. . . .

I

As we shall discuss, the wearing of armbands in the circumstances of this case was entirely divorced from actually or potentially disruptive conduct by those participating in it. It was closely akin to "pure speech" which, we have repeatedly held, is entitled to comprehensive protection under the First Amendment.

First Amendment rights, applied in light of the special characteristics of the school environment, are available to teachers and students. It can hardly be argued that either students or teachers shed their constitutional rights to freedom of speech or expression at the schoolhouse gate. This has been the unmistakable holding of this Court for almost 50 years. . . .

In *West Virginia State Board of Education v. Burnette*, the Court said:

> The Fourteenth Amendment, as now applied to the States, protects the citizen against the State itself and all of its creatures—Boards of Education not excepted. These have, of course, important, delicate, and highly discretionary functions, but none that they may not perform within the limits of the Bill of Rights. That they are educating the young for citizenship is reason for scrupulous protection of Constitutional freedoms of the individual, if we are not to strangle the free mind at its source and teach youth to discount important principles of our government as mere platitudes.

On the other hand, the Court has repeatedly emphasized the need for affirming the comprehensive authority of the States and of school officials, consistent with fundamental constitutional safeguards, to prescribe and control conduct in the schools. Our problem lies in the area where students in the exercise of First Amendment rights collide with the rules of the school authorities. . . .

II

Only a few of the 18,000 students in the school system wore the black armbands. Only five students were suspended for wearing them. There is no indication that the work of the schools or any class was disrupted. Outside the classroom, a few students made hostile remarks to the children wearing armbands, but there were no threats or acts of violence on school premises.

The District Court concluded that the action of the school authorities was reasonable because it was based upon their fear of a disturbance from the wearing of the armbands. But, in our system, undifferentiated fear or apprehension of disturbance is not enough to overcome the right to freedom of expression. Any departure from absolute regimentation may cause trouble. Any variation from the majority's opinion may inspire fear. Any word spoken, in class, in the lunchroom, or on the campus, that deviates from the views of another person may start an argument or cause a disturbance. But our Constitution says we must take this risk, and our history says that it is this sort of hazardous freedom—this kind of openness—that is the basis of our national strength and of the independence and vigor of Americans who grow up and live in this relatively permissive, often disputatious, society.

In order for the State in the person of school officials to justify prohibition of a particular expression of opinion, it must be able to show that its action was caused by something more than a mere desire to avoid the discomfort and unpleasantness that always accompany an unpopular viewpoint. Certainly where there is no finding and no showing that engaging in the forbidden conduct would "materially and substantially interfere with the requirements of appropriate discipline in the operation of the school," the prohibition cannot be sustained. . . .

In the present case, school authorities did not purport to prohibit the wearing of all symbols of political or controversial significance. The record shows that students in some of the schools wore buttons relating to national political campaigns, and some even wore the Iron Cross, traditionally a symbol of Nazism. The order prohibiting the wearing of armbands did not extend to these. Instead, a particular symbol—black armbands worn to exhibit opposition to this Nation's involvement in Vietnam—was singled out for prohibition. Clearly, the prohibition of expression of one particular opinion, at least without evidence that it is necessary to avoid material and substantial interference with schoolwork or discipline, is not constitutionally permissible.

In our system, state-operated schools may not be enclaves of totalitarianism. School officials do not possess absolute authority over their students. Students in school as well as out of school are "persons" under our Constitution. They are possessed of fundamental rights which the State must respect, just as they themselves must respect their obligations to the State. In our system, students may not be regarded as closed-circuit recipients of only that which the State chooses to communicate. They may not be confined to the expression of those sentiments that are officially approved. In the absence of a specific showing of constitutionally valid reasons to regulate their speech, students are entitled to freedom of expression of their views. As Judge Gewin, speaking for the Fifth Circuit, said, school officials cannot suppress "expressions of feelings with which they do not wish to contend."

In *Meyer v. Nebraska,* Mr. Justice McReynolds expressed this Nation's repudiation of the principle that a State might so conduct its schools as to "foster a homogeneous people." He said:

> In order to submerge the individual and develop ideal citizens, Sparta assembled the males at seven into barracks and entrusted their subsequent education and training to official guardians. Although such measures have been deliberately approved by men of great genius, their ideas touching the relation between individual and State were wholly different from those upon which our institutions rest; and it hardly will be affirmed that any Legislature could impose such restrictions upon the people of a state without doing violence to both letter and spirit of the Constitution.

This principle has been repeated by this Court on numerous occasions during the intervening years. Mr. Justice Brennan, speaking for the Court, said:

> The vigilant protection of constitutional freedoms is nowhere more vital than in the community of American schools. The classroom is peculiarly the "marketplace of ideas." The Nation's future depends upon leaders trained through wide exposure to that robust exchange of ideas which discovers truth "out of a multitude of tongues," [rather] than through any kind of authoritative selection.

The principle of these cases is not confined to the supervised and ordained discussion which takes place in the classroom. The principal use to which the schools are dedicated is to accommodate students during prescribed hours for the purpose of certain types of activities. Among those activities is personal intercommunication among the students. This is not only an inevitable part of the process of attending school; it is also an important part of the educational process. A student's rights, therefore, do not embrace merely the classroom hours. When he is in the cafeteria, or on the playing field, or on the campus during the authorized hours, he may express his opinions, even on controversial subjects like the conflict in Vietnam, if he does so without "materially and substantially interfer[ing] with the requirements of appropriate discipline in the operation of the school" and without colliding with the rights of others. But conduct by the student, in class or out of it, which for any reason—whether it stems from time, place, or type of behavior—materially disrupts classwork or involves substantial disorder or invasion of the rights of others is, of course, not immunized by the constitutional guarantee of freedom of speech.

Under our Constitution, free speech is not a right that is given only to be so circumscribed that it exists in principle but not in fact. Freedom of expression would not truly exist if the right could be exercised only in an area that a benevolent government has provided as a safe haven for crackpots. The Constitution says that Congress (and the States) may not abridge the right to free speech. This provision means what it says. We properly read it to permit reasonable regulation of speech-connected activities in carefully restricted circumstances. But we do not confine the permissible exercise of First Amendment rights to a telephone booth or the four corners of a pamphlet, or to supervised and ordained discussion in a school classroom.

If a regulation were adopted by school officials forbidding discussion of the Vietnam conflict, or the expression by any student of opposition to it anywhere on school property except as part of a prescribed classroom exercise, it would be obvious that the regulation would violate the constitutional rights of students, at least if it could not be justified by a showing that the students' activities would materially and substantially disrupt the work and discipline of the school. . . .

These petitioners merely went about their ordained rounds in school. Their deviation consisted only in wearing on their sleeves a band of black cloth, not more than two inches wide. They wore it to exhibit their disapproval of the Vietnam hostilities and their advocacy of a truce, to make their views known, and, by their example, to influence others to adopt them. They neither interrupted school activities nor sought to intrude in the school affairs or the lives of others. They caused discussion outside of the classrooms, but no interference with work and no disorder. In the circumstances, our Constitution does not permit officials of the State to deny their form of expression.

We express no opinion as to the form of relief which should be granted, this being a matter for the lower courts to determine. We reverse and remand for further proceedings consistent with this opinion.

Mr. Justice BLACK, dissenting.

The Court's holding in this case ushers in what I deem to be an entirely new era in which the power to control pupils by the elected "officials of state supported public schools . . ." in the United States is in ultimate effect transferred to the Supreme Court. . . .

Assuming that the Court is correct in holding that the conduct of wearing armbands for the purpose of conveying political ideas is protected by the First Amendment, the crucial remaining questions are whether students and teachers may use the schools at their whim as a platform for the exercise of free speech—"symbolic" or "pure"—and whether the courts will allocate to themselves the function of deciding how the pupils' school day will be spent. . . .

While the absence of obscene remarks or boisterous and loud disorder perhaps justified the Court's statement that the few armband students did not actually "disrupt" the classwork, I think the record overwhelmingly shows that the armbands did exactly what the elected school officials and principals foresaw they would, that is, took the students' minds off their classwork and diverted them to thoughts about the highly emotional subject of the Vietnam war. [And I repeat that] if the time has come when pupils of state-supported schools, kindergartens, grammar schools, or high schools, can defy and flout orders of school officials to keep their minds on their own schoolwork, it is the beginning of a new revolutionary era of permissiveness in this country fostered by the judiciary. . . .

I deny [therefore] that it has been the "unmistakable holding of this Court for almost 50 years" that "students" and "teachers" take with them into the "schoolhouse gate" constitutional rights to "freedom of speech or expression." The truth is that a teacher of kindergarten, grammar school, or high school pupils no more carries into a school with him a complete right to freedom of speech and expression than an anti-Catholic or anti-Semite carries with him a complete freedom of speech and religion into a Catholic church or Jewish synagogue. It is a myth to say that any person has a constitutional right to say what he pleases, where he pleases, and when he pleases. Our Court has decided precisely the opposite.

In my view, teachers in state-controlled public schools are hired to teach there . . . certainly a teacher is not paid to go to school and teach subjects the State does not hire him to teach as a part of its selected curriculum. Nor are public school students sent to the schools at public expense to broadcast political or any other views to educate and inform the public. The original idea of schools, which I do not believe is yet abandoned as worthless or out of date, was that children had not yet reached the point of experience and wisdom which enabled them to teach all of their elders. It may be that the Nation has outworn the old-fashioned slogan that "children are to be seen not heard," but one may, I hope, be permitted to harbor the thought that taxpayers send children to school on the premise that at their age they need to learn, not teach. . . .

Change has been said to be truly the law of life but sometimes the old and the tried and true are worth holding. The schools of this Nation have undoubtedly contributed to giving us tranquility and to making us a more law-abiding people. Uncontrolled and uncontrollable liberty is an enemy to domestic peace. We cannot close our eyes to the fact that some of the country's greatest problems are crimes committed by the youth, too many of school age. School discipline, like parental discipline, is an integral and important part of training our children to be good citizens—to be better citizens. Here a very small number of students have crisply and summarily refused to obey a school order designed to give pupils who want to learn the opportunity to do so. One does not need to be a prophet or the son of a prophet to know that after the Court's holding today some students in Iowa schools and indeed in all schools will be ready, able, and willing to defy their teachers on practically all orders. This is the more unfortunate for the schools since groups of students all over the land are already running loose, conducting break-ins, sit-ins, lie-ins, and smash-ins. Many of these student groups, as is all too familiar to all who read the newspapers and watch the television news programs, have already engaged in rioting, property seizures, and destruction. They have picketed schools to force students not to cross their picket lines and have too often violently attacked earnest but frightened students who wanted an education that the pickets did not want them to get. Students engaged in such activities are apparently confident that they know far more about how to operate public school systems than do their teachers, and elected school officials. It is no answer to say that the particular students here have not yet reached such high points in their demands to attend classes in order to exercise their political pressures. Turned loose with lawsuits for damages and injunctions against their teachers as they are here, it is nothing but wishful thinking to imagine that young, immature students will not soon believe it is their right to control the schools rather than the right of the States that collect the taxes to hire the teachers for the benefit of the pupils. This case, therefore, wholly without constitutional reasons in my judgment, subjects all the public schools in the country to the whims and caprices of their loudest-mouthed, but maybe not their brightest, students. I, for one, am not fully persuaded that school pupils are wise enough, even with this Court's expert help from Washington, to run the 23,390 public school systems in our 50 States. I wish, therefore, wholly to disclaim any purpose on my part to hold that the Federal Constitution compels the teachers, parents, and elected school officials to surrender control of the American public school system to public school students. I dissent.

NOTES

1. Pickering v. Board of Educ., 391 U.S. 563 (1968).
2. Swilley v. Alexander, 448 F. Supp. 702 (S.D. Ala. 1978).
3. Connick v. Myers, 103 S. Ct. 1684 (1983).
4. Hesse v. Board of Educ. of Township High School Dist. 211, 848 F.2d 748 (7th Cir. 1988).
5. Daniels v. Quinn, 801 F.2d 687 (4th Cir. 1986).
6. Bowman v. Pulaski City Special School Dist., 723 F.2d 640 (8th Cir. 1983).
7. Allen v. Antauga City Board of Educ., 685 F.2d 1302 (11th Cir. 1982).
8. Bernasconi v. Temple Elementary School Dist., No. 3, 548 F.2d 857 (9th Cir. 1977).
9. Givhan v. Western Line Consol. School Dist., 439 U.S. 410 (1979).
10. Louis Ebeling, Whistleblowing in the Public Schools, paper presented at the NOLPE Convention, San Francisco, Cal. Nov. 18, 1989.

11. Mount Healthy v. Doyle, 429 U.S. 274 (1977).
12. Virgil v. School Board of Columbia County, *Florida*, 862 F. 2d 1517 (11th Cir. 1989).
13. Keefe v. Geanakos, 418 F.2d 359 (1st Cir. 1969).
14. Tinker v. Des Moines Indep. School Dist., 393 U.S. 503 (1969).
15. Bethel School Dist. No. 403 v. Fraser, 478 U.S. 675 (1986).
16. Karp v. Becken, 477 F.2d 171 (9th Cir. 1973).
17. Grayned v. City of Rockford, 408 U.S. 104 (1972).
18. Chaplinsky v. New Hampshire, 315 U.S. 568 (1942).
19. Fenton v. Stear, 423 F. Supp. 767 (W.D. Penn. 1976).
20. Board of Educ. v. Pico, 457 U.S. 853 (1982).
21. Scoville v. Board of Educ. of Joliet Township, 425 F.2d 10 (7th Cir. 1970); Shanley v. Northeast Indep. School Dist., 462 F.2d 960 (5th Cir. 1972).
22. Fujishima v. Board of Educ., 460 F.2d 1355 (7th Cir. 1972); Baughman v. Freienmuth, 478 F.2d 1345 (4th Cir. 1973).
23. Miller v. California, 413 U.S. 15 (1973).
24. Cohen v. California, 403 U.S. 15, 26 (1971).
25. Hinze v. Superior Court of Marin County, 174 Cal. Rptr. 403 (Cal. App. 1981).
26. Hazelwood v. Kuhlmeir 484 U.S. 260 (1988).
27. Healey v. James, 408 U.S. 169 (1972).
28. Ohlson v. Phillips, 304 F. Supp. 1152 (D. Colo. 1969); *aff'd*, 397 U.S. 317 (1970).
29. Baggett v. Bullitt, 377 U.S. 360 (1964).
30. Whitehall v. Elkins, 389 U.S. 54 (1967).
31. Cole v. Richardson, 405 U.S. 676 (1972).
32. Keyishian v. Board of Regents of N.Y., 385 U.S. 589 (1967).
33. Goldsmith v. Board of Educ., 225 P. 783 (Cal. App. 1924).
34. Charles James v. Board of Educ. of Central Dist. No. 1, 461 F.2d 566 (2d Cir. 1972).
35. Montgomery v. White, 320 F. Suppl. 303 (E.D. Tex. 1969).
36. Keckeisen v. Independent School Dist. 612, 509 F.2d 1062 (8th Cir. 1975), *cert. denied*, 423 U.S. 833 (1975).
37. Solomon v. Quinones, 531 N.Y.S.2d 349 (N.Y. 1988).
38. Smith v. Dorsey, 530 So.2d 513 (Miss. 1988).
39. Jones v. Board of Control, 131 So.2d 713 (Fla. 1961).
40. Minielly v. State, 411 P.2d 69 (Ore. 1966).
41. Galer v. Board of Regents of the Univ. Sys., 236 S.E.2d 617 (Ga. 1977).
42. Lisbon School Comm. v. Lisbon Educ. Ass'n, 438 A.2d 239 (Me. 1981).
43. Robinson v. Sacramento City Unified School Dist., 53 Cal. Rptr. 781 (Cal. App. 1966); Passell v. Fortworth Indep. School Dist., 453 S.W.2d 888 (1970), *cert. denied* 402 U.S. 968 (1971).
44. Healey v. James, 408 U.S. 169 (1972); Dixon v. Beresh, 361 F. Supp. 253 (E.D. Mich. 1973).
45. Gay Alliance of Students v. Matthews, 544 F.2d 162 (4th Cir. 1976).
46. Finot v. Pasadena City Bd. of Educ., 58 Cal. Rptr. 520 (1967).
47. Lucia v. Duggan, 303 F. Supp. 112 (D. Mass, 1969).
48. Miller v. School Dist. No. 167, Cook County, Ill., 495 F.2d 658 (7th Cir. 1974).
49. Morrison v. Hamilton Bd. of Educ., 494 S.W.2d 770 (Tenn. 1973).
50. Karr v. Schmidt, 460 F.2d 609 (5th Cir. 1972), (Wisdom, J., dissenting).
51. Richards v. Thurston, 424 F.2d 1281 (1st Cir. 1970).
52. Crews v. Cloncs, 432 F.2d 1259 (7th Cir. 1970).
53. Bishop v. Colaw, 450 F.2d 1069 (8th Cir. 1971).
54. Karr v. Schmidt, 460 F.2d 609 (5th Cir. 1972).
55. Dwen v. Barry, 483 F.2d 1126 (2d Cir. 1973).

56. Kelley v. Johnson, 425 U.S. 238 (1976).

57. Syrek v. Pennsylvania Air Nat'l Guard, 537 F.2d 66 (3d Cir. 1976).

58. Zeller v. Donegal School Dist., 517 F.2d 600 (3d Cir. 1975).

59. Fagan v. National Cash Register Co., 481 F.2d 1115 (D.C. Cir. 1973).

60. Tardif v. Quinn, 545 F.2d 761 (1st Cir. 1976); Domico v. Rapides School Bd., 675 F.2d 100 (5th Cir. 1982).

61. East Hartford Educ. Ass'n v. Bd. of Educ. of the Town of East Hartford, 562 F.2d 838 (2nd Cir. 1977).

62. Bannister v. Paradis, 316 F. Supp. 185 (D.N.H. 1970).

63. Gano v. School Dist. 411 of Twin Falls County, Idaho, 674 F.Supp. 796 (D. Idaho, 1987).

64. Bethel School Dist. No. 403 v. Frazer, 478 U.S. 675 (1986).

65. Scott v. Board of Educ., Hicksville, 305 N.Y.S.2d 601 (1969).

66. Wallace v. Ford, 346 F. Supp. 156 (E.D. Ark. 1972).

67. Russo v. Central School Dist. No. 1, 469 F.2d 623 (2d Cir. 1972), cert. denied, 411 U.S. 932 (1973).

68. West Virginia v. Barnette, 319 U.S. 624 (1943).

69. Banks v. Board of Pub. Instruction of Dade County, 314 F. Supp. 285 (S.D. Fla. 1970).

70. Frain v. Barron, 307 F. Supp. 27 (E.D.N.Y. 1969).

71. Abington School Dist. v. Schempp, 374 U.S. 203 (1963).

72. Zorach v. Clausen, 343 U.S. 306 (1952).

73. Wallace v. Jaffree, 427 U.S. 38 (1985).

74. Lemon v. Kurtzman, 403 U.S. 602 (1971).

75. Lynch v. Donnelly, 465 U.S. 688 (1984).

76. Widmar v. Vincent, 454 U.S. 263 (1981).

77. Brandon v. Board of Educ. of Guilderland School Dist., 635 F.2d 971 (2d Cir. 1980); and Lubbock Civil Liberties Union v. Lubbock Indep. School Dist., 669 F.2d 1038 (5th Cir. 1982).

78. Mergens v. Board of Educ. of Westside Community Schools, 867 F.2d 1076 (8th Cir. 1989).

79. Garnett v. Renton School Dist. No. 403, 865 F.2d 1121 (9th Cir. 1989).

80. Hardwick v. Board of School Trustees, 205 P.49 (Cal. 1921).

81. Spence v. Bailey, 465 F.2d 797 (6th Cir. 1972).

82. Citizens for Parental Rights v. San Mateo City Bd. of Educ., 124 Cal. Rptr. 68 (Cal. App. 1975).

83. "J.B." and "B.B." as Guardians and Natural Parents of "P.B." and "J.B." v. Dumont Bd. of Educ., Dec. of N.J. Comm'r of Education (1977).

84. Mozert v. Hawkins County Public Schools, 827 F.2d 1058 (6th Cir. 1987); cert. denied, 108 S.Ct. 1029 (Feb. 22, 1988).

85. Pierce v. Society of Sisters, 268 U.S. 510 (1925).

86. New Mexico is a state that does not allow home instruction. Such exclusion was upheld in State v. Edgington, 663 P.2d 374 (N. Mex. App. 1983).

87. Wisconsin v. Yoder, 406 U.S. 205 (1972).

88. Everson v. Board of Educ., 330 U.S. 1 (1947).

89. Wolman v. Walter, 433 U.S. 229 (1977).

90. Meek v. Pittenger, 421 U.S. 349 (1975).

91. McLean v. Arkansas Bd. of Educ., 529 F. Supp. 1255 (E.D. Ark. 1982); Edwards v. Aguillard, 482 U.S. 578 (1987).

92. 42 U.S.C.A. § 2000(e) et seq.

93. Wangness v. Watertown School Dist. No. 14–4, 541 F. Supp. 332 (D.S.D. 1982).

94. Pinsker v. Joint Dist. No. 285, 554 F. Supp. 1049 (D. Colo. 1983).

95. California Teachers Ass'n v. Board of Trustees, 138 Cal. Rptr. 817 (Cal. App. 1977).
96. Hunterdon Central School v. Hunterdon High, 416 A.2d 980 (N.J. 1980).
97. Bethel Park School Dist. v. Krall, 445 A.2d 1377 (Pa. 1982).
98. Bassett Unified School Dist. v. Comm'n on Professional Responsibility, 247 Cal. Rptr. 865 (Cal. App. 1988).
99. Morrison v. State Bd. of Educ., 461 P.2d 375 (Cal. 1969).
100. Sarac v. State Bd. of Educ., 57 Cal. Rptr. 69 (Cal. App. 1967).
101. Burton v. Cascade School Dist. Union High School No. 5, 353 F. Supp. 254 (D. Ore. 1973).
102. Gaylord v. Tacoma School Dist. No. 10, 559 P.2d 1340 (Wash. 1977).
103. Stephens v. Board of Educ., School Dist. No. 5, 429 N.W. 2d, 722 (Neb. 1988).
104. National Gay Task Force v. Board of Educ., 729 F.2d 1270 (10th Cir. 1984).
105. Weissman v. Board of Jefferson City School Dist., 547 P.2d 1267 (Colo. 1976).
106. Yang v. Special Charter School Dist. No. 150, Peoria County, 296 N.E.2d 74 (Ill. 1973).
107. Denton v. South Kitsap School Dist. No. 402, 516 P.2d 1080 (Wash. 1973).
108. Pettit v. State Bd. of Educ., 513 P.2d 889 (Cal. 1973).
109. *In re* Grossman, 316 A.2d 39 (N.J. 1974).
110. Acanfora v. Bd. of Educ. of Montgomery County, 491 F.2d 498 (4th Cir. 1974).
111. Sullivan v. Meade Indep. School Dist. No. 101, 530 F.2d 799 (8th Cir. 1976).
112. Avery v. Homewood City Bd. of Educ., 674 F.2d 337 (5th Cir. 1982).
113. New Mexico State Bd. of Educ. v. Stoudt, 571 P.2d 1186 (N.M. 1977).
114. Drake v. Covington County Bd. of Educ., 371 F. Supp. 974 (M.D. Ala. 1974).
115. Eckman v. Board of Educ. of Hawthorne School Dist., 636 F. Supp. 1214 (N.D. Ill. 1986).
116. Watson v. State Bd. of Educ., 99 Cal. Rptr. 468 (Cal. App. 1971).
117. Tracy v. School Dist. No. 22, Sheridan County Wyoming, 243 P.2d 923 (Wyo. 1952).
118. Williams v. School Dist. No. 40 of Gila County, 417 P.2d 376 (Ariz. 1966).
119. Lindgren v. Board of Trustees, High School Dist. No. 1, 558 P.2d 468 (Mont. 1976).
120. Board of Trustees of Santa Maria Joint Union High School Dist. v. Judge, 123 Cal. Rptr. 830 (Cal. App. 1975).
121. Adams v. State Professional Practices Council, 406 So.2d 1170 (Fla. App. 1981).
122. Dominy v. Mays, 257 S.E.2d 317 (Ga. 1979).
123. Woodard v. Professional Practices Council, 388 So.2d 343 (Fla. App. 1980).
124. Board of Educ. of Hopkins County v. Wood, 717 S.W. 2d 837 (Ky. 1986).
125. Skripchuk v. Austin, 379 A.2d 1142 (Del. 1977).
126. Kiner v. State Bd. of Educ., 344 So.2d 656 (Fla. App. 1977).
127. Gary Teachers Union, Local No. 4, American Fed'n of Teachers v. School City of Gary, 332 N.E.2d 256 (Ind. 1975).
128. Golden v. Board of Educ., Harrison City, 285 S.E. 2d 665 (W. Va. 1981).
129. Board of Regents v. Roth, 408 U.S. 564 (1972).
130. Meyer v. Nebraska, 262 U.S. 390, 399 (1923).
131. Lombard v. Board of Educ. of City of New York, 502 F.2d 631 (2d Cir. 1974); Huntley v. North Carolina State Bd. of Educ., 493 F.2d 1016 (4th Cir. 1974); McGhee v. Draper, 564 F.2d 902 (10th Cir. 1977); Perry v. Sindermann, 408 U.S. 593 (1972).
132. Perry v. Sindermann, 408 U.S. 593 (1972).
133. Greminger v. Seaborne, 584 F.2d 275 (8th Cir. 1978).
134. Pred v. Board of Pub. Instruction, 415 F.2d 851 (5th Cir. 1969).
135. Mt. Healthy City School Dist. Bd. of Educ. v. Doyle, 429 U.S. 274 (1977).
136. Hortonville School Dist. v. Hortonville Educ. Ass'n, 426 U.S. 482 (1976).

CHAPTER 10

Rights Related
to Schooling: Part II

OVERVIEW

Equality is recognized as one of the basic values of our culture. Simultaneously, it is recognized that a gap has always existed between the ideal of equality and the actual functioning of our social institutions. Throughout history, people in the United States have practiced discrimination based on race, sex, national origin, religion, handicap, and other grounds as well, although in our efforts to achieve the ideal of equality, we have also sought various means of combating such discrimination. The equal protection clause of the Constitution has been an important legal vehicle in the struggle to achieve equality, and it has been supplemented by various federal and state laws, many of which are more specific than the general provision of the Constitution. In this chapter we examine legal developments based on these various sources as they impact on the work of counselors, psychologists, and social workers in schools.

RACIAL DISCRIMINATION

Today it is a generally accepted fact that, throughout its history, American culture has been permeated with racism. There were regional differences in racial discrimination; it was more open and official in the South, whereas in the North, East, and West it was covert and unofficially practiced. Schools, along with other institutions, reflected this racism, which tended to work to the serious disadvantage of blacks, Hispanics, Native Americans, and Orientals. In recent decades, significant forces have moved to challenge this widespread prejudice. Among these forces were certain legal developments, in both the courts and the legislatures, that often have led the efforts toward the achievement of equality for all, regardless of race. In this chapter we highlight these legal developments as they impact on both students and school employees, including student services professionals.

Why is racial segregation in schools unconstitutional?

The Supreme Court ruled in 1954, in the landmark case of *Brown v. Board of Education,*[1] that separate educational facilities are *inherently* unequal. In this historic decision it overruled the "separate but equal" doctrine established in 1896 in *Plessy v. Ferguson,*[2] which borrowed the phrase and some of its reasoning from the case of *Roberts v. City of Boston,*[3] decided by the Supreme Court of Massachusetts in 1850. Many controversies and cases were the legal stepping stones to *Brown,* where Chief Justice Earl Warren, writing for a unanimous Court, held that the equal protection clause of the fourteenth amendment makes unconstitutional any official or state-mandated separation of the races. The Court emphasized the importance of education in modern life: "In these days, it is doubtful that any child may reasonably be expected to succeed in life if he is denied the opportunity of an education. Such an opportunity, where the state has undertaken to provide it, is a right which must be available to all on equal terms."

The Court, relying on evidence from the social sciences, concluded that segregation has a serious detrimental effect on black children. "The impact is greater when it has the sanction of the law; for the policy of separating the races is usually interpreted as denoting the inferiority of the Negro group." Therefore, concluded the Court, "In the field of public education the doctrine of 'separate but equal' has no place. Separate educational facilities are inherently unequal."

Did schools follow the Supreme Court's mandate in the *Brown* case?

In general, no. First, we must realize that the Court faced the difficult practical question of how soon schools must desegregate. Since each community had its own unique history of segregation, its separate local schools, and its own geography including residential and traffic patterns, no single desegregation order could meet all needs. Thus, after considering all arguments for implementing its basic decision, the Court ordered schools to desegregate "with all deliberate speed"[4] and gave the responsibility for supervising compliance with this order to the federal district courts closest to each locality. Local school officials were given the task of creating desegregation plans under the supervision of local courts, which were to monitor "good faith implementation of the governing constitutional principles."

How speedily did schools comply with the Supreme Court's ruling in the *Brown* case that public schools must end racial segregation with "all deliberate speed"?

Their compliance turned out to be not speedy at all. Local school officials created a variety of arrangements to delay and even to defeat the intended consequences of the *Brown* decision. Noteworthy among such efforts were the so-called freedom-of-choice plans, struck down by the Court as a subterfuge,[5] and the closing of public schools and use of public funds to support segregated private schools, similarly declared unconstitutional.[6]

What is the difference between *de jure* and *de facto* segregation?

The early attacks on desegregated schooling took place in southern states, where dual school systems were mandated by law. When segregation exists mandated by law, by officially created policy or action, it is called *de jure* segregation; if it came about through people choosing to live in separate neighborhoods and sending their children to neighborhood schools, that is *de facto* segregation. Under the fourteenth amendment, ruled the Court, only *de jure* segregation is unconstitutional.

As efforts to desegregate all schools moved north, it became clear that unlawful segregation was not just a southern problem. Courts have found unconstitutional segregation in many northern cities, from Boston to Los Angeles, from Cleveland to Seattle, and in most cities in between. The key difference between southern and northern segregated schooling seemed to be that, whereas it was done blatantly and through open official action in the South, it was usually accomplished in the North through complex and not-so-open arrangements between public officials and leaders in business and industry to control housing, real estate development, and finance, as well as through the location of business, industry, and schools. Courts, however, ruled that such actions violate the fourteenth amendment just as the more open official actions of the South[7] had done.

Some justices have argued that the distinction between *de jure* and *de facto* segregation is untenable and should be discarded; however, the majority of the Supreme Court considers it an important distinction and it continues to require proof of intent to discriminate on the part of officials.[8] The requirement of intent was reaffirmed by the Supreme Court in 1989.[9]

Are all one-race schools unconstitutional?

No. Rather than promulgate simple rules, courts consider factors such as population concentrations, location of schools, traffic patterns, and other geographic and demographic factors, in determining whether or not good faith efforts have been made to desegregate the schools. As Chief Justice Burger noted in the *Swann* case,[10] minority groups in large cities often are concentrated in one part of the city and even good faith efforts to desegregate might require some schools to remain "one-race schools" until new schools can be built or the population changes. Although the mere existence of such schools is not necessarily unconstitutional, courts will examine such arrangements, and the burden of proof is on the school officials to show that these schools are genuinely nondiscriminatory.

Must communities use busing to desegregate the schools?

No. Courts tend to be quite pragmatic and will consider alternative plans proposed to achieve the goal of desegregation. If there are ways of desegregating the schools of a community without using busing, the Constitution will be satisfied. On the other hand, in many communities, busing has been used to transport millions of school children to all kinds of schools; although buses have been widely used to maintain segregated schooling, they can also be used as one of the means to desegregate schools. The Court recognized in the *Swann* case that there may be limits to the use of buses. Such limits are reached "when the time or distance of travel is so great as to either risk the health of the children or significantly impinge on the educational process."

Have any desegregated schools become resegregated?

Yes. In Pasadena, California, such resegregation occurred as a result of population shifts. When efforts were made to force school officials to act again to desegregate the schools, the Court ruled that there was no such duty to act because there were no official acts that created the resegregation.[11] The new imbalance was a case of *de facto* segregation and thus it was not unconstitutional.

May state laws and state constitutions regulate desegregation?

Yes, and some of them do. However, since the Constitution is the basic law of the land, state constitutions and laws may not contradict it. They may go further and grant additional rights, but they may not mandate actions that are inconsistent with the national Constitution. Some states, for example, have eliminated the *de jure—de facto* distinction by state constitutional provision, state law, or policies of local school boards. Among them are New York, Connecticut, Illinois, and New Jersey. An interesting case arose in California, where the distinction was erased by the state constitution. When voters in 1979 ratified Proposition I, amending the equal protection clause of their state constitution, they provided that there shall be no mandatory busing or pupil assignment beyond what is required by federal law. In a case challenging the validity of Proposition I, the Supreme Court upheld the right of the voters to act as they did. The Court rejected the notion that "once a state chooses to do 'more' than the Fourteenth Amendment requires, it may never recede."[12]

May courts require interdistrict plans for desegregation?

That depends on the facts of the particular case. Efforts were made in the Detroit area to include the schools of Detroit and its suburbs in one overall desegregation plan. Since Detroit was 64 percent black and 36 percent white and its suburbs 81 percent white and 19 percent black, neither could be substantially desegregated without an overall plan for the metropolitan area. Although the lower courts agreed with the metropolitan plan that included cross-district busing, the Supreme Court rejected it.[13]

The Court ruled that the desegregation remedy must take place within the city limits of Detroit because that is where the unlawful segregation occurred. The Court noted, however, that "an inter-district remedy might be in order where the racially discriminatory acts of one or more districts caused racial segregation in an adjacent district, or where district lines have been deliberately drawn on the basis of race." Such a case arose in Wilmington, Delaware, where evidence showed cross-district collaboration that created segregated schooling. When the lower court ordered an interdistrict remedy, the Supreme Court affirmed the decision.[14]

Interdistrict school desegregation has been upheld in several other cases where the facts indicated that pupil transfers or the drawing of boundaries between districts exacerbated the separation of races in schools. Courts upheld such remedies in Indiana,[15] Michigan,[16] Delaware, Texas,[17] and in other states.

In these cases, courts tend to scrutinize not only the racial composition of the student group, but the faculty and staff as well. District courts, which are closest to the local community, often incorporate lengthy, detailed desegregation plans in their decrees, spelling out specific requirements including such details as in-service education related to "student expectations, teacher expectations, minority culture, human relations, testing of students, the student code of conduct and the administration of discipline," as well as emphasizing the importance of counseling services in "easing the process of desegregation."[18]

How does the *Brown* case apply to counselors?

Although pupil desegregation has received the most public attention, the *Brown* decision and its progeny apply with equal force to school employees, including counselors, teachers, administrators, and staff. Among its guiding principles when considering the proper implementation of the first *Brown* decision, the Court noted, in *Brown II*, that we should consider "the physical condition of the school plant, the school transportation system, personnel," and other factors in determining whether or not there is good faith compliance.[19]

How soon must faculty and staff be desegregated?

That depends on the situation. Courts will consider the local situation, the racial composition of the faculty and staff, the availability of qualified personnel, and the overall desegregation plan. The Supreme Court has indicated, time and again, that it has recognized faculty and staff desegregation "to be an important aspect of the basic task of achieving a public school system wholly free from racial discrimination."[20]

To achieve the spirit of the equal protection clause and of the *Brown* decision, various federal and state laws have been enacted. The best known among these are Title VI and Title VII of the Civil Rights Act of 1964, included here as part of Appendix C.

May minorities be dismissed when reductions are necessary in a school's work force?

Yes, but nonracial criteria must be used in such personnel decisions. Furthermore, in school districts that are under court orders to desegregate because of a past history of racial discrimination, objective criteria might have to be used to determine who is laid off.

This question first arose in school districts that maintained a dual school system for reasons of race prejudice. When they were mandated to desegregate and create a "unitary system," they often found themselves with a surplus of teachers, counselors, and administrators. More often than not, a disproportionate number of black educators were dismissed. When such practices were challenged, the so-called Singleton principle was created. This principle requires that if a reduction of staff is necessitated by a court-ordered desegregation of a heretofore dual system, faculty, staff, or administrators to be demoted or dismissed "must be selected on the basis of objective and reasonable and nondiscriminatory standards from among all the staff of the school district."[21] Such objective criteria must be developed by the school district in question and must be available for public inspection.

Does seniority take precedence over an affirmative action plan?

It probably does. This question has arisen in a variety of school districts, particularly in those that have collective bargaining contracts with provisions protecting seniority. In school districts under court order to desegregate the faculty and staff, a disproportionate number of recently hired minorities are most likely to be hit the hardest if layoffs become necessary. Some court orders specified that seniority plans would have to be modified in order to assure that not all recently hired minorities would lose their jobs.[22] However, in June 1984, the Supreme Court ruled that courts do not have authority to suspend or modify a valid seniority system. The decision was based on Title VII of the Civil Rights Act of 1964, which explicitly protects "bona fide" seniority systems that were not themselves put in place for the purpose of discrimination.[23]

May affirmative action plans be used in hiring and promotion?

Yes they may be, held various courts, including the Supreme Court. However, even voluntary affirmative action plans will be closely scrutinized by the courts, for any official policy or action that takes race or ethnicity into account is suspect and can be justified only if it furthers a compelling governmental interest.[24] In general, courts will uphold affirmative action plans for hiring and/or promotion, to overcome vestiges of past discrimination. Preferential layoff plans, however, have been struck down as too hurtful of identifiable employees.

Must objective criteria* always be used before minority staff members can be demoted or dismissed?

No, only when such action is taken in connection with a reduction of personnel that accompanies school desegregation. In a school district that is not undergoing desegregation, the regular policies and procedures related to personnel decisions do

---

*Objective criteria are measurable qualifications such as years of formal schooling, degrees held, and length of teaching experience.

apply to members of minorities as well, and such decisions may be based on both objective and subjective considerations. Policies and procedures of this type must, of course, be racially neutral and fair in other respects.

An example of this principle appears in the case of Eduardo Molina, a Mexican-American school counselor who was demoted to classroom teaching after serving as counselor for three years at two different schools. Although the school officials maintained that his demotion was based on unsatisfactory performance as a counselor and his inability to get along with students, faculty, and other counselors, Molina insisted that the action was based on ethnic prejudice and his involvement in Mexican-American affairs. The court concluded that sufficient evidence existed to establish Molina's unsatisfactory performance as a counselor. Though the school system at large manifested evidence of discrimination, there were sufficient nondiscriminatory reasons for this particular demotion.[25]

May objective tests be used to screen applicants for counseling positions if a disproportionate number of minorities fail the test?

Yes, if the tests are valid, reasonable, and relevant to the job for which people are applying.

The guiding principle, announced by the Supreme Court in *Washington v. Davis,* is that the Court has "not embraced the proposition that a law or other official act, without regard to whether it reflects a racially discriminatory purpose, is unconstitutional solely because it has a racially disproportionate impact."[26] Under this principle, the Court upheld the use by South Carolina of the National Teacher Examination (NTE) to screen people for teacher certification.[27] When more blacks than whites failed to acquire the minimum score they challenged the test, claiming that it created a racial classification in violation of the fourteenth amendment and also Title VII of the Civil Rights Act of 1964. Because the NTE was created for a legitimate purpose, namely to assess the presence or absence of relevant knowledge, and because there was no proof of an intent to discriminate, the Court upheld its use.

May private schools exclude student applicants because of their race?

No. Because the fourteenth amendment applies only to "state action," it would seem that private schools could select their students at will. The Supreme Court ruled, however, that a federal law (42 U.S.C. § 1981) protects the equal rights of blacks to enter into contracts.[28] Under this law even private schools may not deny an applicant admission simply on the basis of race or ethnicity. The only possible exception to this would be a private, sectarian school that based its admissions decisions on the applicant's adherence to religious beliefs that forbid interracial contact. Such was the claim of Bob Jones University, whose claim to tax-exempt status was denied by the Internal Revenue Service because it maintained racially discriminatory admission policies.

The Supreme Court upheld the IRS interpretation of section 501(c)(3) of the Internal Revenue Code of 1954: "It would be wholly incompatible with the concepts underlying tax exemption to grant tax-exempt status to racially discriminatory private educational entities." Furthermore, "[t]he government's fundamental overriding interest in eradicating racial discrimination in education substantially outweighs whatever burden denial of tax benefits places on petitioner's exercise of their religious beliefs."[29]

An interesting case involving racial policies in a private religious school arose when two white female students were expelled by a school operated by the Marumsco Baptist Church. The girls were dismissed because of "romantic relationships" with black students, which they continued despite warnings from the principal. The federal court of appeals held that federal law (42 U.S.C. § 1981) forbids race discrimination by private sectarian schools and, specifically, the termination of a contract with a white student because of her association with a black student. When the church-school claimed its action was protected by the free exercise clause of the first amendment, the court held that it had failed to substantiate its claim.[30]

In sum, the constitutional mandate against racial or ethnic discrimination pervades the life of public schools. Both the equal protection clause and federal legislation apply to students, faculty, and staff, as well as to curricular content. State constitutions and laws often go beyond the federal requirements and further attempt to erase all vestiges of racial prejudice from the functioning of schools.

SEX DISCRIMINATION

The history of discrimination based on sex is well documented in our culture. As one of society's fundamental institutions, schools have reflected this discrimination; its impact is discernible on students, the curriculum, adult employees, and most other aspects of schools. As one of the consequences of the "civil rights revolution" of the 1960s and the "women's movement" of the 1970s, these discriminatory policies and practices have been seriously challenged. Some quickly crumbled and disappeared, but others persist and have found their way to our courts. In this section we examine the way the equal protection clause of the fourteenth amendment as well as Title VII of the Civil Rights Act of 1964 and Title IX of the Education Amendments of 1972 have been used to challenge these historic patterns of discrimination.

May schools pay male counselors more than women counselors?

No, if the men and the women have the same qualifications and experience and if they do the same type of work. Although even raising this question seems absurd to some people, many communities in the past paid male school employees more than females, for identical work. Such a differential in pay could be challenged under the equal protection clause of the fourteenth amendment, Title VII of the Civil Rights Act of 1964, and Equal Pay Act[31] (see Appendix C). This act allows differences in wages paid pursuant to "(i) a seniority system; (ii) a merit system; (iii) a system which measures earnings by quantity or quality of production; or (iv) a differential based on any factor other than sex." However, the Equal Pay Act does not require that the jobs performed by males and females be identical for them to receive equal pay. Substantial equality is all that is required; case-by-case comparisons must be made wherein the plaintiff has to show that her work requires similar skills, effort, and responsibility to that required by the higher-paid male. Once a *prima facie* case is thus established, the burden shifts to the employer to show that the differential is justified under the Equal Pay Act.[32]

For example, a federal district court dismissed a claim that Title VII was violated where elementary school principals were paid less than high school principals. The fact that the lower-paid job was "traditionally female" is not enough to establish a Title VII violation, ruled the court. Examining the situation, the court found that the salary differences were justified by factors other than sex: the high school principal's job entailed greater responsibility and effort due to the size of the staff and student body, as well as a larger budget to manage, and other nonsex factors.[33]

May schools prefer males over females for counseling positions?

No. In matters of promotion and in the selection of administrators and teachers, sexual preference must not be used, according to the law. Such preference would violate equal employment opportunities secured by Title VII of the Civil Rights Act of 1964,[34] and would also violate the equal protection clause of the fourteenth amendment. The selection of a dean of girls or a dean of boys might be an exception to this principle, if the job descriptions for these positions make it clear that some duties of the job call for particular activities for which being a male or a female is a job-related qualification.

May schools make an effort to have a balanced representation of males and females on the faculty and staff?

They probably may, although there are no cases reported on this issue so we do not know how courts would rule. Many schools prefer to have a roughly equal number of male and female teachers and administrators to serve as "role models" for students. It is for the same reason that minority representation is so important on the faculty and staff of schools.

When schools or other federal or state agencies classify people according to race or ethnicity (but not sex), they bear a heavy burden to justify such classification. Courts have determined that these are "suspect classifications" that will bring on "strict scrutiny" and will require officials to show a "compelling state interest" that justifies the need for such classification.* In ordinary situations that involve no suspect classification, courts apply the "rational basis" test, which requires the government to show only that there were some legitimate reasons for its actions. This is a rather easy test to meet, whereas the test of strict scrutiny is very difficult to satisfy.

The Supreme Court has gone beyond the "rational basis" test in cases involving gender-based classification, but has not applied to them the much more demanding "strict scrutiny" test. It is searching for an intermediate level of scrutiny, whereby the Court views with "special sensitivity" any official arrangements that use sex as a basis for classification.[35] This intermediate level of review requires that a gender-based classification, in order to withstand constitutional challenge, must serve important governmental objectives and bear a substantial relationship to the accomplishment of such goals.[36]

If this intermediate test were applied, it is quite likely that schools could make a successful argument justifying efforts to have a balanced representation of males and females on the faculty, in counseling positions, in administration, and on the staff. They would need to present social-psychological evidence verifying the significance for growing children of male and female adult role models. In light of the currently large number of single-parent families, such evidence should be useful in presenting a successful case.

Does Title IX apply to counselors?

The primary purpose of Title IX (20 U.S.C. § 1681–86) is set forth in its section 901(a) as follows: "No person in the United States shall, on the basis of sex, be excluded from participation in, be denied the benefits of, or be subjected to discrimination under any education program or activity receiving Federal financial assistance." (See Appendix C.) Because the specific wording of Title IX nowhere includes the word "employees," various schools argued that Congress intended the law to apply only to students. This argument was rejected by the Court: "While chapter 901(a) does not expressly include employees within its scope or expressly exclude them, its broad directive that 'no person' may be discriminated against on the basis of gender, on its face, includes employees as well as students."[37] Thus, it is clear that Title IX applies to counselors.

What is the penalty for violating Title IX?

The penalty for sexual discrimination in violation of Title IX is the loss of federal financial assistance. Major controversies have arisen over what constitutes a "program or activity" within the meaning of Title IX. Some claimed that Congress intended the phrase to apply only to specific activities within an institution for which funds were earmarked, whereas others argued that an institution that received federal

---

*The Court has ruled that classification on the basis of race, alienage, and national origin are suspect. Such classification will be closely examined for legitimacy and therefore the test is called "strict scrutiny."

funds would lose all of it if any one or more of its specific programs practiced discrimination.

In the highly controversial *Grove City* case[38] the Supreme Court accepted the more restricted view expressed in the first of these interpretations. According to this ruling, if a school received federal funds for a variety of activities and was found to have discriminated only in athletics, only the funds for athletics would be lost. Thus, a narrow "programmatic" approach to Title IX enforcement could create a very curious and complex situation where some students, staff, and activities would be protected by Title IX, although others in the same institution would not be, depending on the source of funding for the program.

Furthermore, the Court's ruling in the *Grove City* case could affect interpretations of Title VI of the Civil Rights Act of 1964 and Section 504 of the Rehabilitation Act of 1973, because they contain language similar to that of Title IX. As a consequence of the Court's ruling and the ensuing public reaction, Congress passed the Civil Rights Restoration Act of 1987,[39] an amendment to Title IX and other civil rights acts, to provide that a "program or activity" means all of the operations of an educational institution. Thus, if a school receives federal support for *any* of its programs or departments it may not discriminate on the basis of sex in any program or department within the institution.

May schools require pregnant counselors to take a specified leave of absence?

Yes, depending on the purposes and the reasonableness of the school policy. In cases involving teachers, however, the Supreme Court ruled that schools may not set arbitrary requirements for pregnancy leaves. They may not create a conclusive presumption that all teachers or counselors become incapable of competent work beyond the fourth or fifth month of pregnancy or after any other prespecified date: "Arbitrary cut-off dates embodied in the mandatory leave rules before us have no rational relationship to the valid state interest of prescribing continuity of instruction," concluded the Court, rejecting the mandatory-leave policy of Cleveland, Ohio.[40] Similarly, it struck down the requirement that a teacher on pregnancy leave is ineligible to return until her child reaches a certain age, for example, three months. Thus, as long as she is capable of performing her duties the teacher/counselor and her physician may decide when she should begin her pregnancy leave.

What reasonable restrictions related to pregnancy leaves may schools impose?

If schools are concerned with continuity of instruction, they could probably create a policy that requires pregnant teachers to start their leave at the beginning of the semester during which they expect to deliver. They could also specify in the policy that such teacher may not return until the beginning of the semester following delivery. Because such a policy focuses on the educationally desirable continuity of instruction and because the policy is reasonably related to that end, it is likely to be upheld under the rational basis test. Furthermore, it does not impose arbitrary leave dates on teachers, because different teachers would begin their leaves at different stages of pregnancy.

Schools could also require teachers to give written notice of when they intend to begin their pregnancy leave and when they intend to return. Medical certificates that attest to the competence of the pregnant teacher to continue or to resume work could also be required by schools.

May a counselor breast-feed her baby at school?

That depends on whether it can be done without interfering with the efficient performance of her duties. Such a question arose when a teacher went to court and challenged a school's refusal to permit her to breast-feed her baby during her duty-free lunch period. Although the lower court dismissed her case, the court of appeals ruled in her favor. The court recognized a legitimate interest the teacher had in breast-feeding her child and also the legitimacy of the school's interest in the efficient performance of all duties. It held that a careful consideration of the facts must be undertaken to determine whether or not the two important interests can be reconciled.[41]

Are counselors protected by law against sexual harassment at work?

Yes. Courts have ruled that unwelcome sexual advances by a supervisory employee toward a subordinate female employee is a form of sexual discrimination and thus a violation of Title VII of the Civil Rights Act of 1964.[42] The employer is held liable for the harassment committed by its supervisory employees; however, the extent of the damages is likely to be less if the employer has a clear policy against such sexual advances as well as internal procedures to enforce the policy. Such harassment might be manifested by words and gestures as well as by more overt sexual advances. Because Title VII nowhere makes specific reference to sexual harassment, courts must decide on a case-by-case basis what acts constitute such harassment.

As of this writing, there are no reported cases of unwanted sexual advances toward male employees, but it is likely that such conduct would be regarded as discrimination. On the other hand, it has been suggested that homosexual or lesbian sexual advances are outside the jurisdiction of the Equal Employment Opportunity Commission (EEOC) and, therefore, not actionable under Title VII.[43]

Logic would dictate that unwanted sexual advances toward either sex by either sex ought to be considered harassment; however, because the concern of Congress focused on gender discrimination, and because Congress did not make its intention clear, courts have come up with narrow interpretations, so far, and have protected only female employees. The strongest cases of sexual harassment are those where it can be shown that submission to the advances of the supervisor constitutes a "term or condition" of employment, and is likely to influence one's retention of a job, promotion, or salary increase.[44]

Is the school liable only when top administration knows that sexual harassment is taking place?

Not under the latest guidelines from the EEOC. In 1980, new and broader guidelines were put into effect by the EEOC that expand employers' liability. The new guidelines specify the following three criteria for what constitutes unlawful behavior in cases of unwanted sexual advances: (1) Submission is either an explicit or implicit condition of employment; (2) submission or rejection is used as a basis for employment decision; or (3) the conduct "has the purpose or effect of unreasonably interfering with an individual's work performance or creating an intimidating, hostile, or offensive work environment."[45]

Under the new guidelines, the employer is responsible for harassment by both supervisory and nonsupervisory employees, but the responsibility is greater for the actions of supervisors. The guidelines suggest that employers bear responsibility for the behavior of nonsupervisory employees only if the employer *knew or should have known* about it, whereas the responsibility for the behavior of supervisors exists whether or not the employer knew or should have known about it. Whether or not the courts will adopt the new EEOC guidelines is yet to be seen. If they do, there will be protection for both sexes against any form of sexual harassment, and employer liability will be much broader than under current court decisions. Schools may be wise to purchase appropriate insurance against such claims.

Are students protected against sex discrimination?

Yes. Both the equal protection clause of the fourteenth amendment and Title IX have been used to challenge gender discrimination against students. Furthermore, many states have equal protection clauses in their own constitutions as well as state laws similar to Title IX, which have been used to secure equal treatment for students, faculty, and staff. Areas of conflict adjudicated by courts include equal access to sports and athletic facilities, equal access to courses and programs, sex-segregated schooling, and sex discrimination in extracurricular activities.

Must girls and boys have equal access to school athletic activities?

In general yes, although there are some exceptions to this generalization. This question first reached the federal courts in 1972, when Peggy Brenden challenged the Minnesota state athletic association rule that forbade girls' participation on boys' teams and vice versa.[46] Peggy, a top-ranked tennis player, wanted to play on the boys' team because there was no girls' team at her school. The federal court ruled in her favor, basing its decision on the equal protection clause of the fourteenth amendment. After analyzing all the evidence, the court concluded that Brenden's exclusion was based on "the fact of sex and sex alone." Therefore, as applied to her, the rules were unreasonable, discriminatory, and unconstitutional, and Peggy Brenden must be allowed to try out for the boy's team.

Various courts have ruled that, in noncontact sports, if no teams exist for girls they may compete for positions on the boys' teams. If teams are provided for both sexes, courts generally uphold school rules that separate boys and girls in athletic activities.[47] Specialists in athletics have argued that such separation works to the overall advantage of women's sports, which sports have received a significant boost from Title IX as well as from recent court decisions.

In sports involving bodily contact, courts tend to uphold separate teams for girls and for boys; they also tend to uphold teams for boys only, even when there are no comparable teams for girls, although this is not always the case. For example, a federal court in Ohio struck down a portion of the Title IX regulations as unconstitutional because they supported separation of boys and girls in contact sports. According to the court, school policies based on the presumption that girls are uniformly weaker or inferior to boys are arbitrary and thus violate due process.[48] This case seems to go further than others, because it strikes down the distinction between contact and noncontact sports.

Must both boys and girls have access to all athletic activities a school offers?

There is no uniform law on this point and we find variations among the states and among federal courts. A Massachusetts court ruled that denial of access to a specific sport is a denial of equal protection. even when overall opportunities are equal.[49] Other courts have held that if the overall athletic opportunities are equal, the lack of access for boys to a specific sport is not a violation of the law.[50] This is particularly the case in situations where boys who have had extensive opportunities to participate in athletics have sought access to a specific sport, such as volleyball, where only girls' teams were organized.

Must schools provide equal financial support for girls' and for boys' sports?

In general, yes, although the emphasis is on equity rather than identical treatment. Title IX forbids gender discrimination in financial support for sports equipment and coaching. However, because different sports require different equipment, costs vary significantly among them and it would be simplistic to require identical amounts of money for each. For teams in the same sport, such as swimming, tennis, or golf, there ought to be comparable financial support for boys and for girls. But in high-cost, high-revenue sports, such as football or basketball, questions of comparability are more difficult and case-by-case decisions must be made. Title IX regulations also require that athletic scholarships must be available on an equal basis for boys and for girls.

May girls or boys be excluded on the basis of their sex from some courses or programs offered by schools?

No, they must all have access to the full range of offerings. Throughout history, stereotypic views of sex roles excluded girls from shop courses and boys from cooking, home economics, and, at times, typing courses. Title IX and other laws forbid such discrimination, but might allow the separation of girls and boys only in courses such as sex education, where the sensitivity of content might make such separation educationally justifiable. There are no cases on record concerning the equalization of access to courses, because schools tended to accommodate to the new requirements as soon as they were issued. The formal barriers quickly crumbled, but informal pressures persist, including the influence of counselors, and these forces often perpetuate historical gender-based stereotypes.

May public schools provide separate schools for boys and for girls?

Yes, if the separate schools are genuinely equal in programs offered, size, prestige, and academic quality, the courts ruled in a Philadelphia case.[51] When school officials presented evidence that such separation makes educational sense during the years of early adolescence, the court was unwilling to substitute its judgment for that of educators. Applying the rational basis test, the court concluded that "separate but equal" sex segregation is acceptable as long as the equality is genuine,* and as long as legitimate educational reasons motivate the separation. By contrast, a compulsory sex-segregated educational plan was struck down in Hinds County, Mississippi, when it was offered as part of a racial desegregation plan.[52] Thus, it is possible that courts will look more favorably on *voluntary* plans of separate schooling for boys and girls than on *compulsory* ones and that they will apply strict scrutiny to any plan that might be a vestige of prior racial segregation.

May schools set higher admission standards for girls than for boys?

No. In a case that arose in Boston, Massachusetts, the federal court declared unconstitutional an admission policy that, in order to maintain balance between male and female admissions, set a higher cut-off score for girls than for boys. Girls had to score 133 or above on a standardized test to be admitted to Girls Latin School, whereas boys could be admitted to Boys Latin School with a score of 120 or above. School officials argued that the different scores were based on the different capacities of the respective school buildings, but the federal court struck down the admission plan as discriminatory and thus in violation of the equal protection clause of the fourteenth amendment.[53]

May schools treat married and unmarried students differently?

In general, no. Schools may provide separate classes or alternative schools on a voluntary basis for married and/or pregnant students. Such students may not be compelled to attend separate schools and they may not be compelled to attend adult or evening schools in place of regular day school.[54]

---

*Note, by contrast, that "separate but equal" is not acceptable when classification is by race, in which case courts use the test of strict scrutiny.

Earlier cases tended to uphold school board regulations that excluded married women students from extracurricular activities, as a way of discouraging "teenage marriages," which often led to dropping out of school.[55] More recently, the trend of judicial decisions is to protect the students' right to full participation in school-sponsored activities. In a case that arose in Ohio,[56] the court relied on the language of the *Tinker* case to ask whether the school policy was necessary to maintain discipline or whether it was part of an "enclave of totalitarianism." Because the student's marriage did not lead to any "material or substantial" disruption of school discipline, his right to participate in athletic and other extracurricular activities was protected.

In sum, constitutional interpretations, federal and state laws, and recent changes in public opinion have significantly reduced sex discrimination in our schools. Curricular revision is attempting to infuse equity into courses and teaching materials, classes and programs are available on a more equal basis for girls and boys, and substantial gains have been made toward equal opportunity for participation in athletics.

Males may not legally be given preference over females for staff positions in schools, and equal work must be recognized with equal pay. Maternity leaves may no longer be controlled by arbitrary rules nor can such rules govern when a woman returns to work after delivery.

Thus, inertia and tradition carry forward some vestiges of sex discrimination in the schools, but substantial advances have been made in recent years toward its elimination.

OTHER TYPES OF DISCRIMINATION

The Constitution has been invoked by teachers and other government employees to protect themselves against a variety of other laws, policies, and practices they felt were discriminatory and unfair. Among these we find objections to a mandatory retirement age, to the exclusion of handicapped persons from various jobs, and to restrictions against noncitizens.

Is a mandatory retirement age unconstitutional?

That depends on the retirement age that is mandated and on what type of job one holds. Historically, many school districts forced people to retire at age 65 and some at age 70. When such policies or laws were challenged, the courts applied the rational basis test to see whether there was a legitimate governmental objective that was served by such policies or laws. A kindergarten teacher in New York challenged such a law, claiming it violated the equal protection clause because it created an irrefutable presumption of incompetence based on age.[57] A federal appeals court disagreed with her and upheld the law. According to the court, there are good reasons to mandate retirement for teachers (in this case at the age of 70), in order to open opportunities for younger teachers and for minorities, as a way of bringing fresh ideas into the system, and to assure predictability of administering pension plans. Because a compulsory retirement system is rationally related to each of these objectives, the Constitution is not violated.

The preceding suit was filed prior to 1978, the year in which Congress enacted the Age Discrimination in Employment Act Amendments of 1978.[58] This act prohibits age discrimination in employment against "individuals who are at least 40 years of age but less than 70." A Pennsylvania teacher filed suit under the law when his school district mandated his retirement at the age of 65.[59] Although this law did not become effective until 1979 and the teacher was told to retire in 1978, the court protected him, recognizing the intent of Congress to create a new national policy "to the effect that 70 years is the earliest time for mandatory retirement." Thus, for teachers, counselors, or administrators in public schools, mandatory retirement is illegal under the age of 70 but permissible at that age.

This law does not apply with equal force to all public employment. Some jobs may call for earlier retirement, if there is a reasonable connection between the requirements of the job and age. For example, a New York requirement that school bus drivers retire at age 65 was upheld by the court when evidence showed that drivers over age 65 have a higher accident rate.[60] Similarly, retirement of police officers, foreign service officers, and some others in public employment is likely to be upheld by the courts when good reasons exist to mandate such retirement at some age below 70 and even below 65.[61]

May school districts exclude the handicapped from employment?

No, if an individual is qualified to do the job. Section 504 of the Rehabilitation Act of 1973 has become an important law in this regard, protecting someone who is denied a position "solely by reason of his handicap."[62]

A blind female was protected under this law when she was prevented from taking the Philadelphia Teacher's Examination. The school district's policy prevented anyone with a chronic or acute physical defect, including blindness, from taking the exam. After the passage of federal legislation in 1973, she was allowed to take the examination and she passed. In the final analysis she prevailed, but only after several years of legal action asserting her claims to a job and to retroactive seniority.[63] In her lawsuit she also sought tenure, but she did not succeed in that claim because she had never gone through a probationary period during which she could have been evaluated.

A very different case arose in California, where a blind teacher filed suit after applying without success for promotion to an administrative position, claiming discrimination on the basis of handicap.[64] Applicants for the position were required to undergo both written and oral examinations. The evidence showed that the teacher scored the lowest quartile in the written examination, though assisted by a reader, and also received low evaluation in the oral interview, because his answers to educational problems presented to him were judged quite superficial. The court, applying the rational basis test, upheld the position of the school district and found that there was no discrimination in denying this blind teacher the administrative position. Since he would not have qualified even if he were sighted, he was not denied the position "solely by reason of his handicap."

May certification be denied for lack of citizenship?

Yes, if a state law so provides. In general, federal laws prohibit discrimination on the basis of national origin. Some states require applicants for teaching certificates to be citizens or to be applying for citizenship, although in other states there are no such requirements. If a state has such a law, the Supreme Court will uphold it as a requirement reasonably related to a legitimate state interest; so ruled the Supreme Court in a case of teachers in New York.[65] The Court emphasized that teachers "play a crucial part in developing students' attitudes toward government and understanding of the role of citizens in a democracy" and, furthermore, a teacher "serves as a role model for his students, exerting a subtle but important influence over their perceptions and values." Because all teachers may influence student attitudes toward citizenship responsibilities, schools "may regard all teachers as having an obligation to promote civic virtues." Therefore, in the opinion of the Court, the requirement that teachers be citizens or show an intention to become citizens by their application, is a reasonable state requirement.

May children of noncitizens or of illegal aliens be excluded from public schools?

No. The Supreme Court held in 1982 that children of illegal aliens have the right to attend the public schools of Texas.[66] In this case plaintiffs challenged the laws of Texas, which authorized local school districts to exclude them by denial of enrollment and also withheld state funds from local schools for the education of such children. A claim was made on behalf of the children that the state law violated the fourteenth amendment's provision that no state shall "deny to any person within its jurisdiction the equal protection of the laws." Texas, on the other hand, claimed that "within its jurisdiction" excluded aliens and, furthermore, that the classification was rationally related to the state's interest in preserving its limited funds for the education of children who were legal residents.

The Court ruled that the phrase "within its jurisdiction" was meant to extend the protection of the fourteenth amendment to all people, citizens or not, who are subject to the laws of the state. Aliens, legal and illegal, are subject to the laws of the state while in that state. Although the Court recognized the state's need to educate the children of its legal residents, it would not tolerate the hardships that would be likely to result from a complete denial of schooling to children of illegal aliens. The Court explicitly recognized the importance of schooling in contemporary life and elevated the importance of public schooling above other governmental services. In light of the significance of schooling for both society and the individual, its denial would take an "inestimable toll on the social, economic, intellectual, and psychological well-being of the individual," and would impose a "lifetime of handicap" on a child.

CONSTITUTIONAL TORTS

In Chapter 3 we discussed civil liability for damages caused by an individual's negligent action. The general principles of tort liability discussed there apply to teachers, administrators, and other school personnel. In recent years we have seen the appearance of what has come to be known as a "constitutional tort." Such a tort refers to the right to sue for money damages when one's constitutional rights are violated by government officials, including employees of public schools.

In a landmark case, *Wood v. Strickland*,[67] two Arkansas students were suspended for three months without due process. When their parents sued the school board for money damages the Supreme Court ruled that school officials could be held liable "if they knew or reasonably should have known that the action they took within their sphere of official responsibility would violate the constitutional rights of students."

Historically, school officials were better off not knowing the law, for courts would not hold them liable if they innocently violated students' rights. Thus, in a way, there was a premium on ignorance. This is no longer so. The court said that violating students' constitutional rights cannot be "justified by ignorance or disregard of settled, indisputable law on the part of one entrusted with supervision of students' daily lives"; official action must be based not only on good intentions "but also on knowledge of the basic, unquestioned constitutional rights" of students.

Although the *Wood* case involved members of the school board, other school personnel, including counselors, psychologists, and social workers, would be held to the same standards by the courts.

How much in damages do courts award when students' rights are violated?

That depends on the situation. In a case that arose in Chicago, two students were suspended for 20 days without due process. At the trial no evidence was introduced to show actual damages suffered, but the students' lawyer argued that they should receive a substantial money award because their constitutional rights had been violated.[68]

Nonetheless, the Supreme Court ruled that they should receive only nominal damages. The Court explained that substantial damages should be awarded (1) if evidence showed the actual injury, which may include "mental or emotional distress" as well as financial loss, or (2) if punitive damages were to be used to punish or deter officials who intentionally deprive students of their rights.

However, even when students may not be able to show intentional violation of their rights or actual injury, the court may, in its discretion, require the school officials to pay all court costs and attorney fees, which may be sizeable.

May counselors sue for damages
if their constitutional rights are violated?

Yes. An experienced successful teacher in Texas went to court when his contract was not renewed following a change in school administration,[69] alleging that the new principal and superintendent had violated his constitutional rights of due process and freedom of expression. The court agreed, having found the principal's evaluations to be inaccurate, grossly unfair, and not procedurally consistent with district requirements. The jury awarded the teacher (1) $16,440 for lost salary and $17,000 "for mental anguish accompanying the termination of his employment"; (2) exemplary damages of $25,000 against the principal and superintendent for having acted with malice and intentionally depriving the teacher of his constitutional rights; and (3) attorney fees, which were incurred unnecessarily due to the "school board's unreasonable and obdurate obstinacy."

We may expect further developments in this relatively new area of the law, which puts pressure on all school personnel to become better informed about rights related to schooling. Also, Congress has enacted legislation granting courts discretion to award court costs and attorney fees to prevailing parties in such lawsuits.[70]

SUMMARY AND CONCLUSIONS

It should be clear to any objective observer of American culture that significant gains have been made in recent years in struggles to gain equality under the law. This is not to claim that full equal treatment has now been achieved. The efforts continue and there are various legal means available to fight discrimination. We have seen that both constitutional and statutory attacks have been made on various forms of discrimination in public schools. In a lawsuit, the plaintiff might invoke a particular provision of the Constitution as well as specific federal laws, if any exist related to the issue at hand. Furthermore, state constitutional provisions and state laws might be applicable to the same situation. Whenever possible, courts will attempt to rule on statutory grounds and avoid the constitutional issue; that is why we find discrimination cases decided on such varied grounds. And finally, even beyond the requirements of the law, there might be provisions incorporated into a local policy or a collective bargaining contract that further help to eliminate discrimination in the professional lives of teachers and counselors. It makes good sense to use all such legal means at one's disposal when a difficulty arises.

BROWN V. BOARD OF EDUCATION OF TOPEKA
347 U.S. 483 (1954)

Mr. Chief Justice WARREN delivered the opinion of the Court.

These cases come to us from the States of Kansas, South Carolina, Virginia, and Delaware. They are premised on different facts and different local conditions, but a common legal question justified their consideration together in this consolidated opinion.

In each of the cases, minors of the Negro race, through their legal representatives, seek the aid of the courts in obtaining admission to the public schools of their community on a nonsegregated basis. In each instance, they have been denied admission to schools attended by white children under laws requiring or permitting segregation according to race. This segregation was alleged to deprive the plaintiffs of the equal protection of the laws under the Fourteenth Amendment. In each of the cases other than the Delaware case, a three-judge federal district court denied relief to the plaintiffs on the so-called "separate but equal" doctrine announced by this Court in *Plessy v. Ferguson*. Under that doctrine, equality of treatment is accorded when the races are provided substantially equal facilities, even though these facilities be separate. In the Delaware case, the Supreme Court of Delaware adhered to that doctrine, but ordered that the plaintiffs be admitted to the white schools because of their superiority to the Negro schools.

The plaintiffs contend that segregated public schools are not "equal" and cannot be made "equal," and that hence they are deprived of the equal protection of the laws. Because of the obvious importance of the question presented, the Court took jurisdiction. Argument was heard in the 1952 Term, and reargument was heard this Term on certain questions propounded by the Court.

Reargument was largely devoted to the circumstances surrounding the adoption of the Fourteenth Amendment in 1868. It covered exhaustively consideration of the Amendment in Congress, ratification by the states, then existing practices in racial segregation, and the views of proponents and opponents of the Amendment. This discussion and our own investigation convince us that, although these sources cast some light, it is not enough to resolve the problem with which we are faced. At best, they are inconclusive. The most avid proponents of the post-War Amendments undoubtedly intended them to remove all legal distinctions among "all persons born or naturalized in the United States." Their opponents, just as certainly, were antagonistic to both the letter and the spirit of the Amendments and wished them to have the most limited effect. What others in Congress and the state legislatures had in mind cannot be determined with any degree of certainty.

An additional reason for the inconclusive nature of the Amendment's history, with respect to segregated schools, is the status of public education at that time. In the South, the movement toward free common schools, supported by general taxation, has not yet taken hold. Education of white children was largely in the hands of private groups. Education of Negroes was almost nonexistent, and practically all of the race were illiterate. In fact, any education of Negroes was forbidden by law in some states. Today, in contrast, many Negroes have achieved outstanding success in the arts and sciences as well as in the business and professional world. It is true that public school education at the time of the Amendment had advanced further in the North, but the effect of the Amendment on Northern States was generally ignored in the congressional debates. Even in the North, the conditions of public education did not approximate those existing today. The curriculum was usually rudimentary; ungraded schools were common in rural areas; the school term was but three months a year in many states; and compulsory school attendance was virtually unknown. As a consequence, it is not surprising that there should be so little in the history of the Fourteenth Amendment relating to its intended effect on public education.

In the first cases in this Court construing the Fourteenth Amendment, decided shortly after its adoption, the Court interpreted it as proscribing all state-imposed discriminations against the Negro race. The doctrine of "separate but equal" did not make its appearance in this Court until 1896 in the case of *Plessy v. Ferguson, supra,* involving not education but transportation. American courts have since labored with the doctrine for over half a century. In this Court, there have been six cases involving the "separate but equal" doctrine in the field of public education. In *Cumming v. Board of Education of Richmond County,* and *Gong Lum v. Rice,* the validity of the doctrine itself was not challenged. In more recent cases, all on the graduate school level, inequality was found in that specific benefits enjoyed by white students were denied to Negro students of the same educational qualifications. . . . In none of these cases was it necessary to reexamine the doctrine to grant relief to the Negro plaintiff. And in *Sweatt v. Painter, supra,* the Court expressly reserved decision on the question whether *Plessy v. Ferguson* should be held inapplicable to public education.

In the instant cases, that question is directly presented. Here, unlike *Sweatt v. Painter,* there are findings below that the Negro and white schools involved have been equalized, or are being equalized, with respect to buildings, curricula, qualifications and salaries of teachers, and other "tangible" factors. Our decision, therefore, cannot turn on merely a comparison of these tangible factors in the Negro and white schools involved in each of the cases. We must look instead to the effect of segregation itself on public education.

[1] In approaching this problem, we cannot turn the clock back to 1868 when the Amendment was adopted, or even to 1896 when *Plessy v. Ferguson* was written. We must consider public education in the light of its full development and its present place in American life throughout the Nation. Only in this way can it be determined if segregation in public schools deprives these plaintiffs of the equal protection of the laws.

[2] Today, education is perhaps the most important function of state and local governments. Compulsory school attendance laws and the great expenditures for education both demonstrate our recognition of the importance of education to our democratic society. It is required in the performance of our most basic public responsibilities, even service in the armed forces. It is the very foundation of good citizenship. Today it is a principal instrument in awakening the child to cultural values, in preparing him for later professional training, and in helping him to adjust normally to his environment. In these days, it is doubtful that any child may reasonably be expected to succeed in life if he is denied the opportunity of an education. Such an opportunity, where the state has undertaken to provide it, is a right which must be made available to all on equal terms.

[3] We come then to the question presented: Does segregation of children in public schools solely on the basis of race, even though the physical facilities and other "tangible" factors may be equal, deprive the children of the minority group of equal educational opportunities? We believe that it does.

In *Sweatt v. Painter, supra,* in finding that a segregated law school for Negroes could not provide them equal educational opportunities, this Court relied in large part on "those qualities which are incapable of objective measurement but which make for greatness in a law school." In *McLaurin v. Oklahoma State Regents, supra,* the Court, in requiring that a Negro admitted to a white graduate school be treated like all other students, again resorted to intangible considerations: ". . . his ability to study, to engage in discussions and exchange views with other students, and, in general, to learn his profession." Such considerations apply with added force to children in grade and high schools. To separate them from others of similar age and qualifications solely because of their race generates a feeling of inferiority as to their status in the community that may affect their hearts and minds in a way unlikely ever to be undone. The effect of this separation on their educational opportunities was well stated by a finding in the Kansas case by a court which nevertheless felt compelled to rule against the Negro plaintiffs:

> Segregation of white and colored children in public schools has a detrimental effect upon the colored children. The impact is greater when it has the sanction of the law; for the policy of separating the races is usually interpreted as denoting the inferiority of the negro group. A sense of inferiority affects the motivation of a child to learn. Segregation with the sanction of law,

therefore, has a tendency to [retard] the educational and mental development of Negro children and to deprive them of some of the benefits they would receive in a racial[ly] integrated school system.

Whatever may have been the extent of psychological knowledge at the time of *Plessy v. Ferguson,* this finding is amply supported by modern authority. Any language in *Plessy v. Ferguson,* contrary to this finding is rejected.

[4] We conclude that in the field of public education the doctrine of "separate but equal" has no place. Separate educational facilities are inherently unequal. Therefore, we hold that the plaintiffs and others similarly situated for whom the actions have been brought are, by reason of the segregation complained of, deprived of the equal protection of the laws guaranteed by the Fourteenth Amendment. This disposition makes unnecessary any discussion whether such segregation also violates the Due Process Clause of the Fourteenth Amendment.

[5] Because these are class actions, because of the wide applicability of this decision, and because of the great variety of local conditions, the formulation of decrees in these cases presents problems of considerable complexity. On reargument, the consideration of appropriate relief was necessarily subordinated to the primary question—the constitutionality of segregation in public education. We have now announced that such segregation is a denial of the equal protection of the laws. In order that we may have the full assistance of all the parties in formulating decrees, the cases will be restored to the docket, and the parties are requested to present further argument on Questions 4 and 5 previously propounded by the Court for the reargument this Term. The Attorney General of the United States is again invited to participate. The Attorneys General of the states requiring or permitting segregation in public education will also be permitted to appear as *amici curiae* upon request to do so by September 15, 1954, and submission of briefs by October 1, 1954.

It is so ordered.

NOTES

1. Brown v. Board of Educ., 347 U.S. 483 (1954).
2. Plessy v. Ferguson, 163 U.S. 537 (1896).
3. Roberts v. City of Boston, 59 Mass (5 Cush.) 198 (1850).
4. This decision is known as Brown II, Brown v. Bd. of Educ., 349 U.S. 294 (1955).
5. Green v. County School Bd. of New Kent County, 391 U.S. 430 (1968).
6. Griffin v. Prince Edward County, 377 U.S. 218 (1964).
7. *See, e.g.,* the case of Boston, reported in Morgan v. Kerrigan, 509 F.2d 580 (1st Cir. 1975); cases from Ohio, reported in Columbus Bd. of Educ. v. Penick, and Dayton Bd. of Educ. v. Brinkman, 443 U.S. 449 (1979); and the case of Los Angeles, reported in Crawford v. Bd. of Educ. in City of Los Angeles, 5 P.2d 28 (Cal. 1976).
8. *See* Keyes v. School Dist. No. 1, Denver, Colo., 413 U.S. 189 (1973).
9. Wards Cove Packing Co. v. Antonio, 57 U.S.L.W. 4583 (June 5, 1989).
10. Swann v. Charlotte-Mecklenburg Bd. of Educ., 402 U.S. 1 (1971).
11. Pasadena City Board of Education v. Spangler, 427 U.S. 424 (1976).
12. Crawford v. Los Angeles Bd. of Educ., 458 U.S. 527 (1982).
13. Milliken v. Bradley, 418 U.S. 717 (1974).
14. Evans v. Buckanan, 393 F. Supp. 428 (D. Del. 1975).
15. United States v. Board of School Comm'r, 637 F.2d 1101 (7th Cir. 1980).
16. Berry v. School Dist. of City of Benton Harbor, 515 F. Supp. 344 (W.D. Mich. 1981).

17. Fort Bend Indep. School Dist. v. City of Stafford, 507 F. Supp. 211 (S.D. Tex. 1980).
18. These are from the district court's opinion in United States v. Board of School Comm'r, 506 F. Supp. 657 (S.D. Ind. 1979).
19. Brown, 347 U.S. 483.
20. United States v. Montgomery Bd. of Educ., 395 U.S. 225 (1969).
21. Singleton v. Jackson Mun. Separate School Dist., 419 F.2d 1211 (5th Cir. 1970).
22. Oliver v. Kalamazoo Bd. of Educ., 706 F.2d 757 (6th Cir. 1983).
23. Firefighter Local Union No. 1784 v. Stotts; Memphis Fire Dept. v. Stotts, 467 U.S. 561 (1984).
24. Wygant v. Jackson Bd. of Educ., 476 U.S. 267 (1986); Int'l Ass'n of Firefighters v. City of Cleveland, 478 U.S. 501 (1986).
25. Molina v. El Paso Indep. School Dist., 583 F.2d 213 (5th Cir. 1978).
26. Washington v. Davis, 426 U.S. 229 (1976).
27. United States v. South Carolina, 434 U.S. 1026 (1978).
28. 42 U.S.C. § 1981; Runyon v. McCrary, 427 U.S. 160 (1976). The Supreme Court, however, limited the effectiveness of 42 U.S.C. § 1981 in Patterson v. McLean Credit Union, 57 U.S.L.W. 4705 (June 13, 1989) by holding that this post–Civil War law protects only the right to enter into contracts and to enforce them regardless of race, and does not forbid racial harassment or discrimination *on* the job. Such actions must be litigated under Title VII of the Civil Rights Act of 1964.
29. Bob Jones Univ. v. United States, 103 S.Ct. 2017 (1983).
30. Fiedler v. Marumsco Christian School, 631 F.2d 1144 (4th Cir. 1980).
31. 29 U.S.C.A. § 206.
32. Corning Glass Works v. Brennan, 417 U.S. 188 (1974).
33. Siegel v. Board of Educ. of City School Dist. of New York, 713 F.Supp. 54 (E.D.N.Y. 1989).
34. 42 U.S.C.A. § 2000(e)–2.
35. Frontiero v. Richardson, 411 U.S. 677 (1973).
36. Craig v. Boren, 429 U.S. 190 (1976).
37. North Haven Bd. of Educ. v. Bell, 456 U.S. 512 (1982).
38. Grove City College v. Bell, 465 U.S. 555 (1984).
39. 20 U.S.C. § 1681.
40. Cleveland Bd. of Educ. v. LaFleur, 414 U.S. 632 (1974).
41. Dike v. School Bd. of Orange City, 650 F.2d 783 (5th Cir. 1981).
42. Barnes v. Costle, 561 F.2d 983 (D.C. Cir. 1977); Miller v. Bank of America, 600 F.2d 211 (9th Cir. 1979).
43. See EEOC Doc. No. 76–67, March 2, 1976, and EEOC Doc. No. 77–28, August 11, 1977.
44. Fisher v. Flynn, 598 F.2d 663 (1st Cir. 1979).
45. 20 C.F.R. § 1604.11(a) (1981).
46. Brenden v. Independent School Dist. 742, 342 F. Supp. 1224 (D. Minn. 1972), *aff'd*, 477 F.2d 1292 (8th Cir. 1973).
47. O'Connor v. Board of Educ., 645 F.2d 578 (7th Cir. 1981), *cert. denied*, 454 U.S. 1084 (1981).
48. Yellow Springs Exempted Village School Dist. Bd. of Educ. v. Ohio High School Athletic Ass'n, 443 F. Supp. 753 (S.D. Ohio 1978).
49. Attorney General v. Massachusetts Interscholastic Athletic Ass'n, 393 N.E. 2d 284 (1979).
50. Mularadelis v. Haldane Central School Bd., 427 N.Y.S.2d 458 (1980).
51. Vorcheimer v. School Dist., 532 F.2d 880 (3rd Cir. 1976), *aff'd*, 430 U.S. 703 (1977).
52. United States v. Hinds County, 560 F.2d 619 (5th Cir. 1977).

53. Bray v. Lee, 337 F. Supp. 934 (D. Mass. 1972).
54. Alvin Indep. School Dist. v. Cooper, 404 S.W.2d 76 (Tex. 1966).
55. Kissick v. Garland Indep. School Dist., 330 S.W.2d 708 (Tex. 1959).
56. Davis v. Meek, 344 F. Supp. 298 (N.D. Ohio 1972).
57. Palmer v. Ticcione, 576 F.2d 459 (2d Cir. 1978).
58. 29 U.S.C.A. § 621 (1980).
59. Kuhar v. Greensburg-Salem School Dist., 466 F. Supp. 806 (W.D. Pa. 1979).
60. Kerwick v. New York State Bd. of Equalization, 453 N.Y.S.2d 151 (1982).
61. Vance v. Bradley, 440 U.S. 93 (1979).
62. 29 U.S.C.A. § 790(a) (1973).
63. Gurmankin v. Costanzo, 556 F.2d 184 (3rd Cir. 1977).
64. Upshur v. Love, 474 F. Supp. 332 (N.D. Cal. 1979).
65. Ambach v. Norwick, 99 S. Ct. 1589 (1979).
66. Plyler v. Doe, 457 U.S. 202 (1982).
67. Wood v. Strickland, 420 U.S. 308 (1975).
68. Carey v. Piphus, 435 U.S. 247 (1978).
69. Burnaman v. Bay City Indep. School Dist., 445 F. Supp. 927 (S.D. Tex. 1978).
70. 42 U.S.C. § 1988.

APPENDIX A

Education and the American Legal System

In this appendix we look first at the role of state governments in education. Then we present the organization of U.S. court systems and indicate the way they relate to educational controversies.

EDUCATION AND STATE GOVERNMENTS

Unlike most countries, the United States has no national system of education. In fact, the national Constitution is silent on the matter; however, under its tenth amendment, education is considered to be among the powers reserved to the states. Courts have accepted this interpretation of the Constitution, and the Supreme Court has repeatedly stated that federal courts may interfere with the actions of state and local school officials only when such actions somehow threaten a personal liberty or property right protected by the Constitution or violate federal law.

All 50 states provide in their constitutions for public education. With America's historic commitment to decentralized government and local control, states have delegated much power and responsibility over schooling to local governments. Such delegation is a choice made by the people of a state, who could, like the state of Hawaii, choose to have one statewide school district. In spite of the existence of local school districts, legally schools remain a responsibility of the state government; school officials, teachers, and staff are agents of the state when performing their official duties. This is a significant principle, because the Constitution protects individuals only against actions taken by the government.

The first 10 amendments to the Constitution (more commonly, the Bill of Rights) prohibit certain actions on the part of the federal government. The fourteenth amendment applies to

Appendix adapted from Louis Fischer, David Schimmel, and Cynthia Kelly, *Teachers and the Law* (White Plains, N.Y.: Longman, 1981).

253

actions by the states. Because all actions of school officials and school boards are "state actions," the fourteenth amendment prohibits certain arbitrary and discriminatory practices. What makes this all the more important is the historic development whereby all the guarantees of the first amendment and many other provisions of the Bill of Rights, have been incorporated into the "liberty clause" of the fourteenth and thus made applicable to all the states. Although there is a complex and controversial legal history to this incorporation, for our purposes it will suffice to understand that all protections of the first amendment, and most protections of the other Bill of Rights provisions, apply to the actions of public school officials just as do those of the fourteenth amendment.

Thus, although states have the primary power and responsibility for public schools, their power must at all times be exercised consistently with the rights guaranteed in the national Constitution.

THE FEDERAL COURT SYSTEM

The U.S. Supreme Court is the only court specifically created by the Constitution (art. III, sec. 2); all other federal courts were established by Congress. Below the Supreme Court are 13 federal courts of appeal (see Figure A1), and within each "circuit" or geographical area (except for one centralized federal court of appeals dealing with copyright and other specialized matters) are trial courts, called district courts. There are nearly 100 district courts, at least one in each state, though their exact number may change from time to time. School-related cases involving federal issues may be brought to trial in a district court; from this court an appeal may be taken to a court of appeals and eventually to the Supreme Court (see Figure A2).

The Constitution specifies what cases the Supreme Court will consider (art. III, sec. 2, cl. 1). For all other federal courts, Congress determines which cases will be tried where, the route appeals will take, and the relationship of courts to the many administrative agencies of government. In general, federal courts take only two kinds of cases: (1) those that present substantial questions under federal laws and the Constitution, and (2) those involving different states or citizens of different states. Many cases present questions involving both federal and state laws and may initially be tried in either federal or state courts. If such a case is brought to trial in a federal court, however, the court must decide questions of state law according to the laws of the affected state. Conversely, if the case was initially filed in a state court, that court must follow the federal law governing that area.

Although decisions of the Supreme Court are applicable to the entire nation, the decisions of circuit courts are binding only within their territories; thus different rules may apply in different regions of the country until the Supreme Court decides the issue.

THE STATE COURT SYSTEM

Most school-related cases are litigated in state courts. Because these courts are created by state constitutions and legislatures, however, they vary considerably in titles, procedures, and jurisdiction. A general pattern among the states is a three-tiered system, excluding lower courts of special jurisdiction such as traffic courts and small claims courts. (See Figure A3.)

At the foundation of the state court system, we find the trial courts, often organized along county lines. From these, appeals go to intermediate appeals courts and finally to the highest court of the state, variously named in different states. For example, the highest state

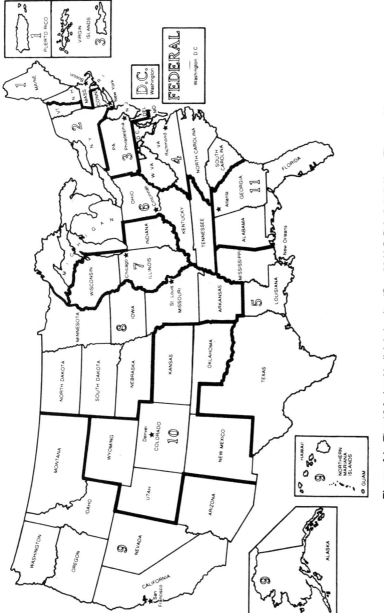

Figure A1. The 13 federal judicial circuits. (See 28 U.S.C.A. § 41.) *Note:* Eleven of the geographical circuits are numbered and one is located in Washington, D.C. The "federal" circuit also is located in D.C.; it deals with specialized matters, e.g., patents and copyrights. (Courtesy of West Publishing Company, St. Paul Minnesota.)

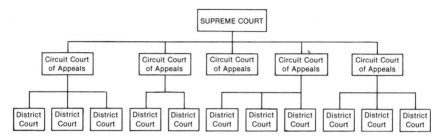

Figure A2. The federal court system.

court is named the Supreme Judicial Court in Massachusetts, the Court of Appeals in Kentucky, the Supreme Court of Errors in Connecticut, and the Supreme Court in California.

THE FUNCTIONS OF TRIAL AND APPEALS COURTS

A school-related controversy that cannot be resolved without a lawsuit first goes to a trial court. Here the facts are established and the relevant legal principles applied to the facts. If the case is appealed, the appellate court will not retry the case; it will usually accept the facts as established by the trial court unless it is very clear that evidence to support such facts was inadequate. The main concern of appeals courts is whether correct legal principles were applied to the facts determined by the court below it.

For example, a school may have expelled Student X for persistent acts of violence and classroom disruption. Student X could seek review of such action in a state trial court of general jurisdiction. If it were alleged that the student had been deprived of a constitutional right to due process, the case could be brought to a federal district court instead. (The student could still proceed in state court, however, because state courts have the power to decide issues of federal constitutional law.) Whichever trial court the student chose would hear

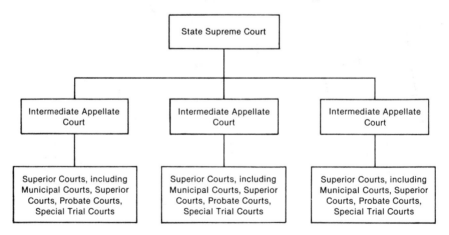

Figure A3. A typical state court system.

evidence from both sides in order to determine what actually happened. Once the facts were established, the judge would apply the law to the facts and arrive at a decision. Even if the judge were a state judge, all laws applicable to the case, both federal and state, would be considered, because article VI of the U.S. Constitution provides that the "Constitution, and the Laws of the United States . . . shall be the supreme Law of the Land; and the Judges in every State shall be bound thereby." If the case were appealed, the appeals court would consider whether or not the principles of law were properly applied by the trial court.

The highest state court will be the final authority on legal questions related to the law of that state unless there is federal law on the same matter. The U.S. Supreme Court is the final authority on matters arising out of the Constitution, treaties, federal laws, or conflicts among state laws. In matters that involve only state laws, the state courts have the authoritative voice.

ADMINISTRATIVE BODIES

It is generally recognized today that the courts are overburdened and their calendars overcrowded. It is all too true that "justice delayed is justice denied," yet in many cities it takes over a year for a criminal case to come to trial and several years for a civil suit to be tried. This situation would be worse if we did not have administrative agencies acting in quasi-judicial capacities. Without a doubt, the largest and most detailed body of law, administrative rules and regulations, is created by agencies that regulate public affairs. Administrative law functions at both federal and state levels, and the lives of educators are heavily influenced by it.

HOW TO FIND REPORTS OF COURT CASES

Every county has a courthouse that contains a law library. Every law school has such a library, and most universities and colleges have legal collections. In each of these places a librarian can help one to find cases of interest. The following constitutes a brief introduction to legal research.

Appellate courts almost always publish their decisions. The decisions of the highest appellate court, the U.S. Supreme Court, can be found in the *United States Reports*. For example, the citation *Brown v. Board of Education of Topeka, Kansas*, 349 U.S. 294 (1955), indicates that the case, decided in 1955, is reported in volume 349 of the *United States Reports* at page 294. Since Supreme Court cases are reported in several publications, the same case may be followed by the notations 75 S. Ct. 753, 99 L. Ed. 1083. This means that the same case also appears in volume 75 of the *Supreme Court Reporter* at page 753 and in volume 99 of the *Lawyers Edition* at page 1083. The most recent cases decided by the Supreme Court appear in a looseleaf volume called *United States Law Week,* cited, for example, as *Irving Independent School District v. Tatro*, 52 U.S.L.W. 5151 (July 5, 1984).

Recent cases decided by the U.S. Courts of Appeals are reported in West's *Federal Reporter, Second Series* (F.2d). For example, *Clark v. Whiting*, 607 F.2d 634 (4th Cir. 1979) would be found in volume 607 of the *Federal Reporter, Second Series* at page 634. The case was decided by the Fourth Circuit Court of Appeals in 1979. When a series becomes too long and thus the volume numbers too large, a second series is begun and cited, for example, "F.2d" rather than "F."

Decisions of the U.S. District Courts are reported in the *Federal Supplement* (F. Supp.), also published by West Publishing Company, and are cited in a manner similar to other federal court cases. For example, *Valencia v. Blue Hen Conference*, 476 F. Supp. 809 (D. Del.

1979), indicates that this case was decided by a district court in Delaware in 1979 and is reported in volume 476 of the *Federal Supplement* at page 809. The *Federal Supplement* does not yet have a second series.

The National Reporter System of the West Publishing Company, in addition to reporting the federal cases noted above, also reports cases from state courts. Most reported state appellate court decisions appear in the following volumes: *Atlantic Reporter* (A.), *North Eastern Reporter* (N.E.), *North Western Reporter* (N.W.), *Pacific Reporter* (P.), *South Eastern Reporter* (S.E.), *South Western Reporter* (S.W.), and *Southern Reporter* (So.). Cases from New York, including some trial court decisions, are available in West's *New York Supplement* (N.Y.S.); cases from California are contained in the *California Reporter* (Cal. Rptr.). Many of these same cases also appear in the respective regional reporters—the *North Eastern Reporter* and the *Pacific Reporter*.

In addition to reading cases, counselors and educators interested in a particular topic might go to one of the standard legal encyclopedias to gain an overview of the topic. The best-known of these encyclopedias are *Corpus Juris Secundum* (C.J.S.) and *American Jurisprudence 2d* (Am. Jur. 2d). School counselors, psychologists, social workers, and other professionals who want to know more about legal research may consult with a law librarian and/or read one of the standard guides on the subject. A good guide is Jacobstein and Merskey, *Fundamentals of Legal Research*.

Selected Provisions
of the U.S. Constitution

ARTICLE I

. . .

Section 8.[1] The Congress shall have Power To Lay and collect Taxes, Duties, Imposts and Excises, to pay the Debts and provide for the common Defence and general Welfare of the United States; . . .

ARTICLE III

Section 1. The judicial Power of the United States, shall be vested in one supreme Court, and in such inferior Courts as the Congress may from time to time ordain and establish. The Judges, both of the supreme and inferior Courts, shall hold their Offices during good Behaviour, and shall, at stated Times, receive for their Services a Compensation, which shall not be diminished during their Continuance in Office. . . .

Section 2.[1] The judicial Power shall extend to all Cases, in Law and Equity, arising under this Constitution, the Laws of the United States and Treaties made, or which shall be made, under their Authority; . . . to Controversies to which the United States shall be a Party;—to Controversies between two or more States;—between a State and Citizens of another State;—between Citizens of different States;—between Citizens of the same State claiming Lands under the Grants of different States, and between a State, or the Citizens thereof, and foreign States, Citizens or Subjects. . . .

ARTICLE VI

[2] This Constitution, and the Laws of the United States which shall be made in Pursuance thereof; and all Treaties made, or which shall be made, under the Authority of the United States, shall be the supreme Law of the Land; and the Judges in every State shall be bound thereby, any Thing in the Constitution or Laws of any State to the Contrary notwithstanding.

. . .

AMENDMENT I [1791]

Congress shall make no law respecting an establishment of religion, or prohibiting the free exercise thereof; or abridging the freedom of speech, or of the press; or the right of the people peaceably to assemble, and to petition the Government for a redress of grievances.

. . .

AMENDMENT IV [1791]

The right of the people to be secure in their persons, houses, papers, and effects, against unreasonable searches and seizures, shall not be violated, and no Warrants shall issue, but upon probable cause, supported by Oath or affirmation, and particularly describing the place to be searched, and the persons or things to be seized.

AMENDMENT V [1791]

No person shall be . . . compelled in any criminal case to be a witness against himself, nor be deprived of life, liberty, or property, without due process of law; nor shall private property be taken for public use, without just compensation.

. . .

AMENDMENT VIII [1791]

Excessive bail shall not be required, nor excessive fines imposed, nor cruel and unusual punishments inflicted.

AMENDMENT IX [1791]

The enumeration in the Constitution, of certain rights, shall not be construed to deny or disparage others retained by the people.

AMENDMENT X [1791]

The powers not delegated to the United States by the Constitution, nor prohibited by it to the States, are reserved to the States respectively, or to the people.

. . .

AMENDMENT XIV [1868]

Section 1. All persons born or naturalized in the United States, and subject to the jurisdiction thereof, are citizens of the United States and of the State wherein they reside. No State shall make or enforce any law which shall abridge the privileges or immunities of citizens of the United States; nor shall any State deprive any person of life, liberty, or property, without due process of law; nor deny to any person within its jurisdiction the equal protection of the laws.

. . .

APPENDIX C

Selected Federal Statutes

EARLY POST–CIVIL WAR STATUTES

Acts of 1866, 1870, 42 U.S.C., sec. 1981 (the right to make contracts regardless of race).

Acts of 1871, 42 U.S.C., sec. 1983 (protects against deprivation of any constitutional right by officials or anyone acting under color of law).

Acts of 1871, 42 U.S.C., sec. 1985 (protects against conspiracy to deprive people of their constitutional rights).

MODERN STATUTES AND EXECUTIVE ORDERS

Equal Pay Act of 1963, 29 U.S.C. 206(d) (sex discrimination in pay).

Civil Rights Act of 1964, 42 U.S.C., sec. 2000. Title VI (general prohibition—sec. 2000(d); Title VII (employment discrimination—sec. 2000(e)).

Education Amendments of 1972 (Title IX), 20 U.S.C., sec. 1681 (discrimination in education programs).

Age Discrimination in Employment Act of 1967, as amended 1978 (92 Stat. 189), 29 U.S.C., sec. 621.

Equal Employment Opportunity Act of 1972, as amending Title VII (*supra*), 42 U.S.C., sec. 2000(e).

Equal Educational Opportunities Act of 1974, 20 U.S.C., sec. 1701 et seq.

Rehabilitation Acts of 1973, 29 U.S.C., sec. 794 (see particularly sec. 504 prohibiting discrimination against the handicapped).

Education of the Handicapped Act, 20 U.S.C., sec. 1400 et seq. (federal funds to provide educational opportunities for handicapped).

Bilingual Education Act, 20 U.S.C., sec. 3221 et seq.

Family Educational Rights and Privacy Act of 1974, 20 U.S.C., sec. 1232(g) (confidentiality of school records and access to them).

42 U.S.C. § 1981—CIVIL RIGHTS ACTS OF 1866, SECTION 1981

Section 1981: All persons within the jurisdiction of the United States shall have the same right . . . to make and enforce contracts, to sue, be parties, give evidence, and to the full and equal benefit of all laws and proceedings for the security of persons and property as is enjoyed by white citizens, and shall be subject to like punishments, pains, penalties, taxes, licenses, and exactions of every kind, and to no other.

42 U.S.C. § 1983—THE CIVIL RIGHTS ACT OF 1871, SECTION 1983

Section 1983: Every person who, under color of any statute, ordinance, regulation, custom or usage, of any State or Territory, subjects or causes to be subjected, any citizen of the United States or other person within the jurisdiction thereof to the deprivation of any rights, privileges or immunities secured by the Constitution and laws, shall be liable to the party injured in an action at law, suit in equity, or other proper proceeding for redress.

42 U.S.C. § 1985—THE CIVIL RIGHTS ACT OF 1871, SECTION 1985

Section 1985(c): If two or more persons in any State or Territory conspire or go in disguise on the highway or on the premises of another, for the purpose of depriving, either directly or indirectly, any person or class of persons of the equal protection of the laws, or of equal privileges and immunities under the laws: or for the purpose of preventing or hindering the constituted authorities of any State or Territory from giving or securing to all persons within such State or Territory the equal protection of the laws . . . : in any case of conspiracy set forth in this section, if one or more persons engaged therein do, or cause to be done, any act in furtherance of the object of such conspiracy, whereby another is injured in his person or property, or deprived of having and exercising any right or privilege of a citizen of the United States, the party so injured or deprived may have an action for the recovery of damages, occasioned by such injury or deprivation, against any one or more of the conspirators.

42 U.S.C § 2000(d)—CIVIL RIGHTS ACT OF 1964, TITLE VI

No person in the United States shall, on the ground of race, color, or national origin, be excluded from participation in, be denied the benefits of, or be subjected to discrimination under any program or activity receiving Federal financial assistance.

42 U.S.C. § 2000(e)—CIVIL RIGHTS ACT OF 1964, TITLE VII

Section 2000(e–1): This title shall not apply to . . . a religious corporation, association, educational institution, or society with respect to the employment of individuals of a particular religion to perform work connected with the carrying on by such corporation, association, educational institution, or society of its activities.

Section 2000(e–2)(a): It shall be an unlawful employment practice for an employer— (1) . . . to discriminate against any individual with respect to his compensation, terms, conditions, or privileges of employment, because of such individual's race, color, religion, sex, or national origin; or (2) to limit, segregate, or classify his employees or applicants . . . in any way which would deprive or tend to deprive any individual of employment opportunities or otherwise adversely affect his status as an employee, because of such individual's race, color, religion, sex, or national origin.

Section 2000(e–2)(e): Notwithstanding any other provision of this subchapter, (1) it shall not be an unlawful employment practice for an employer to hire and employ employees, for an employment agency to classify or refer for employment any individual, for a labor organization to classify its membership or to classify or refer for employment any individual, or for an employer, labor organization, or joint labor-management committee controlling apprenticeship or other training or retraining programs to admit or employ any individual in any such program, on the basis of his religion, sex, or national origin in those certain instances where religion, sex, or national origin is a bona fide occupational qualification reasonably necessary to the normal operation of that particular business or enterprise. . . .

Section 2000(e–2)(h): Notwithstanding any other provision of this title, it shall not be an unlawful employment practice for an employer to apply different standards of compensation, or different terms, conditions, or privileges of employment pursuant to a bona fide seniority or merit system, . . . provided that such differences are not the result of an intention to discriminate because of race, color, religion, sex, or national origin. . . .

20 U.S.C. § 1681—EDUCATION AMENDMENTS OF 1972, TITLE IX

Sec. 1681(a): No person in the United States shall, on the basis of sex, be excluded from participation in, be denied the benefits of, or be subjected to discrimination under any education program or activity receiving Federal financial assistance, except that:

(1) in regard to admissions to educational institutions, this section shall apply only to institutions of vocational education, professional education, and graduate higher education, and to public institutions of undergraduate higher education. . . .

(3) this section shall not apply to an educational institution which is controlled by a religious organization if the application of this subsection would not be consistent with the religious tenets of such organization. . . .

(5) in regard to admissions this section shall not apply to any public institution of undergraduate higher education which is an institution that traditionally and continually from its establishment has had a policy of admitting only students of one sex.

29 U.S.C. § 206(d)—EQUAL PAY ACT

Sec. 206(d): No employer having employees subject to [the minimum wage provisions of the FLSA] shall discriminate, within any establishment . . . , between employees on the basis of sex by paying wages to employees in such establishment at a rate less than the rate at which he pays wages to employees of the opposite sex in such establishment for equal work on jobs the performance of which requires equal skill, effort, and responsibility, and which are performed under similar working conditions, except where payment is made pursuant to: (i) a seniority system; (ii) a merit system; (iii) a system which measures earnings by quantity or quality of production; or (iv) a differential based on any factor other than sex. . . .

29 U.S.C. § 621—AGE DISCRIMINATION ACT

Section 623:
(a) It shall be unlawful for an employer—
(1) to fail or refuse to hire or to discharge any individual or otherwise discriminate against any individual with respect to his compensation, terms, conditions, or privileges of employment, because of such individual's age. . . .
(c) It shall be unlawful for a labor organization—
(1) to exclude or to expel from its membership, or otherwise to discriminate against any individual because of his age. . . .
(3) to cause or attempt to cause an employer to discriminate against an individual in violation of this section. . . .
(f) It shall not be unlawful for an employer, employment agency, or labor organization—
(1) to take any action otherwise prohibited under subsections (a), (b), (c), or (e) of this section where age is a bona fide occupational qualification reasonably necessary to the normal operation of the particular business, or where the differential is based on reasonable factors other than age. . . .
(3) to discharge or otherwise discipline an individual for good cause. . . .

20 U.S.C. § 1703—EQUAL EDUCATION OPPORTUNITIES ACT

Section 1703: No State shall deny equal educational opportunity to an individual on account of his or her race, color, sex, or national origin, by—
(a) the deliberate segregation by an educational agency of students on the basis of race, color, or national origin among or within schools. . . .
(c) the assignment by an educational agency of a student to a school, other than the one closest to his or her place of residence within the school district in which he or she resides, if the assignment results in a greater degree of segregation of students on the basis of race, color, sex, or national origin. . . .
(d) discrimination by an educational agency on the basis of race, color, or national origin in the employment, employment conditions, or assignment to schools of its faculty or staff, except to fulfill the purposes of subsection (f) below. . . .
(e) the transfer by an educational agency, whether voluntary or otherwise, of a student from one school to another if the purpose and effect of such transfer is to increase segregation of students on the basis of race, color, or national origin among the schools of such agency; or
(f) the failure by an educational agency to take appropriate action to overcome language barriers that impede equal participation by its students in its instructional programs.

29 U.S.C. § 794—REHABILITATION ACT OF 1973, SECTION 504

Section 504: No otherwise qualified individual with handicaps . . . shall, solely by reason of his handicap, be excluded from the participation in, be denied the benefits of, or be subjected to discrimination under any program or activity receiving Federal financial assistance. . . .

20 U.S.C. § 1232(g)—FAMILY EDUCATIONAL RIGHTS AND PRIVACY ACT OF 1974

(a) Conditions for availability of funds to educational agencies or institutions; inspection and review of education records; specific information to be made available; procedure for access to education records; reasonableness of time for such access; hearings; written explanations by parents; definitions

(1)(A) No funds shall be made available under any applicable program to any educational agency or institution which has a policy of denying, or which effectively prevents, the parents of students who are or have been in attendance at a school of such agency or at such institution, as the case may be, the right to inspect and review the education records of their children. . . . Each educational agency or institution shall establish appropriate procedures for the granting of a request by parents for access to the education records of their children within a reasonable period of time, but in no case more than forty-five days after the request has been made. . . .

(2) No funds shall be made available under any applicable program to any educational agency or institution unless the parents of students who are or have been in attendance at a school of such agency or at such institution are provided an opportunity for a hearing by such agency or institution, in accordance with regulations of the Secretary, to challenge the content of such student's education records in order to insure that the records are not inaccurate, misleading, or otherwise in violation of the privacy or other rights of students, and to provide an opportunity for the correction or deletion of any such inaccurate, misleading or otherwise inappropriate data contained therein and to insert into such records a written explanation of the parents respecting the content of such records.

(3) For the purposes of this section the term "educational agency or institution" means any public or private agency or institution which is the recipient of funds under any applicable program.

(4)(A) For the purposes of this section, the term "education records" means, except as may be provided otherwise in subparagraph (B), those records, files, documents, and other materials which—

(i) contain information directly related to a student; and

(ii) are maintained by an educational agency or institution or by a person acting for such agency or institution.

(B) The term "education records" does not include—

(i) records of instructional, supervisory, and administrative personnel and educational personnel ancillary thereto which are in the sole possession of the maker thereof and which are not accessible or revealed to any other person except a substitute;

(ii) If the personnel of a law enforcement unit do not have access to education records under subsection (b)(1) of this section, the records and documents of such law enforcement unit which (I) are kept apart from records described in subparagraph (A),

(II) are maintained solely for law enforcement purposes, and (III) are not made available to persons other than law enforcement officials of the same jurisdiction. . . .

(iv) records on a student who is eighteen years of age or older, or is attending an institution of postsecondary education, which are made or maintained by a physician, psychiatrist, psychologist, or other recognized professional or paraprofessional acting in his professional or paraprofessional capacity, or assisting in that capacity, and which are made, maintained, or used only in connection with the provision of treatment to the student, and are not available to anyone other than persons providing such treatment, except that such records can be personally reviewed by a physician or other appropriate professional of the student's choice.

(5)(A) For the purposes of this section the term "directory information" relating to a student includes the following: the student's name, address, telephone listing, date and place of birth, major field of study, participation in officially recognized activities and sports, weight and height of members of athletic teams, dates of attendance, degrees and awards received, and the most recent previous educational agency or institution attended by the student.

(B) Any educational agency or institution making public directory information shall give public notice of the categories of information which it has designated as such information with respect to each student attending the institution or agency and shall allow a reasonable period of time after such notice has been given for a parent to inform the institution or agency that any or all of the information designated should not be released without the parent's prior consent.

(6) For the purposes of this section, the term "student" includes any person with respect to whom an educational agency or institution maintains education records or personally identifiable information, but does not include a person who has not been in attendance at such agency or institution.

(b) **Release of education records; parental consent requirements; exceptions; compliance with judicial orders and subpoenas; audit and evaluation of federally supported education programs; record-keeping**

(1) No funds shall be made available under any applicable program to any educational agency or institution which has a policy or practice of permitting the release of education records (or personally identifiable information contained therein other than directory information, as defined in paragraph (5) of subsection (a) of this section) of students without the written consent of their parents to any individual, agency, or organization, other than to the following—

(A) other school officials, including teachers within the educational institution or local educational agency, who have been determined by such agency or institution to have legitimate educational interest;

(B) officials of other schools or school systems in which the student seeks or intends to enroll, upon condition that the student's parents be notified of the transfer, receive a copy of the record if desired, and have an opportunity for a hearing to challenge the content of the record. . . .

(2) No funds shall be made available under any applicable program to any educational agency or institution which has a policy or practice of releasing, or providing access to, any personally identifiable information in education records other than directory information, or as is permitted under paragraph (1) of this subsection unless—

(A) there is written consent from the student's parents specifying records to be released, the reasons for such release, and to whom, and with a copy of the records to be released to the student's parents and the student if desired by the parents, or

(B) such information is furnished in compliance with judicial order, or pursuant to any lawfully issued subpoena, upon condition that parents and the students are notified of all such orders or subpoenas in advance of the compliance therewith by the educational institution or agency. . . .

(4)(A) Each educational agency or institution shall maintain a record, kept with the education records of each student, which will indicate all individuals (other than those specified in paragraph (1)(A) of this subsection), agencies, or organizations which have requested or obtained access to a student's education records maintained by such educational agency or institution, and which will indicate specifically the legitimate interest that each such person, agency, or organization has in obtaining this information. Such record of access shall be available only to parents, to the school official and his assistants who are responsible for the custody of such records, and to persons or organizations authorized in, and under the conditions of, clauses (A) and (C) of paragraph (1) as a means of auditing the operation of the system.

(B) With respect to this subsection, personal information shall only be transferred to a third party on the condition that such party will not permit any other party to have access to such information without the written consent of the parents of the student. . . .

(d) Students' rather than parents' permission or consent

For the purposes of this section, whenever a student has attained eighteen years of age, or is attending an institution of postsecondary education the permission or consent required of and the rights accorded to the parents of the student shall thereafter only be required of and accorded to the student.

(e) Informing parents or students of rights under this section

No funds shall be made available under any applicable program to any educational agency or institution unless such agency or institution informs the parents of students, or the students, if they are eighteen years of age or older, or are attending an institution of postsecondary education, of the rights accorded them by this section. . . .

20 U.S.C. § 1400 et seq.—EDUCATION OF THE HANDICAPPED ACT

Sec. 1400:

(b) The Congress finds that—

(1) there are more than eight million handicapped children in the United States today;

(2) the special educational needs of such children are not being fully met;

(3) more than half of the handicapped children in the United States do not receive appropriate educational services which would enable them to have full equality of opportunity;

(4) one million of the handicapped children in the United States are excluded entirely from the public school system and will not go through the educational process with their peers;

(5) there are many handicapped children throughout the United States participating in regular school programs whose handicaps prevent them from having a successful educational experience because their handicaps are undetected;

(6) because of the lack of adequate services within the public school system, families are often forced to find services outside the public school system, often at great distance from their residence and at their own expense;

(7) developments in the training of teachers and in diagnostic and instructional procedures and methods have advanced to the point that, given appropriate funding, State and local educational agencies can and will provide effective special education and related services to meet the needs of handicapped children;

(8) State and local educational agencies have a responsibility to provide education for all handicapped children, but present financial resources are inadequate to meet the special educational needs of handicapped children; and

(9) it is in the national interest that the Federal Government assist State and local efforts to provide programs to meet the educational needs of handicapped children in order to assure equal protection of the law.

(c) It is the purpose of this Act to assure that all handicapped children have available to them . . . a free appropriate public education which emphasizes special education and related services designed to meet their unique needs, to assure that the rights of handicapped children and their parents or guardians are protected, to assist States and localities to provide for the education of all handicapped children, and to assess and assure the effectiveness of efforts to educate handicapped children.

§ 1401. Definitions

As used in this chapter—

(1) The term "handicapped children" means mentally retarded, hard of hearing, deaf, speech or language impaired, visually handicapped, seriously emotionally disturbed, orthopedically impaired, or other health impaired children, or children with specific learning disabilities, who by reason thereof require special education and related services. . . .

(16) The term "special education" means specifically designed instruction, at no cost to parents or guardians, to meet the unique needs of a handicapped child, including classroom instruction, instruction in physical education, home instruction, and instruction in hospitals and institutions.

(17) The term "related services" means transportation, and such developmental, corrective, and other supportive services (including speech pathology and audiology, psychological services, physical and occupational therapy, recreation, and medical and counseling services, except that such medical services shall be for diagnostic and evaluation purposes only) as may be required to assist a handicapped child to benefit from special education, and includes the early identification and assessment of handicapping conditions in children.

(18) The term "free appropriate public education" means special education and related services which (A) have been provided at public expense, under public supervision and direction, and without charge, (B) meets the standards of the State educational agency, (C) include an appropriate preschool, elementary, or secondary school education in the State involved, and (D) are provided in conformity with the individualized education program required under section 1414(a)(5) of this title.

(19) The term "individualized education program" means a written statement for each handicapped child developed in any meeting by a representative of the local educational agency or an intermediate educational unit who shall be qualified to provide, or supervise the provision of, specially designed instruction to meet the unique needs of handicapped children, the teacher, the parents or guardian of such child, and, whenever appropriate, such child, which statement shall include (A) a statement of the present levels of educational performance of such child, (B) a statement of annual goals, including short-term instructional objectives, (C) a statement of the specific educational services to be provided to such child, and the extent to which such child will be able to participate in regular educational programs, (D) the projected date for initiation and anticipated duration of such services, and (E) appropriate objective criteria and evaluation procedures and schedules for determining, on at least an annual basis, whether instructional objectives are being achieved. . . .

§ 1412. Eligibility requirements

In order to qualify for assistance under this subchapter in any fiscal year, a State shall demonstrate to the Secretary that the following conditions are met:

(1) the State has in effect a policy that assures all handicapped children the right to a free appropriate public education.

(2) The State has developed a plan pursuant to section 1413(b) of this title in effect prior to November 29, 1975, and submitted not later than August 21, 1975, which will be amended so as to comply with the provisions of this paragraph. Each such amended plan shall set forth in detail the policies and procedures which the State will undertake or has undertaken in order to assure that—

(A) there is established (i) a goal of providing full educational opportunity to all handicapped children, (ii) a detailed timetable for accomplishing such a goal, and (iii) a description of the kind and number of facilities, personnel, and services necessary throughout the State to meet such a goal;

(B) a free appropriate public education will be available for all handicapped children between the ages of three and eighteen within the State not later than September 1, 1978, and for all handicapped children between the ages of three and twenty-one within the State not later than September 1, 1980, except that, with respect to handicapped children aged three to five and aged eighteen to twenty-one, inclusive, the requirements of this clause shall not be applied in any State if the application of such requirements would be inconsistent with State law or practice, or the order of any court, respecting public education within such age groups in the State;

(C) all children residing in the State who are handicapped, regardless of the severity of their handicap, and who are in need of special education and related services are identified, located, and evaluated, and that a practical method is developed and implemented to determine which children are currently receiving needed special education and related services and which children are not currently receiving needed special education and related services. . . .

(5) The State has established (A) procedural safeguards as required by section 1415 of this title, (B) procedures to assure that, to the maximum extent appropriate, handicapped children, including children in public or private institutions or other care facilities, are educated with children who are not handicapped, and that special classes, separate schooling, or other removal of handicapped children from the regular environment occurs only when the nature or severity of the handicap is such that education in regular classes with the use of supplementary aids and services cannot be achieved satisfactorily, and (C) procedures to assure that testing and evaluation materials and procedures utilized for the purposes of evaluation and placement of handicapped children will be selected and administered so as not to be racially or culturally discriminatory. Such materials or procedures shall be provided and administered in the child's native language or mode of communication, unless it clearly is not feasible to do so, and no single procedure shall be the sole criterion for determining an appropriate educational program for a child. . . .

§ 1415 Procedural safeguards

(a) Establishment and maintenance

Any state educational agency, any local educational agency, and any intermediate educational unit which receives assistance under this subchapter shall establish and maintain procedures in accordance with subsection (b) through subsection (e) of this section to assure that handicapped children and their parents or guardians are guaranteed procedural safeguards with respect to the provision of free appropriate public education by such agencies and units.

(b) Required procedures; hearing

(1) The procedures required by this section shall include, but shall not be limited to—

(A) an opportunity for the parents or guardian of a handicapped child to examine all relevant records with respect to the identification, evaluation, and educational placement of the child, and the provision of a free appropriate public education to such child, and to obtain an independent educational evaluation of the child;

(B) procedures to protect the rights of the child whenever the parents or guardian of the child are not known, unavailable, or the child is a ward of the State, including the assignment of an individual (who shall not be an employee of the State educational agency, local educational agency, or intermediate education unit involved in the education or care of the child) to act as a surrogate for the parents or guardian;

(C) written prior notice to the parents or guardian of the child whenever such agency or unit—

(i) proposes to initiate or change, or

(ii) refuses to initiate or change,

the identification, evaluation, or educational placement of the child or the provision of a free appropriate public education to the child;

(D) procedures designed to assure that the notice required by clause (C) fully inform the parents or guardian, in the parents' or guardian's native language, unless it clearly is not feasible to do so, of all procedures available pursuant to this section; and

(E) an opportunity to present complaints with respect to any matter relating to the identification, evaluation, or educational placement of the child, or the provision of a free appropriate public education to such child.

(2) Whenever a complaint has been received under paragraph (1) of this subsection, the parents or guardian shall have an opportunity for an impartial due process hearing which shall be conducted by the State educational agency or by the local educational agency or intermediate educational unit, as determined by State law or by the State educational agency. No hearing conducted pursuant to the requirements of this paragraph shall be conducted by an employee of such agency or unit involved in the education or care of the child.

(c) Review of local decision by State educational agency

If the hearing required in paragraph (2) of subsection (b) of this section is conducted by a local educational agency or an intermediate educational unit, any party aggrieved by the findings and decision rendered in such a hearing may appeal to the State educational agency which shall conduct an impartial review of such hearing. The officer conducting such review shall make an independent decision upon completion of such review.

(d) Enumeration of rights accorded parties to hearings

Any party to any hearing conducted pursuant to subsections (b) and (c) of this section shall be accorded (1) the right to be accompanied and advised by counsel and by individuals with special knowledge or training with respect to the problems of handicapped children, (2) the right to present evidence and confront, cross-examine, and compel the attendance of witnesses, (3) the right to a written or electronic verbatim record of such hearing, and (4) the right to written findings of fact and decisions (which findings and decisions shall also be transmitted to the advisory panel established pursuant to section 1413(a)(12) of this title).

(e) Civil action; jurisdiction

(1) A decision made in a hearing conducted pursuant to paragraph (2) of subsection (b) of this section shall be final, except that any party involved in such hearing may appeal such decision under the provisions of subsection (c) and paragraph (2) of this subsection. A decision made under subsection (c) of this section shall be final, except that any party may bring an action under paragraph (2) of this subsection.

(2) Any party aggrieved by the findings and decision made under subsection (b) of this section who does not have the right to an appeal under subsection (c) of this section, and any

party aggrieved by the findings and decision under subsection (c) of this section, shall have the right to bring a civil action with respect to the complaint presented pursuant to this section, which action may be brought in any State court of competent jurisdiction or in a district court of the United States without regard to the amount in controversy. In any action brought under this paragraph the court shall receive the records of the administrative proceedings, shall hear additional evidence at the request of a party, and, basing its decision on the preponderance of the evidence, shall grant such relief as the court determines is appropriate.

(3) During the pendency of any proceedings conducted pursuant to this section, unless the State or local educational agency and the parents or guardian otherwise agree, the child shall remain in the then current educational placement of such child, or if applying for initial admission to a public school, shall, with the consent of the parents or guardian, be placed in the public school program until all such proceedings have been completed.

(4) The district courts of the United States shall have jurisdiction of actions brought under this subsection without regard to the amount in controversy. . . .

20 U.S.C. § 3221 et seq.—BILINGUAL EDUCATION ACT

§ 3222. Policy . . .

(a) Recognizing—

(1) that there are large numbers of children of limited English proficiency;

(2) that many of such children have a cultural heritage which differs from that of English-speaking persons;

(3) that a primary means by which a child learns is through the use of such child's language and cultural heritage;

(4) that, therefore, large numbers of children of limited English proficiency have educational needs which can be met by the use of bilingual educational methods and techniques;

(5) that, in addition, children of limited English proficiency and children whose primary language is English benefit through the fullest utilization of multiple language and cultural resources;

(6) children of limited English proficiency have a high dropout rate and low median years of education; and

(7) research and evaluation capabilities in the field of bilingual education need to be strengthened,

the Congress declares it to be the policy of the United States, in order to establish equal educational opportunity for all children (A) to encourage the establishment and operation, where appropriate, of educational programs using bilingual educational practices, techniques, and methods, and (B) for that purpose, to provide financial assistance to local educational agencies, and to State educational agencies for certain purposes, in order to enable such local educational agencies to develop and carry out such programs in elementary and secondary schools, including activities at the preschool level, which are designed to meet the educational needs of such children, with particular attention to children having the greatest need for such programs; and to demonstrate effective ways of providing, for children of limited English proficiency, instruction designed to enable them, while using their native language, to achieve competence in the English language. . . .

§ 3223. General provisions

(a) Definitions

The following definitions shall apply to the terms used in this subchapter:

(1) The term "limited English proficiency" when used with reference to individuals means—

(A) individuals who were not born in the United States or whose native language is a language other than English,

(B) individuals who come from environments where a language other than English is dominant, as further defined by the Secretary by regulation, and

(C) individuals who are American Indian and Alaskan Native students and who come from environments where a language other than English has had a significant impact on their level of English language proficiency, subject to such regulations as the Secretary determines to be necessary;

and by reason thereof, have sufficient difficulty speaking, reading, writing, or understanding the English language to deny such individuals the opportunity to learn successfully in classrooms where the language of instruction is English.

(2) The term "native language," when used with reference to an individual of limited English proficiency, means the language normally used by such individuals, or in the case of a child, the language normally used by the parents of the child. . . .

(4)(A) The term "program of bilingual education" means a program of instruction, designed for children of limited English proficiency in elementary or secondary schools, in which, with respect to the years of study to which such program is applicable—

(i) there is instruction given in, and study of, English and, to the extent necessary to allow a child to achieve competence in the English language, the native language of the children of limited English proficiency, and such instruction is given with appreciation for the cultural heritage of such children, and of other children in American society, and, with respect to elementary and secondary school instruction, such instruction shall, to the extent necessary, be in all courses or subjects of study which will allow a child to progress effectively through the educational system. . . .

§ 3231. Bilingual education programs

(a) Programs, activities, etc., subject to grants

Funds available for grants under this part shall be used for—

(1) the establishment, operation, and improvement of programs of bilingual education;

(2) auxiliary and supplementary community and educational activities designed to facilitate and expand the implementation of programs described in clause (1), including such activities as (A) adult education programs related to the purposes of this subchapter, particularly for parents of children participating in programs of bilingual education, and carried out, where appropriate, in coordination with programs assisted under the Adult Education Act [20 U.S.C. 1201 et seq.], and (B) preschool programs preparatory and supplementary to bilingual education programs;

(3)(A) the establishment, operation, and improvement of training programs for personnel preparing to participate in, or personnel participating in, the conduct of programs of bilingual education and (B) auxiliary and supplementary training programs, which shall be included in each program of bilingual education, for personnel preparing to participate in, or personnel participating in, the conduct of such programs; and

(4) planning, and providing technical assistance for, and taking other steps leading to the development of, such programs. . . .

§ 3241. Office of Bilingual Education

(a) Establishment; implementation of functions of Secretary

There shall be, in the Department of Education, an Office of Bilingual Education (hereafter in this section referred to as the "Office") through which the Secretary shall carry out his functions relating to bilingual education.

APPENDIX D

Selected Supreme Court Cases

BOARD OF EDUCATION V. ROWLEY
458 U.S. 176 (1982)

Justice REHNQUIST delivered the opinion of the Court.

This case presents a question of statutory interpretation. Petitioners contend that the Court of Appeals and the District Court misconstrued the requirements imposed by Congress upon States which receive federal funds under the Education for All Handicapped Children Act. We agree and reverse the judgement of the Court of Appeals.

I

The Education for All Handicapped Children Act of 1975 (Act), 20 U.S.C. § 1401 *et seq.*, provides federal money to assist state and local agencies in educating handicapped children, and conditions such funding upon a State's compliance with extensive goals and procedures. The Act represents an ambitious federal effort to promote the education of handicapped children, and was passed in response to Congress' perception that a majority of handicapped children in the United States "were either totally excluded from schools or [were] sitting idly in regular classrooms awaiting the time when they were old enough to 'drop out.' " . . . The Act's evolution and major provisions shed light on the question of statutory interpretation which is at the heart of this case.

Congress first addressed the problem of educating the handicapped in 1966 when it amended the Elementary and Secondary Education Act of 1965 to establish a grant program "for the purpose of assisting the States in the initiation, expansion, and improvement of programs and projects . . . for the education of handicapped children." . . . That program was repealed in 1970 by the Education for the Handicapped Act, . . . Part B of which established a grant program similar in purpose to the repealed legislation. Neither the 1966 nor the 1970 legislation contained specific guidelines for state use of the grant money; both were aimed primarily at stimulating the States to develop educational resources and to train personnel for educating the handicapped.

Dissatisfied with the progress being made under these earlier enactments, and spurred by two district court decisions holding that handicapped children should be given access to a public education, Congress in 1974 greatly increased federal funding for education of the handicapped and for the first time required recipient States to adopt "a goal of providing full educational opportunities to all handicapped children." . . .

The 1974 statute was recognized as an interim measure only, adopted "in order to give the Congress an additional year in which to study what if any additional Federal assistance [was] required to enable the States to meet the needs of handicapped children." . . . The ensuing year of study produced the Education for All Handicapped Children Act of 1975.

. . .

II

This case arose in connection with the education of Army Rowley, a deaf student at the Furnace Woods School in the Hendrick Hudson Central School District, Peekskill, New York. Amy has minimal residual hearing and is an excellent lipreader. During the year before she began attending Furnace Woods, a meeting between her parents and school administrators resulted in a decision to place her in a regular kindergarten class in order to determine what supplemental services would be necessary to her education. Several members of the school administration prepared for Amy's arrival by attending a course in sign-language interpretation, and a teletype machine was installed in the principal's office to facilitate communication with her parents who are also deaf. At the end of the trial period it was determined that Amy should remain in the kindergarten class, but that she should be provided with an FM hearing aid which would amplify words spoken into a wireless receiver by the teacher or fellow students during certain classroom activities. Amy successfully completed her kindergarten year.

As required by the Act, an IEP was prepared for Amy during the fall of her first-grade year. The IEP provided that Amy should be educated in a regular classroom at Furnace Woods, should continue to use the FM hearing aid, and should receive instruction from a tutor for the deaf for one hour each day and from a speech therapist for three hours each week. The Rowleys agreed with the IEP but insisted that Amy also be provided a qualified sign-language interpreter in all of her academic classes. Such an interpreter had been placed in Amy's kindergarten class for a two-week experimental period, but the interpreter had reported that Amy did not need his services at that time. The school administrators likewise concluded that Amy did not need such an interpreter in her first-grade classroom. They reached this conclusion after consulting the school district's Committee on the Handicapped, which had received expert evidence from Amy's parents on the importance of a sign-language interpreter, received testimony from Amy's teacher and other persons familiar with her academic and social progress, and visited a class for the deaf.

When their request for an interpreter was denied, the Rowleys demanded and received a hearing before an independent examiner. After receiving evidence from both sides, the examiner agreed with the administrators' determination that an interpreter was not necessary because "Amy was achieving educationally, academically, and socially" without such assistance. . . . The examiner's decision was affirmed on appeal by the New York Commissioner of Education on the basis of substantial evidence in the record. . . . Pursuant to the Act's provision for judicial review, the Rowleys then brought an action in the United States District Court for the Southern District of New York, claiming that the administrators' denial of the sign-language interpreter constituted a denial of the "free appropriate public education" guaranteed by the Act.

The District Court found that Amy "is a remarkably well-adjusted child" who interacts and communicates well with her classmates and has "developed an extraordinary rapport" with her teachers. . . . It also found that "she performs better than the average child in her class and is advancing easily from grade to grade," . . . but "that she understands considerably less of what goes on in class than she would if she were not deaf" and thus "is not learning as much, or performing as well academically, as she would without her handicap," . . . This disparity between Amy's achievement and her potential led the court to decide that she was not receiving a "free appropriate public education," which the court defined as "an opportunity to achieve [her] full potential commensurate with the opportunity provided to other children." . . .

A divided panel of the United States Court of Appeals for the Second Circuit affirmed. . . .

We granted certiorari to review the lower courts' interpretation of the Act. 454 U.S. 961 (1981). Such review requires us to consider two questions: What is meant by the Act's requirement of a "free appropriate public education?" And what is the role of state and federal courts in exercising the review granted by § 1415 of the Act? We consider these questions separately.

III

A

This is the first case in which this Court has been called upon to interpret any provision of the Act. . . .

We are loath to conclude that Congress failed to offer any assistance in defining the meaning of the principal substantive phrase used in the Act. It is beyond dispute that, contrary to the conclusions of the courts below, the Act does expressly define "free appropriate public education":

> "The term 'free appropriate public education' means *special education* and *related services* which (A) have been provided at public expense, under public supervision and direction, and without charge, (B) meet the standards of the State educational agency, (C) include an appropriate preschool, elementary, or secondary school education in the State involved, and (D) are provided in conformity with the individualized education program required under section 1414(a)(5) of this title." § 1401(18) (emphasis added).

"Special education," as referred to in this definition, means "specially designed instruction, at no cost to parents or guardians, to meet the unique needs of a handicapped child, including classroom instruction, instruction in physical education, home instruction, and instruction in hospitals and institutions." § 1401(16). "Related services" are defined as "transportation, and such developmental, corrective, and other supportive services . . . as may be required to assist a handicapped child to benefit from special education." § 1401(17).

Like many statutory definitions, this one tends toward the cryptic rather than the comprehensive, but that is scarcely a reason for abandoning the quest for legislative intent. Whether or not the definition is a "functional" one as respondents contend it is not, it is the principal tool which Congress has given us for parsing the critical phrase of the Act. We think more must be made of it than either respondents or the United States seems willing to admit.

According to the definitions contained in the Act, a "free appropriate public education" consists of educational instruction specially designed to meet the unique needs of the handicapped child, supported by such services as are necessary to permit the child "to benefit" from the instruction. Almost as a checklist for adequacy under the Act, the definition also requires that such instruction and services be provided at public expense and under public supervision, meet the State's educational standards, approximate the grade levels used in the

State's regular education, and comport with the child's IEP. Thus, if personalized instruction is being provided with sufficient supportive services to permit the child to benefit from the instruction, and the other items on the definitional checklist are satisfied, the child is receiving a "free appropriate public education" as defined by the Act.

. . .

Noticeably absent from the language of the statute is any substantive standard prescribing the level of education to be accorded handicapped children. Certainly the language of the statute contains no requirement like the one imposed by the lower courts—that States maximize the potential of handicapped children "commensurate with the opportunity provided to other children." . . . Although we find the statutory definition of "free appropriate public education" to be helpful in our interpretation of the Act, there remains the question of whether the legislative history indicates a congressional intent that such education meet some additional substantive standard. For an answer, we turn to that history."

B
(i)

As suggested in Part I, federal support for education of the handicapped is a fairly recent development. Before passage of the Act, some States had passed laws to improve the educational services afforded handicapped children, but many of these children were excluded completely from any form of public education or were left to fend for themselves in classrooms designed for education of their nonhandicapped peers. The House Report begins by emphasizing this exclusion and misplacement, noting that millions of handicapped children "were either totally excluded from schools or [were] sitting idly in regular classrooms awaiting the time when they were old enough to 'drop out.' " . . . One of the Act's two principal sponsors in the Senate urged its passage in similar terms:

> "While much progress has been made in the last few years, we can take no solace in the progress until all handicapped children are, in fact, receiving an education. The most recent statistics provided by the Bureau of Education for the Handicapped estimate that . . . 1.75 million handicapped children do not receive any educational services, and 2.5 million handicapped children are not receiving an appropriate education." 121 Cong. Rec. 19486 (1975) (remarks of Sen. Williams).

This concern, stressed repeatedly throughout the legislative history, confirms the impression conveyed by the language of the statute: By passing the Act, Congress sought primarily to make public education available to handicapped children. But in seeking to provide such access to public education, Congress did not impose upon the States any greater substantive educational standard than would be necessary to make such access meaningful. Indeed, Congress expressly "recognize[d] that in many instances the process of providing special education and related services to handicapped children is not guaranteed to produce any particular outcome." . . . Thus, the intent of the Act was more to open the door of public education to handicapped children on appropriate terms than to guarantee any particular level of education once inside.

Both the House and the Senate reports attribute the impetus for the Act and its predecessors to two federal court judgments rendered in 1971 and 1972.

. . .

Mills and *PARC* both held that handicapped children must be given access to an adequate, publicly supported education. Neither case purports to require any particular substantive level of education. Rather, like the language of the Act, the cases set forth extensive procedures to be followed in formulating personalized educational programs for handicapped children.

. . . The fact that both *PARC* and *Mills* are discussed at length in the legislative reports suggests that the principles which they established are the principles which, to a significant extent, guided the drafters of the Act. . . .

That the Act imposes no clear obligation upon recipient States beyond the requirement that handicapped children receive some form of specialized education is perhaps best demonstrated by the fact the Congress, in explaining the need for the Act, equated an "appropriate education" to the receipt of some specialized educational services.

. . .

(ii)

Respondents contend that "the goal of the Act is to provide each handicapped child with an equal educational opportunity." . . . We think, however, that the requirements that a State provide specialized educational services to handicapped children generates no additional requirement that the services so provided be sufficient to maximize each child's potential "commensurate with the opportunity provided other children." Respondents and the United States correctly note that Congress sought "to provide assistance to the States in carrying out their responsibilities under . . . the Constitution of the United States to provide equal protection of the laws." . . . But we do not think that such statements imply a congressional intent to achieve strict equality of opportunity or services.

The educational opportunities provided by our public school systems undoubtedly differ from student to student, depending upon a myriad of factors that might affect a particular student's ability to assimilate information presented in the classroom. The requirement that States provide "equal" educational opportunities would thus seem to present an entirely unworkable standard requiring impossible measurements and comparisons. Similarly, furnishing handicapped children with only such services as are available to nonhandicapped children would in all probability fall short of the statutory requirement of "free appropriate public education"; to require, on the other hand, the furnishing of every special service necessary to maximize each handicapped child's potential is, we think, further than Congress intended to go. Thus to speak in terms of "equal" services in one instance gives less than what is required by the Act and in another instance more. The theme of the Act is "free appropriate public education," a phrase which is too complex to be captured by the word "equal" whether one is speaking of opportunities or services.

The legislative conception of the requirements of equal protection was undoubtedly informed by the two district court decisions referred to above. But cases such as *Mills* and *PARC* held simply that handicapped children may not be excluded entirely from public education. In *Mills*, the District Court said:

> "If sufficient funds are not available to finance all of the services and programs that are needed and desirable in the system then the available funds must be expended equitably in such a manner that no child is entirely excluded from a publicly supported education consistent with his needs and ability to benefit therefrom." . . .

The *PARC* Court used similar language, saying "[i]t is the commonwealth's obligation to place each mentally retarded child in a free, public program of education and training appropriate to the child's capacity. . . ." The right of access to free public education enunciated by these cases is significantly different from any notion of absolute equality of opportunity regardless of capacity. To the extent that Congress might have looked further than these cases which are mentioned in the legislative history, at the time of enactment of the Act this Court had held at least twice that the Equal Protection Clause of the Fourteenth Amendment does not require States to expend equal financial resources on the education of each child. *San Antonio School District v. Rodriguez*, 411 U.S. 1 (1975); *McInnis v. Shapiro*, 293 F. Supp. 327 (ND Ill. 1968), *aff'd sub nom, McInnis v. Ogilvie*, 394 U.S. 322 (1969).

In explaining the need for federal legislation, the House Report noted that "no congressional legislation, has required a precise guarantee for handicapped children, i.e. a basic floor of opportunity that would bring into compliance all school districts with the constitutional right of equal protection with respect to handicapped children." . . . Therefore, Congress' desire to provide specialized educational services, even in furtherance of "equality," cannot be read as imposing any particular substantive educational standard upon the States.

The District Court and the Court of Appeals thus erred when they held that the Act requires New York to maximize the potential of each handicapped child commensurate with the opportunity provided nonhandicapped children. Desirable though that goal might be, it is not the standard that Congress imposed upon States which receive funding under the Act. Rather, Congress sought primarily to identify and evaluate handicapped children, and to provide them with access to a free public education.

. . .

(iii)

Implicit in the congressional purpose of providing access to a "free appropriate public education" is the requirement that the education to which *access* is provided be sufficient to confer some educational benefit upon the handicapped child. It would do little good for Congress to spend millions of dollars in providing access to a public education only to have the handicapped child receive no benefit from that education. The statutory definition of "free appropriate public education," in addition to requiring that States provide each child with "specially designed instruction," expressly requires the provision of "such . . . supportive services . . . as may be required to assist a handicapped child to *benefit* from special education. . . . We therefore conclude that the "basic floor of opportunity" provided by the Act consists of access to specialized instruction and related services which are individually designed to provide educational benefit to the handicapped child.

The determination of when handicapped children are receiving sufficient educational benefits to satisfy the requirements of the Act presents a more difficult problem. The Act requires participating States to educate a wide spectrum of handicapped children, from the marginally hearing-impaired to the profoundly retarded and palsied. It is clear that the benefits obtainable by children at one end of the spectrum will differ dramatically from those obtained by children at the other end, with infinite variations in between. One child may have little difficulty competing successfully in an academic setting with nonhandicapped children while another child may encounter great difficulty in acquiring even the most basic of self-maintenance skills. We do not attempt today to establish any one test for determining the adequacy of educational benefits conferred upon all children covered by the Act. Because in this case we are presented with a handicapped child who is receiving substantial specialized instruction and related services, and who is performing above average in the regular classrooms of a public school system, we confine our analysis to that situation.

The Act requires participating States to educate handicapped children with nonhandicapped children whenever possible. When that "mainstreaming" preference of the Act has been met and a child is being educated in the regular classrooms of a public school system, the system itself monitors the educational progress of the child. Regular examinations are administered, grades are awarded, and yearly advancement to higher grade levels is permitted for those children who attain an adequate knowledge of the course material. The grading and advancement system thus constitutes an important factor in determining educational benefit. Children who graduate from our public school systems are considered by our society to have been "educated" at least to the grade level they have completed, and access to an "education" for handicapped children is precisely what Congress sought to provide in the Act.

C

When the language of the Act and its legislative history are considered together, the requirements imposed by Congress become tolerably clear. Insofar as a State is required to provide a handicapped child with a "free appropriate public education," we hold that it satisfies this requirement by providing personalized instruction with sufficient support services to permit the child to benefit educationally from that instruction. Such instruction and services must be provided at public expense, must meet the State's educational standards, must approximate the grade levels used in the State's regular education, and must comport with the child's IEP. In addition, the IEP, and therefore the personalized instruction, should be formulated in accordance with the requirements of the Act and, if the child is being educated in the regular classrooms of the public education system, should be reasonably calculated to enable the child to achieve passing marks and advance from grade to grade.

IV

A

As mentioned in Part I, the Act permits "[a]ny party aggrieved by the findings and decision" of the state administrative hearings "to bring a civil action" in "any State court of competent jurisdiction or in a district court of the United States without regard to the amount in controversy." . . . The complaint, and therefore the civil action, may concern "any matter relating to the identification, evaluation, or educational placement of the child, or the provision of a free appropriate public education to such child." . . . In reviewing the complaint, the Act provides that a court "shall receive the record of the [state] administrative proceeding, shall hear additional evidence at the request of a party, and, basing its decision on the preponderance of the evidence, shall grant such relief as the court determines is appropriate." . . .

In substituting the current language of the statute for language that would have made state administrative findings conclusive if supported by substantial evidence, The Conference Committee explained that courts were to make "independent decision[s] based on a preponderance of the evidence." . . .

But although we find that this grant of authority is broader than claimed by petitioners, we think the fact that it is found in § 1415 of the Act, which is entitled "Procedural Safeguards," is not without significance. When the elaborate and highly specific procedural safeguards embodied in § 1415 are contrasted with the general and somewhat imprecise substantive admonitions contained in the Act, we think that the importance Congress attached to these procedural safeguards cannot be gainsaid. It seems to us no exaggeration to say that Congress placed every bit as much emphasis upon compliance with procedures giving parents and guardians a large measure of participation at every stage of the administrative process, see, e.g. § 1415(a)–(d), as it did upon the measurement of the resulting IEP against a substantive standard. We think that the Congressional emphasis upon full participation of concerned parties throughout the development of the IEP, as well as the requirements that state and local plans be submitted to the Commissioner for approval, demonstrate the legislative conviction that adequate compliance with the procedures prescribed would in most cases assure much if not all of what Congress wished in the way of substantive content in an IEP.

Thus the provision that a reviewing court base its decision on the "preponderance of the evidence" is by no means an invitation to the courts to substitute their own notions of sound educational policy for those of the school authorities which they review. The very importance which Congress has attached to compliance with certain procedures in the preparation of an IEP would be frustrated if a court were permitted simply to set state decisions at nought. . . .

Therefore, a court's inquiry in suits brought under § 1415 (e)(2) is twofold. First, has the State complied with the procedures set forth in the Act? And second, is the individualized educational program developed through the Act's procedures reasonably calculated to enable the child to receive educational benefits? If these requirements are met, the State has complied with the obligations imposed by Congress and the Courts can require no more.

B

In assuring that the requirements of the Act have been met, courts must be careful to avoid imposing their view of preferable educational methods upon the States. The primary responsibility for formulating the education to be accorded a handicapped child, and for choosing the educational method most suitable to the child's needs, was left by the Act to state and local educational agencies in cooperation with the parents or guardian of the child. . . .

We previously have cautioned that courts lack the "specialized knowledge and experience" necessary to resolve "persistent and difficult questions of educational policy." *San Antonio School District* v. *Rodriguez,* 411 U.S. 1, 42 (1973). We think that Congress shared that view when it passed the Act. As already demonstrated, Congress' intention was not that the Act displace the primacy of States in the field of education, but that States receive funds to assist them in extending their educational systems to the handicapped. Therefore, once a court determines that the requirements of the Act have been met, questions of methodology are for resolution by the States.

V

Entrusting a child's education to state and local agencies does not leave the child without protection. Congress sought to protect individual children by providing for parental involvement in the development of State plans and policies, . . . and in formulation of the child's individual educational program. . . . As this very case demonstrates, parents and guardians will not lack ardor in seeking to ensure that handicapped children receive all of the benefits to which they are entitled by the Act.

VI

Applying these principles to the facts of this case, we conclude that the Court of Appeals erred in affirming the decision of the District Court. Neither the District Court nor the Court of Appeals found that petitioners had failed to comply with the procedures of the Act, and the findings of neither court would support a conclusion that Amy's educational program failed to comply with the substantive requirements of the Act. On the contrary, the District Court found that the "evidence firmly establishes that Amy is receiving an 'adequate' education, since she performs better than the average child in her class and is advancing easily from grade to grade." . . . In light of this finding, and of the fact that Amy was receiving personalized instruction and related services calculated by the Furnace Woods school administrators to meet her educational needs, the lower courts should not have concluded that the Act requires the provision of a sign-language interpreter. Accordingly, the decision of the Court of Appeals is reversed and the case is remanded for further proceedings consistent with this opinion.

So ordered.

NEW JERSEY V. T.L.O.
469 U.S. 325 (1985)

Justice WHITE delivered the opinion of the Court.

We granted certiorari in this case to examine the appropriateness of the exclusionary rule as a remedy for searches carried out in violation of the Fourth Amendment by public school authorities. Our consideration of the proper application of the Fourth Amendment to the public schools, however, has led us to conclude that the search that gave rise to the case now before us did not violate the Fourth Amendment. Accordingly, we here address only the questions of the proper standard for assessing the legality of searches conducted by public school officials and the application of that standard to the facts of this case.

I

On March 7, 1980, a teacher at Piscataway High School in Middlesex County, N.J., discovered two girls smoking in a lavatory. One of the two girls was the respondent T. L. O., who at that time was a 14-year-old high school freshman. Because smoking in the lavatory was a violation of a school rule, the teacher took the two girls to the Principal's office, where they met with Assistant Vice Principal Theodore Choplick. In response to questioning by Mr. Choplick, T. L. O.'s companion admitted that she had violated the rule. T. L. O., however, denied that she had been smoking in the lavatory and claimed that she did not smoke at all.

Mr. Choplick asked T. L. O. to come into his private office and demanded to see her purse. Opening the purse, he found a pack of cigarettes, which he removed from the purse and held before T. L. O. as he accused her of having lied to him. As he reached into the purse for the cigarettes, Mr. Choplick also noticed a package of cigarette rolling papers. In his experience, possession of rolling papers by high school students was closely associated with the use of marihuana. Suspecting that a closer examination of the purse might yield further evidence of drug use, Mr. Choplick proceeded to search the purse thoroughly. The searched revealed a small amount of marihuana, a pipe, a number of empty plastic bags, a substantial quantity of money in one-dollar bills, an index card that appeared to be a list of students who owed T. L. O. money, and two letters than implicated T. L. O. in marihuana dealing.

Mr. Choplick notified T. L. O.'s mother and the police, and turned the evidence of drug dealing over to the police. At the request of the police, T. L. O.'s mother took her daughter to police headquarters, where T. L. O. confessed that she had been selling marihuana at the high school. On the basis of the confession and the evidence seized by Mr. Choplick, the State brought delinquency charges against T. L. O. in the Juvenile and Domestic Relations Court of Middlesex County. Contending that Mr. Choplick's search of her purse violated the Fourth Amendment, T. L. O. moved to suppress the evidence found in her purse as well as her confession, which, she argued, was tainted by the allegedly unlawful search. . . .

II

In determining whether the search at issue in this case violated the Fourth Amendment, we are faced initially with the question whether the Amendment's prohibition on unreasonable searches and seizures applies to searches conducted by public school officials. We hold that it does.

It is now beyond dispute that "the Federal Constitution, by virtue of the Fourteenth Amendment, prohibits unreasonable searches and seizures by state officers." . . . Equally indisputable is the proposition that the Fourteenth Amendment protects the rights of students against encroachment by public school officials:

"The Fourteenth Amendment, as now applied to the States, protects the citizen against the State itself and all of its creatures—Boards of Education not excepted. These have, of course, delicate, and highly discretionary functions, but none that they may not perform within the limits of the Bill of Rights. That they are educating the young for citizenship is reason for scrupulous protection of Constitutional freedoms of the individual, if we are not to strangle the free mind at its source and teach youth to discount important principles of our government as mere platitudes." West Virginia State Bd. of Ed. v Barnette, 319 US 624. . . .

As we observed in Camara v Municipal Court, . . . "[t]he basic purpose of this Amendment, as recognized in countless decisions of this Court, is to safeguard the privacy and security of individuals against arbitrary invasions by government officials." . . . Because the individual's interest in privacy and personal security "suffers whether the government's motivation is to investigate violations of criminal laws or breaches of other statutory or regulatory standards," . . . it would be "anomalous to say that the individual and his private property are fully protected by the Fourth Amendment only when the individual is suspected of criminal behavior." . . .

Notwithstanding the general applicability of the Fourth Amendment to the activities of civil authorities, a few courts have concluded that school officials are exempt from the dictates of the Fourth Amendment by virtue of the special nature of their authority over schoolchildren. . . . Teachers and school administrators, it is said, act in loco parentis in their dealings with students: their authority is that of the parent, not the State, and is therefore not subject to the limits of the Fourth Amendment. . . .

Such reasoning is in tension with contemporary reality and the teachings of this Court. We have held school officials subject to the commands of the First Amendment, see Tinker v Des Moines Independent Community School District, 393 US 503, 21 L Ed 2d 731, 89 S Ct 733, 49 Ohio Ops 2d 222 (1969), and the Due Process Clause of the Fourteenth Amendment, see Goss v Lopez, 419 US 565, 42 L Ed 2d 725, 95 S Ct 729 (1975). If school authorities are state actors for purposes of the constitutional guarantees of freedom of expression and due process, it is difficult to understand why they should be deemed to be exercising parental rather than public authority when conducting searches of their students. More generally, the Court has recognized that "the concept of parental delegation" as a source of school authority is not entirely "consonant with compulsory education law." Ingraham v Wright, 430 US 651, 662, 51 L Ed 2d 711, 97 S Ct 1401 (1977). Today's public school officials do not merely exercise authority voluntarily conferred on them by individual parents; rather, they act in furtherance of publicly mandated educational and disciplinary policies. . . . In carrying out searches and other disciplinary functions pursuant to such policies, school officials act as representatives of the State, not merely as surrogates for the parents, and they cannot claim the parents' immunity from the strictures of the Fourth Amendment.

III

To hold that the Fourth Amendment applies to searches conducted by school authorities is only to begin the inquiry into the standards governing such searches. Although the underlying command of the Fourth Amendment is always that searches and seizures be reasonable, what is reasonable depends on the context within which a search takes place. The determination of the standard of reasonableness governing any specific class of searches requires "balancing the need to search against the invasion which the search entails." . . . On one side of the balance are arrayed the individual's legitimate expectations of privacy and personal security; on the other, the government's need for effective methods to deal with breaches of public order.

We have recognized that even a limited search of the person is a substantial invasion of privacy. . . . We have also recognized that searches of closed items of personal luggage are intrusions on protected privacy interests, for "the Fourth Amendment provides protection to the owner of every container that conceals its contents from plain view." . . . A search of a child's person or of a closed purse or other bag carried on her person, no less than a similar search carried out on an adult, is undoubtedly a severe violation of subjective expectations of privacy.

Of course, the Fourth Amendment does not protect subjective expectations of privacy that are unreasonable or otherwise "illegitimate." . . . To receive the protection of the Fourth Amendment, an expectation of privacy must be one that society is "prepared to recognize as legitimate." . . .

Although this Court may take notice of the difficulty of maintaining discipline in the public schools today, the situation is not so dire that students in the schools may claim no legitimate expectations of privacy. We have recently recognized that the need to maintain order in a prison is such that prisoners retain no legitimate expectations of privacy in their cells, but it goes almost without saying that "[t]he prisoner and the schoolchild stand in wholly different circumstances separated by the harsh facts of criminal conviction and incarceration." Ingraham v Wright, 430 US, at 669, 51 L Ed 2d 711, 97 S Ct 1401. We are not yet ready to hold that the schools and the prisons need be equated for purposes of the Fourth Amendment.

Nor does the State's suggestion that children have no legitimate need to bring personal property into the schools seem well anchored in reality. Students at a minimum must bring to school not only the supplies needed for their studies, but also keys, money, and the necessaries of personal hygiene and grooming. In addition, students may carry on their persons or in purses or wallets such nondisruptive yet highly personal items as photographs, letters, and diaries. Finally, students may have perfectly legitimate reasons to carry with them articles of property needed in connection with extracurricular or recreational activities. In short, schoolchildren may find it necessary to carry with them a variety of legitimate, noncontraband items, and there is no reason to conclude that they have necessarily waived all rights to privacy in such items merely by bringing them onto school grounds.

Against the child's interest in privacy must be set the substantial interest of teachers and administrators in maintaining discipline in the classroom and on school grounds. Maintaining order in the classroom has never been easy, but in recent years, school disorder has often taken particularly ugly forms: drug use and violent crime in the schools have become major social problems. . . . Even in schools that have been spared the most severe disciplinary problems, the preservation of order and a proper educational environment requires close supervision of schoolchildren, as well as the enforcement of rules against conduct that would be perfectly permissible if undertaken by an adult. "Events calling for discipline are frequent occurrences and sometimes require immediate, effective action." . . . Accordingly, we have recognized that maintaining security and order in the schools requires a certain degree of flexibility in school disciplinary procedures, and we have respected the value of preserving the informality of the student-teacher relationship. . . .

How, then, should we strike the balance between the schoolchild's legitimate expectations of privacy and the school's equally legitimate need to maintain an environment in which learning can take place? It is evident that the school setting requires some easing of the restrictions to which searches by public authorities are ordinarily subject. The warrant requirement, in particular, is unsuited to the school environment: requiring a teacher to obtain a warrant before searching a child suspected of an infraction of school rule (or of the criminal law) would unduly interfere with the maintenance of the swift and informal disciplinary procedures needed in the schools. Just as we have in other cases dispensed with the warrant requirement when "the burden of obtaining a warrant is likely to frustrate the governmental purpose behind the search," . . . we hold today that school officials need not obtain a warrant before searching a student who is under their authority.

The school setting also requires some modification of the level of suspicion of illicit activity needed to justify a search. Ordinarily, a search—even one that may permissibly be carried out without a warrant—must be based upon "probable cause" to believe that a violation of the law has occurred. . . . However, "probable cause" is not an irreducible requirement of a valid search. The fundamental command of the Fourth Amendment is that searches and seizures be reasonable, and although "both the concept of probable cause and the requirement of a warrant bear on the reasonableness of a search, . . . in certain limited circumstances neither is required." . . .

We join the majority of courts that have examined this issue in concluding that the accommodation of the privacy interests of schoolchildren with the substantial need of teachers and administrators for freedom to maintain order in the schools does not require strict adherence to the requirement that searches be based on probable cause to believe that the subject of the search has violated or is violating the law. Rather, the legality of a search of a student should depend simply on the reasonableness, under all the circumstances, of the search. Determining the reasonableness of any search involves a twofold inquiry: first, one must consider "whether the . . . action was justified at its inception," . . . second, one must determine whether the search as actually conducted "was reasonably related in scope to the circumstances which justified the interference in the first place," . . . Under ordinary circumstances, a search of a student by a teacher or other school official will be "justified at its inception" when there are reasonable grounds for suspecting that the search will turn up evidence that the student has violated or is violating either the law or the rules of the school. Such a search will be permissible in its scope when the measures adopted are reasonably related to the objectives of the search and not excessively intrusive in light of the age and sex of the student and the nature of the infraction.

This standard will, we trust, neither unduly burden the efforts of school authorities to maintain order in their schools nor authorize unrestrained intrusions upon the privacy of schoolchildren. By focusing attention on the question of reasonableness, the standard will spare teachers and school administrators the necessity of schooling themselves in the niceties of probable cause and permit them to regulate their conduct according to the dictates of reason and common sense. At the same time, the reasonableness standard should ensure that the interests of students will be invaded no more than is necessary to achieve the legitimate end of preserving order in the schools.

IV

There remains the question of the legality of the search in this case. . . . Our review of the facts surrounding the search leads us to conclude that the search was in no sense unreasonable for Fourth Amendment purposes.

The incident that gave rise to this case actually involved two separate searches, with the first—the search for cigarettes—providing the suspicion that gave rise to the second—the search for marihuana. Although it is the fruits of the second search that are at issue here, the validity of the search for marihuana must depend on the reasonableness of the initial search for cigarettes, as there would have been no reason to suspect that T. L. O. possessed marihuana had the first search not taken place. Accordingly, it is to the search for cigarettes that we first turn our attention.

. . .

T.L.O. had been accused of smoking, and had denied the accusation in the strongest possible terms when she stated that she did not smoke at all. Surely, it cannot be said that under these circumstances, T. L. O.'s possession of cigarettes would be irrelevant to the charges against her or to her response to those charges. T. L. O.'s possession of cigarettes, once it was discovered, would both corroborate the report that she had been smoking and undermine the credibility of her defense to the charge of smoking. To be sure, the discovery of the cigarettes would not prove that T. L. O. had been smoking in the lavatory; nor would it, strictly speaking, necessarily be inconsistent with her claim that she did not smoke at all. But it is universally recognized that evidence, to be relevant to an inquiry, need not conclusively prove the ultimate fact in issue, but only have "any tendency to make the existence of any fact that is of consequence to the determination of the action more probable or less probable than it would be without the evidence." . . . The relevance of T. L. O.'s possession of cigarettes to the question whether she had been smoking and to the credibility of her denial that she smoked supplied the necessary "nexus" between the item searched for and the infraction under investigation. . . . Thus, if Mr. Choplick in fact had a reasonable suspicion that T. L. O. had cigarettes in her purse, the search was justified despite the fact that the cigarettes, if found, would constitute "mere evidence" of a violation.

Of course, the New Jersey Supreme Court also held that Mr. Choplick had no reasonable suspicion that the purse would contain cigarettes. This conclusion is puzzling. A teacher had reported that T. L. O. was smoking in the lavatory. Certainly this report gave Mr. Choplick reason to suspect that T. L. O. was carrying cigarettes with her; and if she did have cigarettes, her purse was the obvious place in which to find them. Mr. Choplick's suspicion that there were cigarettes in the purse was not an "inchoate and unparticularized suspicion or 'hunch,' " . . . rather, it was the sort of "common-sense conclusio[n] about human behavior," upon which "practical people"—including government officials—are entitled to rely. . . . Of course, even if the teacher's report were true, T. L. O. *might* not have had a pack of cigarettes with her; she might have borrowed a cigarette from someone else or have been sharing a cigarette with another student. But the requirement of reasonable suspicion is not a requirement of absolute certainty: "sufficient probability, not certainty, is the touchstone of reasonableness under the Fourth Amendment. . . ." . . . Because the hypothesis that T. L. O. was carrying cigarettes in her purse was itself not unreasonable, it is irrelevant that other hypotheses were also consistent with the teacher's accusation. Accordingly, it cannot be said that Mr. Choplick acted unreasonably when he examined T. L. O.'s purse to see if it contained cigarettes.

Our conclusion that Mr. Choplick's decision to open T. L. O.'s purse was reasonable brings us to the question of the further search for marihuana once the pack of cigarettes was located. The suspicion upon which the search for marihuana was founded was provided when Mr. Choplick observed a package of rolling papers in the purse as he removed the pack of cigarettes. Although T. L. O. does not dispute the reasonableness of Mr. Choplick's belief that the rolling papers indicated the presence of marihuana, she does contend that the scope of the search Mr. Choplick conducted exceeded permissible bounds when he seized and read certain letters that implicated T. L. O. in drug dealing. This argument, too, is unpersuasive. The discovery of the rolling papers concededly gave rise to a reasonable suspicion that T. L. O. was carrying marihuana as well as cigarettes in her purse. This suspicion justified further exploration of T. L. O.'s purse, which turned up more evidence of drug-related activities: a pipe, a number of plastic bags of the type commonly used to store marihuana, a small quantity of marihuana, and a fairly substantial amount of money. Under these circumstances, it was not unreasonable to extend the search to a separate zippered compartment of the purse; and when a search of that compartment revealed an index card containing a list of "people who owe me money" as well as two letters, the inference that T. L. O. was involved in marihuana trafficking was substantial enough to justify Mr. Choplick in examining the letters to determine whether they contained any further evidence. In short, we cannot conclude that the search for marihuana was unreasonable in any respect.

Because the search resulting in the discovery of the evidence of marihuana dealing by T. L. O. was reasonable, the New Jersey Supreme Court's decision to exclude that evidence from T. L. O.'s juvenile delinquency proceedings on Fourth Amendment grounds was erroneous. Accordingly, the judgment of the Supreme Court of New Jersey is reversed.

HONIG V. DOE
484 U.S. 305 (1988)

Justice BRENNAN delivered the opinion of the Court.

As a condition of federal financial assistance, the Education of the Handicapped Act requires States to ensure a "free appropriate public education" for all disabled children within their jurisdictions. In aid of this goal, the Act establishes a comprehensive system of procedural safeguards designed to ensure parental participation in decisions concerning the education of their disabled children and to provide administrative and judicial review of any decisions with which those parents disagree. Among these safeguards is the so-called "stay-put" provision, which directs that a disabled child "shall remain in [his or her] then current educational placement" pending completion of any review proceedings, unless the parents and state or local educational agencies otherwise agree. 20 U.S.C. § 1415(e)(3). Today we must decide whether, in the face of this statutory proscription, state or local school authorities may nevertheless unilaterally exclude disabled children from the classroom for dangerous or disruptive conduct growing out of their disabilities. In addition, we are called upon to decide whether a district court may, in the exercise of its equitable powers, order a State to provide educational services directly to a disabled child when the local agency fails to do so.

I

In the Education of the Handicapped Act (EHA or the Act), 84 Stat. 175, as amended, 20 U.S.C. § 1400 *et seq.,* Congress sought "to assure that all handicapped children have available to them . . . a free appropriate public education which emphasizes special education and related services designed to meet their unique needs, [and] to assure that the rights of handicapped children and their parents or guardians are protected." . . . When the law was passed in 1975, Congress had before it ample evidence that such legislative assurances were sorely needed: 21 years after this Court declared education to be "perhaps the most important function of state and local governments," *Brown* v. *Board of Education,* 347 U.S. 483, 493 (1954), Congressional studies revealed that better than half of the Nation's eight million disabled children were not receiving appropriate educational services. . . . Indeed, one out of every eight of these children was excluded from the public school system altogether . . . ; many others were simply "warehoused" in special classes or were neglectfully shepherded through the system until they were old enough to drop out. . . . Among the most poorly served of disabled students were emotionally disturbed children: Congressional statistics revealed that for the school year immediately preceding passage of the Act, the educational needs of 82 percent of all children with emotional disabilities went unmet. . . .

Although these educational failings resulted in part from funding constraints, Congress recognized that the problem reflected more than a lack of financial resources at the state and local levels. Two federal-court decisions, which the Senate Report characterized as "landmark," . . . demonstrated that many disabled children were excluded pursuant to state statutes or local rules and policies, typically without any consultation with, or even notice to, their parents. . . . Indeed, by the time of the EHA's enactment, parents had brought legal challenges to similar exclusionary practices in 27 other states. . . .

In responding to these problems, Congress did not content itself with passage of a simple funding statute. Rather, the EHA confers upon disabled students an enforceable substantive right to public education in participating States, . . . and conditions federal financial assistance upon a State's compliance with the substantive and procedural goals of the Act. Accordingly, States seeking to qualify for federal funds must develop policies assuring all disabled children the "right to a free appropriate public education," and must file with the Secretary of Education formal plans mapping out in detail the programs, procedures and timetables under which they will effectuate these policies. . . . Such plans must assure that, "to the maximum extent appropriate," States will "mainstream" disabled children, *i.e.*, that they will educate them with children who are not disabled, and that they will segregate or otherwise remove such children from the regular classroom setting "only when the nature or severity of the handicap is such that education in regular classes . . . cannot be achieved satisfactorily." . . .

The primary vehicle for implementing these congressional goals is the "individualized educational program" (IEP), which the EHA mandates for each disabled child. Prepared at meetings between a representative of the local school district, the child's teacher, the parents or guardians, and, whenever appropriate, the disabled child, the IEP sets out the child's present educational performance, establishes annual and short-term objectives for improvements in that performance, and describes the specially designed instruction and services that will enable the child to meet those objectives. . . . The IEP must be reviewed and, where necessary, revised at least once a year in order to ensure that local agencies tailor the statutorily required "free appropriate public education" to each child's unique needs. . . .

Envisioning the IEP as the centerpiece of the statute's education delivery system for disabled children, and aware that schools had all too often denied such children appropriate educations without in any way consulting their parents, Congress repeatedly emphasized throughout the Act the importance and indeed the necessity of parental participation in both the development of the IEP and any subsequent assessments of its effectiveness. . . . Accordingly, the Act establishes various procedural safeguards that guarantee parents both an opportunity for meaningful input into all decisions affecting their child's education and the right to seek review of any decisions they think inappropriate. These safeguards include the right to examine all relevant records pertaining to the identification, evaluation and educational placement of their child; prior written notice whenever the responsible educational agency proposes (or refuses) to change the child's placement or program; an opportunity to present complaints concerning any aspect of the local agency's provision of a free appropriate public education; and an opportunity for "an impartial due process hearing" with respect to any such complaints. . . .

At the conclusion of any such hearing, both the parents and the local educational agency may seek further administrative review and, where that proves unsatisfactory, may file a civil action in any state or federal court. . . . In addition to reviewing the administrative record, courts are empowered to take additional evidence at the request of either party and to "grant such relief as [they] determine[] is appropriate." . . . The "stay-put" provision at issue in this case governs the placement of a child while these often lengthy review procedures run their course. It directs that:

> "During the pendency of any proceedings conducted pursuant to [§1415], unless the State or
> local educational agency and the parents or guardian otherwise agree, the child shall remain
> in the then current educational placement of such child. . . ." §1415(e)(3).

The present dispute grows out of the efforts of certain officials of the San Francisco Unified School District (SFUSD) to expel two emotionally disturbed children from school indefinitely for violent and disruptive conduct related to their disabilities. In November 1980, respondent John Doe assaulted another student at the Louise Lombard School, a developmental center for disabled children. Doe's April 1980 IEP identified him as a socially and physically awkward 17 year old who experienced considerable difficulty controlling his impulses and anger. Among the goals set out in his IEP was "[i]mprovement in [his] ability to relate to [his] peers [and to] cope with frustrating situations without resorting to aggressive acts." . . . Frustrating situations, however, were an unfortunately prominent feature of Doe's school career: physical abnormalities, speech difficulties, and poor grooming habits had made him the target of teasing and ridicule as early as the first grade . . . ; his 1980 IEP reflected his continuing difficulties with peers, noting that his social skills had deteriorated and that he could tolerate only minor frustration before exploding. . . .

On November 6, 1980, Doe responded to the taunts of a fellow student in precisely the explosive manner anticipated by his IEP: he choked the student with sufficient force to leave abrasions on the child's neck; and kicked out a school window while being escorted to the principal's office afterwards. . . . Doe admitted his misconduct and the school subsequently suspended him for five days. Thereafter, his principal referred the matter to the SFUSD Student Placement Committee (SPC or Committee) with the recommendation that Doe be expelled. On the day the suspension was to end, the SPC notified Doe's mother that it was proposing to exclude her child permanently from SFUSD and was therefore extending his suspension until such time as the expulsion proceedings were completed. The Committee further advised her that she was entitled to attend the November 25 hearing at which it planned to discuss the proposed expulsion.

After unsuccessfully protesting these actions by letter, Doe brought this suit against a host of local school officials and the state superintendent of public education. Alleging that the suspension and proposed expulsion violated the EHA, he sought a temporary restraining order cancelling the SPC hearing and requiring school officials to convene an IEP meeting. The District Judge granted the requested injunctive relief and further ordered defendants to provide home tutoring for Doe on an interim basis; shortly thereafter, she issued a preliminary injunction directing defendants to return Doe to his then current educational placement at Louise Lombard School pending completion of the IEP review process. Doe re-entered school on December 15, 5½ weeks, and 24 school days, after his initial suspension.

Respondent Jack Smith was identified as an emotionally disturbed child by the time he entered the second grade in 1976. School records prepared that year indicated that he was unable "to control verbal or physical outburst[s]" and exhibited a "[s]evere disturbance in relationships with peers and adults." . . . Further evaluations subsequently revealed that he had been physically and emotionally abused as an infant and young child and that, despite above average intelligence, he experienced academic and social difficulties as a result of extreme hyperactivity and low self-esteem. . . . Of particular concern was Smith's propensity for verbal hostility; one evaluator noted that the child reacted to stress by "attempt[ing] to cover his feelings of low self worth through aggressive behavior[,] . . . primarily verbal provocations." . . .

Based on these evaluations, SFUSD placed Smith in a learning center for emotionally disturbed children. His grandparents, however, believed that his needs would be better served in the public school setting and, in September 1979, the school district acceded to their requests and enrolled him at A. P. Giannini Middle School. His February 1980 IEP recommended placement in a Learning Disability Group, stressing the need for close supervision and a highly structured environment. . . . Like earlier evaluations, the February 1980 IEP noted that Smith was easily distracted, impulsive, and anxious; it therefore proposed a half-day schedule and suggested that the placement be undertaken on a trial basis. . . .

At the beginning of the next school year, Smith was assigned to a full-day program; almost immediately thereafter he began misbehaving. School officials met twice with his grandparents in October 1980 to discuss returning him to a half-day program; although the grandparents agreed to the reduction, they apparently were never apprised of their right to challenge the decision through EHA procedures. The school officials also warned them that if the child continued his disruptive behavior—which included stealing, extorting money from fellow students, and making sexual comments to female classmates—they would seek to expel him. On November 14, they made good on this threat, suspending Smith for five days after he made further lewd comments. His principal referred the matter to the SPC, which recommended exclusion from SFUSD. As it did in John Doe's case, the Committee scheduled a hearing and extended the suspension indefinitely pending a final disposition in the matter. On November 28, Smith's counsel protested these actions on grounds essentially identical to those raised by Doe, and the SPC agreed to cancel the hearing and to return Smith to a half-day program at A. P. Giannini or to provide home tutoring. Smith's grandparents chose the latter option and the school began home instruction on December 10; on January 6, 1981, an IEP team convened to discuss alternative placements.

After learning of Doe's action, Smith sought and obtained leave to intervene in the suit. The District Court subsequently entered summary judgment in favor of respondents on their EHA claims and issued a permanent injunction. In a series of decisions, the District Judge found that the proposed expulsions and indefinite suspensions of respondents for conduct attributable to their disabilities deprived them of their congressionally mandated right to a free appropriate public education, as well as their right to have that education provided in accordance with the procedures set out in the EHA. . . .

On appeal, the Court of Appeals for the Ninth Circuit affirmed the orders with slight modifications. *Doe v. Maher*, 793 F.2d 1470 (1986). . . . Lastly, the court affirmed that portion of the injunction requiring the State to provide services directly to a disabled child when the local educational agency fails to do so.

Petitioner Bill Honig, California Superintendent of Public Instruction, sought review in this Court, claiming that the Court of Appeals' construction of the stay-put provision conflicted with that of several other courts of appeals which had recognized a dangerousness exception. . . . We granted certiorari to resolve these questions . . . and now affirm.

II
. . .

III

The language of §1415(e)(3) is unequivocal. It states plainly that during the pendency of any proceedings initiated under the Act, unless the state or local educational agency and the parents or guardian of a disabled child otherwise agree, "the child *shall* remain in the then current educational placement." §1415(e)(3) (emphasis added). Faced with this clear directive, petitioner asks us to read a "dangerousness" exception into the stay-put provision on the basis of either two essentially inconsistent assumptions: first, that Congress thought the residual authority of school officials to exclude dangerous students from the classroom too obvious for comment; or second, that Congress inadvertently failed to provide such authority and this Court must therefore remedy the oversight. Because we cannot accept either premise, we decline petitioner's invitation to re-write the statute.

Petitioner's arguments proceed, he suggests, from a simple, common-sense proposition: Congress could not have intended the stay-put provision to be read literally, for such a construction leads to the clearly unintended, and untenable, result that school districts must return violent or dangerous students to school while the often lengthy EHA proceedings run their course. We think it clear, however, that Congress very much meant to strip schools of the *unilateral* authority they had traditionally employed to exclude disabled students, particularly emotionally disturbed students, from school. In so doing, Congress did not leave school administrators powerless to deal with dangerous students; it did, however, deny school officials their former right to "self-help," and directed that in the future the removal of disabled students could be accomplished only with the permission of the parents or, as a last resort, the courts.

As noted above, Congress passed the EHA after finding that school systems across the country had excluded one out of every eight disabled children from classes. In drafting the law, Congress was largely guided by the recent decisions in *Mills* v. *Board of Education of District of Columbia*, 348 F. Supp. 866 (1972), and *PARC*, 343 F. Supp. 279 (1972), both of which involved the exclusion of hard-to-handle disabled students. *Mills* in particular demonstrated the extent to which schools used disciplinary measures to bar children from the classroom. There, school officials had labeled four of the seven minor plaintiffs "behavioral problems," and had excluded them from classes without providing any alternative education to them or any notice to their parents. . . . After finding that this practice was not limited to the named plaintiffs but affected in one way or another an estimated class of 12,000 to 18,000 disabled students, . . . the District Court enjoined future exclusions, suspensions, or expulsions "on grounds of discipline." . . .

Congress attacked such exclusionary practices in a variety of ways. It required participating States to educate *all* disabled children, regardless of the severity of their disabilities, . . . and included within the definition of "handicapped" those children with serious emotional disturbances. . . . It further provided for meaningful parental participation in all aspects of a child's educational placement, and barred schools, through the stay-put provision, from changing that placement over the parent's objection until all review proceedings were completed. Recognizing that those proceedings might prove long and tedious, the Act's drafters did not intend §1415(e)(3) to operate inflexibly, . . . and they therefore allowed for interim placements where parents and school officials are able to agree on one. Conspicuously absent from §1415(e)(3), however, is any emergency exception for dangerous students. This absence is all the more telling in light of the injunctive decree issued in *PARC*, which permitted school officials unilaterally to remove students in extraordinary circumstances. . . . Given the lack of any similar exception in *Mills*, and the close attention Congress devoted to these "landmark" decisions, . . . we can only conclude that the omission was intentional; we are therefore not at liberty to engraft onto the statute an exception Congress chose not to create.

Our conclusion that §1415(e)(3) means what it says does not leave educators hamstrung. The Department of Education has observed that, "[w]hile the [child's] placement may not be changed [during any complaint proceeding], this does not preclude the agency from using its normal procedures for dealing with children who are endangering themselves or others." . . . Such procedures may include the use of study carrels, timeouts, detention, or the restriction of privileges. More drastically, where a student poses an immediate threat to the safety of others, officials may temporarily suspend him or her for up to 10 school days. This authority, which respondent in no way disputes, not only ensures that school administrators can protect the safety of others by promptly removing the most dangerous of students, it also provides a "cooling down" period during which officials can initiate IEP review and seek to persuade the child's parents to agree to an interim placement. And in those cases in which the parents of a truly dangerous child adamantly refuse to permit any change in placement, the 10-day respite gives school officials an opportunity to invoke the aid of the courts under §1415(e)(2), which empowers courts to grant any appropriate relief.

Petitioner contends, however, that the availability of judicial relief is more illusory than real. . . . It is true that judicial review is normally not available under §1415(e)(2) until all administrative proceedings are completed, but as we have previously noted, parents may by-pass the administrative process where exhaustion would be futile or inadequate. . . . ("[E]xhaustion . . . should not be required . . . in cases where such exhaustion would be futile either as a legal or practical matter"). While many of the EHA's procedural safeguards protect the rights of parents and children, schools can and do seek redress through the administrative review process, and we have no reason to believe that Congress meant to require schools alone to exhaust in all cases, no matter how exigent the circumstances. The burden in such cases, of course, rests with the school to demonstrate the futility or inadequacy of administrative review, but nothing in §1415(e)(2) suggests that schools are completely barred from attempting to make such a showing. Nor do we think that §1415(e)(3) operates to limit the equitable powers of district courts such that they cannot in appropriate cases, temporarily enjoin a dangerous disabled child from attending school. As the EHA's legislative history makes clear, one of the evils Congress sought to remedy was the unilateral exclusion of disabled children by *schools,* not courts, and one of the purposes of §1415(e)(3), therefore, was "to prevent *school* officials from removing a child from the regular public school classroom over the parents' objection pending completion of the review proceedings." . . . The stay-put provision in no way purports to limit or pre-empt the authority conferred on courts by §1415(e)(2) . . . ; indeed, it says nothing whatever about judicial power.

In short, then, we believe that school officials are entitled to seek injunctive relief under §1415(e)(2) in appropriate cases. In any such action, §1415(e)(3) effectively creates a presumption in favor of the child's current educational placement which school officials can overcome only by showing that maintaining the child in his or her current placement is substantially likely to result in injury either to himself or herself, or to others. In the present case, we are satisfied that the District Court, in enjoining the state and local defendants from indefinitely suspending respondent or otherwise unilaterally altering his then current placement, properly balanced respondent's interest in receiving a free appropriate public education in accordance with the procedures and requirements of the EHA against the interests of the state and local school officials in maintaining a safe learning environment for all their students.

IV

We believe the courts below properly construed and applied §1415(e)(3), except insofar as the Court of Appeals held that a suspension in excess of 10 school days does not constitute a "change in placement." We therefore affirm the Court of Appeals' judgment on this issue as modified herein. Because we are equally divided on the question whether a court may order a State to provide services directly to a disabled child where the local agency has failed to do so, we affirm the Court of Appeals' judgment on this issue as well.

Affirmed.

DESHANEY V. WINNEBAGO COUNTY DEPARTMENT OF SOCIAL SERVICES
109 S.CT. 998 (1989)

Chief Justice REHNQUIST delivered the opinion of the Court.

Petitioner is a boy who was beaten and permanently injured by his father, with whom he lived. The respondents are social workers and other local officials who received complaints that petitioner was being abused by his father and had reason to believe that this was the case, but nonetheless did not act to remove petitioner from his father's custody. Petitioner sued respondents claiming that their failure to act deprived him of his liberty in violation of the Due Process Clause of the Fourteenth Amendment to the United States Constitution. We hold that it did not.

I

The facts of this case are undeniably tragic. Petitioner Joshua DeShaney was born in 1979. In 1980, a Wyoming court granted his parents a divorce and awarded custody of Joshua to his father, Randy DeShaney. The father shortly thereafter moved to Neenah, a city located in Winnebago County, Wisconsin, taking the infant Joshua with him. There he entered into a second marriage, which also ended in divorce.

The Winnebago County authorities first learned that Joshua DeShaney might be a victim of child abuse in January 1982, when his father's second wife complained to the police, at the time of their divorce, that he had previously "hit the boy causing marks and [was] a prime case for child abuse." . . . The Winnebago County Department of Social Services (DSS) interviewed the father, but he denied the accusations, and DSS did not pursue them further. In January 1983, Joshua was admitted to a local hospital with multiple bruises and abrasions. The examining physician suspected child abuse and notified DDS, which immediately obtained an order from a Wisconsin juvenile court placing Joshua in the temporary custody of the hospital. Three days later, the county convened an ad hoc "Child Protection Team"— consisting of a pediatrician, a psychologist, a police detective, the county's lawyer, several DDS caseworkers, and various hospital personnel—to consider Joshua's situation. At this meeting, the Team decided that there was insufficient evidence of child abuse to retain Joshua in the custody of the court. The Team did, however, decide to recommend several measures to protect Joshua, including enrolling him in a preschool program, providing his father with certain counselling services, and encouraging his father's girlfriend to move out of the home. Randy DeShaney entered into a voluntary agreement with DSS in which he promised to cooperate with them in accomplishing these goals.

Based on the recommendation of the Child Protection Team, the juvenile court dismissed the child protection case and returned Joshua to the custody of his father. A month later, emergency room personnel called the DSS caseworker handling Joshua's case to report that he had once again been treated for suspicious injuries. The caseworker concluded that there was no basis for action. For the next six months, the caseworker made monthly visits to the DeShaney home, during which she observed a number of suspicious injuries on Joshua's head; she also noticed that he had not been enrolled in school and that the girlfriend had not moved out. The caseworker dutifully recorded these incidents in her files, along with her continuing suspicions that someone in the DeShaney household was physically abusing Joshua, but she did nothing more. In November 1983, the emergency room notified DSS that Joshua had been treated once again for injuries that they believed to be caused by child abuse. On the caseworker's next two visits to the DeShaney home, she was told that Joshua was too ill to see her. Still DSS took no action.

In March 1984, Randy DeShaney beat 4-year-old Joshua so severely that he fell into a life-threatening coma. Emergency brain surgery revealed a series of hemorrhages caused by traumatic injuries to the head inflicted over a long period of time. Joshua did not die, but he suffered brain damage so severe that he is expected to spend the rest of his life confined to an institution for the profoundly retarded. Randy DeShaney was subsequently tried and convicted of child abuse.

Joshua and his mother brought this action under 42 U.S.C. §1983 in the United States District Court for the Eastern District of Wisconsin against respondents Winnebago County, its Department of Social Services, and various individual employees of the Department. The complaint alleged that respondents had deprived Joshua of his liberty without due process of law, in violation of his rights under the Fourteenth Amendment, by failing to intervene to protect him against a risk of violence at his father's hands of which they knew or should have known. The District Court granted summary judgment for respondents.

The Court of Appeals for the Seventh Circuit affirmed, 812 F.2d 298 (1987), holding that petitioners had not made out an actionable §1983 claim. . .

Because of the inconsistent approaches taken by the lower courts in determining when, if ever, the failure or a state of local governmental entity or its agents to provide an individual with adequate protective services constitutes a violation of the individual's due process rights . . . and the importance of the issue to the administration of state and local governments, we granted certiorari. . . . We now affirm.

II

The Due Process Clause of the Fourteenth Amendment provides that "[n]o State shall . . . deprive any person of life, liberty, or property, without due process of law." Petitioners contend that the State deprived Joshua of his liberty interest in "free[dom] from . . . unjustified intrusions on personal security," see *Ingraham* v. *Wright*, 430 U.S. 651, 673 (1977), by failing to provide him with adequate protection against his father's violence. The claim is one invoking the substantive rather than procedural component of the Due Process Clause; petitioners do not claim that the State denied Joshua protection without according him appropriate procedural safeguards . . . but that it was categorically obligated to protect him in these circumstances. . . .

But nothing in the language of the Due Process Clause itself requires the State to protect the life, liberty, and property of its citizens against invasion by private actors. The Clause is phrased as a limitation on the State's power to act, not as a guarantee of certain minimal levels of safety and security. It forbids the State itself to deprive individuals of life, liberty, or property without "due process of law," but its language cannot fairly be extended to impose an affirmative obligation on the State to ensure that those interests do not come to harm through other means. Nor does history support such an expansive reading of the constitutional text. Like its counterpart in the Fifth Amendment, the Due Process Clause of the Fourteenth Amendment was intended to prevent government "from abusing [its] power, or employing it as an instrument of oppression." . . . Its purpose was to protect the people from the State, not to ensure that the State protected them from each other. The Framers were content to leave the extent of governmental obligation in the latter area to the democratic political processes.

Consistent with these principles, our cases have recognized that the Due Process Clauses generally confer no affirmative right to governmental aid, even where such aid may be necessary to secure life, liberty, or property interests of which the government itself may not deprive the individual. . . .

If the Due Process Clause does not require the State to provide its citizens with particular protective services, it follows that the State cannot be held liable under the Clause for injuries that could have been averted had it chosen to provide them. As a general matter, then, we conclude that a State's failure to protect an individual against private violence simply does not constitute a violation of the Due Process Clause.

Petitioners contend, however, that even if the Due Process Clause imposes no affirmative obligation on the State to provide the general public with adequate protective services, such a duty may arise out of certain "special relationships" created or assumed by the State with respect to particular individuals. . . . Petitioners argue that such a "special relationship" existed here because the State knew that Joshua faced a special danger of abuse at his father's hands, and specifically proclaimed, by word and by deed, its intention to protect him against that danger. . . . Having actually undertaken to protect Joshua from this danger—which petitioners concede the State played no part in creating—the State acquired an affirmative "duty," enforceable through the Due Process Clause, to do so in a reasonably competent fashion. Its failure to discharge that duty, so the argument goes, was an abuse of governmental power that so "shocks the conscience," *Rochin* v. *California*, 342 U.S. 165, 172 (1952), as to constitute a substantive due process violation. . . .

We reject this argument. It is true that in certain limited circumstances the Constitution imposes upon the State affirmative duties of care and protection with respect to particular individuals. In *Estelle* v. *Gamble*, 429 U.S. 97 (1976), we recognized that the Eighth Amendment's prohibition against cruel and unusual punishment, made applicable to the States through the Fourteenth Amendment's Due Process Clause, *Robinson* v. *California*, 370 U.S. 660 (1962), requires the State to provide adequate medical care to incarcerated prisoners. . . . We reasoned that because the prisoner is unable " 'by reason of the deprivation of his liberty [to] care for himself,' " it is only "just" that the State be required to care for him. . . .

In *Youngberg* v. *Romeo*, 457 U.S. 307 (1982), we extended this analysis beyond the Eighth Amendment setting, holding that the substantive component of the Fourteenth Amendment's Due Process Clause requires the State to provide involuntarily committed mental patients with such services as are necessary to ensure their "reasonable safety" from themselves and others.

. . . As we explained, "[i]f it is cruel and unusual punishment to hold convicted criminals in unsafe conditions, it must be unconstitutional [under the Due Process Clause] to confine the involuntarily committed—who may not be punished at all—in unsafe conditions." . . .

But these cases afford petitioners no help. Taken together, they stand only for the proposition that when the State takes a person into its custody and holds him there against his will, the Constitution imposes upon it a corresponding duty to assume some responsibility for his safety and general well-being. . . . when the State by the affirmative exercise of its power so restrains an individual's liberty that it renders him unable to care for himself, and at the same time fails to provide for his basic human needs—*e.g.*, food, clothing, shelter, medical care, and reasonable safety—it transgresses the substantive limits on state action set by the Eighth Amendment and the Due Process Clause. . . . The affirmative duty to protect arises not from the State's knowledge of the individual's predicament or from its expressions of intent to help him, but from the limitation which it has imposed on his freedom to act on his own behalf. . . . In the substantive due process analysis, it is the State's affirmative act of restraining the individual's freedom to act on his own behalf—through incarceration, institutionalization, or other similar restraint of personal liberty—which is the "deprivation of liberty" triggering the protections of the Due Process Clause, not its failure to act to protect his liberty interests against harms inflicted by other means.

The *Estelle-Youngberg* analysis simply has no applicability in the present case. Petitioners concede that the harms Joshua suffered did not occur while he was in the State's custody, but while he was in the custody of his natural father, who was in no sense a state actor. While the State may have been aware of the dangers that Joshua faced in the free world, it played no part in their creation, nor did it do anything to render him any more vulnerable to them. That the State once took temporary custody of Joshua does not alter the analysis, for when it returned him to his father's custody, it placed him in no worse position than that in which he would have been had it not acted at all; the State does not become the permanent guarantor of an individual's safety by having once offered him shelter. Under these circumstances, the State had no constitutional duty to protect Joshua.

It may well be that, by voluntarily undertaking to protect Joshua against a danger it concededly played no part in creating, the State acquired a duty under state tort law to provide him with adequate protection against that danger. See Restatement (Second) of Torts §323 (1965) (one who undertakes to render services to another may in some circumstances be held liable for doing so in a negligent fashion). . . . But the claim here is based on the Due Process Clause of the Fourteenth Amendment, which, as we have said many times, does not transform every tort committed by a state actor into a constitutional violation. . . . A State may, through its courts and legislatures, impose such affirmative duties of care and protection upon its agents as it wishes. But not "all common-law duties owed by government actors were . . . constitutionalized by the Fourteenth Amendment." . . . Because, as explained above, the State had no constitutional duty to protect Joshua against his father's violence, its failure to do so—though calamitous in hindsight—simply does not constitute a violation of the Due Process Clause.

Judges and lawyers, like other humans, are moved by natural sympathy in a case like this to find a way for Joshua and his mother to receive adequate compensation for the grievous harm inflicted upon them. But before yielding to that impulse, it is well to remember once again that the harm was inflicted not by the State of Wisconsin, but by Joshua's father. The most that can be said of the state functionaries in this case is that they stood by and did nothing when suspicious circumstances dictated a more active role for them. In defense of them it must also be said that had they moved too soon to take custody of the son away from the father, they would likely have been met with charges of improperly intruding into the parent-child relationship, charges based on the same Due Process Clause that forms the basis for the present charge of failure to provide adequate protection.

The people of Wisconsin may well prefer a system of liability which would place upon the State and its officials the responsibility for failure to act in situations such as the present one. They may create such a system, if they do not have it already, by changing the tort law of the State in accordance with the regular law-making process. But they should not have it thrust upon them by this Court's expansion of the Due Process Clause of the Fourteenth Amendment.

Affirmed.

Student Records Policies and Procedures for the Alpha School District

(A model that elementary and secondary school districts may use as one example of a student records policy to meet the standards of the Family Educational Rights and Privacy Act of 1974)

PREFACE

School districts should use this model student records policy statement as one of several instruments to help formulate their own policies and procedures to implement the Family Educational Rights and Privacy Act of 1974 (FERPA).

While the statement probably meets the minimum requirements of the FERPA, it is not intended to reflect what the [Department of Education] would approve as a proper policy for a specific school district. In writing the statement, the author exercised for the hypothetical Alpha School District several of the many options the FERPA regulations leave to local school districts. Therefore, unless a given school district maintains the same types of records, operates under the same philosophies, has the same administrative organization as the author imagined, it is not likely that this policy statement will adequately meet the needs of the district.

Under each chapter title in the policy, there is a guide to the section of the FERPA regulation which school district officials should study before they formulate and adopt their own policies. Also, the word "optional" or "required" appears after each title. Where the word "required" appears, it indicates that a policy must include the item. It does not indicate that the item should appear in the same form.

Persons writing student records policies should read the act, study the regulations, compare these with State laws dealing with education records, review the current school district policies and administrative practices, then examine the policy statement as an example of one way to formulate a policy.

Interested parties wishing additional help or guidance in writing policies may contact:

The Family Policy and Regulations Staff
U.S. Department of Education
Room 4511 Switzer Building
Washington, D.C. 20202
Telephone: (202) 732–2057

INTRODUCTION

(Optional)

This policy and the procedures included with it are designed to meet the provisions of the Family Educational Rights and Privacy Act (FERPA), and the Alpha School District is committed to implement the policy and follow the procedures.

The Board of Education authorizes the school superintendent to inform parents, students, and the public of the policy and to exercise his administrative resources to implement the policy as well as to deal with individuals who violate it.

In case a parent of a student, an eligible student, or a citizen of the Alpha School District believes that the district is violating the FERPA, that person has a right to file a complaint with the [Department of Education]. The address is:

The Family Policy and Regulations Staff
U.S. Department of Education
Room 4511 Switzer Building
Washington, D.C. 20202
Telephone: (202) 732–2057

DEFINITIONS

(Optional) (Study 99.3, FERPA regulations.)
For the purposes of this policy, the Alpha School District has used the following definitions of terms.

Student—any person who attends or has attended a program of instruction sponsored by the Board of Education of the Alpha School District.

Eligible student—a student or former student who has reached age 18 or is attending a postsecondary school.

Parent—either natural parent of a student unless his or her rights under the FERPA have been removed by a court order, a guardian, or an individual acting as a parent or guardian in the absence of the student's parent or guardian.

Education records—any record (in handwriting, print, tapes, film, or other medium) maintained by the Alpha School District, an employee of the district, or an agent of the district which is related to a student except:

1. A personal record kept by a school staff member which meets the following tests:
   a. It was made as a personal memory aid.

    b. It is in the personal possession of the individual who made it.

    c. Information contained in it has never been revealed or made available to any other person except the maker's temporary substitute.

2. An employment record which is used only in relation to a student's employment by the Alpha School District. (Employment for this purpose does not include activities for which a student receives a grade or credit in a course.)

3. Alumni records which relate to the student after he or she no longer attends classes provided by the Alpha School District and the records do not relate to the person as a student.

Personal identifier—is any data or information that makes the subject of a record known. This includes the student's name, the student's parent's or other family member's name, the student's address, the student's social security number, a student number, a list of personal characteristics, or any other information which would make the student's identity known.

ANNUAL NOTIFICATION

(Required. Form and method optional) (Study 99.6, FERPA regulations.)

    Within the first three weeks of each school year, the Alpha School District will publish in the Alpha Gazette a notice to parents and eligible students of their rights under the FERPA and this policy. The district will also send home with each student a bulletin listing these rights and the bulletin will be included with a packet of material provided parents or an eligible student when the student enrolls during the school year.

    The notice will include the following:

1. The right of a student's parents and eligible students to inspect and review the student's education records.

2. The intent of the Alpha School District to limit the disclosure of information contained in a student's education records except: (1) by the prior written consent of the student's parent or the eligible student, (2) as directory information, or, (3) under certain limited circumstances, as permitted by the FERPA.

3. The right of a student's parent or an eligible student to seek to correct parts of the student's education record which he or she believes to be inaccurate, misleading, or in violation of student rights. This right includes the right to a hearing to present evidence that the record should be changed if the district decides not to alter it according to the parent or eligible student's request.

4. The right of any person to file a complaint with the Department of Health, Education and Welfare if the Alpha School District violates the FERPA.

5. The procedure that a student's parent or an eligible student should follow to obtain copies of this policy and the locations where copies may be obtained.

The district will arrange to provide translations of this notice to non-English speaking parents in their native language.

STATEMENT OF RIGHTS

(Required) (Study sections 99.11, 99.30, 99.20, 99.6, 99.37, 99.5, 99.60, FERPA regulations.)

Parents and eligible students have the following rights under the Family Educational Rights and Privacy Act and this policy.

1. The right to inspect and review the student's education record.
2. The right to exercise a limited control over other people's access to the student's education record.
3. The right to seek to correct the student's education record, in a hearing if necessary.
4. The right to report violations of the FERPA to the [Department of Education].
5. The right to be informed about FERPA rights.

All rights and protections given parents under the FERPA and this policy transfer to the student when he or she reaches age 18 or enrolls in a postsecondary school. The student then becomes an "eligible student."

PROCEDURE TO INSPECT EDUCATION RECORDS

(Required. Method optional) (Study 99.5 (a) (2) (i), 99.11, FERPA regulations.)

Parents of students and eligible students may inspect and review the student's education records upon request. In some circumstances, it may be mutually more convenient for the record custodian to provide copies of records. See the schedule of fees for copies on page 303.

Since a student's records may be maintained in several locations, the school principals will offer to collect copies of records or the records themselves from locations other than a student's school, so they may be inspected at one site. However, if parents and eligible students wish to inspect records where they are maintained, school principals will make every effort to accommodate their wishes.

Parents or eligible students should submit to the student's school principal a written request which identifies as precisely as possible the record or records he or she wishes to inspect.

The principal (or other custodian) will contact the parent of the student or the eligible student to discuss how access will be best arranged (copies, at the exact location, or records brought to a single site).

The principal (or other custodian) will make the needed arrangements as promptly as possible and notify the parent or eligible student of the time and place where the records may be inspected. This procedure must be completed in 45 days or less from the receipt of the request for access.

If for any valid reason such as working hours, distance between record location sites, or health, a parent or eligible student cannot personally inspect and review a student's education record, the Alpha School District will arrange for the parent or eligible student to obtain copies of the record. See below for information regarding fees for copies of records.

When a record contains information about students other than a parent's child or the eligible student, the parent or eligible student may not inspect and review the records of the other students.

FEES FOR COPIES OF RECORDS

(Required. Actual fee and conditions for denial of copies is optional. Also, a school district may state that it provides copies at no cost and on request.) (Study sections 99.5 (2) (iii) 99.8, FERPA regulations.)

Locations of Education Records (Required) (Study 99.5 (a) (2) (iv), FERPA regulations)

Types	Location	Custodian
Cumulative School Records	School Principal's Office	School Principal Pine Elementary School 312 A Street Oak Elementary School 500 First Street Cherry Elementary School 111 M Street Alpha High School 614 Third Street
Cumulative School Records (Former Students)	Office of School Archives	Chief Archivist Alpha Public Library 509 A Street
Health Records	Health Supervisor's Office	Director of Health Services Alpha School District Administration 615 Third Street
Speech Therapy Records Psychological Records	Office of Education for the Handicapped	Chief Speech Pathology, Chief School Psychologist Alpha School District Administration 615 Third Street
School Transportation Records	School Bus Garage	Director of Pupil Transportation 24 Fifteenth Street
Special Test Records	Office of Pupil Personnel Services	Director of School Counseling Alpha School District Administration 615 Third Street
Occasional Records (Student Education Records not identified above, such as those in superintendent's office, in the school attorney's office, or in the personal possession of teachers)	Principal will collect and make available at student's school	School Principal

The Alpha School District will not deny parents or eligible student any rights to copies of records because of the following published fees. Where the fee represents an unusual hardship, it may be waived in part or entirely by the record custodian. However, the district reserves the right to make a charge for copies such as transcripts it forwards to potential employers or to colleges and universities for employment or admissions purposes. The school district may deny copies of records (except those required by the FERPA) in the following situations:

1. The student has an unpaid financial obligation to the school.
2. There is an unresolved disciplinary action against the student which warrants the denial of copies.

The FERPA requires the school district to provide copies of records:

1. When the refusal to provide copies effectively denies access to the records by a parent or eligible student.
2. At the request of the parent or eligible student when the school district has provided the records to third parties by the prior consent of the parent or eligible student.
3. At the request of the parent or eligible student when the school district has forwarded the records to another school where the student seeks or intends to enroll.

The fee for copies provided under the FERPA may not include the costs for search and retrieval. This fee will be from no cost to 10 cents per page (actual copying cost less hardship factor).

The fee for all other copies, such as copies of records forwarded to third parties with prior consent or those provided to parents as a convenience, will be from 10 cents to 35 cents per page (actual search, retrieval, and copying cost) plus postage if that is involved.

DIRECTORY INFORMATION

(Optional. If option is exercised, procedure required.) (Study sections 99.3, 99.37, 99.5 (3), FERPA regulations.)

The Alpha School District proposes to designate the following personally identifiable information contained in a student's education record as "directory information," and it will disclose that information without prior written consent.

1. The student's name
2. The names of the student's parents
3. The student's address
4. The student's date of birth
5. The student's class designation (i.e. 1st grade, 10th grade, etc.)
6. The student's extracurricular participation
7. The student's achievement awards or honors
8. The student's weight and height if a member of an athletic team
9. The student's photograph
10. The school or school district the student attended before he or she enrolled in the Alpha School District

Within the first three weeks of each school year, the Alpha School District will publish in the Alpha Gazette the above list, or a revised list, of the items of directory information it proposes to designate as directory information. For students enrolling after the notice is published, the list will be given to the student's parent or the eligible student at the time and place of enrollment.

After the parents or eligible students have been notified, they will have two weeks to advise the school district in writing (a letter to the school superintendent's office) of any or all of the items they refuse to permit the district to designate as directory information about that student.

At the end of the two-week period, each student's records will be appropriately marked by the records custodians to indicate the items the district will designate as directory information about that student. This designation will remain in effect until it is modified by the written direction of the student's parent or the eligible student.

USE OF STUDENT EDUCATION RECORDS

(Optional. If school officials have access, first two paragraphs are required. A school district should establish its own criteria and definition of legitimate educational interest.) (Study sections 99.30, 99.31, 99.34, 99.35, 99.36, 99.32, 99.33, 99.37, FERPA regulations.)

To carry out their responsibilities, school officials will have access to student education records for legitimate educational purposes. The Alpha School District will use the following criteria to determine who are school officials. An official is:

1. A person duly elected to the school board.
2. A person certified by the State and appointed by the school board to an administrative or supervisory position.
3. A person certified by the State and under contract to the school board as an instructor.
4. A person employed by the school board as a temporary substitute for administrative, supervisory, or instructional personnel for the period of his or her performance as a substitute.
5. A person employed by or under contract to the school board to perform a special task such as a secretary, a clerk, the school board attorney or auditor for the period of his or her performance as an employee or contractor.

School officials who meet the criteria listed above will have access to a student's records if they have a legitimate educational interest in doing so. A "legitimate educational interest" is the person's need to know in order to:

1. Perform an administrative task required in the school employee's position description approved by the school board.
2. Perform a supervisory or instructional task directly related to the student's education.
3. Perform a service or benefit for the student or the student's family, such as health care, counselling, student job placement, or student financial aid.

The Alpha School District will only release information from or permit access to a student's education record with a parent or eligible student's prior written consent except that the school superintendent or a person designated in writing by the superintendent may permit disclosure:

1. When a student seeks or intends to enroll in another school district or a postsecondary school. The district will not further notify parents or eligible students prior to such a transfer of records. Parents and students have a right to obtain copies of records transferred under this provision.
2. When certain Federal and State officials need information in order to audit or enforce legal conditions related to Federally supported education programs in the district.
3. To parties who provide or may provide financial aid to a student to:
   a. Establish the student's eligibility for the aid.
   b. Determine the amount of financial aid.
   c. Establish the conditions for the receipt of the financial aid.

d. Enforce the agreement between the provider and the receiver of financial aid.
4. If a State law adopted before November 19, 1974 required certain specific items of information to be disclosed in personally identifiable form from student records to State or local officials.
5. When the Alpha School District has entered into a written agreement or contract for an organization to conduct studies on the school district's behalf to develop tests, administer student aid, or improve instruction.
6. To accrediting organizations to carry out their accrediting functions.
7. To parents of eligible students if the parents claim the student as a dependent as defined by the Internal Revenue Code of 1954.
8. To comply with a judicial order or lawfully issued subpoena. The district will make a reasonable effort to notify the student's parents or the eligible student before making a disclosure under this provision.
9. If the disclosure is an item of directory information and the student's parent or the eligible student has not refused to allow the district to designate that item as directory information for that student.

The Alpha School District will permit any of its officials to make the needed disclosure from student education records in a health or safety emergency, if:

1. He or she deems it is warranted by the seriousness of the threat to the health or safety of the student or other persons.
2. The information is necessary and needed to meet the emergency.
3. The persons to whom the information is to be disclosed are qualified and in a position to deal with the emergency.
4. Time is an important and limiting factor in dealing with the emergency.

Alpha School District officials may release information from a student's education record if the student's parent or the eligible student gives his prior written consent for the disclosure. The written consent must include at least:

1. A specification of the records to be released.
2. The reasons for the disclosure.
3. The person or the organization or the class of persons or organizations to whom the disclosure is to be made.
4. The parent or student's signature.
5. The date of the consent and, if appropriate, a date when the consent is to be terminated.

The student's parent or the student may obtain a copy of any records disclosed under this provision.

The Alpha School District will not release information contained in a student's education records, except directory information, to any third parties except its own officials, unless those parties agree that the information will not be redisclosed without the parent or eligible student's prior written consent.

RECORDS OF REQUESTS FOR ACCESS
AND DISCLOSURES MADE FROM EDUCATION RECORDS

(Required) (Study sections 99.32 of the FERPA regulations.)

The Alpha School District will maintain an accurate record of all requests for it to disclose information from or to permit access to a student's education records, and of information it discloses and access it permits, with some exceptions listed below. This record will be kept with, but will not be a part of, each student's Cumulative School Records. It will be available only to the record custodian, the eligible student, the parent of the student, or to Federal, State, or local officials for the purpose of auditing or enforcing Federally supported educational programs.

The record will include at least:

1. The name of the person or agency that made the request.
2. The interest the person or agency had in the information.
3. The date the person or agency made the request.
4. Whether the request was granted and, if it was, the date access was permitted or the disclosure was made.

The district will maintain this record as long as it maintains the student's education record.

The record will not include requests for access or access granted to parents of the student or to an eligible student, requests for access or access granted to officials of the Alpha School District who have a legitimate educational interest in the student, requests for or disclosures of information contained in the student's education record if the request is accompanied by the prior written consent of a parent of the student or the eligible student or the disclosure is authorized by such prior consent, or for requests for, or disclosures of directory information designated for that student.

PROCEDURES TO SEEK TO CORRECT EDUCATION RECORDS

(A procedure is required. District may have an option to establish a procedure so long as it meets the requirements of the FERPA regulations.) (Study Subpart C of the FERPA regulations.)

Parents of students and eligible students have a right to seek to change any part of the student's record they believe is inaccurate, misleading, or in violation of student rights. (Note: under the FERPA, the district may decline to consider a request to change the grade a teacher assigns for a course.)

For the purpose of outlining the procedure to seek to correct education records, the term "incorrect" will be used to describe a record that is inaccurate, misleading, or in violation of student rights. The term "correct" will be used to describe a record that is accurate, not misleading, and not in violation of student rights. Also, in this section, the term "requester" will be used to describe the parent of a student or the eligible student who is asking the school district to correct a record.

To establish an orderly process to review and correct an education record for a requester, the district may make a decision to comply with the request for change at several levels in the procedure.

First Level Decision. When a parent of a student or an eligible student finds an item in the student's education record which he or she believes is inaccurate, misleading, or in violation of student rights, he or she should immediately ask the record custodian to correct it. If the record is incorrect because of an obvious error and it is a simple matter to make the record change at this level, the record custodian will make the correction. However, if the record is changed at this level, the method and result must satisfy the requester.

If the custodian cannot change the record to the requester's satisfaction or the record does not appear to be obviously incorrect, he will:

1. Provide the requester a copy of the questioned record at no cost,
2. Ask the requester to initiate a written request for the change, and
3. Follow the procedure for a second level decision.

Second Level Decision. The written request to correct a student's education record through the procedure at this level should specify the correction the requester wishes the district to make. It should at least identify the item the requester believes is incorrect and state whether he or she believes the item:

1. Is inaccurate and why,
2. Is misleading and why, or
3. Violates student rights and why.

The request will be dated and signed by the requester.

Within two weeks after the record custodian receives a written request, he or she will: study the request, discuss it with other school officials (the person who made the record or those who may have a professional concern about the district's response to the request), make a decision to comply or decline to comply with the request, and complete the appropriate steps to notify the requester or move the request to the next level for a decision.

If, as a result of this review and discussion, the record custodian decides the record should be corrected, he will effect the change and notify the requester in writing that he has made the change. Each such notice will include an invitation for the requester to inspect and review the student's education record to make certain the record is in order and the correction is satisfactory.

If the custodian decides the record is correct, he will make a written summary of any discussions with other officials and of his findings in the matter. He will transmit this summary and a copy of the written request to the school superintendent.

Third Level Decision. The school superintendent will review the material provided by the record custodian and, if necessary, discuss the matter with other officials such as the school attorney or the school board (in executive session). He will then make a decision concerning the request and complete the steps at this decision level. Ordinarily, this level of the procedure should be completed within two weeks. If it will take longer, the superintendent will notify the requester in writing of the reasons for the delay and a date when the decision will be made.

If the superintendent decides the record is incorrect and should be changed, he will advise the record custodian to make the changes. The record custodian will advise the requester of the change as he would if the change had been made at the second level.

If the superintendent decides the record is correct he will prepare a letter to the requester which will include:

1. The school district's decision, that the record is correct, and the basis for the decision.
2. A notice to the requester that he or she has a right to ask for a hearing to present evidence that the record is incorrect and that the district will grant such a hearing.
3. Instructions for the requester to contact the superintendent, or an official he designates, to discuss acceptable hearing officers, convenient times, and a satisfactory site for the hearing. (The district will not be bound by the requester's positions on these items but will, so far as possible, arrange the hearing as the requester wishes.)
4. Advice that the requester may be represented or assisted in the hearing by other parties, including an attorney at the requester's expense.

Fourth Level Decision. After the requester has submitted (orally or in writing) his wishes concerning the hearing officer and the time and place for the hearing, the superintendent will, within a week, notify the requester when and where the district will hold the hearing and who he has designated as the hearing officer.

At the hearing, the hearing officer will provide the requester a full and reasonable opportunity to present material evidence and testimony to demonstrate that the questioned part of the student's education record is incorrect as shown in the requester's written request for a change in the record (second level).

Within one week after the hearing, the hearing officer will submit to the school superintendent a written summary of the evidence submitted at the hearing. Along with the summary, the hearing officer will submit his or her recommendation, based solely on the evidence presented at the hearing, that the record should be changed or remain unchanged.

The school superintendent will prepare the district's decision within two weeks of the hearing. That decision will be based on the summary of the evidence presented at the hearing and the hearing officer's recommendation. However, the district's decision will be based solely on the evidence presented at the hearing. Therefore, the superintendent may overrule the hearing officer if he believes the hearing officer's recommendation is not consistent with the evidence presented. As a result of the district's decision, the superintendent will take one of the following actions:

1. If the decision is that the district will change the record, the superintendent will instruct the record custodian to correct the record. The record custodian will correct the record and notify the requester as at the second level decision.
2. If the decision is that the district will not change the record, the superintendent will prepare a written notice to the requester which will include:
   a. The school district's decision that the record is correct and will not be changed.
   b. A copy of a summary of the evidence presented at the hearing and a written statement of the reasons for the district's decision.
   c. Advice to the requester that he or she may place in the student's education record an explanatory statement which states the reasons he or she disagrees with the school district's decision and/or the reasons he or she believes the record is incorrect.

Final Administration Step in the Procedure. When the Alpha School District receives an explanatory statement from a requester after a hearing, it will maintain that statement as part of the student's education record as long as it maintains the questioned part of the record. The statement will be attached to the questioned part of the record and whenever the questioned part of the record is disclosed, the explanatory statement will also be disclosed.

ADOPTION

(Required) (Study section 99.5 (5) (b).)

The Board of Education of the Alpha School District adopted this student records policy at its December 1978 meeting and thereby directs and authorizes the appropriate school officials to establish and put in effect the procedures to implement the policy beginning January 1, 1979.

Copies of the policy will be available for parent and eligible student review in the principal's office of each school building and at the superintendent's office.

Materials Related to Child Abuse

THE EDUCATOR'S ROLE IN THE PREVENTION
AND TREATMENT OF CHILD ABUSE AND NEGLECT

OUTLINE OF A MODEL CHILD ABUSE AND NEGLECT POLICY FOR SCHOOLS

Policy	Procedures
Statement of School System Commitment to Maltreated Children and Families.	• Disseminate school board statement.
	• Define areas of child abuse and neglect.
	• Recognize parent feelings and rights.
Reporting Requirements that Reflect State Law.	• Publish legal requirements, with immunities and liabilities.
	• Provide in oral and written form.
	• Designate reporting responsibility.
	• Appoint an internal coordinator and outline specific procedural action.
	• Identify a feedback/follow-up system.
Inservice Training and Staff Development Programs.	• Appoint a training team.
	• Select training materials.
	• Plan a schedule of inservice events.
	• Offer education incentives.
Designation of School Personnel to Collaborate with the Community Multi-Disciplinary Child Abuse and Neglect Case-Consultation Team.	• Appoint a school representative/liasion on the case-consultation team.
	• Designate school personnel who can be used in advisory capacity.
	• Specify attendance procedures for case-related personnel.

(Continued)

OUTLINE MODEL POLICY FOR SCHOOLS (*continued*)

Policy	Procedures
Identification of School/Community Resources as Support Services.	• Assess available resources. • Publish a list of service providers and programs with eligibility requirements. • Establish or utilize existing school-based teams for program planning.
Promotion of Primary Prevention Programs.	• Authorize schools to sponsor parent education programs. • Initiate a public awareness effort. • Designate school facilities to be used for family-support services. • Develop parent-education curriculum at secondary level.

SOURCE: *Diane D. Broadhurst,* The Educator's Role in the Prevention and Treatment of Child Abuse and Neglect, *U.S. Department of Health, Education and Welfare, National Center on Child Abuse and Neglect, DHEW Publication No. (OHDS) 79-30172, 1979.*

EXAMPLE OF A CHILD ABUSE AND NEGLECT POLICY FOR EDUCATORS*

Students: Elementary and Secondary

Child abuse and neglect

1. Physical Abuse and Sexual Abuse

Under Maryland Law an abused child is any child under the age of eighteen (18) who (a) has sustained physical injury as a result of cruel or inhumane treatment or a malicious act or acts by his parent or any other person responsible for his care or supervision; (b) has been sexually molested or exploited, whether or not he has sustained physical injury, by his parent or any other person responsible for his care or supervision. Sexual abuse includes, but is not limited to, incest, rape, carnal knowledge, sodomy, or unnatural or perverted sexual practices.

Suspected physical abuse and sexual abuse cases are investigated by the Baltimore County Department of Social Services and the Youth Division of the Baltimore County Police Department. Each case is professionally evaluated to determine the necessity of treatment for the family. Criminal prosecution is not the primary purpose of the investigation or the reports made by the educator.

The law provides immunity from any civil liability or criminal penalty to all who participate, in good faith, in the making of a report in an investigation, in physical and sexual abuse, or in any judicial proceedings resulting from such a report. The procedures below are to be followed in suspected physical abuse and sexual abuse cases *only*.

    a. Reporting Procedure

        (1) School staff members and any employee of the Board of Education shall orally report suspected child abuse to the *Baltimore County Department of Social Services*

---

*Provided by the Baltimore County, Maryland, Public School System.

between 8:30 a.m. and 4:30 p.m. on business days. For reports made outside of business hours, telephone the *Baltimore County Police, Youth Division,* and request the emergency worker for the Department of Social Services contact you.

(2) In addition to reporting orally to the Department of Social Services school staff members shall also inform the local school principal that a case of suspected child abuse has been reported to the Department of Social Services. The obligation of the principal to report cases of suspected child abuse brought to his/her attention by staff members is not discretionary and the principal shall assure that the case is duly reported if this has not already been done.

(3) The person making the oral report to the Department of Social Services is also responsible for submitting a written report. (See form *Suspected Child Abuse Referral* attached.) The written report must follow the oral report and be made within forty-eight (48) hours of the contact which disclosed the existence of possible abuse.

Copies of the written report shall be sent to:

Protective Services
Department of Social Services
Investment Building
620 York Road
Towson, Md. 21204

Youth Division of the
Baltimore County Police
Department
400 Kenilworth Drive
Towson, Md. 21204

State's Attorney for Baltimore County
Court House
Towson, Md. 21204

and to the Carver Office of Pupil Personnel and the assigned pupil personnel worker. Forms are available in each school office.

b. School Procedure

(1) School staff members may initially question the child to determine if the child's injuries resulted from cruel or inhumane treatment, sexual abuse or malicious acts by the child's caretaker. However, in no case should the child be subjected to undue pressure in order to validate the suspicion of abuse. Validation of suspected child abuse is the responsibility of the Department of Social Services, assisted by the police. *Any doubt about reporting a suspected situation is to be resolved in favor of the child and the report made immediately.*

(2) The principal, or his designee, will have the responsibility of notifying the pupil's parents and/or guardian that an incident of child abuse has been reported to the Department of Social Services or the Youth Division of the Baltimore County Police Department. An exception to this rule may be made in a case where in the judgment of the principal, after consultation with the Director of Pupil Services, such a disclosure to the parents would create a threat to the well-being of the child. In these cases the principal and Director of Pupil Services would jointly determine a follow-up procedure which would insure intervention by an appropriate social agency.

(3) In suspected cases of physical and sexual abuse, the suspect victim may be questioned by the police or social worker at the school without the principal obtaining permission of the victim's parent or guardian.

(4) Consultation service to school staff members is available from the Department of Social Services between 8:30 a.m. and 4:30 p.m.

2. Child Neglect

School staff members who have reason to believe a child is suffering from neglect, may make referrals to any school administrator or counselor for team review. Initially, suspected child neglect cases are evaluated by the appropriate school personnel in team or case conferences. The various members of the school multidisciplinary team utilize their skills in assessing the problem and establishing a positive program of action. The pupil personnel worker has the primary responsibility for visiting the home and evaluating the family conditions. A neglected child may be one of the following:

"a. Malnourished; ill-clad, dirty; without proper shelter or sleeping arrangements; lacking appropriate health care
 b. Unattended; without adequate supervision
 c. Ill and lacking essential medical care
 d. Denied normal experiences that produce feelings of being loved, wanted, secure (Emotional neglect)
 e. Unlawfully kept from attending school
 f. Exploited; overworked
 g. Emotionally disturbed due to continuous friction in the home, marital discord, mentally ill parents
 h. Exposed to unwholesome and demoralizing circumstances"*

The families may require assistance in many areas and a variety of different treatment strategies. The pupil personnel worker will assist the family in obtaining the appropriate help needed within the school situation or community.

In severe cases of child neglect or when efforts have been unsuccessful in working towards constructive changes within the family, the pupil personnel worker will refer the case to the Department of Social Services. The pupil personnel worker will also have the responsibility of informing the parents of this action. A written summary outlining the specific conditions of the family situation shall be forwarded to the Baltimore County Department of Social Services.

A referral to the specialized service such as the Department of Social Services may be indicated. However, a well-coordinated multidisciplined approach that stresses interagency cooperation among school, Social Services and other pertinent community agencies must be emphasized. A constructive program of services will result from the coordianted efforts of social and educational representatives.

The Baltimore County Department of Social Services has the legal responsibility for evaluating reports of suspected child neglect and for taking legal action to protect a child where necessary. Under the Annotated Code of Maryland any educator who acts upon reasonable grounds in the making of any report required by law, rule, or regulation or who participated in judicial proceedings which result from such report shall be immune from any civil liability which occurs.

SUSPECTED CHILD ABUSE REFERRAL

TO: Baltimore County Department of Social Services
       Youth Division of Baltimore County Police Department
FROM: (Name of School and Individual making report)

_____

_____

NAME OF CHILD _____

---

*Maryland State Department of Social Services *Goal and Guides,* 1972.

ADDRESS OF CHILD _____

PRESENT WHEREABOUTS OF CHILD _____

AGE OF CHILD _____

BIRTHDATE OF CHILD _____

NAME OF PARENT/ADULT RESPONSIBLE FOR CARE OF CHILD

PHONE _____

ADDRESS _____

RELATIONSHIP _____

NATURE AND DESCRIPTION OF INJURY*

Include description of circumstances and any evidence and/or information available pertaining to present or previous injuries and "all such information available to the reporter which would be of aid in establishing the cause of the injuries or injury and identity of the person or persons responsible therefor."

Signature of person making report:	Date of Oral Report	Date of Written Report	To Whom Reported
_____	_____	_____	_____

Check List

Baltimore County Department of Social Services	_____
Youth Division of Baltimore County Police Dept.	_____
Baltimore County States' Attorney Office	_____
School Office	_____
Office of Pupil Personnel	_____
Pupil Personnel Worker	_____

STATE CHILD PROTECTION STATUTES†

ALABAMA	ALA. CODE §§ 26-14-1 TO -13 (1975 & SUPP. 1981).
ALASKA	ALASKA STAT. §§ 47.17.010-.070 (1979 & SUPP. 1981).
ARIZONA	ARIZ. REV. STAT. ANN. §§ 8-531 TO -546.06 (1974 & SUPP. 1981–1982), 13-3620, -3623 (1978 & SUPP. 1981–1982).
ARKANSAS	ARK. STAT. ANN. §§ 42-807 TO -818 (1977 & SUPP. 1981).

*Article 27, Section 35A, subsection (d), *Form and Contents of Report.*

†Notes, *Unequal and Inadequate Protection Under the Law: State Child Abuse Statutes,* 50 GEO. WASH. L. REV. 243, 272–4 (1982).

CALIFORNIA	CAL. PENAL CODE §§ 11165–11174 (DEERING SUPP. 1982).
COLORADO	COLO. REV. STAT. §§ 19-10-101 TO -115 (1973 & SUPP. 1981).
CONNECTICUT	CONN. GEN. STAT. ANN. §§ 17-38a to -38f (WEST 1975 & SUPP. 1981).
DELAWARE	DEL. CODE ANN. TIT. 16, §§ 901–909 (1974 & SUPP. 1980).
DISTRICT OF COLUMBIA	D.C. CODE ANN. §§ 6-2101 TO -2127 (1981).
FLORIDA	FLA. STAT. ANN. §§ 827.01-.07 (WEST 1976 & SUPP. 1982).
GEORGIA	GA. CODE ANN. §§ 15-11-55, 19-7-4 TO -5 (1982).
HAWAII	HAWAII REV. STAT. §§ 350-1 TO -5 (1976 & SUPP. 1981).
IDAHO	IDAHO CODE §§ 16-1601 TO -1629 (1979).
ILLINOIS	ILL. ANN. STAT. CH. 23, §§ 2051-2061.1 (SMITH-HURD SUPP. 1981-1982), CH. 37, § 704-5 (1972 & CUM. SUPP. 1980–1981) (GUARDIAN *ad litem*).
INDIANA	IND.CODE §§ 31-6-11-1 TO -21 (WEST SUPP. 1981–1982).
IOWA	IOWA CODE ANN. §§ 232.67-.77, 235A.12-.24 (1969 & SUPP. 1981–1982).
KANSAS	KAN. STAT. ANN. §§ 38-716 TO -724, 38-815B (1973 & SUPP. 1980).
KENTUCKY	KY. REV. STAT. § 199.335 (1980) (REPEALED EFFECTIVE JULY 1, 1982).
LOUISIANA	LA. REV. STAT. ANN. TIT. 14, § 403 (WEST 1974 & SUPP. 1982).
MAINE	ME. REV. STAT. ANN. TIT. 22, §§ 4001-4015 (WEST 1980 & SUPP. 1980–1981).
MARYLAND	MD. CODE ANN. ART. 27, § 35A (1982) (ABUSE), ART. 72A, §§ 4-11 (1978 & SUPP. 1981) (NEGLECT).
MASSACHUSETTS	MASS. ANN. LAWS CH. 119, §§ 51A-51F (MICHIE/LAW. CO-OP, 1975 & SUPP. 1981).
MICHIGAN	MICH. STAT. ANN. §§ 25.248 (1)- (16) (CALLAGHAN SUPP. 1981).
MINNESOTA	MINN. STAT. ANN. §§ 260.155(4)-165, 626.556 (WEST 1971 & SUPP. 1982).
MISSISSIPPI	MISS. CODE ANN. §§ 43-21-101 TO -105, -351 TO -357, 43-23-3 (1981).
MISSOURI	MO. ANN. STAT. §§ 210.110-.165 (VERNON SUPP. 1982).
MONTANA	MONT. CODE ANN. §§ 41-3-101 TO -407 (1981).
NEBRASKA	NEB. REV. STAT. §§ 28-710 TO -727 (1979).
NEVADA	NEV. REV. STAT. §§ 200.501-.5085 (1979).
NEW HAMPSHIRE	N.H. REV. STAT. ANN. §§ 169-C:1 TO :40 (SUPP. 1981).

NEW JERSEY	N.J. Stat. Ann. §§ 9:6-1 to -8.50 (West 1976 & Supp. 1981–1982).
NEW MEXICO	N.M. Stat. Ann. §§ 32-1-15 to -16 (1981).
NEW YORK	N.Y. Soc. Serv. Law §§ 411-428 (McKinney 1976 & Supp. 1981–1982).
NORTH CAROLINA	N.C. Gen.Stat §§ 7A-516 to -524, -542 to -552 (1981).
NORTH DAKOTA	N.D. Cent. Code Ann. §§ 50-25.1-01 to -14 (1974 & Supp. 1981).
OHIO	Ohio Rev. Code Ann. §§ 2151.03, .031, .42.1, .31 (Page 1976 & Supp. 1981).
OKLAHOMA	Okla. Stat. Ann. tit. 21 §§ 843-848 (West Supp. 1981–1982).
OREGON	Or. Rev. Stat. §§ 418-740 to -755 (1979).
PENNSYLVANIA	Pa. Stat. Ann. tit. 11, §§ 2201–2224 (Purdon Supp. 1981–1982).
RHODE ISLAND	R.I. Gen. Laws §§ 40-11-1 to -16 (1977 & Supp. 1981).
SOUTH CAROLINA	S.C. Code Ann. §§ 20-7-480 to -690, -735 (Law. Co-op. Supp. 1981).
SOUTH DAKOTA	S.D. Codified Laws Ann. §§ 26-10-1 to -16 (1976 & Supp. 1981).
TENNESSEE	Tenn. Code Ann. §§ 37-202, -248, 37-1201 to 1213 (1977 & Supp. 1981).
TEXAS	Tex. Fam. Code Ann. §§ 34.01-.08, 35.04 (Vernon 1975 & Supp. 1982).
UTAH	Utah Code Ann. §§ 78-3b-1 to -13 (Supp. 1981).
VERMONT	Vt. Stat. Ann. tit. 13, §§ 1351–1356 (Supp. 1981–1982).
VIRGINIA	Va. Code §§ 16.1-266 (1975 & Supp. 1981), 63.1-248.1 to -248.17 (1980 & Supp. 1981).
WASHINGTON	Wash. Rev. Code Ann. §§ 26.44.011-.900 (Supp. 1981).
WEST VIRGINIA	W.Va. Code §§ 49-6-1 to -9 (1980).
WISCONSIN	Wis. Stat. Ann. §§ 48.981 (West 1979 & Supp. 1981–1982), 905.04 (West 1975 & Supp. 1981–1982).
WYOMING	Wyo. Stat. §§ 14-3-201 to -215 (1978).

States and Territories	Orally, Followed By Writing	Time When Writing is Due	As Soon As Possible (ASAP) or Not Specified (NS)	Orally Only	Orally or In Writing	Orally, Then In Writing If Requested	Time When Due, If Requested	Procedure Not Specified	Receipt of Report		
									Social Services Agency	Law Enforcement Agency	Other Agency
Alabama	X		NS						X	X	X
Alaska								X	X		
Arizona								X	X	X	
Arkansas						X	48 hours		X		
California	X	36 hours							X	X	X
Colorado	X		NS						X	X	
Connecticut	X	72 hours							X	X	
Delaware						X	NS		X		
District of Columbia						X	NS		X	X	
Florida	X		ASAP						X		
Georgia						X	NS		X		
Hawaii	X		ASAP						X		
Idaho								X		X	
Illinois	X	24 hours							X		
Indiana				X					X	X	
Iowa	X	48 hours							X		
Kansas						X	NS				X
Kentucky						X	48 hours		X		
Louisiana	X	5 days							X	X	
Maine						X	48 hours		X		
Maryland	X	48 hours							X	X	
Massachusetts	X	48 hours							X		
Michigan	X	72 hours							X		
Minnesota	X		ASAP						X	X	
Mississippi	X		ASAP						X		
Missouri	X	48 hours							X		
Montana								X	X		X
Nebraska	X		NS							X	
Nevada	X		ASAP						X	X	X
New Hampshire						X	48 hours		X		
New Jersey								X	X		
New Mexico								X	X		X
New York	X	48 hours							X		X
North Carolina					X				X		
North Dakota					X	X	48 hours		X		
Ohio						X	NS		X	X	X
Oklahoma	X		ASAP						X		
Oregon				X					X	X	
Pennsylvania	X	48 hours							X		
Rhode Island	X		NS						X		
South Carolina				X					X	X	
South Dakota				X					X		X
Tennessee								X	X	X	X
Texas	X	5 days							X	X	X
Utah						X	48 hours		X	X	
Vermont	X	7 days							X		
Virginia	X		NS						X		
Washington						X	NS		X	X	
West Virginia						X	48 hours		X		
Wisconsin						X	NS		X	X	
Wyoming						X	NS		X	X	
America Samoa						X	48 hours				X
Guam	X	48 hours							X		
Puerto Rico								48	X		
Virgin Islands						X	48 hours				X

Source: Child Abuse & Neglect: State Reporting Laws, National Center on Child Abuse and Neglect, U.S. Department of Health and Human Services. DHHS Publication # (OHDS) 80-30265. Reports law in effect as of January 1, 1979.

AIDS Guidelines

EDUCATION AND FOSTER CARE OF CHILDREN INFECTED WITH HUMAN T-LYMPHOTROPIC VIRUS TYPE III/LYMPHADENOPATHY-ASSOCIATED VIRUS

The information and recommendations contained in this document were developed and compiled by CDC in consultation with individuals appointed by their organizations to represent the Conference of State and Territorial Epidemiologists: the Association of State and Territorial Health Officers, the National Association of County Health Officers, the Division of Maternal and Child Health (Health Resources and Services Administration), the National Association for Elementary School Principals, the National Association of State School Nurse Consultants, the National Congress of Parents and Teachers, and the Children's Aid Society. The consultants also included the mother of a child with acquired immunodeficiency syndrome (AIDS), a legal advisor to a state education department, and several pediatricians who are experts in the field of pediatric AIDS. This document is made available to assist state and local health and education departments in developing guidelines for their particular situations and locations.

These recommendations apply to all children known to be infected with human T-lymphotropic virus type III/lymphadenopathy-associated virus (HTLV-III/LAV). This includes children with AIDS as defined for reporting purposes; . . . children who are diagnosed by their physicians as having an illness due to infection with HTLV-III/LAV but who do not meet the case definition; and children who are asymptomatic but have virologic or serologic

These guidelines were developed by the Centers for Disease Control, U.S. Dept. of HHS, Public Health Service, and were published on August 30, 1985. The AIDS virus, which was then referred to as HTLV-III/LAV, is now referred to as HIV. References have been omitted from the document; it was published in Vol. 34, No. 34 of *Morbidity and Mortality Weekly Report* at page 517.

evidence of infection with HTLV-III/LAV. These recommendations do not apply to siblings of infected children unless they are also infected.

. . .

Legal Issues. Among the legal issues to be considered in forming guidelines for the education and foster care of HTLV-III/LAV- infected children are the civil rights aspects of public school attendance, the protections for handicapped children under 20 U.S.C. 1401 et seq. and 29 U.S.C. 794, the confidentiality of a student's school record under state laws and under 20 U.S.C. 1232g, and employee right-to-know statutes for public employees in some states.

Confidentiality Issues. . . . School, day-care, and social service personnel and others involved in educating and caring for these children should be sensitive to the need for confidentiality and the right to privacy in these cases.

ASSESSMENT OF RISKS

Risk Factors for Acquiring HTLV-III/LAV Infection and Transmission. In adults and adolescents, HTLV-III/LAV is transmitted primarily through sexual contact (homosexual or heterosexual) and through parenteral exposure to infected blood or blood products. . . .

The majority of infected children acquire the virus from their infected mothers in the perinatal period. . . .

Risk of Transmission in the School, Day-Care or Foster-Care Setting. None of the identified cases of HTLV-III/LAV infection in the United States are known to have been transmitted in the school, day-care, or foster-care setting or through other casual person-to-person contact.
. . .

Based on current evidence, casual person-to-person contact as would occur among schoolchildren appears to pose no risk. . . .

Risks to the Child with HTLV-III/LAV Infection. HTLV-III/LAV infection may result in immunodeficiency. Such children may have a greater risk of encountering infectious agents in a school or day-care setting than at home. Foster homes with multiple children may also increase the risk. In addition, younger children and neurologically handicapped children who may display behaviors such as mouthing of toys would be expected to be at greater risk for acquiring infections. Immunodepressed children are also at greater risk of suffering severe complications from such infections as chickenpox, cytomegalovirus, tuberculosis, herpes simplex, and measles. Assessment of the risk to the immunodepressed child is best made by the child's physician who is aware of the child's immune status. . . .

RECOMMENDATIONS

1. Decisions regarding the type of educational and care setting for HTLV-III/LAV-infected children should be based on the behavior, neurological development, and physical condition of the child and the expected type of interaction with others in that setting. These decisions are best made using the team approach including the child's physician, public health personnel, the child's parent or guardian, and personnel associated with the proposed care or educational setting. In each case, risks and benefits to both the infected child and to others in the setting should be weighed.

2. For most infected school-aged children, the benefits of an unrestricted setting would outweigh the risks of their acquiring potentially harmful infections in the setting and the apparent nonexistent risk of transmission of HTLV-III/LAV. These children should be allowed to attend school and after-school day-care and to be placed in a foster home in an unrestricted setting.

3. For the infected preschool-aged child and for some neurologically handicapped children who lack control of their body secretions or who display behavior, such as biting, and those children who have uncoverable, oozing lesions, a more restricted environment is advisable until more is known about transmission in these settings. Children infected with HTLV-III/LAV should be cared for and educated in settings that minimize exposure of other children to blood or body fluids.

4. Care involving exposure to the infected child's body fluids and excrement, such as feeding and diaper changing, should be performed by persons who are aware of the child's HTLV-III/LAV infection and the modes of possible transmission. In any setting involving an HTLV-III/LAV-infected person, good handwashing after exposure to blood and body fluids and before caring for another child should be observed, and gloves should be worn if open lesions are present on the caretaker's hands. Any open lesions on the infected person should also be covered.

5. Because other infections in addition to HTLV-III/LAV can be present in blood or body fluids, all schools and day-care facilities, regardless of whether children with HTLV-III/LAV infection are attending, should adopt routine procedures for handling blood or body fluids. Soiled surfaces should be promptly cleaned with disinfectants, such as household bleach (diluted 1 part bleach to 10 parts water). Disposable towels or tissues should be used whenever possible, and mops should be rinsed in the disinfectant. Those who are cleaning should avoid exposure of open skin lesions or mucous membranes to the blood or body fluids.

6. The hygienic practice of children with HTLV-III/LAV infection may improve as the child matures. Alternatively, the hygienic practices may deteriorate if the child's condition worsens. Evaluation to assess the need for a restricted environment should be performed regularly.

7. Physicians caring for children born to mothers with AIDS or at increased risk of acquiring HTLV-III/LAV infection should consider testing the children for evidence of HTLV-III/LAV infection for medical reasons. For example, vaccination of infected children with live virus vaccines, such as the measles-mumps-rubella vaccine (MMR), may be hazardous. These children also need to be followed closely for problems with growth and development and given prompt and aggressive therapy for infections and exposure to potentially lethal infections, such as varicella. In the event that an antiviral agent or other therapy for HTLV-III/LAV infection becomes available, these children should be considered for such therapy. Knowledge that a child is infected will allow parents and other caretakers to take precautions when exposed to the blood and body fluids of the child.

8. Adoption and foster-care agencies should consider adding HTLV-III/LAV screening to their routine medical evaluations of children at increased risk of infection before placement in the foster or adoptive home, since these parents must make decisions regarding the medical care of the child and must consider the possible social and psychological effects on their families.

9. Mandatory screening as a condition for school entry is not warranted based on available data.

10. Persons involved in the care and education of HTLV-III/LAV-infected children should respect the child's right to privacy, including maintaining confidential records. The number of personnel who are aware of the child's condition should be

kept at a minimum needed to assure proper care of the child and to detect situations where the potential for transmission may increase (e.g., bleeding injury).

11. All educational and public health departments, regardless of whether HTLV-III/ LAV-infected children are involved, are strongly encouraged to inform parents, children, and educators regarding HTLV-III/LAV and its transmission. Such education would greatly assist efforts to provide the best care and education for infected children while minimizing the risk of transmission to others.

Glossary

Adversary system. System of law in America, where the truth is thought to be best revealed through a clash in the courtroom between opposite sides to a dispute.

Affidavit. A written statement sworn to before a person officially permitted by law to administer an oath.

Amicus curiae. "Friend of the court"; a person or organization allowed to appear in a lawsuit, to file arguments in the form of a brief supporting one side or the other, even though not party to the dispute.

Answer. The first pleading by the defendant in a lawsuit. This statement sets forth the defendant's responses to the charges contained in the plaintiff's "complaint."

Appeal. Asking a higher court to review the actions of a lower court in order to correct mistakes or injustice.

Beyond a reasonable doubt. The level of proof required to convict a person of a crime. This is the highest level of proof required in any type of trial, in contrast to *a fair preponderance of the evidence,* the level of proof in civil cases.

Brief. A written summary or condensed statement of a case. Also a written statement prepared by one side in a lawsuit to explain its case to the judge.

By a fair preponderance of the evidence. The level of proof required in a civil case. This level is lower than that required in criminal cases.

From *Teachers and the Law* by Louis Fischer, David Schimmel, Cynthia Kelly. Copyright © 1981 by Longman Inc. Reprinted with permission of Longman Inc.

Cause of action. Facts sufficient to allow a valid lawsuit to proceed.

Certiorari. A request for review of a lower court decision, which the higher court can refuse.

Circumstantial evidence. Evidence that indirectly proves a main fact in question. Such evidence is open to doubt, since it is inferential, e.g., a student seen in the vicinity of the locker room at the time of a theft is the thief.

Civil case. Every lawsuit other than a criminal proceeding. Most civil cases involve a lawsuit brought by one person against another and usually concern money damages.

Class action. A lawsuit brought by one person on behalf of himself or herself and all other persons in the same situation; persons bringing such suits must meet certain statutory criteria and must follow certain notice procedures.

Code. A collection of laws. Most states have an education code containing all laws directly relevant to education.

Common law. "Judge- made" rather than "legislature-made" law. The body of law developed from judicial decisions based on customs and precedents, as distinct from laws enacted by legislatures and written in statutes and codes.

Compensatory damages. Damages that relate to the actual loss suffered by a plaintiff, such as loss of income.

Complaint. The first main paper filed in a civil lawsuit. It includes, among other things, a statement of the wrong or harm done to the plaintiff by the defendant and a request for specific help from the court. The defendant responds to the complaint by filing an "answer."

Criminal case. Cases involving crimes against the laws of the state; unlike civil cases, the state is the prosecuting party.

De facto. In fact, actual; a situation that exists in fact whether or not it is lawful. *De facto* segregation is that which exists regardless of the law or the actions of civil authorities.

Defamation. Injuring a person's character or reputation by false or malicious statements. This includes both *libel* and *slander*.

Defendant (appellee). The person against whom a legal action is brought. This legal action may be civil or criminal. At the appeal stage, the party against whom an appeal is taken is known as the appellee.

De jure. Of right, legitimate; lawful. *De jure* segregation is that which is sanctioned by law.

De minimus. Small, unimportant; not worthy of concern.

Demurrer. The formal means by which one party to a lawsuit argues against the legal sufficiency of the other party's claim. A demurrer basically contends that even if all the facts that the other party alleges are true, they do not constitute a legal cause of action.

De novo. New, completely new from the start; for example, a trial *de novo* is a completely new trial ordered by the trial judge or by an appeals court.

Dictum. A digression; a discussion of side points or unrelated points. Short for *obiter dictum;* plural is *dicta.*

Disclaimer. The refusal to accept certain types of responsibility. For example, a college catalogue may disclaim any responsibility for guaranteeing that the courses contained therein will actually be offered since courses, programs, and instructors are likely to change without notice.

En banc. The full panel of judges assigned to a court sit to hear a case, usually a case of special significance.

Equity. Fairness; the name of a type of court originating in England to handle legal problems when the existing laws did not cover some situations in which a person's rights were violated by another person. In the United States, civil courts have both the powers of law and equity. If only money is represented in a case, the court is acting as a law court and will give only monetary relief. If something other than money is requested— injunction, declaratory judgment, specific performance of a contractual agreement, etc.—then the court takes jurisdiction in equity and will grant a decree ordering acts to be done or not done. There is no jury in an equity case. Actions at law and suits in equity involve civil cases, not criminal.

Et al. "And others." When the words "et al." are used in an opinion, the court is thereby indicating that there are unnamed parties, either plaintiffs or defendants, also before the court in the case.

Ex parte. With only one side present; an *ex parte* judicial proceeding involves only one party without notice to, or contest by, any person adversely affected.

Ex post facto law. A law that retrospectively changes the legal consequences of an act that has already been performed. Article I, section 10 of the U.S. Constitution forbids the passage of ex post facto laws.

Expunge. Blot out. For example, a court order requesting that a student's record be expunged of any references to disciplinary action during such and such a time period means that the references are to be "wiped off the books."

Ex rel. On behalf of; when a case is titled *State ex rel. Doe v. Roe,* it means that the state is bringing a lawsuit against Roe on behalf of Doe.

Fiduciary. A relationship between persons in which one person acts for another in a position of trust.

Hearing. An oral proceeding before a court or quasi-judicial tribunal. Hearings that describe a process to ascertain facts and provide evidence are labeled "trial-like hearings" or simply, "trials." Hearings that relate to a presentation of ideas as distinguished from facts and evidence are known as "arguments." The former occur in trial courts and the latter occur in appellate courts. The terms "trial," "trial-type hearing," "quasi-judicial hearing," "evidentiary hearing," and "adjudicatory hearing" are all used by courts and have overlapping meanings. See *trial.*

Hearsay. Secondhand evidence; facts not in the personal knowledge of the witness, but a repetition of what others said that is used to prove the truth of what those others said. Hearsay is generally not allowed as evidence at a trial, although there are many exceptions.

Holding. The rule of law in a case; that part of the judge's written opinion that applies the law to the facts of the case and about which can be said "the case means no more and no less than this." A holding is the opposite of *dictum.*

In camera. "In chambers"; in a judge's private office; a hearing in court with all spectators excluded.

Incriminate. To involve in a crime, to cause to appear guilty.

Informed consent. A person's agreement to allow something to happen (such as being the subject of a research study) that is based on a full disclosure of facts needed to make the decision intelligently.

Injunction. A court order requiring someone to do something or refrain from taking some action.

In loco parentis. In place of the parent; acting as a parent with respect to the care, supervision, and discipline of a child.

In re. In the matter of; this is a prefix to the name of a case often used when a child is involved. For example, "*In re John Jones*" might be the title of a child neglect proceeding though it is really against the parents.

Ipso facto. By the fact itself, by the mere fact that.

Judicial review. The power of a court to declare a statute unconstitutional; also the power to interpret the meaning of laws.

Jurisdiction. A court's authority to hear a case; also the geographical area within which a court has the right and power to operate. Original jurisdiction means that the court will be the first to hear the case; appellate jurisdiction means that the court reviews cases on appeal from lower court rulings.

Law. Basic rules of order as pronounced by a government. Common law refers to laws originating in custom or practice. Statute law refers to laws passed by legislatures and recorded in public documents. Case law refers to the pronouncements of courts.

Libel. Written defamation; published false and malicious written statements that injure a person's reputation.

Mandamus. A writ issued by a court commanding that some official duty be performed.

Material. Important, going to the heart of the matter; for example, a material fact is one necessary to reach a decision.

Misrepresentation. A false statement; if knowingly done, misrepresentation may be illegal and result in punishment.

Mitigation. The reduction in a fine, penalty, sentence, or damages initially assessed or decreed against a defendant.

Moot. Abstract; not a real case involving a real dispute.

Motion. A request made by a lawyer that a judge take certain action, such as dismissing a case.

Opinion. A judge's statement of the decision reached in a case.
> **Majority opinion.** The opinion agreed in by more than half the judges or justices hearing a case, sometimes called the opinion of the court.
> **Concurring opinion.** Agrees with the majority judgment, but gives different or added reasons.

Dissenting opinion. Disagrees with the majority opinion.

Ordinance. The term applied to a municipal corporation's legislative enactments.

Parens patriae. The historical right of all governments to take care of persons under their jurisdiction, particularly minors and incapacitated persons.

Per curiam. An unsigned decision and opinion of a court, as distinguished from one signed by a judge.

Petitioner. One who initiates a proceeding and requests some relief be granted on his or her behalf. A plaintiff. When the term "petitioner" is used, the one against whom the petitioner is complaining is referred to as the respondent.

Plaintiff. One who initiates a lawsuit; the party bringing suit.

Pleading. The process of making formal, written statements of each side of a case. First the plaintiff submits a paper with facts and claims; then the defendant submits a paper with facts and counterclaims; then the plaintiff responds; and so on until all issues and questions are clearly posed for a trial.

Political question. A question that the courts will not decide because it concerns a decision more properly made by another branch of government such as the legislature.

Precedent. A court decision on a question of law that gives authority or direction on how to decide a similar question of law in a later case with similar facts.

Prima facie. Clear on the face of it; presumably, a fact that will be considered to be true unless disapproved by contrary evidence. For example, a *prima facie* case is a case that will win unless the other side comes forward with evidence to dispute it.

Punitive damages. Money awarded to a person by a court that is over and above the damages actually sustained. Punitive damages are designed to serve as a deterrent to similar acts in the future.

Quasi-judicial. The case-deciding function of an administrative agency.

Redress. To set right, remedy, make up for, remove the cause of a complaint or grievance.

Remand. Send back. A higher court may remand a case to a lower court with instructions to take some action in the case.

Res judicata. A thing decided. Thus, if a court decides a case, the matter is settled and no new lawsuit on the same subject may be brought by the persons involved.

Respondent. One who makes an answer in a legal appellate proceeding. This term is frequently used in appellate and divorce cases, rather than the more customary term, defendant.

Sectarian. Characteristic of a sect.

Secular. Not specifically religious, ecclesiastical, or clerical; relating to the worldly or temporal.

Sine qua non. A thing or condition that is indispensable.

Slander. Oral defamation; the speaking of false and malicious words that injure another person's reputation, business, or property rights.

Sovereign immunity. The government's freedom from being sued for money damages without its consent.

Standing. A person's right to bring a lawsuit because he or she is directly affected by the issues raised.

Stare decisis. "Let the decision stand"; a legal rule that when a court has decided a case by applying a legal principle to a set of facts, the court should stick by that principle and apply it to all later cases with clearly similar facts unless there is a good reason not to. This rule helps promote fairness and reliability in judicial decision making and is inherent in the American legal system.

Statute of limitation. A statute that sets forth the time period within which litigation may be commenced in a particular cause of action.

Tort. A civil wrong done by one person to another. For an act to be a tort, there must be: a legal duty owed by one person to another, a breach of that duty, and harm done as a direct result of the action.

Trial. A process occurring in a court whereby opposing parties present evidence, subject to cross-examination and rebuttal, pertaining to the matter in dispute.

Trial court. The court in which a case is originally tried, as distinct from higher courts to which the case might be appealed.

Ultra vires. Going beyond the specifically delegated authority to act; for example, a school board that is by law restricted from punishing students for behavior occurring wholly off-campus acts *ultra vires* in punishing a student for behavior observed at a private weekend party.

Waiver. An intentional or uncoerced release of a known right.

Index